In the Variorum Collected Studies Series:

CHARLES B. SCHMITT
The Aristotelian Tradition and Renaissance Universities

CHARLES B. SCHMITT
Studies in Renaissance Philosophy and Science

WILLIAM J. COURTENAY
Covenant and Causality in Medieval Thought

FRANCIS OAKLEY
Natural Law, Conciliarism and Consent in the Late Middle Ages

STEPHAN KUTTNER
The History of Ideas and Doctrines of Canon Law in the Middle Ages

YVES CONGAR
Droit ancien et structures ecclésiales

YVES CONGAR
Thomas d'Aquin. Sa vision de théologie et de l'Eglise

JAN PINBORG
Medieval Semantics
Selected Studies on Medieval Logic and Grammar

JOHN WHITTAKER
Studies in Platonism and Patristic Thought

S. M. STERN
Medieval Arabic and Hebrew Thought

DAVID C. LINDBERG
Studies in the History of Medieval Optics

EDWARD GRANT
Studies in Medieval Science and Natural Philosophy

JOHN W. O'MALLEY
Rome and the Renaissance. Studies in Culture and Religion

CECIL H. CLOUGH
The Duchy of Urbino in the Renaissance

PAUL GRENDLER
Culture and Censorship in Late Renaissance Italy and France

History, Law
and the Human Sciences

Professor Donald R. Kelley

Donald R. Kelley

History, Law and the Human Sciences

Medieval and Renaissance Perspectives

VARIORUM REPRINTS
London 1984

British Library CIP data

Kelley, Donald R.
History, law and the human sciences.
—(Collected studies series; CS205)
1. Historiography—History
I. Title
907′.2 D13

ISBN 0-86078-153-4

Published in Great Britain by Variorum Reprints
20 Pembridge Mews London W11 3EQ

Printed in Great Britain by Paradigm Print
Gateshead, Tyne and Wear

VARIORUM REPRINT CS205

CONTENTS

This volume contains a total of 334 pages.

PUBLISHER'S NOTE

The articles in this volume, as in all others in the Collected Studies Series, have not been given a new, continuous pagination. In order to avoid confusion, and to facilitate their use where these same studies have been referred to elsewhere, the original pagination has been maintained wherever possible.

Each article has been given a Roman number in order of appearance, as listed in the Contents. This number is repeated on each page and quoted in the index entries.

INTRODUCTION

It is not retrospective illusion, I hope, that gives these essays a certain coherence and constancy of direction, despite their chronological and international sprawl. The underlying question is one that has preoccupied me even before beginning my historical apprenticeship. "How curious, after all, is the way in which we moderns think about our world!" I remember being struck by this opening sentence from E. R. Burtt's *Metaphysical Foundations of Modern Science* and thinking later how much more curious, perhaps, was the way in which we think about the world of culture — our culture and those which we can penetrate to some extent. I still think so, even though we may be, many of us, post-modern and little subject to such sentiments of wonderment.

All of these papers, stretching back over some twenty years, are directed to the question of how western scholars have tried to investigate and to interpret their (and to some extent our) cultural world. My point of departure was the sixteenth-century phase of Renaissance humanism. This is the subject of essays III, V and VIII-X, all of them byproducts of my *Foundations of Modern Historical Scholarship* (1970), which I hoped would recall and cut a small parallel to Burtt's classic work. From this limited base I moved into other cultural contexts, especially Italian, German and English (e.g., essays VI, XI, and XIV); ranged backwards and forwards in time from antiquity and the middle ages (I and II) to the present century (XV); and shifted emphasis from historiography to the European legal tradition, which has always seemed to me the principal vehicle of social and cultural thought.

More especially, my first area of study was the study of history, its theory as well as practice, in the sixteenth century, including not only humanist perspectives on "antiquity" but also more conservative notions of "tradition". The link with law was essential for two reasons. The first is the importance of jurisprudence for historical method (the Italian *ars historica* being transformed into the French *methodus*) and universal history —

the "law of nations" (*jus gentium*) becoming the target of a series of historical and comparative studies leading from Bodin to the work of Vico, Montesquieu and others (nos. VII, XII, XIII). The second reason is the potential of legal scholarship for the development of political, institutional and social history. This in turn encouraged me to examination of the mainstream tradition of professional jurisprudence, extending ultimately from Gaius to Savigny (and his student Marx, who was in a sense a renegade jurist) and beyond, especially as it related to the history of society and culture. Most important here were legal discussions of the origins of laws and particular institutions (such as feudalism) and the importance of history in the development of legal hermeneutics.

Various expeditions into the European legal tradition, especially in the medieval period, persuaded me that interest in "historical consciousness," even very broadly defined, did not at all adequately express the value of jurisprudence for social and cultural studies. For "civil science" (as medieval jurists called their discipline) entailed a philosophy of society as well as a normative art of judgment and legislation; and it posed many fundamental questions about the human condition and its shifting patterns. A growing awareness of the "philosophical significance" of jurisprudence led me to examine the grand tradition of legal systematics, "Gaianism" I termed it, which established an anthropocentric and voluntaristic model of social thought which had stood in somewhat the same relation to the human sciences as Aristotelian naturalism has stood to natural philosophy. Like Aristotelian philosophy, Romanoid legal thought has been expanded, interpreted, criticized, transmuted and displaced over the centuries under the impact of various lines of thought and investigation, including scholasticism, humanism ("civil humanism", as I think of it) and modern natural law. Through inspiration, interpretation and various sorts of revulsion it has helped to spawn a number of newer and more specialized human disciplines, including political economy, sociology and anthropology; and it served as a sort of archetype for modern cultural philosophies, such as those of Marx, Weber, Betti and Gadamer. Different aspects of this argument are presented in historical terms in essays I, IV, VI-IX, XII-XIV, and more philosophically in essay XV.

This hypothesis has provided the conceptual map on which I have located and chosen particular soundings. I realize that such a view entails concessions to that "Whig fallacy" identified by Herbert Butterfield, but the internal history of intellectual and professional disciplines requires a recognition of conceptual continuity as well as of historical context. For to some extent the history of historiography, of legal scholarship and of the various human sciences do form traditions which link the present with Renaissance, medieval and ancient intellectual efforts; and to that extent certain values and aims have persisted over many generations despite fundamental changes in mentality and social conditions. A literary tradition may be (in Harold Bloom's phrase) a "map of misreading", but a scientific tradition — even a social-scientific tradition — depends on a certain continuity of understanding and even a sort of "dialogue" over time. To some extent earlier scholars are our colleagues, and lines of communication should be kept open through historical and hermeneutical effort.

Lamentations about a "crisis" in various social and cultural disciplines have been widespread and chronic, and they are unparallelled, it seems to me, in the fields of natural science. One reason for this disparity is perhaps that the sciences can operate — at least "normally", as Thomas Kuhn has taught us to say — without much resort to disciplinary memory. This is not the case with the human sciences — or rather, the human sciences cannot afford professional amnesia without, apparently, disaffection and feelings of being caught in a uniquely threatening predicament. The feeling is common, but it has been common over many generations, and indeed in an important sense the sense of "crisis" is part of the human condition. It is probably true that "crises" occur more frequently in the human than in the scientific disciplines, though without necessarily resulting in a Kuhnian "revolution"; and this is all the more reason to urge a "role for history" in the examination of these fields. To this effort of *anamnesis*, in any case, these essays are devoted.

DONALD R. KELLEY

Rochester, N.Y.
February 1984

I

Gaius Noster: Substructures of Western Social Thought

"tu regere imperio populos, Romane, memento . . ."[1]

GAIUS, THE MOST INFLUENTIAL OF CLASSICAL JURISTS, is apparently a modern discovery. The dramatic story of his resurrection has often been told. In 1816 the historian Barthold Georg Niebuhr came across a manuscript in Verona, a text from Saint Jerome written over a much earlier work. He reported this palimpsest (at some points *ter scriptus*, a double palimpsest) to his friend Friedrich Karl von Savigny, the greatest legal scholar of the age and the emerging leader of the so-called Historical School of Law. Savigny immediately recognized it as the work of the second-century jurist Gaius, otherwise preserved only in fragmentary form in that great sixth-century anthology, the *Digest* of Justinian. "Let us hope that we can decipher more of Gaius in these pages," he wrote to Niebuhr. (So it fortunately turned out, for over eleven-twelfths of the *Institutes of Civil Law* were recovered with the help of this manuscript.) "This will surely give new life to our jurist," Savigny predicted.[2] This book, the only nearly complete pre-Justinianian text, has indeed had a profound impact upon Roman legal history and scholarship since its publication in 1820.

Yet in a deeper sense Gaius had never really been lost to view. Despite the elementary and defective form in which his work was transmitted, the structure of his *Institutes* can be traced in the thought of many generations not only of jurists but also of historians and of political and social philosophers. Whether consisting of notes by Gaius himself or by a student (the same sort of debate that has raged around the works of Aristotle), the book became more influential than those of more authoritative jurists like Ulpian and Pomponius (who, unlike Gaius, possessed the right to interpret the law, the *jus respondendi*). Distilling, simplifying, and organizing the resources of ancient legal

As so often before, I must express gratitude to friends and colleagues at the Institute for Advanced Study for sympathetic stimulation and, for material support, to the National Endowment for the Humanities.

[1] Vergil, *Aeneid*, 6. 851. Also see note 85, below.

[2] Savigny to Niebuhr, December 5, 1816, in A. Stoll, *Karl Friedrich von Savigny*, 2 (Berlin, 1929): no. 321. Also see Savigny to Eduard Schrader, July 16, 1817, in *ibid.*, no. 33: "Das muss ein neues Leben unter unseren Juristen geben!"

wisdom, Gaius became the mentor not only of Rome but also of Byzantium and Europe. He was "the true architect of Justinian's collection," his most recent commentator has told us;[3] he was the model for many later constructions as well, including national codes like the *Siete Partidas* and the *Code Napoléon*, legal treatises like Antoine Loisel's *Institutes of Customary Law*, Savigny's own *System of Modern Roman Law*, and a variety of more tangential philosophical ventures. Gaius' pedagogical role has been almost as various and substantial as that of Aristotle. To Justinian he was "Noster Gaius," and so he has remained for centuries to many others, including Savigny. He was, so to say, "our teacher."

"Gaianism" is not a conventional term, but in view of his role perhaps it should be. Many lesser authors—jurists as well as philosophers—have engendered eponymous "isms" with inferior claims, while Gaius formulated (if he did not create) one of the most distinctive and enduring systems of thought in Western history. It is not too much to say that Gaius established a dominant archetype of social thought, a more practical and human paradigm to rival the metaphysical structure of Aristotelianism.[4] Though by intent a method of teaching law, his book suggested an epistemology, a potentially "scientific" method and various guiding principles for the systematic study of society and culture. His work exhibits, it seems to me, the fundamental kinship between the old science of jurisprudence (*legitima*, *legalis*, or *civilis scientia*, as jurists liked to call it) and the modern science of society.

In recent times, however, the Gaian tradition has been virtually unappreciated, and most likely unperceived, by historians of philosophy and of culture in general. What is the reason for this? Why has such neglect fallen on Gaius' *Institutes* and not, for instance, on Cicero's relatively vacuous *De Legibus*? One answer is surely that the study of law, even in Savigny's time, has diverged from history, literature, philosophy, and other fields with which it formerly had so many vital connections. A more important answer, perhaps, is that the significance of Gaianism—even for those disciplines apparently closest to jurisprudence, such as political and social philosophy—cannot be perceived merely from the literal and legalistic surface of the text. To appreciate this significance we must try to grasp the underlying meaning of the text by deciphering another—a historical and conceptual sort of—palimpsest. Not in any sense, however, should this approach be tried through speculative interpretation or what textual critics used to call "divination." Rather, we should proceed by trying to assess some of the implications that have in fact been

[3] A. M. Honoré, *Gaius* (Oxford, 1962), 128. In general, see H. Wagner, *Studien zur allgemeinen Rechtslehre des Gaius* (Zutphen, 1978); and Pauly-Wissowa. RE 21, pt. 1 (1951): 286. The secondary (and tertiary) literature on Gaius and his text is enormous. The text, for example, is the subject of a periodical, *Gaius Studien*, begun in 1968, edited by R. G. Böhm, and published out of Freiburg. Here, as elsewhere, I will not attempt to provide bibliographical references on law and legal history, except as they bear upon relevant questions of social thought and, even then, only selectively in terms of the argument.

[4] For the standard study, see F. X. Affolter, *Das römische Institutionen-System* (Berlin, 1897). Also see Helmut Coing, *Juristische Methodenlehre* (Berlin, 1972); and H. Jolowicz, *Roman Foundations of Modern Law* (Oxford, 1957), 61–81. For the most recent survey with an excellent bibliography, see G. Fassò, *Storia della filosofia del diritto*, 3 vols. (Bologna, 1966–70).

drawn out, some of the transformations that historically have been attempted: the aim is not to read between the lines of Gaius but, instead, to survey the career of Gaianism. The subject of these remarks is not *ille* but *noster* Gaius.

Of the jurisconsult Gaius little is known, not even his full name, and his doctrinal background is not clear. When he began to teach and to assemble his book, there were already two schools of legal thought in Rome. One was the conservative and republican "Proclian," the other the imperial-minded "Sabinian." It may or may not be significant that Gaius belonged to the latter, more innovative group. Whatever its provenance, the power of Gaianism derives in general from three distinguishing features. The first is his basically historical approach, displayed most prominently in the fragment heading the famous second title of the *Digest*: "On the Origin of Law."[5] His historical orientation is, however, most concretely evident in the substance of the *Institutes*, which constitutes a kind of ordered cornucopia of Roman legal wisdom. The second is his dialectical method, which generated essential distinctions, divisions, and methods of interpretation. The last, and the most important, is the celebrated tripartite arrangement of social categories, a sequence of rubrics that entail not only moral priorities and a means of ordering reality but also a characteristic mode of perceiving and construing the world. What Gaianism suggests is not quite a doctrine (on the analogy, say, of Calvinism) but rather a methodological system (on the analogy of sixteenth-century "Ramism," which accommodated Calvinism, yet was distinct from it), a framework for a *Weltanschauung* encompassing natural as well as social experience.

Although never satisfactorily explained, the Gaian triad, set forth under the rubric *De juris divisione*, has fascinated scholars for centuries. Down to the present day it has enjoyed, if not self-evident rationality, at least extraordinary authority in some circles.[6] According to this anthropocentric, secular trinity, judicial and pedagogical cognizance had to be taken first of persons (*de personis*), second of things (*de rebus*), and last of actions (*de actionibus*): (1) "personality"—the *sine quo non*, so to speak—including degree of "liberty," kinship, citizenship, and other social relations;[7] (2) the "real" world, though for Gaius *res* could be intangible (*incorporales*) as well as tangible; and (3) the relations between and among subjects and objects—that is, "actions in a general sense, themselves divided reflexively into "personal" and "real" types. This presumably exhaustive classification represents, in effect, one enduring expression of the metaphysical foundations of social thought.

[5] *Digest*, 1. 2. 1: "*Gaius libro primo ad legem duodecim tabularum:* Facturus legum vetustarum interpretationem necessario prius ab urbis initiis repetendum existimavi. . . ."

[6] *Digest*, 1. 5. 3; and Gaius, *Institutiones*, 1. 8, in J. Baviera, ed., *Fontes Iuris Romani Antejustiniani* (Florence, 1940): "Omne autem ius quo utimur vel ad personas pertinet vel ad res vel ad actiones."

[7] In general, see Fritz Schulz, *Principles of Roman Law* (Oxford, 1936), 42, 140–63. And, in particular, see P. Duff, *Personality in Roman Private Law* (Cambridge, 1938); Paolo Zatti, *Persona giuridica e soggettività* (Padua, 1975); and Carlo Maiorca, *La Cosa in senso giuridico* (Turin, 1937). Also see Adolf Berger's standard *Encyclopaedic Dictionary of Roman Law* (Philadelphia, 1953).

This distinctive form makes it possible to isolate a Gaian tradition, even though Gaius himself had no claim to originality or profundity. For underneath the Gaian text there are still older formulations. In fact, Gaius was not the first systematizer of Roman legal science. This honor seems to belong to Quintus Mucius Scaevola, a first-century B.C. jurist who, according to Fritz Schulz, created "the first dialectical system of law in the grand manner." The Mucian scheme was quadripartite, resting upon the divisions of inheritance law, persons, things, and obligations; but it bore obvious affinities to that of Gaius. As late as the second century Scaevola's work was the subject of commentaries by Pomponius and by Gaius himself. Thereafter, it disappeared and was unknown to Justinian's editors. "Well may we complain of a fate which has preserved so utterly worthless a work as Cicero's *De Legibus*," Schulz has written with characteristic assertiveness, "but which has allowed the book which laid the foundations of not merely of Roman, but of European, jurisprudence to perish."[8] Paleographical fortune more than intellectual merit, then, leads us to celebrate a Gaian instead of a Mucian tradition, derivative and perhaps even degenerate as it might be in terms of Roman legal history.

What more fundamentally qualifies Gaian claims, of course, is the manifold indebtedness of Roman legal science in general to Greek philosophy and, more particularly, to Greek rhetoric. No one places much stock in the story (told by Pomponius and included in the *Digest*—paired, incidentally, with Gaius' celebration of history) about the visit of the *Decemviri* to Athens before the establishment of the law of the Twelve Tables, but the tale does nicely symbolize the cultural contribution of Greek thought. Although the channels of transmission are obscure, Platonic ideals, Aristotelian categories, sophistic *topoi*, and especially dialectical method constitute the original level, unfortunately illegible in detail, of the Gaian palimpsest. It was Greek conceptualization, especially the theory of interpretation so central to jurisprudence, that transformed the practice and teaching of Roman law into a Hellenistic "science" in the classical (as well as medieval and, before the present century, modern) sense of the term.[9]

More specific Greek influence can be detected at certain crucial points. Among the most important are the practice of making divisions (*divisio*, *differentia*, or, especially among medieval commentators, *distinctio*, corresponding to the Aristotelian διαίρεσις), the setting down of initial definitions (*definitio* or *regula*, corresponding to ὅροι or κανόνες), and a number of rhetorical topics, such as the contrast between the letter and the spirit, or meaning, of a statement (*verba* and *voluntas* or *ratio*). Indeed, many of the basic terms of civil law are simply translations from Greek terminology, such as the distinction between natural and civil law (*jus naturale* and *civile*, corresponding to

[8] Schulz, *History of Roman Legal Science* (Oxford, 1953), 94. Also see G. Scherillo, 'Il civilistico pre-Gaiano," in *Studi in onore di Vicenzo Arangio-Ruiz*, 3 (Naples, 1953): 445–67. On "abstraction," see Schulz, *Principles of Roman Law*, 53–65.

[9] Schulz, *History of Roman Legal Science*, 62–69. In general, see the monumental work of Erich Wolf, *Griechisches Rechtsdenken*, 6 vols. (Frankfurt, 1950–).

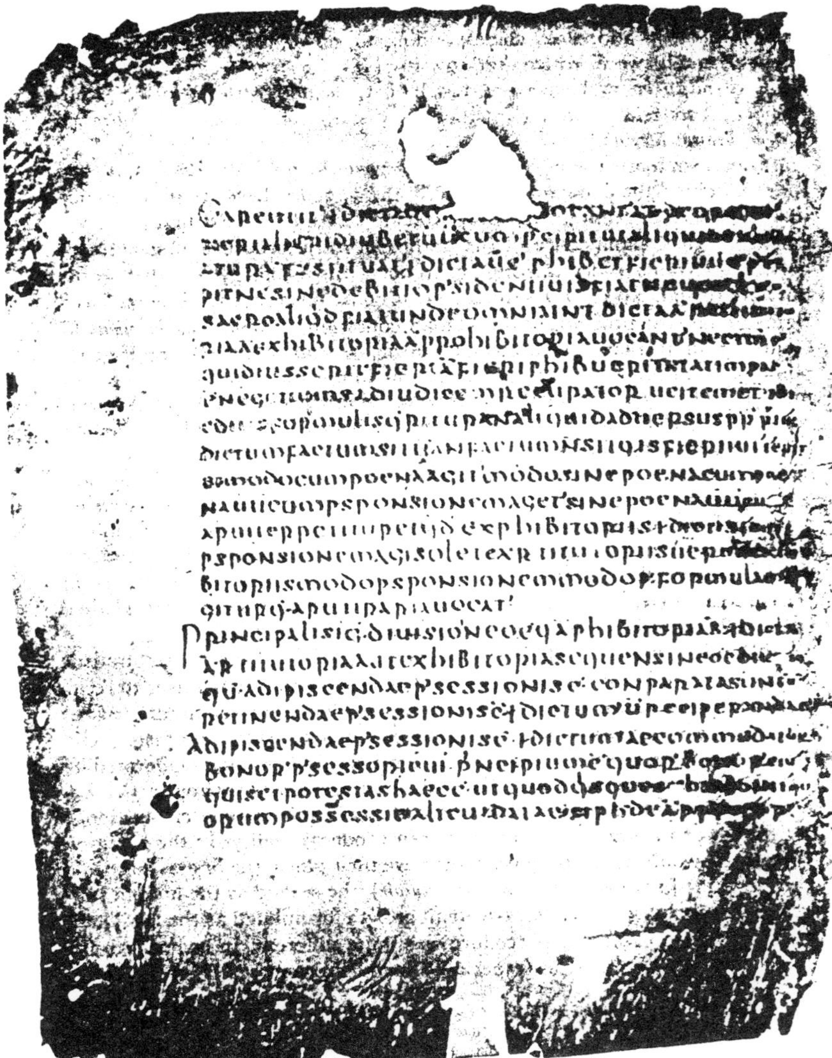

Gaius, *Institutionum*, 4. 139-44, f. singulare.

φύσει δίκαιον and θέσει or νόμῳ δίκαιον), between the law of nations and civil law (*jus gentium* and *civile*, corresponding to κοινὸν δίκαιον and πολιτικόν δίκαιον), and between written and unwritten law (*jus scriptum* and *non scriptum*, νόμος γεγραμμένος and νόμος ἄγραφος). So it was, too, with the idea of equity (*aequitas*, ἐπιείκεια) and the method of disputation (*disputatio in utramque partem*, δισσοὶ λόγοι).[10]

If Gaianism made use of Greek forms, it gave them a Latin dress and style. Indeed, behind the pedagogical intent of the *Institutes* there are philosophical implications that seem distinctively Roman. Consider, in the first place, the epistemological significance of the anthropocentric ordering of social categories. For Gaius understanding began not with cosmology, in other words, but with the human subject—the subject of consciousness, that is, as well as of rights. Thus, the problem of the human condition (*De condicione hominum* for Gaius, encompassed by the civilian rubric *De statu hominis*[11]) provided the point of departure, and the philosophical implication was a sort of rudimentary sociology of knowledge. Having established the subject, horizons could be expanded to include other individuals and natural objects, potentially possessions; and, finally, the social field could be completed with consideration of actions and interactions of various sorts. Secondly, and correlative to this, the Gaian system was aimed not merely at causal explanation—value-free science, so to speak—but also at human problems and the rendering of practical judgments. On these grounds jurisprudence was useful as well as theoretical, concerned with the life active as well as the life contemplative, and enabled jurists to argue for the superiority of their "science" and to identify it with "true philosophy."[12]

In a fundamental way, then, Gaianism was set apart from the naturalistic tradition of Greek philosophy. Perhaps the best way to clarify this is to recall the fundamental polarity that arose in Greek thought between nature (φύσις) and convention, or law (νόμος).[13] "By convention exist color and taste," said Democritus; "in reality there are atoms and the void." As later elaborated by rhetoricians, Roman as well as Greek, the opposition was by implication between the world of human will and behavior (of symbols and "civilization") and that of extra-human (objective or transcendent) reality. In the tradition of Roman law, of course, both concepts have their place: the first as a rational norm identified with natural law (*jus naturale*), the second as the human substance of civil law and that extra-Roman growth formulated as the law of nations (*jus gentium*). But the procedure was quite different. In contrast to the naturalistic or mathematical (especially Euclidean) strategy of starting with

[10] See H. Hübner, "Subjektivismus in der Entwicklung des Privatrechts," in *Festschrift für Max Kaser* (Munich, 1976), 5–42; and Giovanni Pugliese, " 'Res corporales,' 'res incorporales,' e il problema del diritto soggetivo," in *Studi in onore di Vicenzo Arangio-Ruiz*, 223–60. Also see the works cited in note 7, above.

[11] *Digest*, 1. 5; and Gaius, *Institutiones*, 1. 3.

[12] For this related subject, see my "Vera Philosophia: The Philosophical Significance of Renaissance Jurisprudence," *Journal of the History of Philosophy*, 14 (1976): 267–79, and the references cited therein.

[13] F. Heinemann, *Nomos und Physis* (Basel, 1945); and Wolf, *Griechisches Rechtsdenken*, *passim*. Also see C. A. Maschi, *La Coscienza naturalistica del diritto et degli istituti giuridici romani* (Milan, 1937); and F. Lanfranchi, *Il Diritto nei retori romani* (Milan, 1938).

general principles and reasoning from them, Gaianism gave prominence and priority to the human aspect, to what from the twelfth century onward would be termed "positive law,"[14] and then advanced, empirically in a sense, to higher degrees of rationality and universality.

What about the structural significance of Gaianism? Does the secular trinity of persons-things-actions reflect some religious or procedural convention? Does it have some logical or linguistic base? Or is it merely, as one modern expert has suggested, one more manifestation of a general Roman fixation on "trichotomy"?[15] Whatever the prehistorical source, the arrangement was repeated and elaborated in countless ways for many centuries down to the present day. It antedated, and became hardly less ingrained than, the Christian trinity; and, because of its function in liberal as well as legal education, it may have played a larger role in the history of thought than has generally been recognized. Almost seventeen centuries after Gaius the young Karl Marx complained about the trichotomizing (*trichotomisch*) method forced on him by Savigny and other of his teachers—but not before Marx composed a three-hundred-page treatise of private law based on the Gaian scheme.[16] And, though he abandoned both this scheme and the "idealism" associated with it, Marx went on, under Hegel's influence, to adopt another not dissimilar trichotomy likewise based on a dialectic of subject-object. In other ways, too, ghosts from the Roman past haunted Marx's mature works, but of course this discussion goes beyond the confines of the direct tradition of Gaianism.

After Gaius' death (a.d. 178 or later) his authority grew in legal as well as pedagogical terms, especially from 426 onward, when the law of citations named him as one of five jurists to be followed in the courts.[17] The worldwide appeal of his *Institutes* is suggested by various survivals outside Italy, such as the excerpts made for the *Breviarium* of Alaric and the sixth-century commentary made for the law school of Autun. At about the same time, Justinian remarked that Gaius' work was the only elementary textbook assigned to law students in the Byzantine schools, though by 533 it was already obsolete in some respects.[18] In fact, Justinian, or rather his editor Tribonian, preserved Gaius for posterity, until the nineteenth century at any rate, not only by citing him often (531 times to be exact) in the *Digest* but also by making his book the model for Justinian's own *Institutes*. In his preface the emperor revealed his philosophic intention of "bringing into bright harmony" (*in luculentam ereximus*

[14] Steven Kuttner has shown that "positive law" (*jus positivum*) comes from a misreading of "posited law" (*jus positum*); Kuttner, "Sur les origines du terme 'droit positif,' " *Revue historique du droit français et étranger*, 15 (1936): 728–30.

[15] H. Goudy, *Trichotomy in Roman Law* (Oxford, 1910); and Karl Friedrich von Savigny, *System des heutigen römischen Rechts*, 1 (Berlin, 1940): 322–26.

[16] Marx to Heinrich Marx, November 10–11, 1837, in *Marx-Engels Gesamtausgabe*, 1, pt. 1 (Berlin, 1927): 213–31; and see note 87, below.

[17] *Codex Theodosianus*, 1. 4. 3.

[18] "Deo auctore," Constitution prefacing the *Digest*

consonantiam) the confused mass of ancient jurisprudence and legislation, and, indeed, just at this point he made the famous proprietary claim that his manual was largely based on the work of "our Gaius" (*praecipue ex commentariis Gaii nostri. . .*).[19] Through this Byzantine vehicle and, secondarily, through the *Digest* the form and substance of Gaianism was transmitted to modern European culture.

The *Institutes* of Justinian began with the same premise as the *Institutes* of Gaius: "All of our law is related either to persons or to things or to actions." Justinian then explained the reason for that order—"it is of little purpose to know the law if we do not know the persons for whom the law was made."[20] Accordingly, Book I is a topical discussion of the title, "De personis," including analyses of the levels and limitations of personal liberty, especially in terms of paternal and marital power (the *patria potestas* of the father and the *potestas de manu* of husband and wife). Books II and III continued "De rebus" and were devoted to particular problems of possession and property, exchange and inheritance, except for those things designated as public, common to all, or unpossessable because of their ecclesiastical character (*res sacrae*). Finally, Book IV treated "De actionibus"—logically and interlockingly divided into personal and real things—and concluded with judicial procedure and criminal actions.

This Byzantine effort at remodeling differs in two fundamental respects from the Gaian original. One difference is the considerable emphasis placed upon public law, illustrated above all in the notorious, post-Gaian text from Ulpian, "What pleases the prince has the force of law" (*Quod principi placuit legis habet vigorem*).[21] This emphasis, of course, arose from Justinian's determination to exalt, if not to deify, his imperial authority above all previously recognized sources of law, including juristic responses (*responsa prudentum*); but it did not directly affect the social categories encompassed by private law. The other difference is that Justinian, drawing on later classical jurisprudence and rhetorical hyperbole, made larger philosophical claims for the science of law, even claiming for it the status of true wisdom (*divinarum ac humanarum notitia*, the equivalent of the Ciceronian formulation of *sapientia*). But his hyperbole only served to enhance the attractions of Gaianism.[22] There is no denying that from this point most of the words of the Roman legal canon are those of Justinian (or rather his paraphrase of many generations of jurists), but in many respects the assumptions and conceptual base continue to be those of "our Gaius." In any case, in this somewhat disguised form Gaianism was passed on to the West and preserved for the next phase of its posthumous career.

[19] "Imperatoriam maiestatem," Constitution prefacing the *Institutes*. And, in general, see L. Wenger, *Die Quellen des römischen Rechts* (Vienna, 1953), 600–37.

[20] *Institutes*, I. 2. 12. Also see Gaius, *Institutiones*, I. 8.

[21] *Institutes*, 7. 21. 6.

[22] *Digest*, I. I. I. The system of the *Digest*—and, indeed, that of the *Code*—has its own character and history; but it is closely related to, and in some ways dependent on, that of the *Institutes*, and it was much more severely criticized in later centuries. Because of its pedagogical and "methodical" purpose and because of its broader impact, the *Institutes* has been chosen for examination here.

The third level of the Gaian palimpsest, historically *ter scriptus*, began during the twelfth-century revival of Roman law and the establishment of professional faculties of law at the University of Bologna and elsewhere.[23] At this stage the problem of deciphering becomes increasingly complicated by the intrusion of other intellectual forces, including canon and feudal law and Aristotelian philosophy in its scholastic form. Henceforth, the Gaian tradition was enmeshed in glosses, commentaries, questions, opinions, and—though strictly forbidden by Justinian himself—more or less distorting "interpretations."[24] As Gaius' work was lost, so Gaianism became increasingly difficult to perceive.

Nevertheless, the basic principles were preserved, and certainly no alternatives were suggested. The most authoritative of glosses, that by Accursius, remains mostly grammatical corrections, small quibbles, and large justifications. About the first Gaian text in the *Digest*—the law "omnes populi" declaring that "all people are ruled by civil law or the law of nations"—Accursius wondered, "But what of those who are not so ruled?" The answer was not difficult: "I respond that these are uncivilized men."[25] This simplified version of the *disputatio in utramque partem* Accursius also applied to the broader question whether Gaius' threefold division might be false (*hoc videtur esse falsum*), and again he resolved the difficulty, in this case by arguing for a more than merely literal view of "things" and "actions." There was also a tendency, illustrated by Petrus de Bellapertica, to replace "action" by the more sophisticated concept of "obligation," which arose from an agreement (*obligatio nascens ex contractu*) and was guaranteed by natural law.[26] But despite such rationalizing tendencies the Gaian system was not seriously questioned.

Following the Glossators from the late thirteenth century, the still more philosophically minded Commentators began to diverge more basically from Gaian principles. Concerning the same law "Omnes populi," for example, Baldus had a different answer to the problem whether "all people" were indeed ruled as Gaius had asserted. "I respond that not all are," said Baldus, "for many cities have their own statutes by which they are ruled."[27] Although technically the emperor was still the only source of law, the right of people to make their own law (*jus proprium* or *jus proprissimum*) could be justified in legal

[23] For general orientation on the Roman legal tradition, see Paul Koschaker, *Europa und das römische Recht* (3d ed., Berlin, 1958). And, for bibliography, see Franz Wieacker, *Privatrechtsgeschichte der Neuzeit* (2d ed., Göttingen, 1967); and Walter Ullmann, *Law and Politics in the Middle Ages* (Ithaca, N.Y., 1975). On particular themes, see E. Cortese, *La Norma giuridica*, 2 vols. (Milan, 1962–64); and my "Clio and the Lawyers: Forms of Historical Consciousness in Medieval Jurisprudence," *Medievalia et Humanistica*, new. ser., 5 (1974): 25–29.

[24] M. Fuhrman, "Interpretatio," in *Sympotica Franz Wieacker* (Göttingen, 1970), 80–110; F. Pringelsheim, "Justinian's Prohibition of Commentaries to the Digest," in his *Gesammelte Abhandlungen*, 2 (Heidelberg, 1961): 86–106; and V. Piano Mortari, "Il Problema dell'interpretatio nei commentatori," *Annali di storia del diritto*, 2 (1958): 29–109.

[25] Accursius, *Ad Digestum*, 1. 5. 1, which is the equivalent of Gaius, *Institutiones*, 1. 8.

[26] Petrus de Bellapertica, *In libros Institutionum commentarii* (Lyon, 1536), 111. And, in general, see C. Karsten, *Die Lehre von Verträge bei den italienischen Juristen des Mittelalters* (Rostock, 1882).

[27] Baldus, *Super Digesto veteri* (Venice, 1535), f. 26. In general, see *L'Opera di Baldo, per cura dell'Università di Perugia nel V centenario della morte del grande giureconsulto* (Perugia, 1901); and, in particular, see J. Tarducci's essay in *ibid.*, 409–66; Norbert Horn, *Aequitas in den Lehren des Baldus* (Cologne, 1968); and, for the classic work, C. N. S. Woolf, *Bartolus of Sassoferrato* (Cambridge, 1913).

terms, Baldus argued; for did not the imperial rule against a people making "illicit statutes" imply that they could make *licit* ones? In this way Baldus, following his master Bartolus and other Italian jurists, built up the case for the legitimacy of city-states and other political units that were independent of imperial jurisdiction and so, presumably, of Roman forms. For some jurists, of course, there was an answer to this problem, too: such post-Roman statutes and customs should be included in the *jus gentium*.

Gaius' famous statement about the legal "condition of men" likewise received expanding interpretation—and "interpretations," as Accursius reminded his students, implied correction. In the first place the topic "De statu hominum" was an invitation to some jurists to philosophize about the human condition in general, about the natural as well as the social state of that "most worthy of creatures" (*dignissima creaturarum*), as Alberigo de Rosate called man. But the main theme was the historical change that had occurred since the time of Gaius, the difference between the ancient and the "modern state of men" (*status modernus hominum*). "In modern times" (*secundum moderna tempora*), observed Alberigo, "there are various states of men that are not treated under the title" of Gaius. "And, because the state of men is in constant motion and never at rest," he proposed to bring the discussion up to date by treating a variety of more recent questions, including those of the Jews and Saracens and different sorts of Christians (real and supposed)—laymen and clerics.[28] In fact, the general problem that absorbed most of the energies of European jurists was how to accommodate their own experience and institutions, feudal as well as ecclesiastical, to Roman forms and rules or, in other words, how to transform, as Justinian had transformed, the *jus antiquum* into a *usus modernus*. In this effort jurists increasingly turned to extra-Roman experience, but they did so in orthodox terms of custom (*consuetudo*) and the *jus gentium*, based (as Gaius had said) on "natural reason."

Another major force that acted to transform Gaianism was the intrusion, or rather re-intrusion, of Aristotelian philosophy. Attempts to find or to impose logical species, especially the use of the famous "four causes," again illustrates the infiltration of naturalism and metaphysics into jurisprudence and social thought. Accursius had accepted Gaius' demand for the study of the "origin of law," though he interpreted "necessary" as "useful" and justified it simply on grounds of logic and propriety—that it provided a way of introducing basic elements (*principia*) and that it agreed with the method of a lawyer (*advocatus*), which was to start with his exordium. For commentators like Baldus, however, concern for origins and sources was translated into the system of Aristotle's efficient, material, formal, and final causes; and, indeed, this procedure was associated with the growing claims of scholastic jurisprudence to be a rational "science" because it was universal and treated its material in terms of cause and effect (*per causas*).[29] The long-range implica-

[28] Alberigo, *In primam FF* [Digesti] *Veter. part.* (Venice, 1585), f. 44v.

[29] See R. Weigand, *Die Naturrechtslehre der Legisten und Dekretisten von Irnerius bis Accursius und von Gratian bis Johannes Teutonicus* (Munich, 1967); and my "Vera Philosophia: The Philosophical Significance of Renaissance Jurisprudence," 274.

tions of these tendencies were momentous; they continued to inform professional jurisprudence down to Savigny's time and after. Yet Gaianism was modified rather than replaced; another level was added to the multilayered Gaian text.

SERIOUS CRITICISM AND TRANSFORMATION of the Gaian paradigm began in the sixteenth century. The first condition of this mutation was the rise of humanistic jurisprudence, beginning in fifteenth-century literary circles and then infiltrating the academic and professional study of law.[30] From the second quarter of the century deepening historical perspectives and expanding geographical horizons encouraged by humanism led certain jurists to begin the task of "reforming" the Roman system of jurisprudence fixed by Gaius, codified by Justinian, and canonized by the medieval Glossators. The "reformers" wanted to fulfill the famous Ciceronian ideal of "reducing law to an art" (*jus in artem redigendo*)—or, better, Justinian's ideal of elevating it to a science, a concept that was vital and a prime rubric of Romanist jurisprudence. Pursued by elaborate violations of Justinian's strictures against "interpretation," the task was justified in the name of that abstract reason contained in the law (*recta ratio*; *ratio juris*) as well as a novel concern for "method," which was a dominant force in the intellectual life of the sixteenth century. The men involved in this enterprise were the founders of that modern school of jurisprudence that Savigny designated "the systematists" (*die Systematiker*) and that represents a latter-day Gaianism—the last, or perhaps next-to-last, layer of the Gaian palimpsest.[31]

Underlying this tradition was another movement for "reform" associated with humanism, namely the attempt to improve and to re-order dialectic by bringing it into contact with, or even submerging it in, rhetoric.[32] This aim of various pedagogical reformers, including Rudolf Agricola and Petrus Ramus, was carried over by like-minded jurists into their own field of study, which, of course, had other longer-standing ties with rhetoric in technical ways. In 1520, building on Agricola's work, Claudius Cantiuncula published his *Topica legalia* in an effort to find a better arrangement for the major "commonplaces"

[30] On the historical implications of "legal humanism," see D. Maffei, *Gli Inizi dell'umanesimo giuridico* (Milan, 1956); and my *Foundations of Modern Historical Scholarship* (New York, 1970). For the philosophical implications, see Hans Troje, *Graeca Leguntur* (Cologne, 1971), which is useful for orientation, new insights, and bibliography if not for all of its judgments.

[31] Savigny, *Das Recht des Besitzes* (7th ed., Vienna, 1865), 10. For the classic and still indispensable work on this tradition, see R. Stintzing and E. Landsberg, *Geschichte der deutschen Rechtswissenschaft*, 4 vols. (Munich, 1880–1910).

[32] See, in general, Neal Gilbert, *Renaissance Concepts of Method* (New York, 1956); and Walter Ong, *Ramus, Method, and the Decay of Dialogue* (Cambridge, 1958). On law in particular, there has been an upsurge of work lately; see, for example, Hans Troje, "Wissenschaft und System in der Jurisprudenz des 16. Jahrhunderts," in J. Blühdorn and J. Ritter, eds., *Philosophie und Rechtswissenschaft* (Frankfurt, 1969), 63–88; Aldo Mazzacane, *Scienza, logica, e ideologia nella giurisprudenza tedesca del sec. XVI* (Milan, 1971); F. Carpintero, " 'Mos italicus,' 'mos gallicus,' y el humanismo racionalista," *Ius Commune*, 6 (1977): 108–71; C. Vasoli, "La Dialettica umanistica e la metodologia giuridica nel secolo XVI," in *La Formazione storica del diritto moderna in Europa*, 1 (Florence, 1977): 237–79; and A. Giuliani, "The Influence of Rhetoric on the Law of Evidence and Pleading," *Juridical Review* (1962), 216–51.

of law (*locorum divisio*).[33] This work was pursued further in the *Methodica dialecticis ratio* by Johann Apel, who illustrated his topical reform with a series of diagrams showing the logic of social, especially as contrasted to natural, structure and process. Among German jurists like Johann Frey and Nicolaus Vigelius the influence of Ramus was particularly strong, partly because they hoped with his help to restore jurisprudence to a more central position in general learning and, through its association with oratory, to enhance its social utility. As Frey suggested in his schematic prescription for an "idea of the good and complete jurisconsult," the finished product, a paradigm of practical and theoretical knowledge, would be the "political man" (*homo politicus*).[34] But most of all, raising their sights from pedagogy to philosophy, these jurists wanted to fashion the Roman legal tradition into an orderly system; for "order," wrote Christopher Ehem, another of these legal reformers, "is the soul of things themselves" (*ordinem esse animam ipsarum rerum*).[35]

Although not generally appreciated or even admitted, the movements to reform dialectic and jurisprudence continued to have recourse to old traditions of naturalism and scholasticism, despite a lot of careless anti-Aristotelian rhetoric. Johann Oldendorp, in another treatise on "legal topics," used Aristotelian categories to organize his *materia* and *exempla* and the idea of the four causes to interpret "actions" in particular.[36] Even more systematically, Vigelius, who indeed set out to reorganize in such dialectical terms the whole *Institutes* of Justinian (*resolutio Institutionum Imp. Justiniani*), relied upon Aristotle.[37] Similar attitudes are evident in contemporary theories of "interpretation," which, despite Justinian's prohibition, had become a recognized part of law.[38] The "order" sought by critical methodologists like Jean Coras and Pietro Gammaro was a natural order, which they contrasted sharply with civil law. The latter was founded "not on nature," as Coras observed, "but only on opinion and the authority of legislators."[39] This social authority might suffice for law as an "art," but a science needed to judge "through causes"—precisely what the new theories of interpretation proposed to accomplish. A rational method, or methodical rationale (*methodica ratio*), as

[33] Cantiuncula listed twenty-five places or means of making distinctions; see his *Topica legalis*, printed with Johann Apel, *Methodica dialecticis ratio ad iurisprudentiam* (Basel, 1545).

[34] Nicholas Reusner, ed., ΧΕΙΡΑΓΩΓΙΑ *sive Cynosura iuris*, 2 (Speier, 1588), no 32: Freigius, "Idea boni et perfecti iuris consulti" (fold-out diagram in the appendix). Also see Mazzacane, *Scienza, logica, e ideologia*.

[35] Ehem, *De principis iuris libri septem* (Basel, 1556), 1.

[36] Oldendorp, *Actionum forensium progymnasmata in septem classes distincta* (Lyon, 1566), f. 3v. Also see his *Topica legalis* (Lyon, 1555). On Johann Oldendorp, see E. Wolf, *Grosse Rechtsdenker der deutschen Geistesgeschichte* (2d ed., Tübingen, 1951), 134–75; and Guido Kisch, *Erasmus und die Jurisprudenz seiner Zeit* (Basel, 1960), 227–59, *Claudius Cantiuncula* (Basel, 1970), 57–71 ("Methodenlehre"); and *Melanchthons Rechts- und Soziallehre* (Basel, 1967). For a topical analysis of Bartolus, see A. Brederode, *Loci communes . . . novi et uberrimi in Bartoli . . . opera omnia* (Basel, 1589).

[37] Vigelius, *Dialectici iuris civilis libri III* (Basel, 1620). Also see his *Methodus universi iuris civilis absolutissima* (Lyon, 1591).

[38] See V. Piano Mortari, *Ricerca sulla teoria dell'interpretazione del diritto nel sec. XVI* (Milan, 1956). Also see H. Schürpf, "Ratio interpretandi," in Stintzing and Landsberg, *Geschichte der deutschen Rechtswissenschaft*, 1: 1071.

[39] Coras, *De iure civile in artem redigendo*, in *Tractatus universi iuris*, 1 (Venice, 1584): 59; and Gammaro, *De extensionibus*, in *ibid.*, 18: 247. On Coras, see A. Fell, "The Classical Four Causes in the Renaissance Art of Law" (Ph. D. dissertation, Columbia University, 1974).

Oldendorp put it, "requires that the interpreter of law have recourse to the law of nature."[40]

Yet this widespread search for system—"methodus," "schemata," "ratio," and "partitiones" are among the operative terms—by no means implied abandoning the human and positive aspects of jurisprudence. The jurist had to judge fact as well as law; he had to find authorities as well as devise arguments. The dual aim of jurisprudence, according to Conrad Lagus, was to answer both the historical and the philosophical questions: Philosophy, he explained, was no doubt "the first part of law, that is, the truth and reason of law insofar as the human mind can attain them"; but no less essential was "the second part" (that is, history), "the bare narration of facts . . . to show the forms of law observed by Roman legislation in particular cases."[41] Precisely in this sense of "history" could law be analyzed in terms of persons, things, and actions. In the preface to his standard anthology of legal treatises on method, Nicolas Reusner provided the aphorism that best expresses the enduring importance of the Gaian scheme: "Bonus Institutionalista," he stated, "bonus Jurista."[42]

The continuing and cumulative critique of the Roman canon was an international enterprise; but the major efforts of revision were begun in France, especially by disciples of Andrea Alciato at the University of Bourges. Alciato was the founder of humanistic jurisprudence, of the *mos gallicus* as it was later called, although he personally lacked any particular systematic interests. The most notable of his followers—François Connan, Eguinaire Baron, François le Douaren, and Hugues Doneau—were deeply indebted to the humanist movement; but each made a practice of also introducing modern materials and ideas, not only feudal law, which was regularly taught at Bourges, but a variety of historical issues, such as the influence of Celtic and Frankish institutions. Each of them also contributed massively to the criticism of the Roman legal canon, and none hesitated to break with Roman forms in their attempts to realize the ideal of law as "true philosophy."

Connan's master work, published posthumously in 1557, was called *Commentaries on Civil Law*; but its general purpose was actually to shift emphasis away from civil law and to discuss instead such topics as obligation and property in terms of the law of nations, as Gaius had defined it. For Connan the *jus gentium* was equivalent to the "form of a people" (*forma populi*), and it was, logically if not chronologically, "prior to civil law." As a consequence, he tended to examine conventional topics of civil law in the context not only of natural law, identified with the "first law of nations" (*ius hoc gentium primum*), but also of European, often comparative, history. He also gave large and continuing roles to custom in the progress of legal institutions and to jurists in rationalizing these customs. "Custom interprets law," he wrote, and "judgments confirm custom" (*consuetudo legum interpretatur; res judicatae consuetudinem*

[40] Oldendorp, *Iuris naturalis gentium et civilis* εἰσαγωγή (Antwerp, 1539), sig. Aiii.
[41] Lagus, *Methodus iuris utriusque traditio* (Lyon, 1566), 3.
[42] Reusner, ΧΕΙΡΑΓΩΓΙΑ *sive Cynosura iuris*, 1: 13.

confirmat).[43] Law was, of course, grounded in nature, but the first laws (*priscae leges*) were barbaric; there was no original "golden age" (*aetas aurea*), only "the rule of lusts, factions, evils, seditions, plunderings, war, and an absence of equity and justice."[44] The perfection of law only developed over the course of time, with the ratiocinations of jurists and especially with the efforts to establish a rational system of law. Connan had reservations about the triadic system of Gaius and argued that the rubric of actions was unnecessary since it could be divided between persons and things. On a more general level, however, Connan carried on the spirit of the Gaian tradition.

So, in even more modernizing and vernacularizing terms, did Eguinaire Baron, the eldest and in some ways the most original of these four French pioneers. In addition to a manifesto of the new jurisprudence, Baron produced a series of commentaries on all parts of civil law according to a unique and self-consciously comparative method that he termed *commentaria bipertita*, by which he "accommodated civil law to French customs and legislation" (*accommodata hujus tituli ad mores Galliarum et leges regias*).[45] He "accommodated" both the *Institutes* of Gaius and the *Digest* of Justinian, in part simply by translation. He explained, for example, that "among the French the *plebs* is the Third Estate" and went on to point out parallels and contrasts in the respective social and legal systems. He agreed with Gaius that all law concerned persons, things, or actions, but his experience prompted him to expand "the condition of man" beyond the distinction of free and unfree. Women were "persons" too, and, like Connan, he was aware of their peculiar position (*quia status foeminarum deterior in multis causis*). There were also the problems of foreigners and naturalization (*aulbains, ou etrangers, et lettres de naturalité*); and, in fact, Baron composed a monograph on succession among foreigners.[46] Other difficulties, such as the antiquated Roman paternal power (*patria potestas*), likewise led him to depart from Roman convention, though without rejecting the entire Roman framework of jurisprudence. The work of Baron, a marvelous and many-sided illustration of the cultural shock that antiquity could inflict on sensitive and learned moderns, certainly deserves closer study.

Better known and probably more influential is the work of Baron's colleague and rival Le Douaren. Although these two "Alciateans" had a variety of disputes, personal and religious as well as professional and political, they fundamentally agreed about "method"; and Baron subscribed to his younger colleague's formulation that emphasized the systematic-pedagogical (*ars docendi*) as well as the humanistic-philological (*sermonis proprietas*) aspects of the

[43] Connan, *Commentariorum iuris civilis libri X* (Paris, 1557), f. 43. For analyses, see C. Bergfeld, *Franciscus Connanus* (Graz, 1968); and V. Piano Mortari, "La sistematica come ideale umanistico dell'opera di Francisco Connano," in *La Storia del diritto nel quadro delle scienze storiche* (Florence, 1966), 521–31. The same formula appears in Lagus' *Methodus iuris utriusque traditio*, 42, from the *Digest*, 1. 3. 37.

[44] Connan, *Commentariorum iuris civilis libri X*, ff. 32v, 16.

[45] Baron, *Opera omnia*, ed. F. Baudouin (Paris, 1562), *Commentarii*, *passim*, and *Institutionum civilium ab Iustiniano Caesare editarum libri IIII* (Poitou, 1550). On Baron there is no useful study of any sort.

[46] Baron, *Opera omnia*, 1: 52, 78 ("De statu hominum"), 92.

new jurisprudence.[47] For Le Douaren legal education ought to begin with the *Institutes* and, despite the humanist prejudice against scholasticism, ought to include the works of Bartolus, Baldus, and the best of the philosophical commentators. Like his friend Connan, Le Douaren was devoted to the ideal of "true philosophy," and he declared that "there is nothing either divine or human that the jurisconsult does not treat and that is not relevant to civil science." He wrote extensively on both canon law and, under the civilian heading of "custom," feudal law; and he denied that Roman law had in any sense been "received" into France. Nevertheless, civil law continued to provide the terms and framework of his legal philosophy. In his discussion of the problems of legal system, he leaned perhaps more toward the naturalistic interpretation, making an analogy to mathematics in particular, since he believed that "the elements of law, the grounds of its maxims and basic issues are as points, lines, surfaces, etc., are to geometry."[48] Such was the basis of Le Douaren's various "methodical" discussions (*methodica enarratio*, *methodica partitio*, and *tractatio*, as he characterized his interpretations of the Roman canon).

Of all of the work of the great "systematists," that of Hugues Doneau, disciple and successor of Le Douaren at Bourges, is probably the most comprehensive and influential. For Savigny, Doneau's *Commentaries on Civil Law* marked the introduction of the French school into Germany, and for Savigny's disciple R. Stintzing, the great authority in the field, Doneau was "the creator of modern jurisprudence."[49] At Bourges and later at the Universities of Altdorf and Heidelberg, Doneau carried on the work of transforming Romano-Byzantine law into a universal system in accordance with the ideal of law as "true philosophy," as an expression of "right reason."[50] Like many other contemporary "anti-Tribonianists," Doneau was much disturbed by the state of the *Code* and especially of the *Digest* of Justinian, although it was the form, or rather the formlessness, instead of the substance (the post-classical interpolations, or "Tribonianisms") that he wanted to correct. The *Institutes*, on the other hand, he continued to admire, especially the tripartite classification; and, in fact, much of his work of "reformation" consisted of trying to gather together and to arrange the scattered and sometimes contradictory material on persons, things, and actions into an intelligible and symmetrical system. For Doneau each of these headings had three subheadings: (1) divine and human, with the latter divided into public and private; (2) obligations, which followed the discussion of rights and which were grouped under "things"; and (3) forms of procedure to obtain rights, which appeared under "actions." Doneau's work, like that of his elder colleagues, shows the strong imprint of formal philosophy, including the four

[47] Le Douaren, *Opera omnia*, 1: 1. For an analysis, see W. Vogt, *Franciscus Duarenus* (Stuttgart, 1971).

[48] Le Douaren, *Opera omnia*, 1: 1. Also see Coras, *Opera omnia*, 1 (Wittemberg, 1603): 1.

[49] Stintzing, *Hugo Donellus in Altdorf* (Erlangen, 1869), 42.

[50] Doneau, *Opera omnia*, 1 (Rome, 1828): 133. On Doneau, see the old appreciation and analysis by A. Eyssell, *Doneau* (Dijon, 1860); on Doneau's significance for French systematizing and codifying efforts, see A.-J. Arnaud, *Les Origines doctrinales du Code civil français* (Paris, 1969), 121.

Aristotelian causes, and at least a touch of Ramist, or Ramoid, method; but in general the *Commentaries* remains within the Gaian tradition.

In the generation after Doneau the rising tide of "vernacular humanism" brought this tradition into contact with the tangled question of customary law. In France two close colleagues who studied at Bourges, Étienne Pasquier and Antoine Loisel, took Justinian's *Institutes* as the model and guide for their efforts to bring some system to vernacular law. Pasquier found parallels to the Gaian model in other "institutes"—Quintilian's "oratorical," Lactantius's "divine," and Ramus's "dialectical" (to which we might add Calvin's "institutes" of religion)—and began his work with a short history of Roman systematizing from the time of Scaevola.[51] Pasquier argued that law was more closely allied to rhetoric than to philosophy and that, because of the jurist's reliance on memory and human judgment, his art was called *juris prudentia* instead of *juris scientia*. Like his Latinate colleagues, Pasquier operated in the domain of the *jus gentium*, which he equated simply with "human law" (*droit humain*). His *Interpretation of the Institutes of Justinian* (unpublished until the nineteenth century) started out as a translation but ended up as a comparative study of Roman and French legal institutions, following the Gaian pattern very much in the style of Baron's work. Pasquier, however, was generally hostile to civil law, deplored its tyrannical and rigid tendencies, and was at pains to point out contrasts with French customs. With respect to the first division, for example, all French "persons" were free (*libres et franches*) except in a few antiquated provincial *coutumiers*. In most ways Loisel agreed with and, indeed, consulted Pasquier on these matters, and was more insistent on the differing status of French "persons," arguing that the primary division was between *noble* and *roturier* (itself divided into *bourgeois* and *vilain*), since all men were or could become free by baptism. Loisel's *Customary Institutes*, again following the Gaian pattern but composed of native proverbs, literary expressions of folk wisdom, and maxims of customary law, moved even further from Romanism toward some sort of national system.[52]

There were other efforts at system-building in the sixteenth century, but these works, like the celebrated *Republic* of Jean Bodin, tended to be concerned with political rather than social or legal thought. One instructive exception, abused when not neglected, is the curious construction fashioned by Bodin's rival, Pierre Grégoire of Toulouse. For Grégoire "method" was an "imitation of nature," and in his own grandiose *Republic* he tried to assemble a man-centered cosmology to emulate the natural cosmos.[53] Grégoire, like Bodin, denied the universality of the Roman tradition and, specifically, French subjection to it; but on the fundamental point, the nature of the commonwealth, he had a very different emphasis. The center of his political cosmos was occupied not

[51] Pasquier, *L'Interprétation des Institutes de Justinian, avec la conference de chaque paragraphe aux ordonnances royaux, arrestz de Parlement et coustumes génerales de la France*, ed. M. le duc Pasquier (Paris, 1847), 9, 45.

[52] Loisel, *Institutes coustumiers*, ed. M. Reulos (Paris, 1935).

[53] Grégoire, *De republica libri sex et viginti* (Frankfurt, 1609), 10: 54, 13: 12, 21. And see the discussion by C. Collot, *L'École doctrinale de droit public de Pont-à-Mousson* (Paris, 1965).

by the prince—as it was for Bodin and for that "most pernicious man, Machiavelli"—but by that Roman form of wisdom called law. This emphasis is even clearer in Grégoire's other systematic effort, his *Syntagma juris universi*, a book treating "all law, divine, human, and natural," according to a "new method."[54] The novelty of this method, however, fades on examination, not only because it relies on traditional views of hierarchy but also because its principal categories turn out to be variations on the old Gaian theme. The first volume (books 1–6) covers a wide range of things—natural, divine, and human (including "communal" and "feudal")—and then (books 7–19) persons and the various conditions thereof. The second volume concludes with an elaborate consideration of human "actions," criminal as well as legitimate, collective as well as individual, public as well as private. Reversing the position of the first two categories was done for the orthodox reason that in Creation things had in fact preceded persons. In general, Grégoire's work illustrates a crucial turning point in the career of Gaianism—the shift from a normative legal doctrine to a descriptive interpretation of society and culture.

Other endeavors, apart from the tinkering with the Roman system, were operating to transform modern views of jurisprudence. One was the gigantic contemporary enterprise in the field of classical and historical scholarship, although this effort may have served to confuse as well as to broaden perspectives on the old legal tradition. Jacques Cujas was the symbol and leading spirit of this critical assault on the textual aspect of this tradition. Also positive and empirical in a certain sense was the growing appreciation even among academic jurists of the value of modern judicial experience. Cujas's student, Pierre Ayrault, for example, turned from theory to practice (*usus*) as the best means of access to legal wisdom. For him the true source of law lay in particular judgments (*res judicatae* is the civilian rubric). These Ayrault regarded as the first or only or "supreme" part of the law; and he compiled a modern digest (*pandectae*) of such judgments that followed, of course, the conventional order. "Look to the practitioners," he advised, "for those things that pertain to their art."[55] Finally, there were the long-standing ideological objections to Romanism, especially national jealousy of imperial-papal intrusions and claims to universalism. In France the standard formula was "that the civil laws of the Romans may not be alleged in the courts of France or in any inferior courts on the basis of their authority but only on the basis of their rationality" (*pro ratione*).[56] In this way, though in few others, nationalism can be said to have reinforced rationalism. In all of these ways the intimidating position of the Roman canon and of Gaianism in a general sense was increasingly undermined, or at least relocated, in a more pluralistic and rational conception of human history and society.

[54] Grégoire, *Syntagma iuris universi* (Cologne, 1623). Also see his *De iuris arte, methodo, et praeceptis* (Lyon, 1580).

[55] Ayrault, *Rerum ab omni antiquitate iudiciarum Pandectae*, 1 (Geneva, 1677): 84. On *Digest*, 42. 1 ("Res judicatae"), also see Ulrich Zasius, *Opera omnia*, 3 (Lyon, 1550): col. 360. There is no modern study on Ayrault.

[56] Charles de Grassaille, *Regalium Franciae libri duo* (Paris, 1545), 45.

AT THIS POINT THE GAIAN PALIMPSEST seems to be exhausted: between the historical and empirical assaults on the one hand and the efforts of rationalization on the other, academic jurisprudence could hardly retain its conventional form; it moved, in a sense, from the letter to the spirit of Roman jurisprudence. In general, the seventeenth century was suffused not only with *l'esprit de système* but also with *l'esprit de géometrie*, and these combined with the enthusiasm for the "new science" of Galileo and Descartes to ensure that legal scholarship would be intimidated if not dominated by what has inelegantly been termed "jusnaturalism." For the next two centuries, so it seemed to many observers at that time and since, legal and social as well as political philosophy was captive to this modern idea—"antique-modern," as Otto Gierke preferred to call it—of natural law.[57] This cast of mind is a deflection from Gaianism. The resurgence and prominence of the idea of "nature" was used in the explanation and legitimation of human categories, social as well as legal (that is, descriptive as well as normative). Indeed, the "state of nature" tended to take over the function both of the moral basis of social behavior and of the historical interpretation of civilization. Thus, the significance of "convention," so essential to Gaius and other Romanists, was subordinated or distorted. Moreover, the principle of authority—and with it the force of custom, prescription, tradition, and even "interpretation" in a usual sense—tended to be overshadowed by the claims of universal reason. The result was that the "law" seemed in many ways to be dehumanized: man himself—his will, his history, his cultural individuality as well as his irrationality and perhaps sinfulness—was increasingly lost to view.

Gottfried Wilhelm Leibniz, who published his own "new method" of jurisprudence in 1667, provides the most extreme example of legal rationalism (*jurisprudentia rationalis*). Although thoroughly grounded in legal scholarship and attached to the "reformed" dialectic associated with Ramus, Leibniz turned to mathematics, specifically to Euclid, for his model of rationality. He rejected the threefold division of Gaius because, as so many others had pointed out, "actions derive from both persons and things." Most fundamental to his objection was the apparently random empiricism of conventional jurisprudence. "Its method," he remarked, "was taken from the inmost parts not of law but of fact" (*haec Methodus non ex Juris sed Facti visceribus sumpta*), "for persons and things are terms of fact, as power, obligation, and the like are terms of law."[58] The confusion and irrationality inherent in such an approach was too absurd for a modern conception of law: "Who would not laugh at such a new Euclid?" For Leibniz, however, jurisprudence, along with other humanistic studies, was subordinated to metaphysics, ultimately

[57] Still fundamental, in addition to Stintzing and Landsberg, *Geschichte der deutschen Rechtswissenshaft*, is Otto Gierke, *Das deutsche Genossenschaftsrecht*, the relevant part of which has been translated by Ernest Barker as *Natural Law and the Theory of Society, 1500–1800* (Boston, 1957); but, in general, the subject of natural law is too peripheral and too voluminous to allow bibliographical comment here.

[58] Leibniz, *Nova methodus discendae docendaeque iurisprudentiae* (Frankfurt, 1667), in *Sämtliche Schriften und Briefe*, 6, pt. 1 (Berlin, 1971): 298. On Leibniz in general, see K. Dickerhof, *Leibniz' Bedeutung für die Gesetzgebung seiner Zeit* (Freiburg, 1941), and F. Sturm, *Das römische Recht in der Sicht von Gottfried Wilhelm Leibniz* (Göttingen, 1968).

to mathematics; and his position represents a pole rather than a school of thought in the range of legal and social doctrines.

The major figure in the re-emergence of natural law was Hugo Grotius, though he, too, was steeped in humanistic and legal erudition. His main legal works were devoted to that anarchic arena of international relations, which itself seemed to represent a pre- or extra-legal "state of nature." Like Leibniz a generation later, Grotius had a basic contempt for unclassifiable particulars. "For the principles of the law of nature," he wrote in the prolegomena to the *Law of War and Peace*, "since they are always the same, can easily be brought into a systematic form; but the elements of positive law, since they often undergo change and are different in different places, are outside the domain of systematic treatment, just as other notions of particular things are."[59] In a youthful work on prizes and booty he took the same view and, reasoning from a set of general rules and law, affected an even more deliberately mathematical plan.

Yet this renewed emphasis on nature and reason is by no means the whole story of social and legal thought in the age of reason. The *ius naturale* was, after all, an essential part of the Roman legal tradition; and, as Richard Zouche reminded his seventeenth-century contemporaries, Gaius himself had explained that the basis of the law of nations was that "natural reason among men" (*naturalis ratio inter omnes homines*).[60] Indeed, the continuing association of the *jus gentium* and the *jus naturale* permitted the legal tradition to maintain its human groundings. Grotius, for example, was not only a jusnaturalist and "father of international law" but also, as Giambattista Vico later called him, the "jurisconsult of the human race."[61] Like Vico, Grotius neither forgot history nor despised tradition. He persisted in citing ancient "authorities," including not only the Bible, jurists, and scholastic philosophers but also literary and especially historical writers, who provided judgments as well as illustrations. Grotius's intentions were, perhaps, less rationalizing than universalizing; for his primary field of operations was indeed "positive law," specifically the kind of "voluntary human law" (*jus humanum voluntarium*) defined as the law of nations (*jus gentium*, exclusive of the *jus civile* as posited by Gaius). Universal law, according to Grotius, arises not only from nature and from divine ordinance but also from custom or tacit consent—that is, from human will. "And the Law of Nations is proved in the same manner as the unwritten Civil Law," he wrote, "namely, by long usage and the testimony of its professors; for this law, as Dio Chrysostom says, is 'the invention of time and experience,' and here the great historians are of the greatest service to

[59] Grotius, *De iure belli ac pacis libri tres*, trans. W. Knight (London, 1922), prolegomena, 22, and *De iure praedae commentarius*, trans. G. Williams and Q. Zeydel (Oxford, 1950), 7.

[60] Zouche, *Iuris et iudicii fecialis* (1650), ed. T. Holland (Washington, 1911), 1. Also see J. W. Textor, *Synopsis iuris gentium*, ed. L. von Bar (Washington, 1916), 2.

[61] See Dario Faucci, "Vico and Grotius: Jurisconsults of Mankind," in G. Tagliacozzo and H. White, eds., *Giambattista Vico: An International Symposium* (Baltimore, 1969), 61–76; L. Rosa, "Grozio fra il giusnaturalismo scolastico e il giusnaturalismo moderno," in *Miscellanea Adriano Gazzana*, 2 (Milan, 1960); Wolf, *Grosse Rechtsdenker der deutschen Geistesgeschicte*; and Fassò, *Storia della filosofia del diritto*.

use."[62] In these ways Grotius managed to retain at least indirect contact with the old Roman tradition.

In France at the very height of the enthusiasm for Cartesianism and that "geometric spirit" sensed and to some degree resisted by Blaise Pascal, the persistence of Gaianism is apparent in a sublimated form. The clearest example, as well as the greatest monument of jurisprudence before Robert Pothier, is the work of Pascal's friend, Jean Domat, whose great system began to appear in 1695. Although Domat's *Civil Laws . . .* were arranged *. . . in Their Natural Order* (an excellent illustration of the craving to reduce convention or history to nature), they remained, in effect, a rationalizing commentary on Roman experience. And, though he affected to seek out fundamental (natural, perhaps prehistorical) principles, Domat found their human expression in the usual texts of civil law. He gave precedence to the natural over the civil state, but he continued to conceptualize within the Roman paradigm, keeping the rubrics of persons, things, and actions. Convention and not nature, for example, led him to define persons in terms of "liberty" (or the lack thereof), citizenship (or the exclusion therefrom, as in foreign or exiled status), and fatherhood (or subjection thereto).[63] The general impression is of rationality, or the rhetoric of rationalism, imposed on the old Roman categories. Even Domat's ultimate goal, famously defined as the "spirit of the laws," was a more rationalized version of the old juristic aim of getting at the true meaning.

Montesquieu's *L'Esprit des lois* of 1748 is, of course, the work that made this phrase and concept universally famous, although the connection with the earlier legal tradition was effectively obscured by the author himself, whose claims to originality have never been disputed and seldom even examined. "My ideas are new," wrote Montesquieu, "and therefore I have been obliged to find new words, or give new acceptations to old terms, in order to convey my meaning."[64] To point out the relation of Montesquieu's system to the old Roman tradition, which he had surveyed historically in his *Grandeur and Decadence of the Romans* (1734), is not to deny its novelty or conceptual force. His basic concern was not with antecedent "laws of nature" but rather with the old law of nations and civil laws; and, if he construed his subject in an extraordinarily wide-ranging fashion, he followed the lead of Baron, Bodin, and others in adopting a comparative approach, in taking universal history and the law of (all) nations as his field, and in emphasizing climate, geography, and cultural tradition. In more specific ways, too, he retained contact with Roman forms as well as with the texts and modern scholarship of civil law, and the book has with some justice been regarded as a "new *De Legibus*." As Le Douaren and others who commented consecutively on the *Corpus juris*

[62] Grotius, *De iure belli ac pacis*, xiv.

[63] Domat, *Les Loix civiles dans leur ordre naturel*, 1 (Paris, 1835). On Domat, see R. F. Voeltzel, *Jean Domat (1625–1696)* (Paris, 1936), 107; and, most recently, G. Tarello, ed., *Materiali per una storia della cultura giuridica*, 2 (Florence, 1972): 127–57.

[64] Montesquieu, *L'Esprit des lois* (Paris, 1748), preface. On the problem of the work's structure, see Franz Neumann's introduction to the English translation, *The Spirit of the Laws*, trans. T. Nugent (New York, 1949), and, more recently, Mark Waddicor, *Montesquieu and the Philosophy of Natural Law* (The Hague, 1970); S. Goyard-Fabre, *Philosophie du droit de Montesquieu* (Paris, 1973); and Tarello, *Materiali per una storia*, vol. 1.

began with a definition of the law, its species, and its sources (*quid jus*, *de divisione juris*, and *unde jus*), so Montesquieu began with general definitions, continued with the species of constitutions (corresponding to democratic, aristocratic, and monarchical sources of law) and then likewise proceeded to the law of persons (liberty and servitude) and of things (commerce), family, and succession. Montesquieu also ended up with a discussion of feudal law (corresponding to the *Libri feudorum*, which modern jurists had accepted as a continuation of "Roman law"). Although Montesquieu's book may have been "without a mother" (*prolem sine matrem creatam* was its motto), it did have a kind of conceptual godfather: the "spiritual consanguinity" of the basic Roman paradigm. *The Spirit of the Laws* can be read as a set of variations, however remote and figurative, on Gaian and Justinianian themes.

As Cartesianism did not entirely efface the old Roman canon in France, *Naturrecht* did not exclude the study of positive law or even end the tradition of Gaianism in Germany. Most representative of jusnaturalism in Germany was the encyclopedic work of Johann Gottlieb Heineccius, though he belonged as well to the continuing enterprise of humanistic scholarship and looked back in particular to Le Douaren. Like Le Douaren, Heineccius worked along both philological and philosophical lines. His historical surveys of civil and Germanic law and his various investigations into crucial topics of modern critical jurisprudence—including Justinian's prohibition against "interpretation," the ignorance of Greek (that is, the "specious dictum," *Graecum est, non potest legi*), the "anti-Tribonianist sect," and biographical sketches of Cujas and other jurists—exemplify his philological analysis.[65] The second line of endeavor consists of a series of commentaries—"Elements," he called them in Euclidean style—not only of philosophy in general but also of natural law, the law of nations, and especially civil law, from the Twelve Tables down to his own day. The Gaian tradition is represented by his *Syntagma* of 1718, a systematic treatise "according to the order of the *Institutes*," but also making use of Oldendorp and other modern scholars.[66] In general, his first concern was with the human condition (*de statu hominis*), and he expressly repudiated Thomas Hobbes's naturalistic tendency to derive all law from contractual agreement. For Heineccius the mainstream of wisdom, though it certainly originated in Greek philosophy, was that "knowledge of things divine and human" (the title of another of his dissertations) identified with jurisprudence.[67] In a number of ways Heineccius—like Grotius, Domat, and others—provides a link between enthusiasm for natural law and older traditions of positive scholarship—and also, not accidentally, between the old jurisprudence and newer views of how to go about studying society.

The importance of the Roman experience in the thought of the Enlightenment is most conspicuous in the historical works of Montesquieu and Edward

[65] Heineccius, *Opera omnia*, 4 vols. (Geneva, 1744), 3: 17, 21, 171, 203. On Heineccius, see Stintzing and Landsberg, *Geschichte der deutschen Rechtswissenschaft*, 3: 179–97.

[66] Heineccius, *Antiquitatem Romanarum iurisprudentiam illustrantium syntagma secundum ordinem Institutionum Justiniani digestum*, in *Opera omnia*, 4. Also see *Opera omnia*, 1: 191.

[67] Heineccius, "De iurisprudentia divinarum humanarumque rerum notitia," in *Opera omnia*, 3: 374–89.

Gibbon, but it was not only decadence and decline that fascinated scholars. The positive force of Gaianism persisted in a variety of ways and so did the grand tradition of Renaissance scholarship that had accumulated around Roman law. François de Boutaric, like Loisel more than a century earlier, offered a comparative analysis of French customary law within the framework of Justinian's *Institutes*.[68] And Damiano Romano, in the fashion of Bodin almost two centuries earlier, offered a treatise "on the true law of nature and of nations" that was organized according to universal history and drew upon the scholarly work of François Hotman, Cujas, Doneau, Le Douaren, and many other, especially Protestant, jurists of the sixteenth and seventeenth centuries.[69] Other examples of adherence to older scholarly traditions can be found among jurists who ostensibly belonged to the natural school but who were repelled by the naturalistic excesses of Hobbes, Samuel von Pufendorf, Christian Thomasius, and Wolf. This repugnance was especially clear in the continuing efforts to improve international law, the roots of which went back directly to Gaius via Grotius. Gaian notions also continued to inform encyclopedic enterprises; for instance, Joachim Daries' *Institutions of Universal Jurisprudence*, somewhat like Grégoire de Toulouse's *Republic*, proposed to describe the nature of man, society, and public and private law in a "systematic," "methodical," and "scientific" fashion, yet again following the old Roman forms.[70]

But the clearest expression of Gaian influence during the age of Enlightenment was surely the effort to codify positive law, which came to maturity during the next century and, indeed, became a central political issue in Savigny's time. Once again the center of attention was France, where the codification movement had arisen in the sixteenth century in connection with the work of Charles Dumoulin and other "systematic" jurists already discussed. What was required for such an enterprise to succeed, according to A. -J. Arnaud, a recent historian of the movement, was the "juridical rationalism" and "modern philosophy" of the age of Descartes, especially the work of Domat and his eighteenth-century successors, including Montesquieu but even more Pothier and Henri Daguesseau, who were more directly significant for the Napoleonic Code.[71] Yet, as Arnaud himself has shown, the "order" achieved by modern philosophy retained much of its Roman composition, especially the tripartite Gaian scheme, which carried over into the French civil code. The "philosophic" ideal of the rationalizing jurists, of course, was itself a central feature of the Roman legacy. Antoine Terrasson was, perhaps, "the first historian of law really concerned with the philosophy of law"; but

[68] De Boutaric, *Les Institutes de Justinien conférés avec le droit français* (Toulouse, 1738). In general, see Klaus Luig, "Institutionen-Lehrbücher des nationalen Rechts im 17. und 18. Jahrhunderts," *Ius Commune*, 3 (1970): 64–97.

[69] Romano, *Del vero diritto della natura e delle genti* (Naples, 1757).

[70] Daries, *Institutiones iurisprudentiae universalis in quibus omnia iuris naturae socialis et gentium capta in usum auditorii sui methodica scientifica explanantur* (3d ed., Jena, 1748).

[71] Arnaud, *Les origines doctrinales du Code civil français*, 27, *passim*; and Ph. Sagnac, *La Législation civile de la revolution française* (Paris, 1898), 51.

Terrasson's history is specifically of Roman law as an embodiment of this philosophy. And, when he wrote, "Philosophy is the true source of jurisprudence," he was thinking of Ulpian, not of Descartes or Leibniz.[72] In any case, what was really required to achieve a code in France was not a conceptual effort; it was a revolution.

Paralleling these rationalizing tendencies in the eighteenth century were various and increasingly obvious survivals of older humanistic traditions. Indeed, this resurgence of historical and literary erudition divided the Enlightenment from the earlier "age of reason." Despite attacks by naturalizing philosophers on "authority" (and, by inference, on history), positive legal and literary scholarship continued to flourish among a variety of unfashionable *érudits*, who refused to allow the new philosophy to cast everything in doubt. Neither Descartes's skepticism nor Galileo's scorn for historians ("memory experts") could stem the flow of antiquarian social, legal, and institutional history. In Germany Hermann Conring, Heineccius, and Leibniz (!), in the Netherlands Perizonius and Grotius, in France Jacques Godefroy, Terrasson, and Montesquieu, in Italy Giovanni Gravina and Ludovico Muratori, and even in England John Selden and Henry Spelman carried on the great enterprise begun by earlier humanists.[73] Without them, it is too seldom recalled, the work not only of Gibbon and other historians of the Enlightenment but also of Niebuhr and Savigny, however original and ground-breaking, would have been impossible. Indeed, Savigny's famous manifesto of the Historical School, "The Vocation of Our Age for Legislation and Jurisprudence" (1814), may be regarded as a celebration of the monumental efforts of this (philosophically) tenuous tradition of scholarship as well as an assault on naturalism and its attendant fallacies.[74] Under cover of these tendencies, Gaianism could maintain a certain precarious existence even outside of narrow professional circles.

In fact, resistance to a physical, or metaphysical, approach to the study of humanity long antedated the rise of the nineteenth-century historical schools. The first great nemesis of radical naturalism was Giambattista Vico, who was at the same time a leading champion of Roman jurisprudence. Vico waged his campaign not only against the current Cartesian form of naturalism but also against its earlier philosophical manifestations. For him a true "science" of humanity had to accommodate not only nature but also convention, not only reason but also authority (and unreason), not only determinism (*necessitas naturae*) but also the free and creative wills of men. As Le Douaren, Lagus,

[72] Terrasson, *Histoire de la jurisprudence romaine* (Paris, 1750), 101.

[73] In addition to Stintzing and Landsberg, *Geschichte der deutschen Rechtswissenschaft*, volume three, there are various specialized studies. For two notable ones, see C. Chisalberti, *Gian Vincenzo Gravina, giurista e storico* (Milan, 1962); and K. Kossert, *Hermann Conrings rechtsgeschichtliches Verdienst* (Cologne, 1939).

[74] See, for example, Savigny, *Das Recht des Besitzes*. For other works by and about Savigny, see notes 80–81, below.

Grotius, and many others had said, human science had to combine historical-philological with philosophical investigations. And according to Vico the model for such a science was neither Greek philosophy nor rhetoric, which had unfortunately remained conceptually separate, but instead that characteristic Roman kind of "wisdom" (*sapientia*) that was jurisprudence—or, rather, the modern expression of this "civil doctrine" born of humanism and best expressed by Grotius.[75] In the context of Vico's epistemology, itself derived from or, at least, analogous to civil law, the "new jurisprudence" combined the study of the cultural products of human will, the "certain," with the study of the products of God's will, or nature, which was the "true." It had to combine, in other words, an understanding of "authority," or history, with a search for "reason," or the divine ideal, in just the same way that philosophical jurists proceeded. Such was the argument of Vico's treatise, *Universal Law*, which was indeed the first version of the *New Science*—the bottom level of an intellectual palimpsest hardly less complex than Gaius' own.

Vico was one of the great transformers as well as champions of jurisprudence. His method—indeed, his obsession—to reformulate everything into historical terms meant he could not directly take over the static Gaian triad. Yet Vico himself was notoriously a trichotomizer; and his own neotrinitarian structures displayed certain analogies with those of Gaius. On the level of epistemology, or psychology, the Vichian classes were *nosse*, *velle*, and *posse*; and they might be rendered respectively as self-consciousness (perhaps self-possession or self-control), vitality (or the urge to live and to relate to others), and activity (or desire to act and to achieve). In the course of the historical process these three basic faculties of human nature were transformed into what can be considered as social, beyond a mere individual, consciousness (*mens*), rationality (*ratio*), and awareness of divinity (*Deus*). In the sphere of civil society, another homologous triad, the institutional categories, again were produced by historical development: *dominium*, which can be understood as control of things, the basis of civil possession, or property; *libertas*, in social terms the legal order, the rule of law; and *tutela*, active control over and direction of society on behalf of its values and goals—that is, government.[76]

It will not do to make too close an identification between the Vichian and the Gaian systems. For one thing Vico was inordinately proud of the "geometric" design of his "new science," and increasingly the Romanoid structure was lost in the successive and increasingly sublimated versions of the system. But both the *Universal Law* and the *New Science* contained a common denominator: both systems retained, on the one hand, a primary category of personality (that is, the subject of rights and obligations) and, on the other, a secondary category of natural reality (that is, objective "otherness," which represented the field for acquisition—both natural and civil possession). In

[75] For a fuller treatment of the place of rhetoric, see my "Vico's Road: From Philology to Jurisprudence and Back," in G. Tagliacozzo and D. Verene, eds., *Giambattista Vico's Science of Humanity* (Baltimore, 1976), 15–29.

[76] Vico, *De universi juris uno principio et fine uno*, ed. F. Nicolini (Bari, 1936).

both systems actions were defined in terms of these two classes. These remarks hardly begin to reveal Vico's relations to the legal tradition, not only to the ancient sources but to the scholarship of Domat, Grotius, the French "systematists," and other commentators of the preceding two centuries; they may, however, serve to suggest some of his importance as a link between jurisprudence and a modern philosophy of society and culture—another way in which a traditional legal science could become the point of departure for a modern social science.

In various ways Vico anticipated, even if he had no direct impact on, the new view of jurisprudence that began to appear in the late eighteenth century—the Historical School of Law, which became more fully defined, and in some ways even dominant, in the wake of the Napoleonic wars. The point of departure of this school was a historically minded—whether conservative, nationalistic, or "romantic"—rejection of theories of natural law or, at least, a reformulation of them. Its home territory was, of course, Germany, where the wars of liberation were directed not only against Napoleonic domination but also against Bonapartist and Jacobin ideology.[77] To simplify a very complex matter, the assault on rationalism and jusnaturalism (and, related to this attack, the emergence of the Historical School) took its strength from three interrelated traditions. First, the continuing efforts of antiquarian research into the national as well as the classical past followed the work of Heineccius and earlier historians and ultimately stemmed from the philological achievements of Renaissance humanism. Second, again related to sixteenth-century concerns with practical matters, "cameralistic science" (whatever its politics and goals) acted as a solvent upon grand theories of natural law, whether older rationalist schemes or newer idealistic constructs, such as that of Kant. Third, most immediate and most emotional was opposition to that concrete embodiment (or, at least, symbol) of oppressive and arbitrary systems, the Napoleonic Code (and, to some extent, its earlier Prussian and Austrian counterparts). These were the grounds on which the *Historische Rechtsschule* was established in the early nineteenth century.

The man most often regarded as the founder of this school—*Altervater*, Marx called him, and *Naturmensch*—was Gustav Hugo, whose attitudes stemmed quite directly from the tradition of classical humanism. Among other works, he published a new edition of the famous fragments of Ulpian (first published by Cujas and referred to by both Montesquieu and Vico) and a translation of Gibbon's forty-fourth chapter surveying the history of Roman law, likewise based on humanist scholarship; he also wrote voluminously on and taught legal history. He began publishing his systematic and historical works in 1789, taking as his special target "dogmatic" jusnaturalism and setting in its place his own realistic sort of natural law.[78] His system was founded on a "juristic

[77] Like Gaius himself, the *Historische Rechtsschule* has spawned a literature too voluminous to mention and a long concatenation of journals starting with those of Savigny and Hugo and ending with the *Zeitschrift der Savigny-Stiftung für Rechtsgeschichte*. See, for example, Georges Gurvitch, *L'Idée du droit social* (Paris, 1932).

[78] Hugo, *Lehrbuch des Naturrechts als eine Philosophie des positiven Rechts*, which was part of his *Lehrbuch eines civilistisches Cursus*, which began to appear in 1789.

anthropology," in which he considered the animal characteristics of persons (*der Mensch als Tier*) and went on to consider law as "natural" in the sense not of rationality but of a *de facto* growth. In one sense, Hugo recapitulated the method of Gaius, who likewise accepted without question the "reality" of past Roman experience, thereby giving "authority" to history, and then rationalized it through dialectical argument. Not surprisingly, Hugo was, like Gaius, open to charges of being arbitrary and authoritarian; and, as conventional Romanism came under fire from rationalists like Leibniz, so the Historical School was attacked by idealists—especially Hegelians, the most famous of whom was the young Marx. Although he recognized that Hugo represented a "reaction against the frivolous spirit of the eighteenth century," Marx objected to the irrationality of the alternative. About Hugo's historical method Marx observed, "Everything serves him as an authority, every authority serves him as an argument"; and about the true principles of justice he concluded that Hugo "desecrates them in the eyes of reason in order afterwards to make them honorable in the eyes of history."[79] So Hugo seemed even to justify slavery; and, in general, Marx reduced Hugo's philosophy of law to the proposition that "the sole juridical feature of man is his animal nature."

Savigny, Marx's teacher, who first joined and then superseded Hugo in the leadership of the Historical School, regarded this attack, of which he was only an indirect target, as unfair and obtuse. Throughout his life Savigny rejected the charge that his view supported the "tyranny of the past" (*Herrschaft der Vergangenheit*), and he argued that the basis of his thought was not authority but realistic human perspective. His views were expressed first in his youthful yet magisterial treatise on possession, *Das Recht des Besitzes* (1803).[80] Here Savigny decisively contributed to a discussion that had been going on for centuries, a discussion that had indeed begun with Gaius and that included other jurists, especially Le Douaren, Doneau, and Pothier. The controlling assumption of this book was that practical questions of law had to be settled in terms of Roman law understood not only systematically but also historically—that is, in terms of a process that included not only ancient forms but also medieval interpretations and modern (*heutige*) transformations. Savigny later followed this method in his treatise on the law of obligations and, above all, in his *System of Modern Roman Law*; presumably, he also maintained the same stance in his teaching and in his career as minister of justice for the reform of Prussian law. Savigny was involved, of course, in other contemporary controversies, most notably that between the "idealists" (especially the Hegelians) and the "realists," with whom he was identified; but the extent to which his ideas can be understood in terms of the longer legal tradition as well as the more immediate context of German philosophy is surprising.

[79] Marx, "Das philosophische Manifesto der historischen Rechtsschule," in *Marx-Engels Gesamtausgabe*, 1, pt. 1 (Berlin, 1927): 251–59. Also see H. Jaeger, "Marx et Savigny," *Archives de Philosophie du droit*, 12 (1967): 65–89; and J. Blühdorn, "Naturrechtskritik und 'Philosophie des positiven Rechts,' " *Tijdschrift voor Rechtsgeschiedenis*, 45 (1974): 3–17.

[80] Savigny, *Das Recht des Besitzes*, 124, and A. Rudorff's addition, 543–62. Also see Vogt, *Franciscus Duarenus*, 89–108.

From the first, Savigny, like Gaius, had systematic ambitions; and his age, like that of Gaius, was similarly divided, both ideologically and pedagogically, over jurisprudence. The basic question of the suitability of a modern code of laws for German society was the issue on which Savigny and the Historical School rose to prominence.[81] Savigny ridiculed the "positivist" notion advanced by A. F. J. Thibaut of constructing an abstract and academic code as simplistic and outmoded naturalism already discredited historically by the evident failures of the Napoleonic, Prussian, and Austrian codes of the previous half-century. Arguing that law, like language, was the product of a long and gradual development, Savigny concluded that the answer lay in the tradition of Roman law, which had been officially "common law" for three centuries and, in fact, for longer than that. As a result, he came to replace Hugo as the leader of the Historical School, especially after the publication of his manifesto of 1814 and the founding of his journal, *Zeitschrift fur geschichtliche Rechtswissenschaft*, in the following year. The premise of this journal, that a true "science" must be the product of centuries of development, was another illustration of the affinity between Savigny and Gaius. Thus, it is appropriate that in the next year came the miraculous discovery of that most ancient relic and deepest root of Roman legal science—Gaius' *Institutes*.

Ironically, gaius appeared too late to be of practical value for the science of jurisprudence; it was too late in the evening for the Roman owl to take flight. The principal significance of the discovery lay in the field of historical scholarship and Roman antiquities. Even more ironically—tragically, in fact, for Savigny—the Historical School was itself more important in the long run for academic—scholarly and philosophical—than for professional achievements. In a sense this culmination of a long process of "historicizing" (*Historizierung*, as a recent historian of eighteenth-century universities calls it[82]) underlies the great works of Theodor Mommsen, Rudolf von Jhering, and others of the next century. In fact, Savigny's reputation today rests largely on his massive *History of Roman Law in the Middle Ages*, even though it was intended originally to be a preliminary study of the sources of law and, thus, ancillary to its author's professional aims and ambitions. Nevertheless, Savigny's *System of Modern Roman Law* was the principal monument of the Historical School; and in many ways it proposed, in modern terms, to carry out the same sort of task, philosophical as well as pedagogical, that Gaius had set for himself. In a sense, it was a move back toward Gaianism.

Savigny's neglected masterwork represents not only the culmination of the Historical School but also a kind of historically oriented *summa* of the legal

[81] Savigny, *Vom Beruf unserer Zeit für Gesetzgebung und Rechtswissenschaft* (Heidelberg, 1814), published with Thibaut's article and other material in J. Stern, *Thibaut und Savigny* (Darmstadt, 1959). On the problem of codification, see J. Vanderlinden, *La Concept du code en Europe occidentale du XXIIIe au XIXe siècle* (Brussels, 1967); G. Tarello, *Le Ideologie della codificazione nel secolo XVIII* (Genoa, 1971); W. Ebel, *Geschichte der Gesetzgebung in Deutschland* (2d ed., Göttingen, 1958); S. Gagnér, *Studien zur Ideengeschichte der Gesetzgebung* (Stockholm, 1960); and Koschaker, *Europa und das römische Recht*.

[82] Notker Hammerstein, *Jus und Historie* (Göttingen, 1972), 216.

tradition going back to the classical period of jurisprudence—most specifically to Gaius himself, who figures prominently in as well as provides the prototype for this treatise. Like Gaius, Savigny proposed to give shape to a vastly "rich heritage" through critical and selective judgment.[83] He rejected the current fallacy of both historical and legal scholarship, which assumed that a systematic treatment could merely be a collection of monographs (though that treatment, indeed, drew upon such works, including Savigny's own on possession and obligation). "Scientific" jurisprudence was the creation not of amateur philosophers like Cicero (or even Montesquieu, despite his training) but only of men of professional authority (*auctoritas prudentium*) like Gaius and Savigny himself. To Savigny's system in general Gaius had made at least three contributions. One was the transmission of particular formulas derived from more ancient Roman legal wisdom. Another was the distinction between the two basic kinds of law—that is, civil law and the law of nations, which was properly identified with natural law (as Savigny thought, in contradiction to those who recognized it as a third type) since it was based on "natural reason." And, almost unavoidably, the third was the notorious Gaian triad. Although Savigny had critical remarks to make about the triad, he did incorporate it into his own structure. What is more, he went on to point out a number of analogous trichotomies of Roman law that history, if not nature, had endorsed.

At the center of Savigny's (as of Gaius') cosmos was, of course, the individual "person," the first member of the Gaian trinity, which perhaps not originally but eventually opened up the whole question of the "status" and "condition" of man in a philosophical as well as a legal sense. In this connection he referred to Doneau, one of the most important of his systematizing predecessors, who elaborated on the concept of personhood by distinguishing aspects not only of life and security but also of liberty and belief (*existimatio*), all of which stemmed from an "original" rather than an "acquired" right. As Savigny described the basic *conditio hominum*, "Man stands in the midst of the outer world, and the most important element, to him in this surrounding of his, is the contact with those who are like him, by their nature and destination." From the individual Savigny moved to the social sphere, where as he put it, "in the richness of living reality all jural relations form a systematic whole." On the level of this web of jural relations (*Rechtsverhältnisse*), the counterpart of the individual was the "people" (*Volk*—that is, the Roman *gens*), and the law thereof was an expression of the old law of nations (*jus gentium*, rendered as *Volksrecht*).[84] Then, in Gaian fashion, he took up the law of things, actions, and their various derivatives and interactions. Romantic and organistic imagery aside, Savigny's strategy was quite in keeping with the Romanist tradition, which he was, in his "historicist" way, espousing.

[83] Savigny, *System des heutigen römischen Rechts*, ix, 413, 393, 38. And, for a very important article, see Aldo Mazzacane, "Savigny et la storiografia giuridica tra storia e sistema," in *Scritti in onore di Salvatore Pugliatti*, 4 (Milan, 1978): 515–29.

[84] Savigny, *System des heutigen römischen Rechts*, 357, 331, xix, 17.

Savigny's influence, though restricted in the long run to the intellectual sphere (his struggle against modern jusnaturalism was defeated with the adoption of the German civil code in 1900), was profound and in many ways pervasive, illustrating again the humanist commonplace that Rome, although it had collapsed as a political structure, continued its dominance through linguistic, literary, and especially legal channels. Gibbon opened his forty-fourth chapter with the observation that "the public reason of the Romans has been silently or studiously transfused into the domestic institutions of Europe . . . ," but even deeper and more enduring has been the effect upon legal, historical, and social thought. Before Savigny this Roman influence was most conspicuously evident in the work of Montesquieu and Vico, who had also striven to recapture the essence of the tradition and give it modern form; after him, it was evident in the work of many others, not only disciples but also critics like Rudolf von Jhering, whose magisterial *Spirit of Roman Law* was devoted to the same purpose. To illustrate this purpose, both Vico and Jhering quoted the famous lines of Vergil,

> Remember, O Romans, you keep universal rule over nations
> In these ways: by maintaining peace through law,
> By doing justice to the lowly, by bringing down the haughty. . . .[85]

This prophecy might be taken as the epitaph of Savigny and his school—not only in their efforts to reform and to regulate society but also in their impact on modern social thought in general.

THE ACHIEVEMENT OF THE HISTORICAL SCHOOL had repercussions far beyond the legal scholarship of Savigny, Johann Eichhorn, and their disciples and the parallel historical writings of Barthold Georg Niebuhr and of Leopold von Ranke and his academic offspring. Based upon a total and "organic" view of culture, this approach involved many other areas of cultural study, most notably language, religion, and political economy. Out of the inter-disciplinary matrix created by these complementary and overlapping "historical schools" emerged one phase of a new discipline called sociology. One of the first historians (and in this country a founder) of that discipline pointed to the Historical School of Law, especially to the Savigny-Thibaut controversy, as seminal for the growth of sociology.[86] A more concrete illustration of this connection is Marx, whose social thought arose in the context of his legal education and, specifically, in the quarrel between the Hegelians and the Historical School; and a number of his ideas, including class structure and "alienation," were directly linked with the civilian tradition.[87] Other particular instances could be added—including, perhaps, the systematic work of Max Weber and, certainly, his sociology of law.

[85] Vico, *Diritto universale*, 214; and Rudolf von Jhering, *Der Geist des römischen Rechts auf den Stufen seiner Entwicklung*, 1 (Berlin, 1852): 306.

[86] Albion Small, *Origins of Sociology* (Chicago, 1924), 37–62.

[87] See my article, "The Metaphysics of Law: An Essay on the Very Young Marx," *AHR*, 83 (1978): 350–67, which is a continuation of the present discussion.

A central remaining question is the significance of the old Roman and Gaian paradigm for modern social thought, especially in its systematic sociological forms. Although to provide an answer moves the discussion from the historical dimension to transhistorical speculation, the question at least provides a logical *terminus ad quem* for this discussion of the afterlife of Roman forms and of Gaianism in particular. To conclude with a retrospective glance at this tradition, it seems clear that the first, and perhaps the most fundamental, continuing influence was pedagogical. Civil law was a major vehicle of secular higher education in European universities from the thirteenth to the nineteenth century (as it had been in Gaius' time), and the *Institutes* (first in a Gaian, then in a Justinianian, and finally in a national form for various European states) constituted one of the basic textbooks of Western civilization, arguably the single most influential introduction to social thought. Certainly, the overwhelming majority of social thinkers prior to Savigny were juridically trained. Secondly, Roman civil law was an almost inexhaustible source of assumptions, insights, terminology, methods, formulas, and concepts for systematic thinking about social structure and process; and even for those who, like Marx, reacted against it, the importance of civil law in negative ways was considerable. Finally, through its ideals, systematic form, and practical intentions, Roman jurisprudence furnished a "scientific" and "philosophical" model for the understanding of human society. The specific relationships between the old legal tradition and the new fields of human study, including economics, sociology, and anthropology, for the most part still await investigation.

In assessing the significance of civil law in Western social thought, let us, in conclusion, return to the original epistemological basis of the Gaian tradition. The ancient dualism of nature and convention implied a distinction between the natural and the social or historical condition of man; and Gaius' subjective and "personal" starting point gave priority to the latter, in contrast both to the intimidating political philosophy of Aristotelianism and to modern naturalism. Jurisprudence could not extricate itself from the conventional, however much it reached toward the natural: as "true philosophy," it was incorrigibly man-centered, value-laden, and action-oriented. It had to view the human condition not as a natural process or a logical construct but as a human epic or drama that focused on the conflict of wills and the means of resolving them within the overall communal pattern. Ultimately, perhaps, the natural and the conventional—reason and custom, the "spirit of law," and the reality of society—might be reconcilable; but men cannot judge, act, and live "ultimately," though they can talk about doing so. Of this human yet global approach to "science," the symbol and in some contingent (and "conventional") sense the starting point is "our Gaius."

II

Clio and the Lawyers

FORMS OF HISTORICAL CONSCIOUSNESS IN MEDIEVAL JURISPRUDENCE

DISCUSSING the question of historical consciousness in medieval law may seem at first to be like writing the famous work on the snakes, or the owls, in Iceland. The judgment of such authorities as Fritz Schultz on Roman legal science, Paul Koschaker on medieval civilians, and Stephan Kuttner on the canonists is that none existed.[1] Even scholars willing to concede a "sense of history" to the middle ages usually talk about Otto of Freising or Joachim of Flora or, at most, Chaucer.[2] Yet such an opinion surely needs modification unless we are satisfied to accept the narrowest and most self-congratulatory view of "history," denying it to all ages but our own, and unless we insist upon interpreting texts in the most superficial and rationalistic fashion, confounding the professed ideals of medieval scholars with their perceptions of reality. To medieval jurists in particular, as to idealists in all ages, history usually seemed more of a burden than a legacy; but it by no means follows that history did not penetrate their consciousness. On the contrary it may be suggested that they had at least as profound an understanding of the processes of history—know thy enemy!—as historians. The question remaining is just how medieval jurists perceived and tried to account for these processes.

Humanist hyperbole to the contrary notwithstanding, it is not only in the Renaissance that law and history have been conjoined: from the beginning the courses run by these disciplines were not only congruent but often contiguous. This circumstance was due above all to their situation in the western scheme of learning derived from antiquity. Both in particular were allied to— and from the standpoint of classical pedagogy practically equated with—rhetoric; so that in terms of training and public function the orator became the model both for the lawyer and for the historian. In the middle ages, with the decline of the oratorical ideal (among other things), their relationship became still closer, both of them, in effect, drawn down into the *trivium* and subsumed under rhetoric, or the *ars dictaminis.*[3] Irnerius himself, the twelfth-century restorer of Roman legal science, was in fact a *magister artium,* and only his disciples, the so-called "four doctors," received professional status. Even then close ties were preserved, and as Odofredus declared, "The orator may properly be called an advocate." [4] Much the same was true for historians after receiving a measure of "professorial" standing in the sixteenth-century, and they continued to identify their function with the "office of the orator" *(munus oratoris).* In a sense, then, the sixteenth-century "conjunction of law and history" which produced the movement modern historians call "legal humanism" was little more than an attempt to recall each to its "trivial" origins, and so it was characterized by its professional opponents.

Such academic consanguinity was reinforced by deeper and sometimes crasser coincidences. On the one hand both law and history represent the racial or public memory of a people and so express their ideals, values, and views of human nature and society; on the other hand both reflect national fears, prejudices, and myths, and so are bound up with national ideology, whether popular or official. Frequently, therefore, historians and jurists have shared not only sources and methods but also issues and political goals. Belonging to overlapping professions, they have waged similar and sometimes mutual ideological battles; committed to common causes, they were not infrequently rewarded—or punished—by the same masters. It cannot be concluded from this that lawyers and historians have always shared the same code of values, much less trusted each other completely; but they have belonged to the same world of discourse (set off by convention from the alien field of natural philosophy) and often have shared the same perspective. This was especially true in the Middle Ages—moreso in a sense than in the sixteenth century, when the war of the *mores italicus* and *gallicus* created a rift between lawyers and historians of law. If it is legitimate to speak in any sense of the "birth of history" in the twelfth century, surely the medieval jurists should not be left out of account.

Jus Civile

In the longest perspective, the medieval phase of the western legal tradition may be said to span a dozen centuries, beginning with the collections made by the Emperor Justinian in the sixth century and continuing well into what on most grounds we think of as "modern times," including the work of such philosophers as Bodin, Grotius, and even Vico, which cannot be fully appreciated apart from the structure and methods of medieval jurisprudence. In the west, however, direct knowledge of the Corpus Juris hardly existed before the "Renaissance of the twelfth century," which began to fulfill the hopes expressed by one enthusiast for the empire, that "with the ancient laws the whole world will be restored." [11] What happened, in more prosaic terms, was that the study of law was taken from its concealment in the liberal arts to the level of a science, sanctioned by the formation of its own university faculty and professional organization.

Out of this came the European "legist tradition" (as canonists referred to it), [12] beginning with the Glossators, dominant from the late eleventh to the late thirteenth century, and carried on by the Commentators, or Post-Glossators, through the sixteenth century and beyond. The distinction was established by the sixteenth century and fixed by humanist critics, who called the two schools Accursiani and Bartolisti, or Bartolo-Baldisti, respectively; [13] but it should be added that the jurists themselves were aware of a pattern of change in their ranks, and like their theological and philosophical rivals they distinguished between "ancients" and "modern"—even "ancients, more recent, and moderns" *(antiqui, noviores, modernique)*[8]—as well as between old and new law. By the thirteenth century the originally Romano-Byzantine canon had expanded in several ways, not only spilling over into ecclesiastical law but also sweeping into its own course certain later north Italian jurisprudence and imperial legislation incorporated into the so-called *Consuetudines Feudorum,* which came to be recognized as the "tenth collation" of "Roman" law. Such were the "authorities" which were technically above suspicion of error and which gave shape, sustenance, and direction to the *legista traditio* for many generations.

It would be a mistake to suppose that this tradition was monolithic in any ideological sense, of course, for there was a wide range of bitter conflicts—canonists versus civilians, Gallicans versus Italians, Germanists versus Romanists, feudists versus advocates of written law, and eventually Protestants versus Catholics. The Italian or "citramontane" jurists lamented "these ultramontane jackasses [*isti asini ultramontani*] who are never happy except when criticizing the Gloss" of Accursius, while the "ultramontanes," especially the French, condemned the servility of their rivals toward the papacy.[9] Indeed, medieval juristic method was founded on the theory and practice of dialectical conflict, and no books aside from the Bible have produced so much controversy over such an extended period. On the most controversial issues there were often not even particular resolutions, not to speak of a *communis opinio;* and well into the eighteenth century scholars were still listing their accumulated pros and cons. Nevertheless, about the manner of formulating issues and about the perception of the underlying social reality there was little disagreement. All medieval jurists, identifying directly with the *antecessores,* or *professores legum,* of Justinian's law schools, shared the same terminology, logic, formulas, apparatus, and to some degree methods. Despite varying allegiances, in short, they spoke the same language, saw the world through the same spectacles, and shared many of what Justice Holmes called "inarticulate major premises."

This consistency of outlook is particularly apparent in the field of history, and the reason for this again attaches to the juridical canon of Justinian. Many of the legists' views about the past were variations on themes found in Byzantine law, especially in the great anthology of classical jurisprudence, the Digest, and in Justinian's prefatory legislation. Here were to be found not only sophisticated conceptions of political and moral philosophy but also a deep consciousness of history—"almost fourteen hundred years" of it. In general, classical Rome had a most subtle appreciation for the workings of legal history. Despite popular notions about founding fathers, Cicero was well aware that the Roman legal tradition was the result not of a single law-giver but of many generations.[10] And despite emphasis upon the rationality of civil law, scholars were aware also of the corrupting force of time—"tempus edax rerum" is the Vergilian phrase. "For long lapse of time has rendered old works and customs obsolete," wrote Aulus Gellius, "and it is in the light of those words that the sense of the laws is to be understood."[11]

Though not publicized, such attitudes inform all the work of Justinian and his editors. The Digest itself was a great act of filial piety toward the first Rome, and the Emperor insisted upon his "reverence for antiquity" *(antquitatis reverentia).*[12] He honored the old jurists (*veteris juris conditores* he called them at one point)[13] by setting down their names in the Digest. Certain laws he included simply because they were "approved by the long usage of this revered city," and even denied that the reasons for some laws were any longer visible. He also emphasized how important it was for beginning law students—"new Justinians" he was pleased to call them—to study the "monuments of ancient learning" *(antiquae eruditionis monumenta).*[14] In recognition of this his editor, Tribonian, placed among the very first titles of the Digest a selection from Pomponius' textbook "On the Origin of Laws" *(De Origine juris)*, which celebrated the great line of jurists from Appius Claudius down to classical times.[15]

But if Justinian could speak in glowing terms of an idealized past, he had no intention of letting its reality get in his way. "For how can antiquity interfere with our authority?" he asked rhetorically. Much as he honored the old jurists, he was careful to stipulate that their decisions (the *responsa prudentum*) no longer had the force of law, and he strictly forbade further "interpretations," permitting only "paratitles," or summaries. Nor did he hesitate to omit, modify, or even reverse what he called the "old learning" or "old laws." In particular he declared his intention of eliminating "superfluities," inequities (such as the law of escheat, derived from the "evil days" of Rome), contradictions (the famous *antinomiae* which it was improper to discuss before the Renaissance), and anachronisms (that is, laws which have fallen *in disuetudinem*).[16] Such were the guidelines for transforming the legacy of Rome into the "new law" *(jus novum)* of Byzantium.

To judge only from the Emperor's rhetoric, his goal was entirely meta-historical. He wanted his law to "prevail for all time," and his transcendent aims were inflated further by imprecations to the Holy Trinity and to his own divine office.[17] Yet behind this heaven-storming project there is apparent a very substantial awareness of the destructiveness of time, the mutability of laws, and the untrustworthiness of posterity. Internal conflicts had rendered Rome unstable for almost fourteen centuries, and the old laws were "oppressed with age." He also realized that "only divine things are perfect," that human nature was incorrigibly weak, and that only a superhuman effort could stem what he called "the vain discord of posterity." The conclusion which Justinian drew from these considerations pointed in quite the opposite direction from his will as legislator. "It is characteristic of human jurisprudence to be always indefinitely extending," he admitted, "and there is nothing in it which can endure forever, for nature is constantly hastening to bring forth new forms." [18] This statement not only illustrates Justinian's considerable "sense of history" but also embodies one of the fundamental arguments for the modern idea of progress, that is, the creativity of nature and the "plenitude of forms." And it makes articulate one of those concealed major premises of legal thought that eventually opened the way to the historical investigation of laws and institutions.

In the event, of course, Justinian's reluctant admissions proved more prophetic than his imperial program: history would not stop for him; later interpreters would not be still. It is true that the Glossators tried to avoid admitting change since Justinian's age, or rather they hoped, like Arnold of Brescia, to revive intact "the good customs and ancient laws" of Rome.[19] They seldom questioned the text of the law, therefore, and never its authority. Justinian had called his collection a "monument," but as Accursius insisted, the word really meant document (from *moneo* not *memoria*).[20] Thus the changes they did effect were largely inadvertent, due to misunderstanding or strict logical necessity. But inadvertence is a powerful force in the history of thought, especially when combined with the enthusiasm and (sometimes) cultural shock which Roman law, like Aristotelian philosophy, tended to generate.

In the Corpus Juris Civilis, furthermore, medieval jurists could not help but recognize the remnants of almost the entire life-cycle of a civilization. "It is called old," observed Azo, "because it contains the confused legislation of almost 1400 years from the founding of Rome at the time of Romulus down to the time of Justinian."[21] In their introductory "materia" they offered information of historical interest, but of course their most direct contact with history was in the *De Origine juris,* all the more because so much of it was so obviously obsolete. So Odofredus and others discussed at some length the five sources (or "species") of law, and yet they realized that four (the *plebiscita,* the *senatusconsulta,* the *responsa prudentum,* and the *lex pretoria*) were of purely antiquarian value.[22] It should be noted that it was this title which provided the point of departure for the modern field of legal history, of which, consequently, the Glossators may be regarded as the earliest pioneers—playing the role of Marco Polo if not Columbus. Among their intellectual descendents were Aymar du Rivail, who compiled the first history of civil and canon law, such historians of feudal law as Marina Freccia and Charles Dumoulin, and Thomas Diplovataccius, author of a biographical dictionary of the legist tradition—none of whom, it may be remarked, owed significant debts to humanism.[23]

But there were more significant manifestations of historical awareness. On the one hand, for example, despite the Christian facade provided by Justinian, the authors of the laws in the Digest were in fact pagans, as Accursius reminded his readers. On the other hand, while in theory admitting no fundamental changes between the time of the Caesars and that of the Hohenstaufen, the Glossators in fact recognized the "barbarous" Lombard accretions that had been given imperial sanction in the eleventh and twelfth centuries. Most interesting of all is the little known fact that Accursius (like his future humanist critics, though they took all the credit) was capable of detecting, on historical grounds, not only contradictions and interpolations but, more generally, an earlier stage of law *(media jurisprudentia)* not quite covered over by Justinian's attempt to bring everything up to date (*hodie per Justiniano* is one formula).[24] Much of the supposed credulity of the Accursians, it may be suggested, arose not so much from ignorance, as humanists charged, but rather from professional scruples.

In some ways the Commentators were more doctrinaire in their clinging to the assumption of consistency in the texts of civil law. Yet again—though again partly through inadvertence—they possessed a broad awareness of historical change even if they did not find much occasion to display it. To some extent this was a result of their dialectical method, which made them face up to difficult problems, to some extent the result of their exaggerated respect for academic authority, which underlay their compulsive tendency to accumulate *opiniones,* itself in effect a historiographical habit.[25] It was the appreciation and criticism of such a legacy of interpretation that led fourteenth-century jurists to compose bibliographical and historiographical essays not unlike modern discussions of the *états des question*. In effect the history of the legist tradition itself begins with such bibliographical notes, including the gloss of Johannes Andrea on Durandus' *Speculum* and (though not extant) Baldus' *Commemoration of the Most Famous Jurists,* which Savigny took as the antecedents of his own work.[26]

What is more striking is that by the fifteenth century the outlawed "interpretation" of legal texts had been transformed by the Commentators from a surreptitious practice into an elaborate theory; and in fact the *defensio interpretationis* sheltered not only a rubric of discussion but a legal genre. "Interpretation is a necessary part of law," declared Pietro Andrea Gammaro, going on to explain that this arose from the law of nations and especially "because laws vary." [27] This conscious mechanism of change was attached to the conventional legal topic "on the meaning of terms" *(de verborum significatione)* and was justified by reference to a number of juridical conventions, including the concept of equity, the force of custom, the conflict of laws, and the so-called "corrective laws" *(leges correctoriae)*. Nevertheless it represented another departure from Justinian's ideal. On this basis professional jurists could claim not merely a mechanical but a "creative function," as a recent historian has remarked—not merely a traditional but also an historical role.[28] It was partly because of such presumptions, it may be added, that humanist critics rejected the adaptive methods of professional lawyers in favor of the static ideals of classicism and Byzantine jurisprudence.

A more conspicuous, though less fortunate, example of the Commentators' encounter with history was their attempts to grapple with the problem of "origins." Two cases in point are the fable about the miraculous recovery of the famous Florentine manuscript of the Digest in the siege of Malfi in 1135 and the assignment of the founding of the University of Bologna to the time of Charlemagne, neither universally accepted.[29] Still more amusing examples appear in the vastly inventive etymologies devised by jurists in their best Isidorean style. But in fact such *obiter dicta* need not be taken too seriously. Some derivations were merely logical (as *jus* from *justitia* instead of the reverse); some honorific (*jus* from Justinian); and others, as Hermann Kantorowicz has remarked, were at least half-facetious.[30] But then etymologies were only incidentally historical; more often than not their purpose was legal or philosophical—to get at the *quidditas* of a term, as Seyssel put it.[31] And as for the problem of ultimate "origins," it is still located largely in the realm of myth, or mystery.

The truth is that the jurists' justification for history was mostly practical. No doubt "antiquities must be studied," in the words of Odofredus, "so that none of the ancient past should be ignored"; but the reason was that history furnished a valuable repository of examples, precedents, and explanatory models to strengthen legal argumentation.[32] For Baldus, investigating origins meant looking for "causes" of a matter—that is, the four Aristotelian causes.[33] These attitudes naturally reinforced the "scientific" rather than the "historical" character of medieval jurisprudence, emphasizing its general, rational, and explanatory basis. "Scire est per causas cognoscere. . ." is the dictum of Chasseneux. "Legista et canonista cognoscunt per causas."[34] But eventually history, too, would come to profess such an analytic concern with human behavior, especially in the political, pragmatic, and neo-Polybian writings of Machiavelli, Bodin, and other Renaissance interpreters of constitutional history.

But if jurisprudence was a "science" in the opinion of many of its practitioners, it had not for that reason lost touch with the humanities and so, in the most rudimentary sense, with history; for like grammar, as John of Salisbury pointed out, law was occupied not only with nature but also with the wills of men.[35] Though divine in origin, the study of law yet turned, in Socratic fashion, to the "human conditon itself"; and because of its public concerns *(utilitas hominum)* it was superior to other professional fields, especially (as argued in endless *quaestiones*) to medicine.[36] Although universal, jurisprudence yet encompassed the particularity of human experience. "Our science," as Baldus put it, "concerns accidents and human deeds, which are as diverse as the minds and wills of men." [37] This emphasis upon the civic and activist ideals of Roman law at the expense of the naturalistic bias of scholastic philosophy, analogous to the attitude of Leonardo Bruni toward political philosophy, also made contributions (though largely unnoticed) to the general phenomenon of "civic humanism." Like Bruni, Bartolus, Baldus, Lucas de Penna, and other classical-minded jurists were drawn toward an even greater appreciation for history, which after all was the chief souce of information about the deeds of men.[38]

It was in the area not of philosophical jurisprudence, not of natural or divine law but in a general sense of human law—*jus positivum* was the term in use from the twelfth century[39]—that medieval jurists most directly confronted problems of legal and institutional history. In a sense the ground had been prepared by discussions of the principle of equity and its function in moderating the rigors of law,[40] and by a growing willingness to question the text of civil law and even to admit the presence of "antinomies"—for as Azo remarked, "to forget nothing and never to err belongs rather to divinity than to humanity" [41]—and by the general principle, stated by Placentinus, that "Man is the author of law, God of justice." [42] But the primary loci of thinking about history were three time-honored doctrines that had always accommodated the idea of change in laws over time. One was simply the legislative principle that "Posterior laws regularly correct prior ones." [43] Another was the doctrine of desuetude—"Leges per desuetudine possunt tolli" is the formula[44]—which Justinian had made an axiom of his legislation. The third was the concept of prescription (especially the *praescriptio longi temporis,* dating from the second century), which jurists elaborated under a varied terminology: *longa, vetera, antiqua consuetudo, vetusta, inveterata mos,* and *usus longevum* are some of the terms listed by Odofredus.[45]

The consequences of these doctrines, or processes, were generally irreversible, and jurists were as often as not content simply to note that "today the law has been changed" *(hodie jus mutatum est).*[46] This insidious though largely unconscious device of *hodie* was applied frequently in the Digest (not only by Tribonian and his assistants but also by classical jurists and so left by the Byzantine editors),[47] and it was very liberally resorted to by the Glossators as well as the Commentators (and also, more self-consciously, by the humanists). Examples from public law were numerous. Formerly, according to the famous *lex regia,* power rested with the people; *hodie* no longer, declared Placentinus, Cino, and others.[48] Formerly, the Roman senators; *hodie,* wrote Baldus, no longer.[49] Formerly, the Emperor had unconditional authority, argued Alberico de Rosate, but *hodie* he had his authority from the church.[50] Formerly, too, usury was accepted; *hodie,* according to Bartolus, not.[51]

Underlying these ad hoc notions of legal change was an attitude that could not help but subvert the uniform and universalist ideals of Roman law which even humanists took over intact: this was a sort of historical and geographical relativism demanding that human institutions should be interpreted in terms of conditions and environment as well as ideal and precept. "Whoever speaks the Latin language. . .is bound by Roman law" was a medieval formula that humanists like Valla could endorse with enthusiasm;[52] but it hardly struck a chord among most Europeans, even educated Europeans, who never saw a toga or a forum or perhaps even a Roman ruin. *Hodie,* things were different. "Human laws," remarked Lucas de Penna, "vary according to the disposition of the land and differences in time [*secundum dispositionum terrarum et varietates temporum*]. . ., and so from the diversity of times flow the diversity of things."[53]

Reflected in this change were the very mechanics and morphology of history, and from the standpoint of medieval law none has better represented the process than that most philosophical of jurists, Baldus. It was a process at once backward- and forward-looking, accommodating both continuity and change. On the one hand, as Ernst Kantorowicz has pointed out, the principle of the "continuity of forms" constituted a link with the past and, for Baldus, a way of preserving the sempiternal ideals of jurisprudence.[54] On the other hand Baldus provided for future change through the idea already expressed by Justinian and, in a somewhat different form, described by Arthur Lovejoy—that is, the "plenitude of forms." "New cases demand new remedies,"

Baldus once observed; and his general conclusion may be taken as one of the first premises of historical consciousness: "Nature and the acts of men always produce new forms" *(natura et actus hominum semper novas producunt formas).* [55]

Consuetudo

The ultimate, and yet in historical terms most immediate, source of these "new forms" is to be found in the realm of custom; and it is here that we enter that penumbral area where law and history overlap— where patterns of social behavior are transformed into enforceable public norms. Whatever the utility of Walter Ullmann's "ascending thesis" for political theory, it does seem to apply to medieval views of the historical process; [56] for before the great lawmaker established laws *de proprio motu,* the people had expressed themselves in their own inarticulate fashion. As Isidore of Seville declared, "Human nature is governed by two rules, namely, natural law and custom." [57] Or according to the often-cited dictum of Irnerius, "Law [*jus*] is threefold, arising from legislation [*lex*], custom [*mos*], and natural necessity [*necessitas naturae*]." [58] It is this quasi-private, sub-political, almost subconscious area of custom (*consuetudo, mos, usus,* or even *stylus*) that has nurtured historical consciousness most successfully.

In Roman law custom is described as *jus non scriptum,* but medieval lawyers also included in it barbarian laws that had been written down and even in a sense codified. "Today," as Bartolus wrote, "feudal law is nothing but custom set down in writing." [59] The justification for accepting custom as law was the alleged "tacit consent of the people," [60] and it had at least two aspects, one geographical and one temporal. The first rested ultimately upon the designation of the *jus gentium* as a recognized form of law (and indeed canonists included civil law itself in this category); the second upon the realization that all legal traditions were born out of unwritten usage, passing from a *de facto* to a *de jure* level. "Law arises out of fact" *(lex ex facto oritur)* is the formula established by later jurists, beginning with Wilhelmus de Cuneo. [61] The relationship between law and custom was endlessly complex, and Bartolus in particular offers an elaborate discussion about "when custom makes law, when it corroborates law, when it imitates law, when it repeals law, and when it is repealed by law." [62] In any case the transforming force of custom was ever present, acting, as jurists admitted, as "the founder, interpreter, and repealer of laws." *Consuetu-*

do est legum condatrix, interpretatrix, et abrogatrix: this opinion of Azo provided not only one of the heaviest counterweights to the authority of civil law but also a fundamental explanation for the process of legal and social change.[63]

Some such assumption was present from the beginning. According to one of the earliest civilian texts in the West, the *Petri Exceptiones* of the late eleventh century, "Usages approved for a long time" were granted as much authority as written law; and the Glossators, though not always the canonists, tended to agree.[64] In his *Book for Poor Scholars,* Vacarius justified customary law by remarking that "things are dissolved by the same process by which they have been created." [65] Given the "fragility of human nature," as Accursius wrote, how could "human justice" be unchanging? [66] Still worse, customs themselves were not always in accord with justice; and it became a commonplace that "evil customs are not to be followed" *(malae consuetudines servandae non sunt).*[67] The function of these flexible and sometimes ambiguous notions was to give judges a freer hand in the interpretation of civil law, but indirectly they served also, by providing a rationale for legal diversity and mutability, to open up legal perspective to problems of what we would call social and cultural history.

Customary law was a matter of some territorial pride as well as privilege for many jurists, who were prone to celebrate the excellence of local unwritten usages by seeing to it that they were given written currency. It was Bracton's proud claim that only England was ruled by customary law;[68] but in truth custom was widely accepted throughout Europe and often, as in the *pays du droit coutumier* in northern France, was dominant. According to the greatest of the early French *feudistae,* Philippe de Beaumanoir, custom had the force of law if it fulfilled two conditions, that it was general and that it had been accepted beyond living memory, and in that case it was to be preferred to written law.[69] The essential ingredient, however, was what would later be called the principle of territoriality—*Consuetudo regionis aut loci servanda est,* in the formula of Azo—which assumes that custom is the expression of and so should be administered to a particular locale or its immediate environs.[70] The idea that "Place determines behavior" *(locus regit actum)* was another premise that was to be shared by lawyers and historians.

The principal text in the discussion of customary law was the *Consuetudines Feudorum* appended to the Corpus Juris of Justinian. Although commonly regarded as authoritative, it was nevertheless often described in terms offensive to the point of scatology—"not writ but shit" *(nec lex sed faex)* would not be an unfair rendering.[71] Yet barbarous as this Italo-Lombard law seemed to classical-minded jurists like Lucas de Penna (not to speak of humanists like Petrarch), it did display conspicuous signs of—and provoked extensive research into—historical change. The redactor Girardus Niger, according to J.G.A. Pocock, "displayed a historical sense not too common at the beginning of the twelfth century"; and his introduction provided, as Ralph Giesey has pointed out, "a convenient synopsis of the historical evolution of feudal succession up to the time of its compilation (about 1125)." [72] An evolutionary pattern may be seen, too, in the glosses and commentaries which accumulated from the thirteenth century onwards, including what amounted to critical historiographical discussions by Baldus, Jacobus Alvarottus, and others from the fourteenth to the sixteenth century.[73]

Most interesting among the rubrics of the *Consuetudines Feudorum* was the one, established on the analogy of the Digest title *De Origine juris,* concerning the "origin of feudal law" *(De Origine juris feudorum).* The formal *quaestio* was that of the "authenticity" of feudal law; and the commentators divided themselves into two schools of thought. One was what I have called the Romanist position, the *communis opinio,* which linked the fief with such civil law precedents as the *precaria* or the *emphyteuma*—the argument being either that feudal law was literally *jus antiquissimum* as the text had it, or else that, in the words of Durandus, it was an "imitation" of antiquity, similar to the Romans' own imitation of the Greeks as reported by Pomponius.[74] The other was the Germanist position, which insisted that feudal vocabulary was made up of "new names" *(nova nomina),* and hence feudal institutions were post-Roman as well as non-Roman.[75] As usual it was the "ultramontane," and especially the French, jurists who followed this anti-imperialist line, and again their achievement represents a story by itself. What finally emerged from this (in a sense still continuing) debate was not only a sharper awareness of national self-consciousness but also one of the most remarkable examples of the common ground between history and jurisprudence.

Jus Canonicum

A common heritage, overlapping careers, mutual concerns, and the fact that many jurists took their degrees *utriusque* make it impossible to discuss civil law without some attention to its ecclesiastical counterpart. Canon law, too, was productive of "new forms" and significant for historical thought. Like civilians, canonists had an appreciation for antiquity, looking back with Gregory VII, for example, to an idealized *ecclesia primitiva* and likewise believing that "the ancient canons must be served." [76] They, too, distinguished between "old law" and "new law," that is, between Gratian's Decretum (c. 1140) and the papal Decretals added over the next two centuries, and were taught to interpret laws literally *(grammaticaliter et ad litteram).* [77] More important, it was the canonists who developed the rules and techniques for determining the authenticity—or exposing the forgery—of particular documents. These devices, established especially by the papal chancery of the twelfth century, were incorporated into canon law under the rubric "De Fide instrumentum," which prescribed ways of assessing a text in terms of style and script as well as seal and general condition.[78] The whole question of the *discrimen veri et falsi,* which again has civilian precedents going back at least to the third century *Lex Cornelia de falsis,* makes a very large story by itself.[79] Suffice it to say that long before the time of Lorenzo Valla the practice of historical and philological criticism had been advanced by canonists. Indeed it is possible that such precedents were known by Valla himself, since canon law was the principal source (as well as principal target) of his famous "Declamation against the Donation of Constantine."

For the most part, however, the focus of canonists was not on restoration but on continuity—not on *antiquitas* but on *traditio.* As Walter Ullmann has pointed out, "the idea of historical continuity was fully made use of in papal disputations;" [80] and this practice became widespread in the legal profession. Canonists and civilians alike shared assumptions about what may be called the morphology of legal tradition. The key to this was again the doctrine of the "continuity of forms," and the emphasis, naturally enough, was on the positive side of legal tradition—not on decline through human weakness but on preservation of nature through right (or at least legal fiction), not on unstable temporality but on idealized, often mystical endurance (represented in particular by the term *aevum,* which, as Fritz Kern pointed out, was sometimes etymologically associated with *ê*, an old Germanic word for law).[81] "When the form does not change," as Baldus argued, on behalf of the immortality of the Roman *populus,* "the thing itself is said not to change." [82] On this basis jurists were able to demonstrate, or at least to save the appearances of, continuity—of asserting various kinds of political or institutional immortality, unchangeable succession, corporate permanence, immutable sovereignty, the "mystical" yet vital body of the commonwealth,[83] and other fictions amenable to *Geistesgeschichte.* That such abstractions have been so largely the preserve of German legal historians, especially since Gierke, should not blind us to their importance in the historical consciousness of an earlier age.

The locus classicus—or should we say locus barbaricus?—of canonist thought about the general structure of human history is the famous theme of "translation of empire." [84] Despite an interesting pre-history from Carolingian times, this idea does not emerge into the full heat of controversy until its appearance in an early gloss (that of "Paucapala") on Gratian and more especially in the decretals, through Innocent III's bull Venerabilem. Thence, through such commentaries as that of Johannes Teutonicus, it made its way into historiography. This theory—tracing the course of empire westward from the Medes and Persians through the Greeks to the Romans and, by agency of the papacy, the Germans—became even more grandiose in the hands of historians, who linked world cultural leadership with world monarchy and affected to find an accompanying "translation of learning" *(translatio studii* or *sapientiae),* including, of course, jurisprudence.[85] Associated with this formula was the legend of Charlemagne's founding of the University of Paris—"Studium de Roma Parisiis transtulit," wrote a twelfth-century grammarian, and the idea persisted until the seventeenth century. Yet beneath this apparent universalism lurked a most parochial view of history, and the idea of translation was not without its critics, especially among the "ultramontane" commentators of northern Europe. Next to the Donation of Constantine, in fact, there was no more controversial thesis in medieval historiography and law.

Perhaps the most amusing thing about this canonist idea is that the weapons ultimately turned against it were themselves canonist in origin. The issue arose from the first law, "Cunctos populos," in the Code, which designated the emperor "lord of the whole world" *(dominus totius mundi),* and around it the "vain discord of posterity" was almost deafening. The *communis opinio,* expressed for example by Cino da Pistoia (and Petrarch), was that he held authority de jure, not de facto;[86] but many voices were raised against this view, especially those of such French jurists as Jacques de Révigny and Jason del Maino.[87] Their position was that the emperor's authority extended only to his subjects *(non ligant nisi subditos imperatoris)* and that, consequently, the law was misleading *(et sic male dicit cunctos etc.).* The clinching argument was always the canonist proposition, again originating with Innocent III, that "the King of the French recognized no superior in temporals"—so, according to the still more notorious formula, was "emperor in his kingdom." [88] And other ultramontane jurists, especially the Spanish and English, followed suit.

But this incipient nationalism had a historical as well as a legal basis, stemming from a refusal to apply the distinction between law and fact in this case. Jason del Maino, for example, pointed out that there were numerous peoples, the Persians and Vandals as well as the French, who had never been subject to the empire; [89] and Cosmo Guymier, glossing the Pragmatic Sanction of Bourges, offered the testimony of the "old chroniclers" in support of the same conclusion. [90] By the fifteenth century, in general, the validity of historical evidence was often recognized, especially in the Gallican branch of the canonist tradition, which was particularly intent upon reestablishing privileges lost and "ancient liberties" usurped, as they saw it, by modern Romanist deviations from the "primitive church." [91] Because of this problem of "usurpation," indeed, Gallicanism was from at least the time of "the lawyers of the last Capetians" a fertile field for the cultivation of historical argumentation; and this attitude was confirmed by the practices of the Parlement of Paris in particular, which like the monarchy itself began to build a tradition out of its own precedents, thus helping to create, though inadvertently again, an interpretation of history. The pluralism implicit in such anti-universalist and anti-authoritarian opinions was another premise shared by lawyers and historians, and they owed it in no small part to canon law.

Despite the weight of tradition, the lure of sempiternal fictions, and the stasis of juridical ideals, reality could not be imprisoned. *Eppur si muove*—the human world at least, and in this case the canonists were prepared to agree. Forms may be undying, as Baldus thought, but he also added, "Nihil perpetuum sub sole." [92] Underlying the *translatio imperii,* too, was something a bit more profound than the notion of a providential succession of Four World Monarchies, or hypostasized Ages. There was also a sense—a tragic sense—of the essential mutability of human societies. The invariably cited text was from the *Liber ecclesiastici:* "God transfers kingdoms from one people to another because of injustice, injuries, blasphemies, and other evils." [93] Nature may have established the basis of political and legal order, but human nature guaranteed that disorder would finally return. In terms of the structure of history this resulted in the rise and fall of individual societies; on the level of the texture of history it involved what a recent historian of canon law has called "a theory of the relativity and mutability of laws, or *leges.*" [94] This theory was reinforced by the controversies within the canonist tradition and by the sense of the national diversity of European society, which no universal system could overcome or conceal.

In their attempts to bring some order out of this disorder, to find some pattern in this mutability, canonists were led, or perhaps driven, to a fundamental sort of relativism. "One must take into consideration," wrote one eleventh-century churchman, "geography, the nature of the time [*qualitas temporum*], the weakness of men, and other unavoidable realities which normally change rules; for by power many things are changed for the common good of the churches. . . .Sometimes contradictory canons are issued in one council and prohibited in another. Yet this should not frustrate those who, in terms of our temporal life, want virtue to overcome vice, and truth falsehood." [95] On the level of policy-making such casuistry lent support to ideas of "equity," which offered protection against the severity of laws, or of "reason of state," which demanded attention to circumstances as well as to principles.[96] On the level of perception, however, it confirmed a historical view of law-making and of social order, and it further justified the canonist assumption that laws had to be interpreted in terms of the places, times, and persons *(locus, tempus, persona).* [97]

Again it was the "ultramontane asses," and especially the Gallicans, who developed most fully these views, turning them as usual against the universalism of the church, extending them into heterodoxy and, eventually, into historiography. "So it is not necessary for all the faithful to live in a common republic," declared John of Paris. "They may live in different climes, regions, and conditions, according to different ways of living and under different governments." [98] With John of Paris, of course, we approach the arena of propaganda, where rather more contrasting and colorful views of history tend to prevail. Yet such protestations of national independence by publicists—which must be counted not only among the most significant manifestations of historical consciousness but also among the most effective incentives for further historical research—were the product most directly of the controversies defined and promoted by medieval jurists.

Jus Gentium

From the later middle ages the historical and comparative investigation of laws and institutions was carried out in a broader context than the "two laws" of professional jurisprudence, yet still in association with the traditions of Roman law. This context was that of the *jus gentium,* which according to Baldus was "applied by all nations." [99] From at least his time, of course, this "law of nations" was not merely that recognized by Justinian but the sum of the legal traditions of all nations, past, present, and to come; and this ever-expanding territory was explored by historians and philosophers as well as jurists. The focus in general was not upon the abstract or normative "source," but upon the positive and individual development of individual nations, which according to one formula of the Commentators were "established by the law of nations." It was their opinion, too, that the *jus gentium* was chronologically posterior to the *jus naturale,* and so necessarily it had to be approached historically, or at least empirically.

In the framework of the *jus gentium* certain general patterns of development were beginning to be perceived by medieval jurists. The starting point was not a bountiful Providence but prehistorical anarchy, not Eden but what amounts to a "state of nature." The basis of this was no doubt the Christian assumption that the social order was a pagan creation of dubious respectability—that the Roman Empire in particular "was built on violence not justice" and that its legitimation was a matter of providential yet *de facto* approval or subsequent rationalization. Combined with this assumption, however, was a kind of evolutionary theory of social history. [100] Formerly men lived in forests, remarked Alberico de Rosate, and only later did they build houses, live in cities, and create laws. The mechanism of this evolution likewise had a human and nonprovidential aspect. "Notice that the two pronouns 'mine' and 'thine'," remarked Lucas de Penna, "procede not from justice but from the iniquity of mortals. . . , that is, from custom." [101] Whence arose—whether through the *jus gentium* or not was debated—slavery, wars, and other evils as well as such useful devices as contracts and other civil institutions. But thereafter the story of human society was one literally of "civilization"—and that largely through the good offices of the grand tradition of professional jurisprudence.

This pattern became much clearer in the works of such modern products of the legist tradition as Jean Bodin, who took a more deliberate interest in history. Like the earlier jurists, Bodin dispensed with the notion of a "golden age" and posited instead a primitive time which, ridden with barbarism and unparallelled crime, was a veritable *bellum omnium contra omnes.*[102] The subsequent pattern, common to both law and history, was one of gradual improvement, in general terms, from oral tradition to increasingly coherent and cultivated written forms. Just as history changed from myth and annals to chronicles to more rational and explanatory narrative to the level of intellectualized and ideologized historiography, so law developed from unwritten customs to more generalized written laws to the rationalized jurisprudence of professional lawyers and judges and finally, perhaps, to a systematized "code." The progression from fact to law, implicit in medieval jurisprudence, becomes explicit in the work of certain early modern social philosophers. Of course, the change could also be interpreted as degeneration, a falling away from virtue and *boni mores,* and indeed was so interpreted by such malcontents as François Hotman;[103] but more often it was looked upon as a manifestation of civilization and enlightenment. At least one form of the modern idea of progress, it may be suggested, was a byproduct of the legist tradition.

In a number of ways the harvest time of the investigation of the *jus gentium*—"universal law" is roughly equivalent—and indeed of medieval jurisprudence in general came in the sixteenth century; and no one represents this fruition better than Jean Bodin, whose work establishes as well the most conspicuous link between the medieval art of law and the modern science of society. Bodin had full command of the methods, apparatus, and aims of professional jurisprudence and in fact, as his most acute commentator remarked, was the inheritor less of Machiavelli than of Bartolus and Beaumanoir.[104] The chief difference was that Bodin shifted emphasis from commentary on standard "authorities" to analysis of historical "sources" (though they were often the same works)—that is, from interpreting texts to interpreting history itself. In line with the assumption of earlier French legists, Bodin rejected Roman claims upon any universal tradition, not only in his famous refutation of the old theory of Four World Monarchies but even more fundamentally by denying the relevance as well as the authority of civil law. "The better part of law," he believed, "is to be found in history;" and so he launched into an empirical and comparative study of the institutions of all nations to which he had access.[105] To this enterprise he brought many of the attitudes displayed by his professional forebears, especially a fascination with "origins," a sense of temporal and geographic relativity, and an appreciation of the mutability of human institutions.

This late and transmuted phase of jurisprudence inspired by Bodin was continued by other scholars and philosophers in succeeding generations and led ultimately to the work of *philosophes* like Montesquieu and Vico, who also wanted, as Montesquieu put it, "to illuminate history through laws and laws through history." [106] The clearest connection can be seen in Vico, whose great treatise of universal law may be regarded not only as a juristic prefiguring of his "new science" but also as a kind of philosophical summing up of the legist tradition. Like Bodin and Montesquieu, Vico discussed various conventional legal topics (such as the origin of feudal law), adapted conventional methods of interpretation (such as etymology), and took as his field of operations the entire world of the *gentes.* His major point of departure (as well as his major goal) was the problem of "origins," and so he focussed upon that "image of antiquity," the Twelve Tables, which in fact inspired his basic insights about the original character of primitive society (law emerging from custom and founded upon violence), the universality of the feudal pattern ("Roman law emerged from feudal law, not feudal from Roman"), and in general about what he termed "poetic wisdom." [107] Indeed there are few aspects of Vico's historical philosophy that did not stem from, or have direct analogies with juridical conventions; and this includes his famous *corso-ricorso* thesis, the *verum ipsum factum* principle, and his ultimate aim of uncovering the most fundamental rules of human behavior (the *jus naturale gentium,* as he called it). [108] Obviously this opens up another world of inquiry altogether, but it does serve to suggest the longer perspective of the present discussion.

In conclusion, it may be said that the task of Vico and Montesquieu was to reconstruct what medieval jurists took on faith, which was the reason underlying law, the *logos* behind the letter. At first, impressed by the structure of Justinian's law (as well as his rhetoric), jurists had looked upon Roman law as itself "written reason" (*ratio scripta*); but increasingly they began to act as if this "reason" were an ideal apart from, or rather behind, the written law and that the authority rested actually in the ideal *(ratio legis est ipsa lex).* In jurisprudence, as in Biblical scholarship, the letter killed but the spirit gave life, and so jurists sought the reason, or intent, of the literal text (*ratio, sententia, voluntas,* or *mens legis* was the formula). [109] By the sixteenth century this rationale (rather than the Emperor) was itself sovereign. So scholars began to look more deliberately beyond the horizons of Roman law to other societies, past and present, and to other methods of interpretation, especially to historical and comparative techniques. The target was still the *mens legum,* but increasingly in the sense not of the meaning of particular laws but rather of the structure of human law in general. Thus a procedure of legal exegesis was, in association with historical investigation, transformed into a philosophical concept, especially by Vico (who adapts the term directly) and by Montesquieu (if one can supply the translation). It is appropriate to conclude by suggesting that, at least from one perspective, one of the major consequences of the legist tradition was the formulation of "the spirit of the laws."

NOTES

1. Schulz, *Principles of Roman Law,* trans. M. Wolff (Oxford, 1936) 98, Koschaker, *Europa und das römische Recht* (Munich, 1953) 88, and Kuttner, *Harmony from Dissonance* (Latrobe, Pa., 1960) 35.
2. Heer, *The Intellectual History of Europe,* trans. J. Steinberg (New York, 1966) 80; cf. Morton Bloomfield, "Chaucer's Sense of History," *Essays and Explorations* (Cambridge, Mass., 1960) 15. An almost unique discussion of the "Senso della Storia" in medieval law is Riccardo Orestano, *Introduzione allo studio del diritto romano* (Turin, 1963) 114, 136. See also the fascinating, if rather doctrinaire, application of structuralist theory to medieval law by Pietro Costa, *Iurisdictio, Semantico del potere publico nella pubblicistica medievale (1100–1433)* (Milan, 1969).
3. On rhetoric and law see Hastings Rashdall, *The Universities of Europe in the Middle Ages,* ed. F. M. Powicke and A. B. Emden (Oxford, 1936) I, 109; on rhetoric and history M. Schulz, *Die Lehre von der historische Methode. . .* (Berlin, 1909). There is a section "de origine juris" in Boncampagni's *Rhetorica novissima* (1226), according to Rockinger, in *Sitzungsberichte der königl. bayerischen Akademie der Wissenschaften zu München,* I (1861) 136.
4. Odofredus, *Lectura super Digesto veteri* (Lyon, 1550; repr. Bologna, 1967) f. 10^{v} (D. I, 1, 2): "Orator proprie dicitur advocatus." Cf. Cassiodorus, *An Introduction to Divine and Human Readings,* trans. L. W. Jones (New York, 1946) 148: "The art of rhetoric. . .is expertness in discourse on civil questions."
5. Cited by Percy Ernst Schramm, *Kaiser, Rom und Renovatio* (Berlin, 1929) 286.
6. Ruffinus, *Summa Decretorum,* cited by R. W. and A. J. Carlyle, *A History of Political Theory in the West* (London, 1903–1936) II, 103.
7. The classic attack on the "Accursiani" is Guillaume Budé, *Annotationes in . . .Pandectas* (Paris, 1508), and on Bartolus, Lorenzo Valla, "In Bartoli de insigniis et armis libellum," *Opera onmia* (Basel, 1546; repr. Turin, 1962) I, 633; *bartolobaldizein* is a coinage of Theodore Beza, *Correspondance,* ed. H. Aubert et al (Geneva, 1960–) I, 35. Odofredus is one who distinguished between "vetustiores" and "moderni." The standard periodization appears in Etienne Pasquier, *Les Recherches de la France* (Paris, 1621) Bk. IX, ch. 34, "les glossateurs," "les docteurs en droict" or "Bartholistes" or "scribentes," and "les docteurs humanistes." In general see my "Rise of Legal History in the Renaissance," *History and Theory,* IX (1970) 174–94.
8. By the Bartolist Claude de Seyssel, *Speculum feudorum* (Basel, 1566) 3. The designation "antiqui" is used from the eleventh century, according to Paul Vinogradoff, *Roman Law in Medieval Europe* (Oxford, 1929) 39.
9. Baldus, cited by Biagio Brugi in *L'Opera di Baldo,* per cura dell'Università di

Perugia nel V centenario della morte del grande giureconsulto (Perugia, 1901) 78. Cf. Chasseneux, *Catalogus gloriae mundi* (Paris, 1529) V, 28, and Walter Ullmann, *Medieval Papalism* (London, 1949) 45.

10. *De Republica,* II, 1, 2.
11. *Noctes Atticae,* XX, 1.
12. Justinian's constitution *Tanta.* Cf. Durandus, *Speculum* (Lyon, 1547) f. 2[r]: "Antiquitas est reverenda." In general see Fritz Schulz, *History of Roman Legal Science* (Oxford, 1953).
13. *Code,* I, 14, 12, 3.
14. *Deo auctore.*
15. *Digest,* I, 2, 2.
16. *Deo auctore.* See Schulz, *Principles of Roman Law,* 14. A fundamental study is still François Baudouin, *Justinianus, sive de jure novo* (Paris, 1556).
17. Constitution *Omnem.*
18. *Tanta*: "Sed quia divinae quidem res perfectissimae sunt, humano vero juris condicio semper in infinitum decurrit est nihil in ea, quod stare perpetuo possit (multas enim formas edere natura novas deproperat), non desperamus quaedam postea emergi negotia, quae adhuc legum laqueis non sunt innodata."
19. Otto of Freising, *The Deeds of Frederick Barbarossa,* trans. C. C. Mierow (New York, 1953) 61.
20. Accursius, *Ad Digestum, in tit.*
21. Azo, *Summa* (Venice, 1566; repr. Turin, 1966) col. 29. See Hermann Fitting, *Summa Codicis des Irnerius* (Berlin, 1894) 3; also Hermann Kantorowicz, *Studies in the Glossators of the Roman Law* (Cambridge, Eng., 1938) 37, and Edwin A. Quain, "The Medieval Accessus ad Auctores," *Traditio,* III (1945) 228 ff.
22. Odofredus, *Super Digesto,* f. 8[r].
23. Aymar du Rivail, *Historia juris civilis,* followed by *Historia juris pontificalis* (Mainz, 1530); cf E. von Moeller, *Aymar du Rivail, der erste Rechtshistoriker* (Berlin, 1907). Thomas Diplovataccius, *De claris juris consultis,* ed. H. Kantorowicz and F. Schulz (Berlin, 1919).
24. Carlo Alberto Maschi, "Accursio precursore del metodo storico-critico nel studio del 'corpus iuris civilis,'" *Atti del Convegno internazionali di studi accursiani,* ed. Guido Rossi (Milan, 1968), II, 610.
25. See M. P. Gilmore, *Humanists and Jurists* (Cambridge, 1963) 158–59.
26. Karl von Savigny, *Geschichte des römischen Rechts im Mittelalter* (Heidelberg, 1834–51; 2nd ed.) III, Anhang II, "Aelteste Beyträge zur juristischen Literärgeschichte" contains the texts; and see Enrico Besta, "Baldo e la storia letteraria di diritto," in *Opera di Baldo,* 81–111.
27. Gammaro, *De Extensionibus,* in *Tractatus universi juris* (Venice, 1584) XVIII, 248.
28. Vincenzo Piano Mortari, *Ricerche sulla teoria dell'interpretazione del diritto nel secolo XVI* (Milan, 1956) 54.
29. Hermann Kantorowicz, "A Medieval Grammarian on the Sources of the Law," *Tijdschrift voor Rechtsgeschiedenis,* XV (1937) 46, and Savigny, III, 97.
30. Kantorowicz, *Studies in the Glossators,* 57.
31. Seyssel, *op. cit.,* 11.
32. Odofredus, *Super Digesto,* f. 12[r].
33. Baldus, *Super Digesto,* f. 4[r].
34. Chasseneux, *Catalogus,* X, 9.
35. John of Salisbury, *Metalogicon,* trans. D. McGarry (Berkeley, 1962) 73.
36. Cited in *Opera di Baldo,* p. 435. Some of the more formal entries in the controversy have been discussed by Lynn Thorndike, *Science and Thought in the Fifteenth Century* (New York, 1929) 24–58, and Eugenio Garin, *La Disputa delle arti nel Quattrocento* (Florence, 1947).

37. *Opera di Baldo, loc. cit.*
38. The point has been made by Peter Riesenberg, "Civism and Roman Law in Fourteenth-Century Italian Society," *Explorations in Economic History,* VII (1969–70) 252; the neglect of the jurists by historians of the Italian Renaissance is practically universal. Baldus' relation to the new idea of *civilità* was discussed by Iulio Tarducci, "Il Temp di Baldo e lo spirito della sua scuola," *Opera di Baldo,* 409–66.
39. Gabriel Lebras (ed.), *L'Histoire du droit et des institutions de l'eglise en occident,* VII (Paris, 1955) 388.
40. See Norbert Horn, *Aequitas in der Lehren des Baldus* (Cologne, 1968).
41. Azo, *Summa,* col. 29. Cf. Odofredus, *Super Digesto,* f. 3[r]: "Jus civile an sit purgatum contrariis."
42. Placentinus, *Summa Institutionum,* cited by Orestano, *op. cit.* 131.
43. Alberico de Rosate, *Super Digesto,* f. 28[v].
44. Odofredus, *Lectura super Codicem* (Lyon, 1552) f. 3[r].
45. Odofredus, *Super Digesto,* f. 15[r]. In general see Noel Vilain, "Prescription et bonne foi du Décret de Gratien (1140) à Jean d'André (+ 1348), *Traditio,* XIV (1958) 129.
46. Odofredus, *Super Codicem, loc. cit.* Francesco Calasso, *I Glossatori e la teoria della sovranità* (Milan, 1951) 19.
47. Emilio Albertario, "Hodie," *Studi di diritto romano,* VI (Milan, 1953) 125–42.
48. Placentinus, *Summa Codicis* (Mainz, 1536; repr. Turin, 1962) 17; Cynus, *In Codicem. . .doctissima commentaria* (Frankfurt, 1578; repr. Turin, 1964) 17. Cf. Charles T. Davis, *Dante and the Idea of Rome* (Oxford, 1957) 17.
49. Baldus, *Super Digesto,* f. 2[r] (prooemium).
50. Alberious de Rosato, *Super Codicem,* f. 7[r].
51. Cited by C. N. S. Woolf, *Bartolus of Sassoferrato* (Cambridge, Eng., 1913) 47.
52. *Summa Lipsiensis,* cited by S. Mochi Onory, *Fonti canonistiche dell'idea moderna dello stato* (Milan, 1951) 174; cf. Valla, *Elegantiae Latinae linguae,* I, praefatio, in *Opera,* I.
53. Cited by Walter Ullmann, *The Medieval Idea of Law* (London, 1946) 57.
54. Kantorowicz, *The King's Two Bodies* (Princeton, 1957) 295.
55. *Opera di Baldo,* 433.
56. *Principles of Government and Politics in the Middle Ages* (London, 1961) 19.
57. Cited by Carlyle, V, 46.
58. Cited by Carlyle, II, 53. In general see Francesco Calasso, *Medio evo del diritto,* I (Milan, 1954) 181 ff, and Horn, *Aequitas,* 82ff.
59. Bartolus, *In Primam Digesti veteris partem* (Venice, 1590) f. 17[r].
60. Ullmann, *Medieval Idea of Law,* 63. Cf. the discussion in Chasseneux, *Consuetudines Ducatus Burgundiae* (Frankfurt, 1574) prooemium.
61. It is commonly used in the sixteenth-century, as e. g., Ulrich Zasius, *Paratitla,* in *Operum omnium* (Lyon, 1550) I, col. 17 (on D. I, 2, 2); Francois Hotman, *Matago de Matagonibus* (s. 1., 1575) 30; Thomas Smith, *De Republica Anglorum,* ed. L. Aston (Cambridge, Eng., 1906) 74. The locus is usually D. IX, 2, 52, 2; see E. Cortese, *La Norma giuridica* (Rome, 1962–64); and Charles Fried, "The *Lex Aquilia* as a Source of Law for Bartolus and Baldus," *American Journal for Legal History,* IV (1960) 142–72. Above all see the discussion of Luigi Prosdocimi, " 'Ius vetus' accursiano e 'Ius novum' postaccursiano," *Atti del Convegno internazionali di studi accursiani,* 950. But there is much more to be said on this question. Special thanks to Domenico Maffei for suggestions on this matter.
62. Bartolus, *In Primam Digesti veteris partem,* f. 18[r].
63. Odofredus, *Super Digesto,* f. 16[r]; cf. Azo, *Summa Codicis,* cited by Carlyle, II, 52.
64. Cited by Carlyle, *loc. cit.*
65. Cited by Vinogradoff, *Roman Law in Medieval Europe,* 57.

66. Accursius, *Ad Digestum,* I, 1, 1.
67. Baldus, cited by Horn, *Aequitas,* 85. In general see F. Olivier-Martin, *Histoire de la Coutume. . .de Paris* (Paris, 1922) I.
68. Bracton, *De Legibus et consuetudines Angliae,* ed. G. Woodbine and trans. S. Thorne (Cambridge, Mass., 1968) I, 1.
69. Carlyle, II, 42.
70. Azo, *Brocardia* (Venice, 1561) col. 123. See P. Meylan, "Les Statutes réels et personels dans la doctrine de Dumoulin," *Mélanges Paul Fournier* (Paris, 1929) 511–26, and Paul Ourliac, *Droit romain et practique méridionale au XVIe siècle, Etienne Bertrand* (Paris, 1937).
71. E. g., Lucas de Penna, cited by Ullmann, *Medieval Idea of Law,* 73.
72. Pocock, *The Ancient Constitution and the Feudal Law* (Cambridge, Eng., 1957) 74, and R. E. Giesey, *The Juristic Basis of Dynastic Right to the French,* Trans. American Philosophical Society, LI (5) (Philadelphia, 1961) 1.
73. The essential texts are in the study by Savigny's disciple, Ernst Adolph Laspeyres, *Ueber die Entstehung und älteste Bearbeitung des Libri Feudorum* (Berlin, 1830).
74. This is studied in detail in my "De Origine Feudorum: the Beginnings on an Historical Problem," *Speculum,* XXXIX (1964) 207–28.
75. Andrea de Isernia, *In Usu feudorum commentaria* (Naples, 1571) f. 6[r].
76. Odofredus, *Super Codicem,* f. 9[v]. In general see Glenn Olsen, "The Idea of the Ecclesia Primitiva in the Writings of the Twelfth-Century Canonists," *Traditio,* XXV (1969) 61–86; and Stanley Chodorow, *Christian Political Theory and Church Politics in the Mid-Twelfth-Century* (Berkeley, 1972).
77. *Sexti Decretalium,* II, t. 12, and *Extravag. Ioann. XXII,* t. 14, rubric "De Verborum significatione," in Emil Friedberg (ed.), *Corpus Iuris Canonici* (Graz, 1959) II. Cf. Lebras, *Institutions ecclesiastiques,* 105.
78. *Decr. Greg. IX,* II, t. 22; cf. V, t. 20 ("De Crimine falsi").
79. Peter Herde, "Römisches und kanonistisches Recht bei der Verfolgung des Fälschungsdelikts im Mittelalter," *Traditio,* XXI (1965) 291-362; also Horst Fuhrmann, "Die Fälschung im Mittelalter," *Historisches Zeitschrift,* CXCVII (1963) 529–601, and R. Lane Poole, *Lectures on the History of the Papal Chancery down to the Time of Innocent III* (Cambridge, Eng., 1915) 145.
80. Ullmann, *Medieval Papalism,* 9.
81. Cited by Kantorowicz, *King's Two Bodies,* 299.
82. Texts cited by Goez, *Translatio Imperii,* 11 ff. See n. 84.
83. Among recent studies see R. E. Giesey, "The French Estates and the Corpus Mysticum Regni," *Album Helen Maud Cam* (Louvain, 1960) 155–71.
84. An excellent and comprehensive study is Werner Goez, *Translatio Imperii* (Tübingen, 1958), discussing jurists as well as historians; see also Ullman, *Medieval Papalism,* 168 ff.
85. Paul Renucci, *L'Aventure de l'humanisme européen au moyen-âge* (Paris, 1953) 139; Hermann Kantorowicz, "A Medieval Grammarian," 47.
86. Summarized in Paulus Castrensis, *In Primam Codicis partem commentaria* (Venice, 1582) f. 3[v]. See J. Baskeiwicz, "Quelques remarques sur la conception de dominium mundi dans l'oeuvre de Bartolus," in *Bartolo da Sassoferrato, Studi e documenti per il centenario* (Milan, 1962) II, 9–25.
87. Iacobus de Ravanis (originally attributed to Petrus de Bella Pertica), *Lectura . . .super prima parte Codicis* (Paris, n. d.; repr. Bologna, 1967) f. II[r]; Jason del Mayno, *In Primam Codicis partem commentaria* (Venice, 1589) f. 2[r].
88. *Per Venerabilem;* of Albericus de Rosate, *Super Codice,* f. 7[v]. The best recent guide to this much discussed topic is Gaines Post, *Studies in Medieval Legal Thought* (Princeton, 1964) 454 ff.
89. Jason, *op. cit.*, f. 3[r].

90. *Pragmatica Sanctio, glossata per Cosmam Guymier* (Lyon, 1488) f.1^r^.
91. E. g., P. Bertrand, *De Origine jurisdictionum,* in *Tractatus universi juris* (Venice, 1584) III (part 1) f. 31^r^. In general see Johannes Haller, *Papsttum und Kirchenreform* (Berlin, 1903) 242, passim; citing Jouvenal des Ursins (e.g.), "quod ecclesia Gallicana ad suas antiquas libertates reduceretur." Also Victor Martin, *Les Origines du Gallicanisme* (Paris, 1939) I, and G. Mollat, "Les Origines du gallicanisme parlementaire au XIVe siècle," *Revue d'histoire ecclésiastique,* XLIII (1948) 90–147.
92. Cited by Kantorowicz, *King's Two Bodies,* 299.
93. Texts cited by Goez, *Translatio Imperii,* 11 ff.
94. Charles Duggan, *Twelfth-Century Decretal Collections* (London, 1963) 14.
95. Cited by J. M. Salgado, "La Methode d'interprétation en usage chez les canonistes," *Revue de l'Université d'Ottawa,* XXI (1951) 209.
96. Classic discussion in Post, *Studies,* p. 241 ff.
97. Lebras, *Institutions ecclésiastiques,* 116.
98. Cited by Ullmann, "The Development of the Medieval Idea of Sovereignty," *English Historical Review,* LXIV (1949) 17. See also the recent study centering on the *Somnium viridarii:* J.-P. Royer, *L'Eglise et le Royaume de France au XIV siècle* (Paris, 1969).
99. Cited by Horn, *Aequitas,* 74.
100. Albericus de Rosate, *Super Codice,* f. 7^r^, and *Super Digesto,* f. 14^r^. Cf. Bertrand, De *Origine jurisdictionum,* f. 29^v^, discussing the founding of the Greek and Roman states "non per viam legitimam. . .sed per meram violentiam potentie."
101. Ullmann, *Medieval Idea of Law,* 47; Albericus de Rosate, *Super Digesto,* f. 14^r^: "Bellum enim qui processerunt a iuregentium processerunt ab istis pronomibus meum et tuum. . . ."
102. Bodin, *Method for the Easy Comprehension of History,* trans. B. Reynolds (New York, 1945) 297 .
103. Hotman, *Antitribonian* (Paris, 1903). On this see the thesis presented by A. H. Saint-Chamaran to the Université de Droit d'Economie et de Science Sociale de Paris in 1973.
104. J. Moreau-Reibel, *Jean Bodin et le droit public comparé* (Paris, 1933) 135, and J. Brejon, *André Tiraqueau* (Paris, 1937) iii.
105. See my "Development and Context of Bodin's Method," *Jean Bodin: Verhandlungen der internationalen Bodin Tagung in München,* ed. H. Denzer (Munich, 1972) 123–50.
106. *L'Esprit des lois,* XXX, 2.
107. *De Universi juris uno principio et fine uno,* in *Opere,* I, ed. G. Gentile and F. Nicolini (Bari, 1914) 1. See my "Vico's Road," in the forthcoming *Giambattista Vico's Science of Humanity,* ed. G. Tagliacozzo and D. Verene.
108. *De Universi juris,* p. 95; of *La Scienza nuova seconda,* in *Opere,* IV, ed. F. Nicolini (Bari, 1928) 102, *passim.*
109. *De Universi juris,* 66. The term "mens legum" is common in the sixteenth-century. The best study is that of Piano Mortari (cited in n. 28).

III

DE ORIGINE FEUDORUM: THE BEGINNINGS OF AN HISTORICAL PROBLEM

Legend has it that Montesquieu originated the historical study of feudalism. This is of course a distortion — one of the many distortions made possible by ignoring the contributions of historical learning prior to the "century of philosophy," by ignoring, that is, the scholarly traditions linking the Enlightenment with the Renaissance. It is an error that Montesquieu would not have made. "Feudal laws offer a remarkable sight," he wrote. "An ancient oak has grown up. From a distance the leaves are visible, closer up the trunk, but the roots are out of sight. To find them one must dig."[1] Much the same might be said of the historical study of feudalism. In the development of this field Montesquieu represents but a single branch: to find the roots we must dig into the more fundamental if less spectacular contributions of earlier generations of historians and jurists.

The historiography of feudalism has been marked by furious controversies and has left the tattered reputation of more than one historian in its wake. About many of the questions there is still no universal agreement. Where, for example, did the fief come from? Was it related to the old Roman *militia* or to the *stipendium?* What about vassalage? Was it derived from the Germanic *comitatus* or from the Roman clientele — or perhaps from both? More generally, was "feudalism" a peculiarly European institution, or is it a stage in the development of every nation? For centuries lawyers and historians have wrangled over these problems, repeating each other's views, producing more heat than light. We have heard often enough how national and "racial" issues have provoked the ire and indiscretion of historians, especially the Romantic school and its more recent beneficiaries. We may be surprised to learn, however, that the nineteenth- and twentieth-century war of Romanists and Germanists was neither the most voluminous nor the most interesting phase of the debate, and certainly not the most original. Over three centuries earlier the central issues of the history of feudalism had become clear: the terms of the discussion had been set down, much of the evidence had been analysed, and the positions, including the poles of

[1] *De l'Esprit des lois*, xxx, 1.

Romanism and Germanism, had been established. In the sixteenth century as in the nineteenth, judgments were made as often on ideological as on scholarly grounds; in both periods, too, the legal-minded and the history-minded clashed; yet both periods, each with its own "historical school of law," witnessed major advances in historical criticism. Not only history, it seems, but also historiography tends to repeat itself.

We cannot, of course, hope to throw light on the already over-illuminated problem of feudalism; nor do the disputes of the nineteenth century, which have been reviewed often enough, concern us here.[2] It is the purpose of this paper to give a hearing to some of the earlier participants in this lengthy debate, to study the case history of a classic historiographical puzzle and perhaps to gain insight into the reasons historians ask certain questions and what kind of answers they expect — to survey, in short, the origins of the question so often glossed by mediaeval and Renaissance jurists: "the origin of feudal law."

* * *

Humanists were always fascinated by historical "origins." In fact it was precisely this curiosity, applied to legal as well as to literary studies, that distinguished them from their more "barbarous" predecessors. Characteristic is Petrarch's lament that "the majority of our legists, caring little or nothing for the origins of law and the first fathers of jurisprudence, or anything except professional gain. . . , did not believe that knowledge of the arts and of literature would be of much use. . . . "[3] Indeed this statement is more than characteristic; it is prescient, for in it we can recognize three essential ingredients of legal humanism, a method which would not be formulated for another century.[4] First, the polemical attitude, most notoriously displayed by Lorenzo Valla and then by Guillaume Budé, toward the *Accursiani* (the glossators) and the *Bartolisti* (the commentators) — in particular toward their venality, toward that "Gothic" style which Valla said "turned his stomach," and toward that unphilosophic disregard of method which so irritated Budé.[5] Second, a concern for the "sources" of law (but in a historical, not a legal, sense), especially through the "De Origine juris." This *Digest* title, which by the early sixteenth century had inspired a new field, the history of law,[6] showed the need for history, said François Baudouin, just as the title "De Verborum significatione" showed the need for philology.[7] This brings us

[2] See, e.g., Carl Stephenson's historiographical discussion, "The Origin and Significance of Feudalism," *American Historical Review*, XLVI (1940–41), 788–812. The earliest stages of the controversy, however, have been largely neglected by modern historians. R. Boutruche, *Seigneurie et Féodalité*, I (Paris, 1959), 11–13, briefly notes some of the contributions. J. G. A. Pocock, *The Ancient Constitution and the Feudal Law* (Cambridge, 1957) has a fine introductory chapter on two relatively late commentators, Cujas and Hotman, but includes no account of the true origin of the problem.

[3] *Epistolae de rebus familiaribus*, ed. Fracassetti (Florence, 1863), III, 18 (1356–57).

[4] In general the best introduction is now D. Maffei, *Gli inizi dell'umanesimo giuridico* (Milan, 1956).

[5] *Annotationes priores et posteriores . . . in pandectas* (Paris, 1556), p. 19; Valla, *Elegantiarum latinae linguae libri VI* (Lyons, 1556), III, Proem.

[6] Beginning with Aymar du Rivail, *Historia iuris civilis* (Paris, 1515).

[7] *Scaevola*, in J. Heineccius, *Jurisprudentia romana et antiqua* (Leiden, 1737), I, 435–436.

to the third factor alluded to by Petrarch, that is, the fundamental importance of *philologia*, as Budé called the "encyclopaedic" method he took from Poliziano.[8] According to Budé, it was the job of the philologian to study legal monuments (especially the great Florentine manuscript of the *Digest*, on which Poliziano had begun work) in the light of all the liberal arts. The convergence and systematization of these attitudes resulted in what sixteenth-century jurists came to call — after Budé and his protégé Andrea Alciato — the *mos gallicus juris docendi*, in contrast to the *mos italicus* of the scholastic Bartolists. This "French method," that is, legal humanism, was perhaps most comprehensively defined by Baudouin. "I have become aware," he wrote, "that law books are the products of history and that historical monuments evolve into the books of law." This insight he raised to the level of a methodological principle: "Historical studies must be placed on a solid foundation of law, and jurisprudence must be joined to history."[9]

This alliance of history and jurisprudence affected other fields besides Roman law. Thus Baudouin, unlike many of his fellow humanists, welcomed into the immaculate domain of legal humanism the study of mediaeval law, including those *labes germanicae* of which Petrarch had wanted to purge the *corpus italicum*, that is, the Lombard *Book of Fiefs*.[10] Just as French scholars had to study Celtic and Germanic as well as Roman legal traditions, so, Baudouin realized, Italians needed to be familiar with these Lombard customs.[11] And Baudouin's bitterest rival, François Hotman, agreed on this point, that the law and history of classical Rome were insufficient for modern students.[12] Such humanist revisionism has sometimes been referred to as "neo-Bartolism," but its purpose was not so much a return to scholastic methods as an acceptance of the goals of "vernacular humanism." "Those of our age who . . . labor to retrieve the writings of the ancient Greeks and Romans . . . have served the sciences well. . . . Following their example, French patriots ought to devote themselves to the recovery of the ancient books of their own language."[13] This statement by the French feudist Louis Le Caron, prefacing his edition of one of the great French legal monuments, is typical of vernacular humanism — or, more precisely, of legal-vernacular humanism. It is also a vindication of mediaeval studies.

Some humanists — "grammariens purifiez" in Hotman's disparaging phrase — looked upon the mediaeval accretions to the civil law as beneath contempt, "nec lex sed faex."[14] Yet such fastidiousness never succeeded in banishing the *jus feudale* from "Roman law"; it did not even stem the flow of commentaries on the

[8] Budé, *De Studio litterarum* [1527] (Paris, 1533), p. 75: "Liberales autem disciplina qui nostra complectitur uno hodie nomine Philologia. . . . "

[9] *De Institutione historiae universae et eius cum iurisprudentia coniunctione* [1561] (Strasbourg, 1608), p. 188.

[10] See Paul Koschaker, *Europa und das römische Recht* (Munich, 1958), p. 71.

[11] *De Institutione*, p. 55.

[12] *Antitribonian* (Paris, 1603), p. 17.

[13] Le Caron's edition of *Le Grand Coustumier de France* (Paris, 1598), introductory letter to his son.

[14] An old wisecrack repeated, e.g., by Charles Dumoulin, *Commentarii in parisiensis . . . parlamenti consuetudines*, in *Opera omnia* (Paris, 1681), I, 9; and by Lucas de Penna in his commentary on the Sicilian customs—see W. Ullmann, *The Medieval Idea of Law* (London, 1946), p. 73.

Book of Fiefs. The members of the great "triumvirate" of legal humanism — Budé, Alciato, and Zasius — each had something to say about the Lombard customs. Alciato's prize pupil, François Le Douaren, and his colleagues at the University of Bourges, Hotman and Jacques Cujas, later published commentaries (based of course on the techniques of "philology"), as did Lelio Torelli, the editor of the Florentine manuscript of the *Digest*. So, even more loquaciously, did their Bartolist adversaries, including the much maligned Étienne Forcadel, the Belgian Guillaume Hanneton, and the Italians Giovanni Ferrari, Guerrini Piso, and Marino Freccia. In fact Freccia provided (in 1579) one of the best summaries of the literature of feudalism, that is, the most complete list of *opiniones*, according to the pack-rat methods of Bartolism.[15] Humanist critics often deplored this bibliographical obsession and lamented that these commentators were more adept at reciting each other's views than in explaining feudal terms. Such criticism, however, was probably due as much to professional resentment as to methodological disagreement. It is true that complaints about lawyers' making "glosses upon glosses of glosses"[16] were registered as frequently — and with as much justification — as charges that historians repeat one another. But if, on the subject of feudal law, the *grammatici* were a bit more critical than the *doctores scholastici*, they were not far behind in adding to the deposit of "opinion."

When did the process of scholarly sedimentation begin? In a sense with the *Liber feudorum* (or better the *Consuetudines feudorum*) itself, a compilation normally attributed to the Milanese jurist Obertus de Orto, perhaps in collaboration with Girardus Niger; more specifically with the vulgate version of the collection and the subsequent commentaries by the "feudists," especially by Andrea de Isernia, Jacopo de Ardizone, Jacopo de Belviso, Jacopo Alvarotto, Lucas de Penna, Giasone del Maino, and Claude de Seyssel.[17] Writing in 1438, Alvarotto counted over forty commentaries "super feudis,"[18] and by the sixteenth century they had reached flood stage. By then too, such topics as "the nature of a fief" or "who succeeds to a fief" or "how a fief is acquired" had become stereotyped.[19] Even humanists could not wholly extricate themselves from the labyrinthine ways of scholasticism. Consequently the historical interpretations of feudalism, as they emerged in historical writing, had the appearance of a palimpsest — conventional legal formulas overlaid with historical qualifications, Bartolism cast in a

[15] Freccia, *De Subfeudis baronum et investitum feudorum* (Venice, 1579), pp. 1 ff. ("De Origine feudorum"). Works of the jurists mentioned will be cited as they bear upon the following discussion. Many may be found in "*Tractatus*," X^1 or X^2; that is, *Tractatus universi juris*, duce et auspice Gregorio XIII (Venice, 1584), vol. x, parts 1 and 2.

[16] "Scribunt nostri doctores moderni lecturas novas, in quibus non glossant glossas sed glossarum glossas," quoted by G. Barni, "Notizie del giurista e umanista Andrea Alciato," *Bibliothèque d'Humanisme et Renaissance*, xx (1958), 25.

[17] K. Lehmann, *Das langobardische Lehnrecht* (Göttingen, 1896), contains critical editions of the three main recensions. The best analysis is still that by Savigny's disciple E. A. Laspeyres, *Über die Entstehung und älteste Bearbeitung der Libri feudorum* (Berlin, 1830), including much biographical information (like Savigny's, not always reliable) on the feudists and an appended selection, "älteste Beiträge zur Literaturgeschichte des Lehnrechts."

[18] Jacopo Alvarotto Patrizzi, *Lectura in usus feudorum* (Frankfurt, 1570), Proem.

[19] These are some of the rubrics of Jacopo de Ardizone's recension, designated "antiqua" by Lehmann.

historical mold. Not of course that there was agreement on every issue. Consider, for example, the question of the "authenticity" of the *Book of Fiefs*. While Bartolists understood the term to mean legally valid, humanists heard historical overtones and so naturally became critical of the collection — attempting perhaps (like Budé) to make it respectable by "classicizing" its vocabulary, perhaps (like Le Douaren) to accept it on its own barbarous terms. But this was an issue mainly of historical pedigree and did not at first disturb the conditioned legal responses of three centuries.

But if the history-mindedness of humanists did not lead to many radical interpretations, it did at least make possible a better understanding of the texts of feudal law. The neo-Bartolist Dumoulin, for example, adopting for the moment the critical techniques of humanism, identified the imperial legislation included in the *Book of Fiefs*. The earliest, he pointed out, was from Lothair II, not Lothair I. "This error arose from the incompetence of Obertus de Orto and his sort, who argue without knowledge of history, saying that the law "Si quis miles" was passed by the same Emperor Lothair at the time of Pope Eugene, which is false and impossible. . . . It should be 'Lothair II.' "[20] And as for the Emperor Conrad, "nothing in this book can be referred to Conrad I, who never was in Italy, . . . but it evidently concerns Conrad II, who came to Rome to be crowned . . . about 1007." Although Dumoulin agreed with his predecessors that Obertus de Orto was responsible for the *Book of Fiefs*, he denied that Obertus, who was only a private person, had compiled an official code; consequently the Lombard customs were merely "local law." Le Douaren, who followed Dumoulin in most matters, went even further, rejecting Obertus' authorship altogether, on the grounds that the mere inclusion of his letters "does not prove him to be the author of this book, any more than Ulpian was the author of the *Pandects*."[21] Next, François Hotman, humanist friend of both Dumoulin and Le Douaren, emphasized the barbaric origin of much of the feudal vocabulary and the incompatibility of feudal and Roman institutions.[22] Finally Cujas, Le Douaren's successor as dean of legal humanists, performed the invaluable task of publishing a critical (by sixteenth-century standards) edition of the *Book of Fiefs*.[23] He, too, denied Obertus' authorship and discussed the vulgar language of feudal law, pointing out differences in French and Italian usages. Thus sixteenth-century scholarship, adopting a historical, though legally inconvenient, attitude toward feudalism, approached the modern view, which is that the *Book of Fiefs* is a *mélange* of imperial constitutions, Milanese statutory law and northern Italian jurisprudence, dating from the eleventh and twelfth centuries, only peripherally significant for the history of feudal institutions.

By the sixteenth century commentaries on feudal law had not only reached flood stage, they had reached fever heat. To a large extent this was due to the efforts of a third school of jurists, who, if they entertained radical notions, never-

[20] *Commentarii*, p. 21.

[21] *Commentarium in consuetudines feudorum*, in *Omnia opera* (Geneva, 1608), p. 133.

[22] *Ad Disputationem de feudis*, in *Operum*, II (Geneva, 1599), 801 ff.

[23] *In Libros quinque feudorum*, in Cujas' *Opera omnia* (Prato, 1840), X, 829 ff. Clearly this is an eclectic edition.

theless made important contributions to the historiography of feudalism. These were the French feudists, who were too practical to be strict humanists and too proud to be Bartolists. These lawyers, who may also be counted among the first mediaevalists — men like Jean Pyrrhus d'Angleberme, Barthélemy de Chasseneuz, and especially Charles Dumoulin and his followers Louis Le Caron, René Choppin, Pierre Pithou, and Jean de Basmaison — were even more critical of the Lombard customs than the humanists. Their objections, however, rested on legal, or ideological, rather than historical grounds, and their anger was roused more by the Hapsburg wars than by the pedantic quarrels of rival methods. What disturbed them was not the anachronisms of Bartolist interpretation but the notion that the "ultramontane book of fiefs," as Dumoulin called it, had any authority in France. Accepting Lombard custom in France was objectionable not only because, as "the Emperor's law," it would derogate from the king's honor, but because it was tainted with the venal and tyrannical practices of Roman law; hence it was socially as well as legally invalid in France. Dumoulin went so far as to deny that it was representative of feudal law at all, of which he considered the French *coutumes* a much more faithful image. Would it be an exaggeration to conclude that the sixteenth-century legal convention that the Parisian *coutume* in particular was "caput omnium consuetudinum Franciae" was an anticipation of the modern view that the most typical form of feudalism appeared in northern France?[24] Unfortunately such sociological sophistication only confused the problem of feudal origins, into which these feudalists, because of the eclectic nature of French law, were forced to inject even more qualifications and complexities than the "duplicitous" civilians. "Among the customs of France," said Dumoulin, "the greatest, most prolix, richest, fullest and most difficult is the title 'De Feudis.' " And the hardest question of all, he realized, was: who first established feudal law, or at least where did it first arise? For years Dumoulin pondered this. His answer, the great *Treatise of Fiefs* of 1539, is also the first comprehensive, critical survey of the problem. It was of course not the last, and even by the French revolution feudists had not resolved the question.

Needless to say, some lawyers scorned such pedantic matters. "Certain solemn men of learning," remarked Dumoulin's rival Bernard d'Argentré, "have pursued those philological problems regarding the origin and division of fiefs, usually with many unprofitable conjectures. But what have we to do with such an obscure affair?"[25] Why should a student of law study history and philosophy, anyway? This is a question professional lawyers have always asked; it is a question Bartolists — the "patricians," as Forcadel designated them — were asking of the "plebeian" humanists in the sixteenth century; it was a question posed most brutally, perhaps, byAlberico Gentile, who had no use at all for the "Cujacians."[26]

[24] *Commentarii*, 1. The inadequacy of the *Consuetudines feudorum* for the study of western feudalism has been pointed out by Ganshof, *Feudalism*, trans. P. Grierson (London, 1952), p. 60, and by Maitland, *History of English Law* (London, 1895), II, 287.

[25] *Commentarii in . . . consuetudines generales antiquis ducatus Britanniae* (Paris, 1661), Preface.

[26] Forcadel, *Sphaera legalis* (Lyons, 1569), p. 41; Gentile, *De Iuris interpretibus dialogi sex* (London, 1582), pp. 50 ff.

Fortunately — for historians at least — it is a question which did not disturb the greatest of sixteenth-century jurists. Professing a classical unconcern with "profit," they absorbed themselves in the study of legal history Their pioneering work greatly enriched the writings of historians who, by the second half of the sixteenth century, were themselves becoming fascinated with the problem of the origins of feudal institutions And so, through the work of such scholars as Étienne Pasquier, Claude Fauchet, and Bernard du Haillan, the technical concerns of feudal law entered into the main stream of historiography

* * *

"Concerning fiefs," wrote Pasquier in 1565, "some attribute the first source to the Franks, some to the Burgundians, the Lombards and other peoples of Germany. . . . Others, seeking to banish barbarism from their discourse, attribute this invention to the most ancient Romans, and others, to gratify our own country, to the Gauls "[27] Whereupon Pasquier — humanist, student of Cujas, intimate of the *Pléiade* and one of the most critical of sixteenth-century historians — entered into a discussion, *à la* Bartolus, of the principal opinions on the origins of fiefs, thus illustrating the convergence of legal and historiographical traditions. In fact, however, the literary history of feudalism begins not with the historians but with the legal commentators, in particular with one of the founding fathers of Bartolism. "Many old glossators," wrote Baldus, "commented on this book [of fiefs] and made very useful summaries of it, among whom were these great men: Pylaeus, Jacobus Columbi, Jacopo de Ardizone, . . . Odofredus, later Jacopo de Belviso, Andrea de Isernia, Petrus de Cernitis and many others of unquestionable authority."[28] And this feudist tradition survived the feudal system itself, since Michael Bellius published his *On Fiefs* in 1792.

In a sense the historical inquiry into feudalism, too, begins with Baldus. "My first question," he said, "is whether the collection called the book of fiefs should be considered authentic. . . . For it is not part of civil or pretorian law, nor does it follow the normal order of the corpus, and . . . it contains many irregularities and inadequacies which are not of the nature of true law, . . . the art of the good and the just."[29] As a good imperialist, Baldus himself had no such doubts about the validity of the *Book of Fiefs*. "On the contrary, this book is by custom proven to be authentic and useful . . . , " he concluded, not only because it was the subject of so many glosses and summaries but because "many decretals follow the imperial law in this volume, and so the feudal customs should be observed not

[27] *Recherches de la France* (Paris, 1621), p. 120. Cf. Édouard Secretan, *Essai sur la féodalité* (Lausanne, 1858), p. 16: "La question des origines de la féodalité du moyen âge a partagé les savants qui ont traité ce sujet; il est peu de questions historiques qui aient été autant controversées. . . . Deux écoles principales existent et luttent encore aujourd'hui avec une vivacité que le temps n'a point ralentie: l'école romaniste, qui deduit les institutions féodales du moyen âge des institutions romaines, et particulièrement de celles de Bas Empire, et l'école germaniste, qui s'efforce de les rattacher aux coutumes des nations germaniques qui, au Ve siècle, s'établirent sur les ruines de l'empire romain. A côté de ces deux écoles, il s'en est formé nouvellement une troisième, qui ne fait découler la féodalité ni de Rome, ni de la Germainie, mais des institutions de la race celtique ou gauloise."

[28] *Opus aureum . . . super feudis* (Venice, 1516), f. 2r.

[29] *Loc. cit.*

only in legal practice but in legal science. . . , for the civil law is partly divine law." No doubt this is a point of law rather than of history, depending on the continuity of imperial authority as expressed in the Emperor's constitutions, his "authentics"; but the context is necessarily historical. "To resolve this question," wrote Guerrini Piso in the later sixteenth century, "it must be recalled that this book consists partly of the imperial constitutions of Conrad [II], Lothair [II], Frederick [I] and others, and so has authority, as no sane person will deny, for 'what pleases the prince has the force of law.' "[30]

If this were true, insanity must have been a common ailment among lawyers, for as Piso admitted, concerning the question of authenticity, "great is the contention among doctors." French feudists were especially reluctant to admit the authenticity — by inference the authority — of feudal law. As legists in the employ of the king (which many of them were), their job was to reject the preeminence of the Emperor, hence any direct connection with ancient Roman, or even Carolingian, tradition. The idea that the *Book of Fiefs* was the "decima collatio" — that is, the tenth collection of imperial authentics[31] — was to Dumoulin ridiculous and illusory. Consequently he presented a "new opinion," that "this book or compilation has the force neither of law nor of custom . . . because it was apparently compiled by Obertus de Orto, who was a lawyer or *pragmaticus* of the Milanese court, . . . a private person, having the public authority neither of a prince nor of the people. . . . It is clear that Obertus had no power to decide at what court or to what place a custom belonged . . . or to judge the force of the law or custom. . . . "[32] The collection could therefore be called authentic only in the sense that it had been accepted *ex post facto* by certain peoples. All of Baldus' "colorful arguments" Dumoulin rejected: that based on "the approval of Frederick . . . is a fictitious and incredible argument of Odofredus," while that based on universal consent is also nonsense "because of the notorious irregularity of feudal customs." Lacking a universal standard, feudal law was by no means "general." Not only the Lombard customs but "even the imperial constitutions may be considered local law, since at that time the Empire itself was limited and local."[33]

But even if the *Book of Fiefs* were both general and authentic, there was no reason to assume that its authority was universal, any more than the authority of the Emperor. "There is a great controversy," admitted Piso, "as to whether it

[30] *In feudorum usus*, in *Tractatus*, X^1, 97v.

[31] Claude de Seyssel, *Speculum feudorum* (Basel, 1566), p. 20: "Aliqui etiam appellant *decimam collationem*, quia iste liber [feudorum] fuit additus post novem collationes Authenticorum."

[32] *Commentarii*, pp. 20–21: "Succedit famigerata illa quaestio, et institut. nostro satis necessaria, Utrum liber ille feudorum habeat vim et authoritatem legis, quod vulgis dicunt, an sit authenticus. Et omissis somniis fere omnium hac in re scribentium, quod ille liber sit decima collatio, quasi ab aliquo imperatore fuerit approbatus, et novem Novellarum Iustiniani collationibus ad decimam complendam annexus, quod ridiculum, et ad placitum confictum puto . . . , quia constat quod fuit compilatus et compositus per Obertum de Horto, qui erat advocatus seu pragmaticus in curia Mediolanensi . . . , nulla authoritate publica, seu principis, seu populi fungens: sed sui ipsius tantum privata opera. . . . Tum ut patet per discursum illius libri, illae consuetudines erant locales, et multum variae. . . . "

[33] *Ibid.*, p. 22.

binds all kings and peoples who, either *de jure* or *de facto*, do not recognize the Empire."[34] While teaching at Turin and even before entering the service of Louis XII, Claude de Seyssel asserted that "those who do not recognize the Emperor are not bound by these laws," referring in particular to the kings of France (who according to the old canonist formula "recognized no superior in temporal things") and Spain.[35] And Le Douaren threw the weight of legal humanism behind this judgment.[36] It became a commonplace for French historians as well as jurists that appeal should be made neither to Roman nor to Lombard law but to the "common law" of France, which according to Dumoulin meant, at least in the *pays de droit coutumier*, the customary law of Paris. Dumoulin fortified his position with historical as well as legal arguments — for example, that Justinian never ruled in Gaul and that the "German Emperor" did not receive the *imperium* by direct translation from Charlemagne but only through a "new creation." Without rejecting all imperialist traditions, certainly not the anti-papal arguments, he asserted the superior dignity and independence of the French king on the grounds that "the concession of the Empire was limited to the king of the Franks, and similarly the law of the Frankish crown was transmitted by the Salic law."[37] Dumoulin's work was rich in such Gallican themes, which reinforced Valois claims in Italy and which cast doubt on the validity, or at least the universality of imperial legislation. In this way the polemical exercises of lawyers gave the issue of authenticity a historical as well as a legal character.

It was Baldus' next *quaestio*, however, that brings history most directly into play. "My second question," he continued, "is the derivation and the definition of the fief."[38] Here again the authority of the *Book of Fiefs* is at stake. This is the essential text: "No investiture ought to be granted him who refuses to owe fealty [*fidelitatem facere*], since 'fief' is said to come from 'fidelity' or 'faith' [*cum a fidelitate feudum dicatur vel a fide*]."[39] This etymology — or should we say this goperism? — was repeated by every jurist from Obertus de Orto to Dumoulin and persisted even into the nineteenth century.[40] In the sixteenth century it was

[34] *In Feudorum usus*, f. 97v.

[35] *Speculum feudorum*, pp. 27–28. Migne, *Patrologia Latina*, CCXIV, 1130: " . . . cum rex *ipse* superiorem in temporalibus minime recognoscat. . . . "

[36] *Commentarium*, p. 133: "An Mediolani servari debeat [liber feudorum], non est magna dubitatio: de aliis regnis major est dubitatio. . . . In Gallia est dubitatio. Etenim falsum est, quod quidam dicunt Galliam subesse Imperio. . . . "

[37] *Commentarii*, p. 13. In his edition of the *Leges Longobardorum* (Lyons, 1512) Nicolas Bohier, too, pressed the French claims in Italy on the grounds that Charlemagne had been "King of the Lombards."

[38] *Super feudis*, f. 2r.

[39] Lehmann, p. 119 (*Consuetudines feudorum*, II, 3). Pierre Rebuffi, *Feudorum declaratio*, in *Tractatus*, X[1], 300v, calls it a "communis opinio."

[40] In addition to the mediaeval commentators, it was accepted both by humanists, such as Cujas, *op. cit.*, p. 830, and by French feudists, such as Bohier, *Consuetudines bituricenses* (Paris, 1543), f. xxxvi v, and Chasseneuz, *Consuetudines ducatus Burgundiae* (Paris, 1548), f. 98v; and still, over two centuries later, by Bellius, *De Feudis commentarius* (Rome, 1792), p. 14. It should be pointed out, that the etymology was often accepted for legal rather than linguistic reasons: "pource que c'est un point de droict . . . ," said the historian Du Haillan, *De l'Estat et succez des affaires de France* (Lyon, 1596), p. 388.

accepted by a number of historians who should have known better and by such philologists as Cujas and Zasius. "According to Obertus *feudum* comes from *fides* or *fidelitas*" — "although," Zasius added, "*feudum* may also be said to come, by analogy, from *foedus* because of certain treaties based on fidelity. . . . "[41] Such derivations naturally implied a "Romanist' position, that is, a belief in the Roman origin of the fief as an institution as well as a term. As early as the fourteenth century, however, there were some independent minds who forgot legal propriety long enough to protest against such unrestricted Romanizing. Thus Andrea de Isernia doubted "whether fief and vassal are new names [*nova nomina*] or are contained in Roman law."[42] And at least some humanists remembered Valla's warning that "when the etymology is false, the definition will be false."[43] One thing is clear in any case: long before the vogue of humanism, philology and law had entered into an alliance, although a somewhat precarious alliance; and for humanists and Bartolists alike, historical proofs were founded on linguistic arguments.

When Isernia dropped the rather vulgar suggestion that feudal terms were post-classical, the topic under discussion was "the origin of fiefs." From this time (about 1320) on, "De Origine feudorum" or "De Origine juris feudorum" became a conventional rubric, perhaps on the analogy of the *Digest*'s "De Origine juris." Nor was this purely a question of etymology; it had also philosophic implications. According to Seyssel, "In order to understand the fief, one must know first whence feudal law takes its origin, next the efficient cause of the collection, and equally the other causes, that is, formal, material and final. . . . "[44] On this topic both Bartolists and humanists commented, and both realized the essentially historical nature of the question. Within the juristic tradition proper as well as the historiographical tradition, this became increasingly explicit, so that by the end of the eighteenth century one feudist could remark, "In studying the origins of fiefs we should distinguish the political from the historical origin. . . . "[45] Not that even at this late date, over a generation after Montesquieu, the problem had been solved to everyone's satisfaction. "The historical origin of the fief," Bellius added, "to what period and to what nation it should be attributed, is somewhat obscure." Over five centuries of discussion by lawyers had not — and over four centuries of discussion by historians have not — radically altered this conclusion.

* * *

How did the Bartolists and humanists stand on this question of feudal origins? All jurists would agree with Baudouin that "in the devastation of these miserable

[41] *In Usus feudorum epitome* (Lyon, 1556), pp. 3–4. Thomas Craig, *Jus feudale* [1603] (Edinburgh, 1732), p. 55, reports an even more fantastic etymology, based on the initial letters of the following phrase, "Fidelis ero ubique domino vero meo."

[42] *In Usu feudorum commentaria* (Naples, 1571), f. 6r.

[43] *Elegantiae*, VI, 52.

[44] *Speculum feudorum*, pp. 11 ff; "Et ille Imperator, qui hunc compilationi dicitur authoritatem praebuisse, potest dici etiam causa efficiens, ratione authoritatis. . . . Causa materialis, sunt leges, constitutiones, decisiones, et consuetudines, de quibus praedixi, ex quibus hic liber constat. . . . Causa vero formalis huius libri, est distinctio, seu divisio per tres libros partiales. Causa autem finalis est . . . ut facilius quaestiones feudales diffiniri possent. . . . "

[45] *De Feudis commentarius*, p. 7.

regions [of Europe], there arose, in the place of Roman law, various customs which today we call *feuda*."[46] The real question, however, was whether feudal law was, in the words of the lawyers, *antiquissimum* or *recentissimum* — "when and by what nation *feuda* took their origin," as Freccia posed the problem, "and whether they were invented by the Romans. . . . "[47] In every jurist's list of *opiniones* three principal "Romanist" arguments appeared. Le Douaren summarized them in this way: "There are those who believe that [feudal law] arose from the Romans, and they refer to the Roman clientele recalled by Dionysius of Halicarnassus. . . . Others . . . think that the *militia* . . . mentioned in Roman law were *feuda*. . . . Others refer to the lands of the *limitanei* recalled by the ancients."[48] Of these views the last may be attributed to the Bartolist Lucas de Penna, the first two to the humanists Budé and Zasius. Thus it seems that, between the commentators and at least the first generation of legal humanists, there was a certain amount of agreement. Each group wanted, in a sense, to establish continuity between classical and feudal institutions; each accepted, initially at least, a "Romanist" position.

Their motives, however, were vastly different: the Bartolist view of "continuity" was as far removed from the humanist view as the Bartolist conception of "authenticity" or of the "origin" of law. What the Bartolists wanted above all was the legal continuity of imperial authority, whereas humanists were more interested in establishing an honorable historical ancestry.[49] Although humanists did not always have more scholarly scruples than the Bartolists, they usually appear more critical because of their anxiety to root out the "corruptions" of latter day historical development. The attitude of the Bartolists stemmed from a systematic — one may almost say a rampant — eclecticism; yet they were concerned with neither comparative law nor, except indirectly, legal history. As lawyers their business was neither to make historical discriminations between usages nor to point out the irrelevancies of Roman law to contemporary problems. Rather it was to make the Justinianian corpus fit the chaotic conditions of a feudal and multi-national society; it was to emphasize similarities, to make identifications, to apply legal formulas in a plausible fashion, and to reconcile contradictions in law on the basis of fidelity not to historical fact or to philology but to utility and to "reason." Just as, in its generation and decay, Rome provided a historical archetype and a treasury of historical examples, so in its codes and jurisprudence — and through the mediaeval commentators — it gave Europe a legal science.

To humanists, on the other hand, Roman law was not *ratio scripta;* it was *effigies antiquitatis:* "it was not a collection of rules and prohibitions . . . but a manifestation of Roman thought."[50] It is not surprising, therefore, that it was the early generation of humanists — in particular that triumvirate, Budé, Alciato,

[46] *Praefata de iure civile,* in Heineccius, *op. cit.*, p. 12.

[47] *De Subfeudis baronum et investitum feudorum,* p. 3.

[48] *Commentarius in consuetudines feudorum,* p. 134.

[49] See P. E. Schramm, *Kaiser, Rom und Renovatio* (Darmstadt, 1957), ch. 8, on this "Rechtskontinuität," which gave Rome a different sort of "eternal" character than that conceived by Petrarch.

[50] Koschaker, *op. cit.*, p. 106.

and Zasius — who first placed the discussion of feudal origins on a strictly historical basis. While these humanists did not get on very well with each other — both Zasius and Budé's heir apparent, Alciato, reproached Budé for his overliterary attitude and his amateur standing —[51] they did agree about the three factors of legal humanism discussed earlier. They each objected to the "squalid and horrid" Latin of the Bartolists; they understood the vital importance of philology; they each followed a historical method. More important, they were in general agreement about the Roman origin of feudal institutions.

Budé's *Annotations on the Pandects* (1508), which revolutionized the study of Roman law, also presented the first humanist view of this problem. "Among the ancients," he wrote, "it was customary for provincials and allies of the Romans to pledge themselves as clients to Roman noblemen, by which patrons they were adopted, privately as well as publicly, and they called themselves clients, that is, πελάται (fem. πελάτιδες), or neighbors. These clients were then obliged to keep themselves and their fortunes forever subjected to their patron and to keep and to venerate his customs."[52] Both Caesar and Cicero furnished evidence for this "patrocinium." The Sequani, for example, "pledged themselves as clients to the Romans, whom they diligently served. . . . " Therefore, Budé concluded, "nobody, I think, can avoid the conclusion that our feudal customs [*nostram feudorum consuetudinem*] arose from the relation of client to patron. Wherefore, I usually apply the Latin term 'clients' to those called vassals and 'clientele' to that relation and ceremony called 'homage.' " Like his predecessor, Valla, Budé was at times concerned more with elegance — "to banish barbarism from his discourse," in Pasquier's phrase — than with accuracy. His method was undeniably "encyclopaedic," his evidence taken from classical historians as well as from jurists, but his argument is based on little more than analogy. Analogical reasoning, which was an obstacle both to comparative law and to historical criticism, was a weakness of jurists of all schools. "I do not doubt," as Ferrari said later, "that a certain likeness and image of that clientele, *militia*, and such ancient institutions could have been passed on to our law of benefices."[53]

But the question, as Ferrari himself realized, was *how* — "how to trace back to that institution which is not ours . . . but which custom has brought to use." His own explanation was unimaginative enough and may be reduced to a simple transformation of vocabulary succeeding the *translatio imperii:* "When the Roman Empire was translated to Charlemagne . . . , the provinces were no longer administered by the Emperor but by the counts, to whom administrative, then legal, authority was granted."[54] And according to the conclusion of Hanneton, "The name of clientele having in the course of time been transformed, feudal concessions and vassals began to replace the name of clients."[55] A standard de-

[51] See L. Delaruelle, *Répertoire de la correspondance de Guillaume Budé* (Paris, 1907), pp. 168 ff, and A. Hartmann, *Die Amerbachkorrespondenz*, III (Basel, 1947), 288; typically, these quarrels over method were intensified by the issue of "plagiarism."

[52] *Annotationes*, f. 192v ff.

[53] Giovanni Ferrari Montano, *Collectanea in usus feudorum*, in *Tractatus*, X^2, 93r.

[54] *Ibid.*, 93v.

[55] Guillaume Hanneton, *Tractatus de iure feudorum*, in *Tractatus*, X^1, 162v.

scription of this transformation was given by Zasius in his famous *Epitome of Feudal Custom* (1535). "We believe," he wrote,

that *feuda* arose from ancient Roman custom. From the founding of the city, the *potentes* accepted pledges from people they called clients, who commended themselves and their possessions to the *potentes*, as Dionysius of Halicarnassus, Aulus Gellius and others recount. . . . It seems likely that, when the Romans conquered the provinces of Gaul, Germany etc, and when they installed there a large group of Roman *militiae*, they invited many natives, since many were peasants, to become clients, and they granted lands and property to them as clientele; and so in the course of time, which transforms all, fiefs and other such concessions emerged. . . . [56]

But since, as Dumoulin was to point out, the clientele was obsolete three centuries before Justinian (except in the sense of one's relation to a lawyer)[57] and since it involved no military obligation, how could it be likened to vassalage? These objections occurred to Cujas. They were not disturbing enough to make him abandon Romanism (for Girardus, one of the compilers of the *Book of Fiefs*, had himself called Lombard feudalism "most ancient"), but they were enough to make him search for a more plausible link with antiquity. This link he found in certain later Roman institutions, that is, with precarial tenures like the *procuratores, custodes* and *actores*. "Later on such grants," explained Cujas, in what amounts to a fourth Romanist thesis, "began to be hereditary, which characterizes the true fief; and so . . . gradually those who had been temporary actors and custodians of lands began to be so permanently, and while keeping the Latin name *homines* accepted the new and foreign names of vassals, *leudes* [allied, he explains, to the Germanic *Lehen*] or feudatories, from their princes and nobles, who preferred to give them hereditary grants if they would agree to military duty. . . . "[58]

The hereditability implied by these "new names" was, as both jurists and historians realized, the final stage in the formation of feudal law. "In earliest times," we read in the *Book of Fiefs*, "the benefice was so far subject to the lord's authority that he might take away at will what he had granted in fief. But afterwards it came about that the vassal had security of tenure for a year only; and then it was ordained that this should be extended to the length of his life. . . . The next stage was that the benefice should pass to the sons. . . . "[59] Writers of history, too, frequently adopted this scheme. According to the royal historiographer du Haillan, for example, "Formerly in France lords had the power to retract at will things given in fief; then came the custom by which the fief was given for a single year, and later for life. . . . Then fiefs became patrimonial, hereditary and transmissable to all the children equally. . . . "[60] They became hereditary, he said elsewhere, "after the example and by imitation of the royal domain of the early Capetians." This allodial tendency was particularly characteristic of France, where such unique institutions as the franc-fief appeared;

[56] *Op. cit.*, p. 3.

[57] *Commentarii*, p. 1.

[58] *In Libros quinque feudorum*, p. 830.

[59] Lehman, p. 84 (*Consuetudines feudorum*, I, 1); cf. Pocock, *op. cit.*, pp. 72 ff.

[60] *Estat et succez*, p. 388.

and in Dumoulin's view it offered another reason why Lombard customs were unsuited to French courts — another reason for asserting the superiority of French law.[61]

What light, according to the teaching of philology, did the *nova nomina* of feudal law shed on this historical development? What precisely was the relationship between feudal institutions and feudal terminology? Like modern historians, many jurists found it hard to decide. For most of them such a distinction was worse than meaningless; it was inconvenient, and so they ignored it. Even Zasius and Cujas are not clear about this, and as Zasius recalled, Haloander, too, the first humanist editor of the *corpus juris*, used the terms *feudum* and *militia* interchangeably. On the other hand, there were a few obstinate souls who rejected such an equation, holding rather that the Lombards first instituted feudal law. This, Zasius sneered, was the view of "Alvarotto and other doctors ignorant of history"; it was the view also of such humanists as Le Douaren and such historians as du Haillan.[62] Such a contrary — we might say such a terminist — point of view, which Piso attributes to the "moderns,"[63] was actually expressed as early as the fourteenth century. Andrea de Isernia, as we have seen, cast doubt on the Romanist position, suggesting "that [fief and vassal] are new names and that neither is contained in the text of Roman law . . . ," while Gulielmus Durandus held that homage was not introduced through civil law but "through manners and daily use, which imitate law."[64] In the late fifteenth century Claude de Seyssel wrote in his *Feudal Mirror*, "It is very obvious that fiefs were wholly unknown to the ancient jurists and only came to be used by later men"; and Barthélemy de Chasseneuz, a humanist and admirer of Budé, agreed that "the feudal contract was unknown before the *Book of Fiefs*, at least as regards its name."[65] Later generations of jurists, especially those espousing a historical view of philology, took up this argument enthusiastically and subjected Zasius to the same charge, ignorance of history, which he had flung at these "terminists."[66]

[61] *Commentarii*, p. 22: "Propius ad materiam nostrarum consuetudinum accedens, praemitto apud nos et in toto hoc regno, maxime in parte consuetudinaria, feuda esse patrimonialia, et patrimoniorum seu alaudiorum jure censeri, hoc est, in plena et libera facultate et dispositione clientum, sicut de jure commune censentur bona, quae pure et simplicitur sunt in patrimonio nostro. . . . Et haec est generalis consuetudo regni."

[62] Zasius, *op. cit.*, p. 3; Le Douaren, *op. cit.*, p. 138; Du Haillan, *Histoire generale des roys de France* (Paris, 1615), pp. 201–203.

[63] *In feudorum usus*, f. 99v: "Moderniores quidam credederunt feudalia a Longobardis originem traxi esse, in quo numero fuit Balduin[us]. . . . Quam opinionem probant ex multis capitulis, in usibus feudorum. . . . "

[64] Isernia, *In Usu feudorum commentaria*, f. 6r: "Dubitatur, et quaeritur, an feudum, et vassalli sint nomina nova; vel iure Romano contineatur aliquid de eis. Videtur quod sint nomina nova, nec in textu Romanarum legum aliquid de eis continetur." *Speculi . . . Durandi* (Lyon, 1547), p. 119; "Quaeritur utrum homagium [in Italia . . . vocatur vasallagium], introductum sit de iure civile, sive de iure scripto. Respond. non, sed moribus et diuturno usu, qui legem imitantur. . . . "

[65] *Speculum feudorum*, p. 1; Chasseneuz, *op. cit.*, f. 99r.

[66] Beginning in 1539 with Dumoulin (see *infra*) and in 1542 with the humanist Lelio Torelli, *De Militiis*, in *Tractatus*, X², 323v.

This *via moderna* of the feudist tradition provided the initial impulse in the shift from Romanism to Germanism.

* * *

Budé, Zasius, and later Cujas made classic statements about the Roman origins of feudalism. Yet it would seem that humanists, as connoisseurs of style, had in general the greatest incentive to reject the clumsy Romanism of most civilians. Consider, for example, the anti-Ciceronian diatribes of Erasmus, who asked, "What is more inappropriate in this wholly new age than to hear religion, empires, magistrates, name of places, cults and manners discussed as Cicero would have spoken of them? If brought back to life, Cicero would have laughed at this kind of Ciceronian."[67] Even Budé, who permitted himself to Latinize feudal terms, was less willing to identify Roman and French institutions — the Senate with the *parlement* of Paris, for instance — because of derogatory republican implications.[68] His young friend Le Douaren went on to apply such implicitly historical criteria to feudal law. Adhering to a precise definition of the fief, he concluded that it had different ingredients than the *militia*, that consequently "it is doubtful that [feudal] law takes its origin from the law of the Romans." "Nor," he added, "is there the same relation [between client and patron] as we require between lord and vassal"; and as for the *limitanei*, "no mention of fealty appears there."[69] And Le Douaren's young colleague Cujas, although he leaned toward a Romanist interpretation, was still more conscious of the innovations brought by the barbarians, that is, of the peculiarly Germanic elements of feudal law. He also referred to the *devotos* of the Gauls (described by Caesar),[70] pointing out that the word "vassal" was of Celtic derivation. These arguments were more usually associated with the thesis of Hotman's late friend, the great humanist François Connan, who attributed feudalism to the Gauls — an argument satisfying to Gallic pride but not accepted by subsequent commentators.[71] In any case, there was agreement among French humanists, even most of the humanists, that an unqualified Romanism was an inadequate as it was distasteful.

The most direct attack on Romanism, however, was not made by humanists at all; it was made by French feudists, who were concerned more with national propaganda and etiquette, with the integrity and status of the monarchy, than with the niceties of philology. Polemical needs forced even the most scholastic-minded of these lawyers to make use of the historians' tools; and if they did not possess the sharp historical sense of scholars like Budé and Cujas, if they were

[67] P. S. Allen, *Opus Epistolarum Des. Erasmi*, VI (1926), 336.

[68] *Annotationes*, f. 69v.

[69] *Commentarius in consuetudines feudorum*, p. 137.

[70] *In Libros quinque feudorum*, p. 832: "Sed et Vvassi, vel Vassalli nomen, quod eisdem competit, servitium significat, sive comitatum cum deducatur non ex eo quod sint quasi in vasario nobilium, et vasa eorum instrumentaque censeantur, sed a Germanica et veteri Gallica voce *Gessel*, qua significatur comes qui nobis servit mercede certa. . . ."

[71] *Commentariorum juris civilis libri X*, ed. B. Faye (Paris, 1558), p. 172.

more interested in celebrating old myths than in uncovering new truths, they at least cultivated a sense of national individuality. In fact it was this belief in the uniqueness of French legal traditions that led these feudists to disparage the Lombard customs and in general to deny the Roman origin of feudal institutions, which added so much luster to their patria. The monarchy itself adopted this attitude. The authority and pedigree of civil (including canon and Lombard) law was expressly repudiated in the quasi-official lists of regalian rights compiled by Jean Ferrault and Charles de Grassaille as well as in the works of such feudists as Jean Pyrrhus d'Angleberme and André Tiraqueau.[72] Such distrust of "ultramontane" institutions, which contemporaries traced back to the introduction of Roman law into the universities and the establishment of the papacy at Avignon, was of course intensified during the religious wars, when Roman law was associated with even more malignant forms of Italian tyranny, such as the Jesuit order or the Tridentine decrees.[73] The religious passions of these years embittered the national enthusiasm of many French scholars, including those who remained orthodox. Thus the learned Pasquier's life-long hatred of the Jesuits spilled over into his *Researches of France;* thus, more spectacularly, the "anti-Tribonianism" of François Hotman and the conventional Gallicanism of Charles Dumoulin were transformed into the most ferocious kind of Italophobia. This helps to account also for the enthusiasm with which these two feudists attacked the Romanist thesis.

In spite of a widely held notion that Dumoulin and Hotman waged a common fight against the "usurpation of the fief" (the phrase is Michelet's), in fact their major objection to feudalism was its lack of uniformity; the real enemy was this hydra-headed monster, Romanism. It was Dumoulin in particular who, a generation before Hotman, carried on this offensive with the greatest effectiveness and originality. His *Treatise on Fiefs* (1539), in form an introduction to his great commentary on the unreformed *coutume* of Paris, was in fact a learned and contentious monograph on the history of feudal law. Based on both legal and historical sources (some of which, like Gaguin's history, had the force of law), it presented a survey of the entire history of the western empire from its translation to the Carolingian "French" down to the fourteenth century, including its relation to the papacy, and a discussion of the dating and composition of the *Book of Fiefs*, finally its relevance to France. Dumoulin's purpose was to demonstrate both the inapplicability of Roman (including Lombard) law to the French legal system and the inferiority of the German empire — because of its elective nature and its defective tradition, that is, its remoter connection with Charlemagne — to the French monarchy.[74] His authority, among feudists at least, was supreme for two and a half centuries.

[72] Thus Grassaille, *Regalium Franciae libri duo* (Paris, 1545), p. 67: "Septimum jus . . . ut legibus Romanorum Imperatorum, vel Jurisconsultorum [rex Francorum] subditus non sit . . . "; p. 75: "Leges seu consuetudines feudorum non habent locum in Francia. . . . " Cf Ferrault, *Iura seu privilegia aliqua regni Franciae*, in *Stilus . . . parlamenti* (Paris, 1542), f. cxviii v.

[73] G. Weill, *Les Théories sur le pouvoir royal en France pendant les guerres de religion* (Paris, 1892), p. 105: "La colère de l'auteur contre la Rome ancienne s'explique par la haine du calviniste contre la Rome pontificale."

[74] *Commentarii*, pp. 12–13.

In spite of his polemical occupations, Dumoulin's point of view was that of a historian and legal antiquarian, a textual critic who did not fear to cross pens with the most distinguished of humanists. Dumoulin began with a summary of the Romanist arguments:

> Those who derive the origin and invention of fiefs from Roman law show a great ignorance of antiquity and produce futile conjectures, such as that doctor Lucas de Penna . . . , who said that the feudal contract existed at the time of Justinian . . . , [that is] the *stipendiaria*, which term stands for the lands given to soldiers so that they could live by the fruits of these stipends and serve the republic without other rewards. . . . And about 150 years after his time our own Ulrich Zasius (who apparently did not read Lucas), in his most learned scholia on . . . "The Origin of law" and in his *Epitome of Fiefs* (which only reached us after our commentary was begun), was of the opinion that vassals arose from Roman law and that held for those mentioned in the *Book of Fiefs* . . . , and considered the common opinion, which was contrary, to be false and mistaken and to have arisen from ignorance of antiquity. . . . [75]

To reinforce his own argument Dumoulin referred to Isernia, who "said that in all of Roman law there appears no word of fief or vassal . . . , neither in the Pandects nor in the twelve books of the Code nor in the constitutions of Justinian called authentics . . . " — nor, Dumoulin added, in any of the contemporary histories. He repeated also the argument of his old mentor Angleberme, that "feudal law is most recent, originating neither with the jurists nor with the ancient emperors of the Romans, but was afterwards introduced as custom."[76] "I have," Dumoulin claimed, "diligently studied all the feudal treatises and summaries as well as glosses of existing books, but nowhere does there appear a statement of the patronage described by [Dionysius of] Halicarnassus. Everyone agrees that vassals, fiefs and the laws thereof are derived originally neither from Roman law nor from Roman laws but only from the customary laws which exist in the feudal usages and were unknown to and unused by the ancient jurists of the Roman Empire."[77] Dumoulin relied, in other words, on *auctoritas* as well as *ratio*, as historians too are accustomed to do. He claimed to be in agreement with the "common opinion" of doctors. "However," he added, "I accept the common opinion not because it is common but because it is true."[78] The same kind of critical premise permitted him even to admire sections of Roman law, "not by reason of empire, but by the empire of reason."

Having disposed of the crude imperialism of the *doctores italici*, Dumoulin, still following Angleberme's lead, went on to criticize the more elegant but no less offensive Romanism of humanists, in particular that of Zasius, Budé, and Alciato. Not, he hastened to add, that he would deny their scholarly eminence, especially that of Budé, "the splendor of all disciplines, glory of all France," who "restored

[75] *Ibid.*, p. 3.

[76] *Consuetudines Aurelianae*, in *Opuscula* (Paris, 1517), f. IIv. Like Dumoulin, Angleberme emphasized that "Rex Franciae non subest imperio" (f. IIIr). In *Commentarii*, p. 4, Dumoulin speaks of "Pyrrhus Englebermeus, Jurisconsultissimus, et utriusque linguae peritissimus, quondam praeceptor meus."

[77] *Commentarii*, p. 1.

[78] E.g., the often cited *Summa feudorum* [c. 1250–60] by Jacopo de Ardizone, *Tractatus*, X^1, 225v: "Iure enim Romano nihil de vasallo vel de feudo potest reperiri, excepto quod de clientulo reperitur. . . . " See also note 64.

the elegance of laws after more than 800 years," or even that of Zasius, although he had shamelessly plagiarized from Budé.[79] His only concern was to correct the historical error and to alleviate the legal discomfort which had resulted from their anachronisms and false analogies — which had been devised simply (as Angleberme had also pointed out) "for the sake of purer speech," although everyone realized that the monuments of feudalism were full of barbarous and "Gothic" language.[80] Dumoulin protested that his objections to such classicizing rested on no mere verbal quibble; the point was not a change in terminology but a difference in historical origin. There was, in other words, no continuity between the clientele and vassalage, "which Zasius so elegantly binds together," or between the *militia* and the feudal tenant, or between a regular *traditio* and the donation of a fief, which involved not transference of domain but only usufruct. Seyssel, too, had lamented that "the difficulty was increased by the fact that ancient, mediaeval and modern commentators [*antiqui, noviores, modernique Commentatores*] referred to Roman and canon law in various feudal passages, joining together what seems impossible to compare."[81] But Dumoulin spelled out his accusations: "I cannot . . . approve that most elegant adaption, first introduced by Budé and imitated by Zasius, of the old patron and client to the vocabulary of fiefs for the sake of purer speech, confirmed by a conventional connection and elegant induction, [nor] other conjectures by [Dionysius of] Halicarnassus and extended to feudal courts. . . . "[82]

It was in this way, building on the argument of Angleberme but going further in depth of historical research, that Dumoulin laid the groundwork for his "Germanist" thesis. By means of the study of ancient monuments and records, he continued, "I have learned that the authors of fiefs were the kings of the Franks, reigning in eastern Franconia even before the birth of Christ. . . . I have seen the ancient records of the donation by Childebert, son of the Frankish King Clovis, to the monastery of St-Germain-des-prés, near the city and house in which I write . . . , made before the time of Justinian the Great, who never had jurisdiction in Gaul. . . . This is the origin of fiefs." It was, of course, only the beginning of a long and complicated story. "These Franks conceded in fief the occupied lands of their frontier in return for recognition, an oath of fealty, the promise of certain military duties for the fief, renewal of investiture and other conditions. . . Whence it has been introduced into Gaul . . . , then Lombardy, the two Sicilies, Apulia and many other regions. . . . " So from these "Francigermani," as Dumoulin called them, feudal institutions had descended; from them, too, the "French" nation and the French kingship. "It is well known," Dumoulin later told Henry II, "that the able, virtuous and wise Charles the Great, first of this name, King of France . . . transmitted to you not less but equal and the same power along with the same crown, as it is also well known that these things are

[79] The controversy referred to in note 51.

[80] Angleberme, *loc. cit.;* Dumoulin, *Commentarii*, p. 6, "purioris sermonis gratia," referring to the discussion of Budé cited in note 52.

[81] *Speculum feudorum*, p. 3.

[82] *Commentarii*, p. 6.

indivisible and inseparable."[83] And of this bequest the institution of fiefs was one of the most illustrious and useful portions.

Such arguments, forming the basis of Dumoulin's "Germanist" position, continued to be popular during the religious wars, with the Huguenots even more than the Gallicans. They were taken up with gusto by three of Dumoulin's younger disciples, who also carried on his exegesis of the Parisian *coutume* — René Choppin, Louis Le Caron, and Pierre Pithou. Choppin not only repeated Dumoulin's arguments about the origin of fiefs but also his specific evidence. "The memory of what we in France call fiefs," he wrote, "is older than the fiefs of the Lombards . . . and such fiefs take their origin from the lands of Paris. . . . When King Childebert founded the Abbey of St Vincent in the faubourg of Paris, now called St-Germain-des-prés, he gave many fiefs and seigneurial rights."[84] Le Caron went so far as to contradict the conventional etymology of the fief (which even Dumoulin and Cujas had accepted), explaining that "fief or *feudum* or *beneficium* . . . were barbaric and known in Italy only after the Lombards descended from Germany, from the island called Scandanavia, . . . so that it should not be derived from or denoted by the Latin term *fides* or *foedus* or *fidelitas* but rather from a German word, which some have *faida* or *feed*, which means emnity, hostility or war."[85] Not that Le Caron was satisfied to attribute the fief to the Lombards, as Le Douaren for instance had done; he agreed with Dumoulin on this point, too. "Long before this fiefs [and] . . . vassalage were known and used in France, having arisen from benefices and recompenses which kings and great lords made to warriors who had followed them in their victories in Gaul. . . . " And Pithou, who was the leading "Cujacian" after Cujas as well as the foremost Gallican theorist, carried on this vernacularized tradition of *philologia*.[86] So, it may be remarked, did a number of the more critical French historians.

The man who most fully realized Dumoulin's thesis, however, was Dumoulin's life-long friend François Hotman who shared not only his Italophobia and his radical religious views but his commitment to Gallicanism.[87] Or would it be more accurate to say that he reduced the Germanist thesis to absurdity? In any case Hotman replaced the traditional conception of the *Francigermani* with the more chauvinistic image of the *Francogalli*, which embellished his view of history and nourished his ideological needs. His notorious *Franco-Gallia* of 1573, heading the

[83] *Commentaire sur l'edict . . . contre les petites dates* [1552] (Lyons, 1554), introductory letter to Henry II.

[84] *Commentaire sur les coustumes . . . de Paris* (Paris, 1662), p. 35.

[85] *Responses et decisions du droict françois* (Paris, 1637), p. 93.

[86] Especially in *Le premier livre des memoires des comtes hereditaires de Champaigne et Brie* (Troyes, 1609).

[87] Hotman and Dumoulin, who first met in Paris in 1540, and who were both converted to Calvinism shortly afterwards, remained in contact until Dumoulin's break with Calvin in 1556. Even after this Hotman — who had published under a pseudonym a defense of Dumoulin's attack on the papacy (*Contra les petites dates, cit. supra*), Francisci Vilerii *De Statu primitivae ecclesiae . . . ad Remundum Rufum defensor pontificis romanis adversus Carolum Molinaeum* (Regensburg, 1553) — continued, in his polemical and legal work, to cite Dumoulin with respect.

list of literary fireworks set off by the massacre of St Bartholomew, provoked the first large scale war between Romanists and Germanists, that is, between "Italogauls" and "Francogauls." But five years before this *Kulturkampf* Hotman had already expressed his almost racist contempt for Roman law as a manifestation of Italianate tyranny unsuited to the pure manners of the free French (*liberi franci, die freyen Francken*);[88] and five years before that, in a more scholarly work, he had stated his Germanist views concerning feudal origins, including not only Dumoulin's critique of humanist theories but the Germanic etymology of the fief.[89] He rejected the arguments associating the fief with Roman tenures because of their non-noble or non-military nature; he also rejected Connan's *gaulois* thesis. More interesting, he proposed (as Cujas had already done) what was to become the standard Germanist derivation of vassalage: "If any scholar shows us a reference to the feudal clientele before the Gothic and Germanic invasions, to him we concede victory. If one seeks the origins of vassalage [*vassallica clientela*], it seems to me not inconsistent to refer it to the original *comitatus* described by Tacitus, . . ." adding, "in which, however, there is mention neither of benefices nor of military rewards, which is basic to our vassalage." Elaborating such historical arguments into a more general defense of representative institutions, Hotman came to represent, for Michelet, the point of intersection of "barbarism and modern liberty." For more recent historians, he was the creator of a real historical myth and so one of the great-grandfathers of the Germanists.[90]

* * *

"What is to be said for so many opinions?" asked Piso, having surveyed most of the literature up to this time, relying especially on Dumoulin's monograph. Like many jurists his own final assessment was unimaginative and historically conservative; the sixteenth century, too, had its eclectics. "I believe," he concluded, "that as to name and form, fiefs have come from the Lombards or Goths, but by emulation from the Romans, who instituted *militiae* and clienteles, to which *feuda* owe some debts."[91] This topos of "emulation" or "imitation" of course suited humanist views of historical development perfectly, but it was also popular among jurists. Le Caron, for example, in spite of his Germanic etymologies, believed that fiefs were granted "after the example of the Romans, who especially under the emperors distributed lands to the soldiers in conquered terri-

[88] *Franco-Gallia* (Frankfurt, 1665), p. 53, uses these terms. *Antitribonian* [1567] (Paris, 1603), e.g., ch. 3, "Que l'estat de la republique Romaine est fort different de celuy de la France," and ch. 17, "Discours sur l'heur ou malheur advenu a la France par les livres de Justinian." The best account of the Francogallic controversy is P. Ronzy, *Un humaniste italianisant, Papire Masson* (Paris, 1924), pp. 163 ff.

[89] *Ad Disputationem de feudis* [1574], was based on lectures given at Strasbourg a dozen years before; col. 807: " . . . veni equidem olim in eam opinionem, ut Feudum a Germanica voce Feed deductum esse existimarem. . . . "

[90] F. W. Maitland, *English Law and the Renaissance* (Cambridge, England, 1901), p. 58, and J. N. Figgis, *Political Thought from Gerson to Grotius*, (Cambridge, England, 1916), p. 173.

[91] *In feudorum usus*, in *Tractatus*, X^1, 99v.

tory."[92] And of the French feudists both Jean de Basmaison, who was a faithful disciple of Dumoulin, and Guy de Coquille, one of Dumoulin's arch foes, would agree. Referring to the *stipendiaria*, Basmaison wrote that "the example of these first fiefs was introduced from nation to nation and from people to people . . . ," further that private fiefs were given "in imitation of public,"[93] while Coquille thought that the Frankish military chiefs "in imitation of the Romans distributed the domains of their conquests to the Frankish warriors."[94] And in 1565 even Pasquier, one of the best historians of the century as well as a competent jurist in his own right, finally reverted (after reviewing all the earlier opinions) to the Romanist thesis: "Many learned men are of the opinion that these fiefs arose from the distribution by the emperors to their armies of the frontier lands, the *limites*. Which opinion seems to me the most probable. . . . "[95] Which opinion may seem to us to bring the whole concatenation of arguments full cycle.

Or did historians' understanding of feudal institutions go beyond that of the jurists? Although such analogical arguments seem to bring us back to our point of departure, is it not true that historians like Pasquier, who spent their lives rummaging among their national antiquities, had the advantage of a broader horizon, if not of a deeper perspective than their more single-minded legal colleagues? It seems true of Pasquier, who was aware not only of the ambiguities of the question of feudal origins but of the qualifications of the Romanist, Gallic, and Germanist theses. Certainly it was true of his friend and fellow antiquarian Claude Fauchet, who was, if anyone, Pasquier's peer as a critical historian. Fauchet, too, was conscious of the complexities and peculiarities of European feudalism, but he preferred to take a broader and more philosophical attitude toward feudal relationships, in a sense going beyond even that loose analogizing of Budé and Zasius which had so irritated Dumoulin, in a sense also anticipating the typological views of historians like Bloch and Mitteis. "They are mistaken who consider fiefs to be an invention of the Lombards," wrote Fauchet, perhaps twenty years after Pasquier,

> for it is certain that there have always been lands pledged to more powerful kingdoms and communities in return for military service, whether they be called *victi*, that is, conquered subjects . . . , or *foederati*, that is, allies. Thus the fiefs and vassalage of antiquity, which I take to be the same (for current usage has been totally corrupted), may be taken from the law of nations, since the same service performed by our old feudatories . . . existed in those times; kings, princes and communities holding of [*prenans . . . saisine de*] their superiors, to whom they were bound by oath; for example, the Persians subject to the Medes, Croesus King of Lydia . . . to the Persians, the kings of India . . . to Alexander the Great. And it is not impossible that these first feudatories had subordinates obliged to them like our sub-vassals.[96]

Without displaying any extraordinary sophistication or (outside of French insti-

[92] *Responses et decisions*, p. 93.

[93] *De l'Origine des fiefs et riere fiefs* [1579] (Paris, 1611), f. 7r.

[94] *Les Coustumes de Nivernois* (Paris, 1610), p. 92.

[95] *Recherches de France*, p. 121.

[96] *Origines des dignitez et magistrats de France* [1584], in *Oeuvres* (Paris, 1610), f. 497r.

tutional history) depth of research, Fauchet was at least approaching a sociological conception of feudal law. This marked an advance in ambition if not in historical understanding.

* * *

For mediaevalists these opinions should have more than a mere antiquarian interest. As Herbert Butterfield has said, "Our knowledge of the past is seriously affected if we learn how that knowledge came into existence and see the part which historical study itself has played in the story of the human race."[97] What conclusions, in particular, can we draw from our historiographical survey of this problem of feudal origins? At first glance the moral of our story would appear to be negative: that ideological factors are often more important in historical judgments than positive evidence; that historians tend to repeat — or to refute — one another; that there is a sort of Malthusian law governing the accumulation of opinions on controversial and ambiguous topics. But, while we may be surprised to see historians outdone in this matter, we can hardly consider it a major revelation. What is far more interesting is the way in which our problem illustrates the awakening of historical consciousness and the enrichment — or should we say the adulteration? — of historical writing by the technicalities of legal scholarship. Even before the convergence of feudal law with historiography, we can see in legal writings the multiplication of historical arguments, the introduction of extra-legal sources and a concern with comparative law and legal history that transcended utilitarianism. More especially we can see an increasing historical emphasis in the discussion of philological questions, an area in which humanist methods made their deepest mark. What finally emerged from these changing attitudes and shifting interests was a more profound understanding of the complexities of feudal law, an understanding based on an awareness both of geographic (hence national) variations in feudal usages and of historical differences in the institutional (hence social) structure of nations, consequently in the differences in historical developments. Jurists and historians alike began to adopt, in other words, an attitude of historical relativism in their attempts to find a pattern in history. The result was perhaps not to permit more conclusive answers, but it was to encourage the asking of more intelligent questions. Could we demand more from these pioneering mediaevalists?

Southern Illinois University

[97] *Man on his Past* (Cambridge, England, 1955), pp. 1–2.

IV

Vera Philosophia: The Philosophical Significance of Renaissance Jurisprudence*

"CIVIL SCIENCE IS THE TRUE PHILOSOPHY," declared the fifteenth-century jurist Claude de Seyssel, "and it is to be preferred to all other fields because of its purpose."[1] From the thirteenth to the eighteenth century, throughout the career of modern legal thought, this conviction was maintained and, in some circles, expanded. Furthermore, many aspects of formal philosophy—including the nature of man and the universe, the problem of knowledge, the processes of cause and effect, and the search for a proper scientific method—were taken up, sometimes productively, by jurists. Yet in histories of philosophy and of thought in general, which often find occasion to discuss such fields as natural science, literature, art, and of course political thought, it is hardly possible to find even recognition of the significance of jurisprudence, to say nothing of discussion of its contributions. This circumstance is another illustration of the specialization and fragmentation of knowledge that has occurred since the Renaissance, and another source of misunderstanding about the history of thought between that age and the Enlightenment.

The identification of law and philosophy was one of the few doctrines that gained almost universal assent in a profession that has never been known for agreement. It was defended by jurists of all sorts—by ancients and moderns, by glossators and post-glossators, by ultramontanes and citramontanes, by civilians and feudists, by scholastics and humanists. It was based upon impeccable, indeed inviolable authority, appearing as it did in the very first title of the Digest, taken from the work of that most classical of jurists, Ulpian. It was glossed and reglossed hundreds of times, elaborated in terms of Platonic, Aristotelian and Ciceronian thought, and confirmed by the hardly less celebrated formula that defined law as "the knowledge of things divine and human," that is, as *sapientia,* wisdom itself.[2] Finally, in more recent times, it was given new life by incorporation in more than one system of thought from Baldus to Giambattista Vico, although again few figure in histories of philosophy.[3]

---

* Versions of this paper have been given at Columbia, Brown, Harvard and the University of Toledo.

1 *In VI. FForum partes* (s. 1. n. d.), f. 1 on Digest I, 1, 1: "Civilis scientia vera est philosophia et aliis omnibus propter eius finem praeferenda." The "FF," as Renaissance jurists liked to explain, was the closest Latin printers could come to the *pi* of the Greek "Pandecta."

2 Digest I, 1, 10, 2. The better known aspects of this idea have been traced by Eugene Rice, *The Renaissance Idea of Wisdom* (Cambridge, Mass., 1957), but for contemporaries fewer texts could have been more familiar than Accursius' Gloss on Digest I, 1, 1: "civilis sapientia vera philosophia dicitur, id est amor sapientiae."

3 Especially Vico, *De Universi juris uno principio et fine uno,* ed. F. Nicolini (Bari, 1936), Proloquium. discussion in my "Vico's Road," in *Giambattista Vico's Science of Humanity,* ed. G. Tagliacozzo and D. Verene (Baltimore, 1976).

In certain ways the ties between philosophy and jurisprudence were strengthened by Renaissance humanism, especially because of the pedagogical conviction that law was associated with the *studia humanitatis* and specifically with moral philosophy. This point was argued countless times, from Coluccio Salutati's *Nobility of Law and Medicine* to Vico's *Study Methods of Our Time,*[4] in a whole genre of methodological treatises (*de modo studiendi et docendi juris*), themselves derived from Justinian's prefatory constitutions instructing his law professors, and in the obiter dicta of the so-called "legal humanists," headed in the sixteenth century by Andrea Alciato. Characteristically, most humanists believed that this association had been lost. "Law is the art of the good and the just, etc.," quoted Guillaume Budé, the only scholar acknowledged as Alciato's peer. "To philosophize on this point is the job of the jurist, and from this we conclude that the study of law has degenerated from its original state. Today there are no longer jurisconsults, or philosophers, but only lawyers" (*jurisperiti*).[5] It was Budé's hope to restore law to its condition as a form of wisdom, "that cycle of learning," as he defined *sapientia,* "which Accursius calls Minerva but which the Greeks call encyclopedia." In fact this restoration was already going on; and even jurists of the older school, much distrusted by Budé, were affected by the same change in scholarly fashion. "The profession of law is regarded as a liberal art," as Barthélemy de Chasseneux put it; "it is a *studium liberale*."[6] For some enthusiasts the jurisconsult was the very model of the universal man of the Renaissance.

Yet recent discussions of Renaissance jurisprudence (mine included) have tended to exaggerate the significance of the humanist movement for the study of law. The truth is that legal humanism changed the style rather than the substance of professional jurisprudence, and in some ways the "historical school of law" was less significant than what may be regarded as the philosophical school.[7] The attempt of amateur scholars like Valla and Budé to treat law as a form of literature was undeniably important for historical scholarship, but as a legal method it was literally "trivializing"—subordinating a science to the *trivium*—and so rejected by professionals like Alciato except for certain pedagogical purposes. To jurists of all persuasions law did not really "belong to," it dominated the *studia humanitatis* and moral philosophy in particular; and its method did not have to be imported from disciplines, especially not from grammar or rhetoric, as Valla had proposed.[8] Law constituted its own "encyclopedia," in short, sweeping into its orbit not only the humanities but even the "queen of sciences" herself. Was theology really necessary for lawyers? "I answer no," replied Accursius in his authori-

---

4 See Eugenio Garin, *La Disputa delle arti nel quatrocento* (Florence, 1947), and Lynn Thorndike, *Science and Thought in the Fifteenth Century* (New York, 1929), pp. 24–58, also the ground-breaking work of Neal Gilbert, *Concepts of Method in the Renaissance* (New York, 1956).

5 *Annotationes in quattuor et viginti Pandectarum libros* (Paris, 1535), f. 3ʳ, on Digest I, 1, 1, and see Guido Kisch, *Erasmus und die Jurisprudenz seiner Zeit* (Basel, 1960).

6 *Catalogus gloriae mundi* (Frankfurt, 1586), f. 207ʳ.

7 See the works of Hans Troje, especially *Graeca leguntur* (Cologne, 1971), Aldo Mazzacane, especially *Scienza, logica e ideologia nella giruisprudenza tedesca del sec. XVI* (Rome, 1971), and Ennio Cortese, *La Norma giuridica* (Rome, 1962–1964). On the historical school see Domenico Maffei, *Gli Inizi dell'umanesimo giuridico* (Milan, 1956), and my *Foundations of Modern Historical Scholarship* (New York, 1970), which the present paper is intended in certain ways to counterbalance.

8 Alciato's strictures against Valla in *Dispunctiones,* IV, 7, and commentary on Digest, L, 16 ("De verborum significatione"), in *Opera omnia* (Frankfurt, 1617), IV, 201, and I, 205. See note 34.

tative thirteenth-century Gloss, "because in the civil law everything is contained."[9] "In the whole body of civil law," declared Chasseneux three centuries later, "one may find true theology" (*vera theologia*).[10] And as one of Alciato's followers concluded, "There is nothing either human or divine which the jurist does not treat and which does not pertain to civil science."[11]

The basic institutional reason for the self-confidence and intellectual imperialism of jurisprudence was an elitism accompanied by a sense of rank that often bordered on the ridiculous. Justinian had called his law professors *antecessores*. The reason for this, according to one glossator (in one of those inventive etymologies that might have come straight out of Isidore of Seville), is that "they antecede other professors in learning and virtue."[12] Academic snobbery has perhaps never been higher than among Renaissance jurists; it led Alciato, for example, to chide Budé for discussing law without the proper credentials, that is, a doctor's degree. For Chasseneux the academic hierarchy had an absolutely cosmological basis, and he celebrated the jurist's place in it in terms derived from Pico's famous oration on the "dignity of man."[13] The dignity of lawyers could be calibrated in a way that might bring a warm glow to college administrators across the centuries. "Among all doctors of law," Chasseneux wrote in his *Catalogue of the Glories of the World*, "those who are to be preferred first who teach, then those who have the larger salary [*maiora stipendia*] . . . , who put together or write books [*libros composerunt seu scripserunt*] . . . , who are appointed by the Pope or Emperor . . . , who have several degrees [*plures habent gradus*] . . . , who teach in the larger, more famous and better universities [*in majore, famosiora et digniora universitate*] . . . , and who have other honors." Jurists, in short, lived in their own world; and while ideally they might be members of the *respublica litterarum*, their first allegiance was, in the phrase of one of their eighteenth-century colleagues, to the *respublica jurisconsultorum*.[14] As such they had their own questions and answers, their own methods and goals, their own language and philosophy. It is no wonder that, like other academic chauvinists, they believed that their philosophy was the true philosophy.

There is an unmistakable analogy between my argument and the view expressed some years ago by P. O. Kristeller about the relations between humanism and scholastic philosophy.[15] My paraphrase would be that so-called legal humanists like Valla and Poliziano were not either good or bad jurists but no jurists at all—though likewise I should by no means want to deny their significance for jurisprudence, above all in textual and historical criticism. I might conclude, too, that humanism and jurisprudence "coexisted and developed all the way through the Renaissance period as different branches of learning"—that the controversy between the two, that is, the conflict between the *mos italicus* and the *mos gallicus*, "is merely a phase in the battle of the arts, not a struggle for existence," and similarly that "all kinds of adjustments and combinations between humanism and phiosophy [here I substitute 'jurisprudence'] were possible and successfully accomplished." In terms of Renaissance discourse it may be said that Alciato's critique of the views of Valla were made on the same methodological grounds

9 *Ad. tit.*
10 *Catalogus gloriae mundi*, just following the *vera philosophia* topos.
11 François le Douaren, *Opera omnia* (Frankfurt, 1598), I, 1. See note 50.
12 Odofredus, *Lectura super Digesto veteri* (Lyon, 1550), f. 2r.
13 *Catalogus gloriae mundi*, f. 220v.
14 Giuseppe Gennaro, *Respublica jurisconsultorum* (Leipzig, 1733).
15 P. O. Kristeller, *Studies in Renaissance Thought and Letters* (Rome, 1956), p. 562.

as the responses made to the philologist Ermolao Barbaro by Pico in his classic defense of all species of philosophy, even the scholastic, as transcending stylistic questions.[16] In the same way Alciato found much to praise in what his opponent regarded as "barbarism," and he too believed in a wisdom beyond eloquence.

There was another reason for the superiority of jurisprudence aside from its encyclopedic breadth, and this was brought out in the rest of Seyssel's statement. "Jurisprudence," he went on to explain, "consists not in speculation but in action."[17] Here again there seems to be an affinity with the humanist tradition, which defended the dignity of rhetoric on exactly the same grounds. Yet again this civic spirit had been an integral part of traditional jurisprudence from the beginning. "The science of jurisprudence concerns the accidents and deeds of men," as Baldus put it, "and these are as diverse as the minds and wills of men."[18] His works and those of Bartolus are filled with celebrations of the *vita activa* and the supremacy of justice and equity over truth and consistency as philosophic values. In all of the recent discussions of "civic humanism," it seems curious that the contributions of jurists, especially contemporaries of Petrarch and Salutati like Bartolus and Baldus, who used to figure so prominently in discussions of the new *civilità* of the Renaissance, are almost universally neglected.[19]

In this area too the effect of humanism was not really to generate but rather to reinforce the civic message. In the sixteenth century the jurist continues to be represented as the highest form of "political animal"; but increasingly Plato joins Aristotle as a witness for the defense. "For the welfare of humanity," wrote François Baudouin, one of Alciato's French disciples, "Socrates said that either philosophers should rule or kings should be philosophers, and if this is true, philosophy should be expressed not in words but in actions. . . . But since public actions are more potent than private, the true and supreme philosophy [*vera et summa philosophia*] is contained in laws which pertain to public actions."[20] One of Baudouin's own disciples, Louis le Caron, who was quite self-consciously a Platonist, put the matter more directly: "I say that true philosophy is contained in the books of law and not in the useless and inarticulate libraries of philosophers, who in effect are men of great learning but incompetent in public affairs. . . . Wherefore jurisprudence may indeed be called the true philosophy."[21]

This association between Roman law and Greek philosophy was not accidental, of course; it had also a historical, or at least a mythical, dimension. For the second title of the Digest, "On the Origin of Law," incorporated and legitimized the old story that, before embarking upon their pioneering work of codification, the Roman "decimvirs" made a trip to Greece to consult with the wise and experienced lawmakers of Athens.[22] The fable added by Accursius, that the decimvirs made a gesture signifying the trinity, was rejected by Renaissance jurists; but the story itself was accepted and so, at least

---

16 See the translation and discussion by Q. Breen in *Journal of the History of Ideas,* XIII (1952), 384–426; also A. Bernardini and G. Righi, *Il Concetto di filologia e di cultura classica* (Bari, 1953), ch. II.

17 See note 1.

18 *L'Opera di Baldo* per cura dell'Università di Perugia nel V centenario della morte del grande giureconsulto (Perugia, 1901), p. 435.

19 See Peter Riesenberg, "Civism and Roman Law in Fourteenth-Century Italian Society," *Explorations in Economic History,* VII (1969–1970), 237–254.

20 *Commentarius in quattuor libros institutionum iuris civilis* (Paris, 1554), *in tit.*

21 *La Claire, ou de la prudence du droit* (Paris, 1554), pp. 23–24. See note 55.

22 Digest I, 2, 2, and see my "The Rise of Legal History in the Renaissance," *History and Theory,* IX (1970), 174–194.

until Vico's time, was the notion of direct Greek influence upon the law of the Twelve Tables, which according to Cicero was not only the first great monument of Roman jurisprudence but also, as he put it, "superior to the libraries of all the philosophers." "Like other sciences," wrote Alberico Rosciate, "legal science takes its origin from the Greeks,"[23] and sixteenth-century jurists developed this theme in philosophical as well as historical terms. Through Roman law, as François Baudouin put it, Athens became the education (*paideia*) not only of Hellas but of the whole world. And with the great work of codification by Justinian in the sixth century this *paideia* was in a sense restored to its original context.[24] "Thus the Romans first took their laws from the Athenians," Baudouin concluded, "and then gave them back."

The sense of holy tradition, of inheriting a body of ancient wisdom and guarding a sacred canon, was formalized in the Corpus Juris Civilis of Justinian. In this the *sacra scriptura* of the legal tradition the Emperor repeatedly declared his "reverence for antiquity" and for the "monuments of ancient learning," and in his prefatory constitutions to his teachers he gave a counsel of absolute perfection.[25] Unlike the previous 1400 years of legal mutability, his collection was, he said, "to prevail for all time"; and commentators, forbidden all further "interpretation," were permitted only "paratitles," or summaries. These were the ideals accepted by most medieval and Renaissance jurists and the rules by which they at least tried to live. They made a direct identification with the "priests of the laws" (*sacerdotes legum*), as the Roman jurists had called themselves; they accepted the universal tradition of the empire, if not the authority of the emperor himself; and they looked upon civil law not only as the highest philosophy but as reason itself in written form (*ratio scripta*).

The one point to which modern jurists took exception—and it was a crucial one—was Justinian's injunction against further interpretation; and it is here that we may see the most fundamental expression of the conceptual independence of jurisprudence. For the method of exegesis in law was neither that of grammar nor of dialectic but had its own traditions and rules. According to the view of Bartolus, which was still retained by Alciato and his followers, the meaning of a text could be established in three ways—by authority, definition, or etymology. *Auctoritas* was the most forceful way, since the power of the emperor lay behind every law and since, as Baldus put it, "Doctors of law may not allege an error in the law."[26] As a good imperialist Alciato accepted this, although for obvious political reasons his French disciples could not follow suit. Definition was either a logical or a philosophical assertion by the commentator, but of course without the benefit of legal authority it was always open to question. "In law," Alciato remarked, "definition is always dangerous."[27] Etymology continued to be a popular device, and especially among lawyers it continued to be as irrelevant to philology as it had been for Isidore of Seville—or as it would be for Giambattista Vico. The reason for this was not ignorance but rather, as Seyssel put it, the purpose of etymology was to get at the essence (*quidditas*) of a term; and the final test was not grammatical or historical but rather legal or philosophical.[28]

---

23 *Commentariorum . . . super Codice* (Lyon, 1545), f. 4ᵛ.

24 *Commentarius de legibus XII tabularum*, in *Tractatus universi juris* (Venice, 1584), I, f. 226ʳ.

25 Constitutions *Omnem* and *Tanta*, and see my "Clio and the Lawyers," *Medievalia et Humanistica*, n. s., V (1974), 25–49.

26 *Super Digesto* (s.l. 1535), 4ʳ.

27 *De Verborum significatione* (Lyon, 1565), p. 17.

28 *Speculum feudorum* (Basel, 1566), p. 11.

Bartolus' formulation was much elaborated in the later Renaissance, notably in Alciato's commentary on the last title of the Digest concerning the meaning of words, "De Vebrorum significatione," which is one of the classic statements of juristic hermeneutics.[29] No more than his friend Erasmus did Alciato, despite his popular image as a founder of legal humanism, advocate a narrowly grammatical method. In his view there were four basic modes of understanding—through propriety, impropriety, custom and interpretation—and none of these was exclusively philological in character. The literal meaning of terms was of course a first and essential step, but the target of *proprietas,* as Alciato designated his first stage, was "not the name but the force of meaning [*vis*], not the word but the conception." The rule that Alciato had in mind here was that of Celsus included in the first title of the Digest: "To understand laws is not to know their words but rather their force and power" (*vis et potestas*), which referred also to the intention (*mens, voluntas, sententia*) of the legislator.[30] *Proprietas* also involved proper use of terms of varying degrees of abstraction whose literal referents could not be so precisely determined—terms with more than one meaning, or more than one term referring to the same thing in different circumstances (such as *adultorium* and *stupra,* the first applying to married, the other to unmarried women), and other complications about which jurists could not usefully be literal-minded. As Erasmus sought the spirit of Biblical texts, so Alciato sought the underlying rationale of laws; "for reason," as he put it, "is the soul and life of a particular law" (*ratio est anima, vigorque ipsius legis*).[31]

What grammar provided, in other words, was not rules but tools. To illustrate his point Alciato told an anecdote about a certain grammarian of his acquaintance who, having taken his horse to a veteranarian on a trip from Milan to Bologna, refused to pay his bill because the horse doctor had set down his written plea in appalling Latin.[32] The question was, Alciato asked, could the grammarian's case really be defended on such grounds? The law itself, if not simple logic, furnished the answer: "Grammatica mala non vitiat instrumentum" was the way Bartolus had expressed the rule.[33] Here we can see the real grounds for Alciato's abhorrence for Lorenzo Valla, "emperor of the grammarians," as he called him, who had done such violence to the texts of law on behalf of literary elegance, and "against ancient authority." The point was that classical usage did not necessarily correspond to juridical usage, nor eloquence to justice, and Alciato gave many examples in his commentary "De verborum significations." One famous and often quoted complaint of Valla (actually lifted from Aulus Gellius) was the derivation of the word *testamentum* from *testatio mentis,* "a testifying of the mind"; but Alciato rejected this argument too.[34] This was not a true etymology, he wrote, but an allusion, that is, a device for getting at the meaning of the term.

The other modes of understanding introduced more qualifications, distinctions, and exceptions than could be dreamed of in the world of grammarians. *Improprietas,* not necessarily a pejorative term, was a designation of something by other than its proper name and included, for example, temporary relationships and legal fictions. Customary usage (*ex usu*) involved everyday, non-technical language, again legitimate, though unfortunately not usually desirable, since common usage (*communis loquendi usus*) was

---

29 *De Verborum significatione,* pp. 14 ff.

30 Digest I, 3, 17.

31 *De Verborum significatione,* p. 20.

32 Ibid., p. 78.

33 *Opera omnia* (Venice, 1590), i, 22v.

34 *De Verborum significatione,* p. 195. Valla's commentaries on "De Verborum significatione" appear in his *Elegantiae latinae linguae,* VI, 35–64.

subject to change, so that the meaning of laws themselves might be effaced by time. This is why Alciato, like Valla, preferred language sanctioned by the learned (*consensus eruditorum* is the phrase used by both)—except of course that Alciato's "learned" were lawyers, not orators, and that the proper language was to be derived from the Digest, not the literary classics from which Valla took his authority.

Last came *interpretatio,* forbidden by Justinian and ostensibly avoided by humanists like Valla and Budé. Now Alciato, too, deplored the endless accumulation of *opiniones* by the scholastic jurists, and yet at the same time he realized that much of the Digest was not self-evident, especially to moderns, and that furthermore corrections had to be made because of Justinian's inconsistency—what he called "Justiniani inconstantia in condendis legibus."[35] Under this rubric he presented an elaborate discussion of the principal places, tropes, and figures, drawn from Quintilian but embellished with legal illustrations; for in the law there was a wealth of literary, historical, and philosophical material that invited such explication and criticism. Alciato's French disciples felt even less compunction about laying their hands upon the texts of law—not only to make necessary emendations but also to correct the philosophical deficiencies of Justinian's handiwork, or rather that of his principal editor, whence the source of that scholarly movement called "anti-Tribonianism." The justification for this offered by another of Alciato's French followers, Hugues Doneau, was that the Byzantine collection was fragmentary, without order and sometimes contradictory and inequitable. In this most fundamental way Doneau undermined the "absolutist" position of Justinian, and contradicting the imperial will established "interpretation" as an essential part (indeed a rubric, "interpretationis defensio") of civil law.[36]

In general Renaissance jurists, because of the conventions of their profession, were bound also to assume a much more complicated and abstractive theory of knowledge than humanists like Valla. Thus Alciato, though he had no use for elaborate logical games (*subtilitates Iurisconsulti Dialecticis*) and admitted that "conjectures about meaning must give way to propriety,"[37] nonetheless accepted some features of scholastic philosophy which Valla had explicitly rejected in the name of humanist usage (*usus humanitatis*). Among these were the practices of distinguishing on logical grounds among individuals, species, and genera, and especially resorting to the so-called *praedicamenta*, such as the notions of quality, quantity, place, and time, which were necessary for the interpretation, qualification, and of course application of individual laws. Among the most important fruits of this admission of general categories was the accommodation of comparative studies in laws and institutions, and sixteenth-century jurists followed up this lead with enthusiasm.

Hardly less complicated than the problem of classification was the problem of process and change, and here perhaps the most striking response was the adaptation of the Aristotelian system of causal explanation, a practice that began with the glossators but was much elaborated in the Renaissance. Following the lead of Baldus in particular, Seyssel showed how this scheme might be applied to the body of feudal law, that is to the *Libri Feudorum,* which many jurists continued to regard as "Roman" law.[38] The

---

35 *Dispunctiones,* in *Opera omnia,* IV, 78.

36 *Opera omnia* (Rome, 1828), I, 88. Cf. P. Gammaro, *De Extensionibus,* in *Tractatus universi juris,* XVIII, 248, "Nam ista interpretatio est pars ipsius iuris." See A. Eyssell, *Doneau* (Dijon, 1860), and in general V. Piano Mortari, *Ricerche sulla teoria dell'interpretazione del diritto nel secolo XVI* (Milan, 1956), and "Il Problema dell'interpretatio iuris nei commentatori," *Annali di storia del diritto,* II (1958), 29–109.

37 *De Verborum significatione,* p. 25.

38 *Speculum Feudorum,* 11.

efficient cause of these feudal customs, as of all laws, Seyssel wrote, was divine authority itself; the material cause included the laws, constitutions and judicial decisions contained in the text; the formal cause was their organization and distribution into books and titles; and the final cause was the light they shed on problems of feudal society (*ut facilius quaestiones feudales deffiniri possent*). The assumption was that all laws had, at least ideally, such a schematic foundation.

The central *quaestio* to which these arguments were attached was whether or not the study of law was a true "science." Some jurists preferred to regard it as an applied "art," others as a kind of non-theoretical "prudence" governed by experience; but the *communis opinio* was that law indeed deserved to be ranked as *scientia*. For this proposition there were two persuasive arguments, each of which had significant philosophical implications. The first was that law, like reason itself, was universal in scope. It was this conviction that sustained jurists in their drive to reform and to unify customs, to rationalize and to reconcile particular laws, and to establish grandiose and symmetrical "institutes," "digests," "codes" and "methods" of law.[39] Second and more to the point, law dealt with the world in terms of cause and effect. "To know is to understand through causes," as Chasseneux explained it (*scire est per causas cognoscere*), and furthermore "legists and canonists know through causas" (*legistae et canonistae cognoscunt per causas*).[40] The conclusion of the syllogism was that jurisprudence had a stake not only in the practical or moral disciplines but also in the natural or theoretical disciplines. This was a claim that social philosophers of later ages, from Hobbes to Marx and beyond, would often make, and often on the same grounds.

There are other, less explicitly formulated but no less significant philosophical themes in the legal tradition that deserve more attention than they have received. One is what may be regarded as a version of the traditional problem of universals. The point was that while laws were in theory universal in application, in fact they varied according to the diversity of national traditions (*gentes*), of which the Roman itself (as canonists in particular were pleased to point out) was one. "God is the author of justice," the formula went, "and man of laws";[41] and so men might well wonder if general laws behind specific formulations existed or not. Or rather, could general laws be grasped directly through reason, or was it necessary to proceed through the investigation of individuals? In the legal tradition of the fourteenth century, as in philosophy, there was what may be called a nominalist school that inclined to an empirical approach. So Andrea de Isernia (+1316) objected to the common practice of identifying feudal with ancient Roman institutions, and he argued that feudal terms were unprecedented (*nova nomina*) and the institutions they denoted were likewise distinctive.[42] The empirical methods encouraged by such an attitude were reinforced by certain tendencies in legal humanism and began to bear scholarly fruit in the sixteenth century. On the other side were "realists" like Baldus and Durandus, for whom feudal law was an "imitation" of the Roman—and both reflections of a universal pattern.[43] In the basis of these assumptions

---

39 See J. Van Kan, *Les Efforts de la codification en France* (Paris, 1929).

40 *Catalogus gloriae mundi*, f. 209r. Cf. A. Favre, *Iurisprudentiae Papinianae scientia* (Cologne, 1631), 8, "De iurisprudentia arsne sit an scientia," and J. Coras, *De Iure civili in artem redigendo*, in *Tractatus universi juris*.

41 Placentinus, cited by R. Orestano, *Introduzione allo studio del diritto romano* (Turin, 1963), p. 141.

42 *In usu feudorum commentaria* (Naples, 1571), 6r; discussion in my "De Origine Feudorum," *Speculum*, XXXIX (1964), 207–228.

43 *Speculum* (Lyon, 1547), p. 119.

there was erected a still more distinguished school of social thought and research, including Jean Bodin, Montesquieu and Vico. In such ways the legal tradition contributed both to modern sociology and political science.

In a number of ways jurists had to deal with permanence and change, with the variety and mutability of human life on the one hand and the stability and continuity of institutions and ideals on the other. They had to face the problems not only of individual behavior, in short, but also of general "forms." Like nature itself jurisprudence contained potentially a "plenitude of forms," in Lovejoy's term, and on these grounds it may be suggested made its own contribution to the modern "idea of progress."[44] "It is characteristic of human jurisprudence to be indefinitely extending," declared Justinian in one of his famous prefaces to the Digest, "and there is nothing in it which can endure forever, for nature is constantly hastening to bring forth new forms." Philosophical minded jurists like Baldus took this as practically an axiom of legal thought: "Nature and the acts of men always produce new forms," he paraphrased.[45] Yet at the same time forms did afford a basis for a certain permanence that humanity alone could not accommodate. This epiphenomenon of the "continuity of forms" has been discussed most perceptively, though by no means exhaustively, by Ernst Kantorowicz; and again may be illustrated by the views of Baldus on the sempiternal character of certain institutions like the Roman populus and the empire. "Note that when the form of a thing does not change," Baldus wrote, "the thing itself is said not to change" (*ubi non mutatur forma rei, non dicitur mutari res*).[46]

Perhaps the key concept, and certainly one of the most controversial among Renaissance jurists, is that of the *imperium,* which refers generally to the sovereign or legislative authority of the emperor. Among classical jurists this was a subject commonly avoided except for vague or rhetorical formulas; nor did Justinian elaborate much upon it, except to stipulate that from his time on the imperial will superseded all other sources of authority. In modern times, however, the subject was debated endlessly, especially by non-Italian jurists; and indeed the idea of the *imperium* became a locus for discussions of countless aspects of public authority. But despite the association of the concept with various concrete powers, privileges, and kinds of jurisdiction, it continued to have a transcendent and even mystical connotation, and once again it was in the sixteenth century that the full potential of the idea was realized. As has been suggested, there is a direct historical as well as a logical connection between the formula of Baldus concerning the indivisibility of imperial authority—*imperium est indivisibile*—and the famous discussion of the idea of sovereignty in the *Republic* of Bodin; but at this point we touch the more familiar ground of political philosophy and natural law into which it does not seem useful to enter.[47]

In general the jurists, no less than the philosophers, believed in a basically intelligible universe and were convinced that their discipline provided the best access to it. Decaring law to be "written reason" (*ratio scripta*) was the way they expressed this conviction. This imperialist formula did not go entirely unquestioned, of course. Neither canonists nor "ultramontane" jurists with national allegiances incompatible with the

44 A. O. Lovejoy, *The Great Chain of Being* (Cambridge, Mass., 1936), p. 52.

45 *Opera di Baldo,* p. 433.

46 Cited by Ernst Kantorowicz, *The King's Two Bodies* (Princeton, 1957), p. 295.

47 On this question see Julian H. Franklin, *Jean Bodin and the Rise of Absolutist Theory* (Cambridge, 1973), arguing against this connection, though it seems to me on logical rather than historical grounds.

empire could accept the identification of the Roman tradition with reason itself. Their general view was that, while Roman law might indeed be a model and superior to other varieties, it was nonetheless merely one national tradition. The point was put best in the sixteenth century by the French lawyer Charles Dumoulin, who accorded much utility but absolutely no authority to civil law in France. Roman laws were to be accepted in French courts "not by reason of empire," he declared, "but by the empire of reason" (*non ratione imperii sed rationis imperio*).[48] Roman law continued to be a model, in other words, but in a sublimated form. A true emulation of Roman jurisprudence entailed not literal imitation in the fashion of those "apes of Cicero" derided by Erasmus but rather the continued pursuit of ancient philosophical ideals in modern terms, which was to say modern customs and perhaps even modern languages. This enterprise was carried on in the sixteenth century above all by French jurists, whose devotion to the encyclopedic ideals of humanism broadened their philosophical horizons, yet whose Gallican convictions were freed from Romanist intimidation. The most important of these were associated with the University of Bourges and included Eguinaire Baron, François le Douaren, François Connan, Hugues Doneau, François Hotman, Louis le Caron, and even François Baudouin and Jacques Cujas, though their respective reputations as legal historian and arch-"grammarian" have obscured their philosophical contributions. As Roderick Stintzing pointed out almost a century ago this group—Alciatei or Alciatani their critics called them—labored not only to restore the texts of civil law but also to establish a more comprehensive and equitable synthesis of jurisprudence.[49]

What these scholars shared above all was an obsession with "method" in a philosophical as well as a pedagogical sense, similar to the systematizing style of Ramus and his "larvae," though not necessarily derived from it. Two of the earliest methodological manifestos were by Baron and Le Douaren; and despite deep personal, religious and political differences, they agreed on this subject.[50] Carrying on from Alciato's discussion of the *ars interpretationis,* Le Douaren proposed as an antidote to barbarism not only Latin eloquence but also logical clarity, which he celebrated in mathematical terms. Jurisprudence should start with "fundamental maxims and basic problems," he wrote, "just as geometry begins with points, lines, surfaces, etc."[51] So the order of reading was crucial, especially as regarded the arrangement of the Digest and the Institutes themselves. This unauthorized trend toward the internal reorganization of civil law, implied in the "methodical" commentaries of Baron and Le Douaren, began to achieve fulfillment in the work of Connan and Doneau, who reordered the rubrics of jurisprudence according to a new and different logic, though still recognizably adaptations of Justinian's. The definition of law as *vera philosophia* was one that "everybody applauded," Connan wrote, but to give it meaning he found it advisable to resort to the well known plans of Cicero and of Caesar to systematize received laws.[52] Thus from

[48] Aubépin, "De l'Influence de Dumoulin sur la législation française," *Revue critique de législation et de jurisprudence,* V (1854), 305.

[49] *Geschichte der deutschen Rechtswissenschaft* (Munich, 1880), I, 367 ff.; see also Friedrich Ebrard, "Über Methode, Systeme, Dogmen in der Geschichte des Privatrechts," *Zeitschrift für Schweizerischen Recht,* LXVII (1948), 95–306, and various works of Troje listed in the bibliography of his *Graeca leguntur.*

[50] These and other treatises on legal method are collected in N. Reusner, ΧΕΙΡΑΓΩΓΙΑ, *Sive Cynosura Iuris* (Spires, 1588); and see now W. Vogt, *Franciscus Duarenus 1509–1559* (Stuttgart, 1971).

[51] *Opera omnia* (Lucca, 1765), I, 1.

[52] *Commentariorum Iuris civilis libri X* (Paris, 1553), 8ᵛ; and see now C. Bergfeld, *Franciscus Connanus 1508–1551* (Cologne, 1968).

the pedagogical goal of making jurisprudence mnemonically more manageable, Connan moved on to the philosophical goal of making it more rational and equitable. "Reducing civil law to an art" *(jus civile in artem redigendo)* was the popular Ciceronian formula that referred to both levels of systematization.

A related, though somewhat less well defined tendency among these French jurists of the mid- and late sixteenth-century was their growing interest in the study of comparative law, inadvertent to begin with, as in the practice of reconciling civil law with feudal or provincial customs, and then more deliberate and academic. As Jean Coras suggested in his discussion of legal method, the *praedicamenta* of place and time invited some such approach, illustrated by the old religious maxim, "When in Rome, behave as the Romans," which corresponded in legal terms to the principle of territoriality.[53] One pioneering, yet almost totally neglected work was Eguinaire Baron's *Civil Institutes* (published in 1550, the year of his and Alciato's death), which was a comparative commentary (*commentarius bipartita*) that aligned Roman institutions with their supposed French counterparts (such as the *merum* and *mixtum imperium* with *haute, moyenne* and *basse justice*), and defended the juxtaposition with reference to Platonic as well as Ciceronian thought.[54] In the next generation such works multiplied, culminating in a variety of attempts, official as well as unofficial, to assemble a unified French "code" in some sense or another.

A striking example of the assimilation of jurisprudence to philosophy that emerged from the school of Bourges is Louis Le Caron, who quite literally identified the *vera philosophia* of Ulpian with that of the "divine Plato"—and the profession of the jurist with the "office du philosophe"—and who in a sense devoted his career to the fulfillment of this eclectic ideal.[55] What Le Caron found must vital in Platonic philosophy was the fusion of systematic philosophy with the conviction that, as he quoted Plato, "true philosophy concerns itself with the life and customs of men." Sustained by this idea, he turned increasingly from the rambling and repetitious celebrations of Platonic philosophy found in his youthful poetry and prose to the task of imposing the values and organization of classical jurisprudence upon the tangled legal traditions of France, combining the comparative interests of his mentors at Bourges with their desire to "reduce law to an art." The major product of this enterprise was his *Digest of French Law,* published first in 1587, which he believed to have restored the customs of his patria to the context of universal law and moral philosophy and so to be a monument to what he called civil wisdom (*la sagesse civile*) or "the royal science."[56]

The best known expression of the philosophical ideals of jurisprudence in the sixteenth century is to be found in the work of Jean Bodin, whose starting point was conventional legal philosophy but whose ultimate goal was a system of philosophy that went beyond the intentions, and indeed the dreams, of contemporary jurists.[57] Bodin was an arch-eclectic, his thought displaying all of the elements discussed here and many others as well, worthy of the overreaching enterprises of those two "princes" of Concord, Pico and Guillaume Postel, with whom Bodin in fact had direct contact. In one

53 *De Iure civili in artem redigendo,* in *Tractatus universi juris,* I, 81r; and see now A. Fell, *The Classical Four Causes in the Renaissance Art of Law* (Ph.D. diss., Columbia University, 1974).

54 *Institutionum civilium ab Justiniano Caesare editarum libri IIII* (Poitiers, 1550).

55 See my "Louis le Caron Philosophe," in *Philosophy and Humanism: Renaissance Essays in Honor of Paul Oskar Kristeller* (New York, 1976).

56 *Pandectes ou Digestes du droict françois* (Paris, 1587), I, 3.

57 See my "The Development and Context of Bodin's Method," *Jean Bodin: Verhandlungen der internationalen Bodin Tagung in München,* ed. H. Denzer (Munich, 1973), pp. 123–150.

successively modified structure Bodin combined many disparate elements—attitudes of legal humanism, old-fashioned scholastic apparatus, new-fangled systematic jurisprudence as exemplified by Connan, Aristotelian political philosophy, Machiavellian statecraft, and Ramist, or at least Ramoid, organization. His aim, appearing first in his youthful attempt to "reduce law to an art," was the formulation of a system of "universal law." Like his Gallican colleagues he regarded civil law as a useful but not an authoritative or sufficient guide, as parochial in legal terms as the Four World Monarchies was in historical terms; and so he rejected an alleged Roman for a truly Platonic universalism, turning in particular from the *jus civile* to the *jus gentium,* in which he included not only the body of law sanctioned by Justinian but all subsequent national traditions. Like Pico, then, Bodin sought the materials for his system of thought in the cultural past, in history which—as Ernst Cassirer characterized Pico's view—"is the sum total of the intellectual forms which man produces from himself."[58] In the pivotal work of his career, the *Method of History* of 1566, Bodin began to ransack the past in order to place political and social philosophy (*civilis disciplina*) on a broader and firmer basis. The operation was completed a decade later with the publication of his *Republic,* in which his eclecticism had become rampant and his systematizing obsessions transcendent. Mixing historical evidence with legal allegations and philosophic authorities, Bodin tried to formulate, in normative as well as naturalistic terms, the structure of society and government. In this way Bodin fulfilled his promise "to do for the Republic of the world," as he put it, "what Plato did for his Republic."

An equally impressive system—grotesque in form, devoid of legal relevance but sublime in conception—was erected by Bodin's rival, the Toulouse jurist Pierre Grégoire, whose efforts were expressed in two encyclopedic works. The first was another Republic, arranged in twenty-six books as contrasted with Bodin's six, which was if anything even more eclectic than Bodin's book. Like Bodin, Grégoire started out wanting to "reduce law to an art" but like him was carried away with the implications of a "republic." To Grégoire this meant not only an ideal society but a total cultural cosmos, and so he was prompted to digress on many aspects of intellectual and religious tradition, on all the arts and sciences including philosophy itself. More of a traditionalist than Bodin, Grégoire took special care in rejecting the "aetheistic and hypocritical" doctrines of that "most pernicious man, Machiavelli," whom Bodin had not scrupled to single out for praise.[59] He was also more of a jurist, turning as he did for his organizing principle to the tripartite division of civil law (persons, things, acts). He did this also in his other systematic work, a synthesis of universal law (*Syntagma iuris universi*), where through a "new method" he tried to organize and to explain all divine, natural and human law. Although Bodin treated the same range of learning, he was surpassed in plan and execution by this encyclopedic effort of Grégoire of Toulouse, misguided as it must seem to modern readers.

In fact, of course, Grégoire has no modern readers; nor for all practical purposes have any of these scholars, even Bodin, except for a few well-worn pages. Yet their world of thought, alien and remote though it may seem from this perspective, must be penetrated if we hope to understand the earlier phases of the history of philosophy. They surely deserve as much attention as, say, the contributors to pre-Galilean mechan-

[58] "Giovanni Pico della Mirandola," *Journal of the History of Ideas,* III (1942), 334.

[59] *De Republica* (Frankfurt, 1609), XIII, 21; and cf. *De Iuris methodo et praeceptis* (Lyon, 1580). E. Joucla, *Les Doctrines politiques de Grégoire de Toulouse* (Toulouse, 1899).

ics, or theological systems builders, or utopian authors, to whom historians of thought so often turn. What especially needs clarification are the connecting links between Renaissance jurisprudence and Enlightenment philosophy. Of these the belief that law is *vera philosophia* is one of the most prominent. Centuries before the philosophes the jurists carried on a philosophic quest for the reason underlying human law, for the logos behind the latter, for what both referred to as the "spirit of the laws." What had been a hermeneutic principle, the focus upon the true meaning of a law (*mens legum*), was transformed into a concern for the spirit of laws in general (*mens legum* is the technical civilian term that Vico, for example, gives such philosophic significance), especially as derived from a critical and comparative canvassing of the "law of nations" (Vico's study of the *majores* and *minores gentes* corresponds to Bodin's study of *maximae* and *minimae respublicae*). The connections might be illustrated through a number of philosophers from the time of Grotius to that of Montesquieu, but they are most clearly exemplified in the work of Vico—which was itself born out of reflections upon Roman legal history, which was well grounded in Renaissance legal scholarship, which included an ideal of a "philosophical grammar," which was aimed at formulating a general law of nations (*jus divinum apud gentes* is one of the phrases) as well as a system of "universal law," before it took the more familiar form of the *Scienza Nuova*.

In general—and in conclusion—it seems incontestible that the legal tradition had a fairly continuous and at least a peripheral effect upon philosophical thought, more, certainly, than has been recognized in conventional historical surveys. The explanation for this is most likely the same as that for the neglect of Renaissance philosophy in general—namely, the intimidating figures of Descartes, Leibniz, Hobbes, and other seventeenth-century thinkers, who were attached in so obsessive a fashion to natural law and to mathematical or mechanical philosophy. Their imposing structures and public impact overshadowed the tenuous traditions of humanistic thought, of which jurisprudence was a significant and sometimes creative part. As the works of Bodin, Le Caron and Grégoire of Toulouse indicate, the practice of system-building itself had other models and other methods than those of natural philosophy. Among the most important of these was jurisprudence, whose categories were not those of metaphysics but those of society—that is, on the most general level, persons, things, actions, contracts and above all the human cosmos of the *respublica,* which could itself serve as a principle of organization and evaluation of the whole range of human knowledge and behavior. Comte said that metaphysics is the ghost of dead theologies. From the perspective of more anthropological-minded thinkers like Vico it might be said with equal justice that social philosophy is the ghost of dead jurisprudences. Unfortunately, this is a transformation that has not even begun to be understood.

University of Rochester

V

THE RISE OF LEGAL HISTORY IN THE RENAISSANCE

In the late 1550's Etienne Pasquier, a rising young lawyer and man of letters, addressed a letter to Jacques Cujas, professor of law at the University of Valence, formerly of the University of Bourges. "I have decided to research the antiquities of France," he wrote, "and so I have called my book 'les recherches.' The enterprise is a great labor requiring the study of many old books. If you have anything on the subject, you would do me a great favor by sending it to me."[1] Now this confession may not be quite so dramatic as Gibbon's account of the decision he took while musing among the Roman ruins, and yet it does have a comparable significance. For here we can see not only the launching of one of the most ambitious and original scholarly enterprises of the Renaissance but also one of the chief sources of modern historical scholarship. I mean that somewhat misunderstood branch of philology which we call legal humanism. A couple of years before, Cujas had begun to publish one of the great classics of legal humanism, his *Observations and Emendations,* a brilliant collection of legal, linguistic, and historical criticisms which grew to monumental proportions in the next forty years. Now Pasquier was beginning to assemble a similar gallery of monographs devoted to the past of French civilization, and he too would devote the better part of his life — almost sixty years — to the task.[2] What Cujas was doing for Roman law, in short, restoring it bit by bit to a proper historical perspective, Pasquier proposed to do for the entire range of French history.

I do not want to exaggerate the parallel between Cujas, the greatest of legal humanists, and Pasquier, one of the greatest of sixteenth-century historians. Between them there were several awkward barriers as well: that between the

1. *Les Lettres* (Paris, 1619), II, 6, also in *Choix des lettres*, ed. D. Thickett (Geneva, 1956), with additional notes.

2. *Les Recherches de la France* (Paris, 1560), including only the first book; the second appeared in 1565 but the next four not until 1596 because of Pasquier's fears of plagiarism; the first complete edition, containing ten books, was that of 1621. Cujas' *Observationum et emendationum libri* grew more gradually, from three books (Paris, 1556) to eighteen in the last edition, 1598.

Latinist and the vernacular humanist, between the "ancient" and the "modern," between the professional and the amateur, and between the cautious academic and the impassioned propagandist. Yet between them, too, were bonds of vital importance for the modern study of history. Both of these scholars had legal training, both had mastered the techniques of philology, and both found a boundless fascination in the origin and growth of human laws, institutions, and customs. They were innovating "historians," but in marked contrast to such analytical writers as Machiavelli, Guicciardini, and Commines, they had only a slight interest in personality, in problems of cause and effect, and in political philosophy. What interested them was not the sequence of political action but the substance of human society and the creations of human intelligence. The reason for this is not that they were "antiquarians," but rather that their interests and training gave them a richer, though more diffuse, perspective on the human past. Their novel concerns, as well as the techniques for pursuing them, arose not out of the tradition of historical writing but rather out of their formal training and everyday work, that is, out of the legal profession. In general, I would suggest, it was not the historians but the lawyers who laid the foundations for the study of legal, institutional, and to some extent social history.

No one should be surprised at this. Intellectually, history has never been a creative field, and its best practitioners have often applied to other disciplines for new ways of asking and answering questions about the past. Such poaching is common today; it was not so easy in the sixteenth century, when historical writing was bound by literary convention or distorted by political pressure, and when academic boundary lines were so strictly patrolled. Still, there were a few fields which seemed to offer new insights and perspectives to the historian, especially classical literature, Biblical studies, and jurisprudence. I have chosen to examine the last of these, because the transformation of legal scholarship in the sixteenth century offers a striking illustration of the way in which historiography has been shaped by an encounter with an ostensibly alien discipline. To put it briefly, what began as a revolution in the science of law, exemplified by the work of Cujas, ended as a revolution in the art of history, exemplified by the work of Pasquier.[3] The result was not only the emergence of a new branch of scholarship, that is, legal history, but the enrichment and expansion of the study of human society in general. My purpose here is to assess some of the early plantings in this field from which Pasquier was to reap so abundant a harvest.

3. These two related phenomena have been studied by Julian Franklin, *Jean Bodin and the Sixteenth-Century Revolution in the Methodology of Law and History* (New York, 1963), but from the perspective of systematic jurisprudence and political thought rather than of historical scholarship.

I. CIVIL LAW

If I disparage the ingenuity of historians, I do not mean to exaggerate that of lawyers, who normally stand in even greater need of outside inspiration. In fact, while the study of legal history had roots in antiquity and grew up largely within the confines of the legal profession, it had another parent: it was equally, if somewhat illegitimately, the offspring of Renaissance humanism. As a consequence, it bore the scars of the conflict between the champions of the liberal arts and the defenders of the established scholastic method. Appropriately, the *locus classicus* of this conflict was provided by Petrarch, who spoke from experience when he denounced the myopic and mercenary attitude of the law professors and called for a return to the "first fathers of jurisprudence," meaning the "classical" authors collected in the *Digest* of Justinian.[4] These battle cries resound throughout the entire history of legal humanism.

In the century after Petrarch the challenge was taken up by various scholars. In the first place, there were more or less popular essays on Roman offices by such antiquarians as Flavio Biondo, Antonio Fiocchi, and Pomponio Leto, whose work on Roman magistrates Savigny accepted as the first legal history.[5] But while these books showed some familiarity with legal sources, on the whole they were superficial and without much scholarly significance. The real pioneers were the philologists, who regarded Roman law as a species of literature and subjected it to the same sort of stylistic criticism. Maffeo Vegio reversed the classic pattern of Petrarch by switching from poetry back to law; he wrote the first important humanist treatise on the language of Roman law. Of course, his work was overshadowed by that of his friend Lorenzo Valla, whose accomplishment it was to establish the philological method — and the polemic against Bartolism — in its most radical form.[6] He was one of the founding fathers of legal humanism as he was of Biblical humanism; but because of the excesses of his rhetorical approach, with its reliance on aesthetic standards and conjecture, many later members of the school he

4. *Epistolae de rebus familiaribus*, ed. Fracassetti (Florence, 1863), III, 18; there is an abridged translation of this amusing letter in *Letters from Petrarch*, transl. Morris Bishop (Bloomington, Ind., 1966), 166-170.

5. Biondo, *De Militia et jurisprudentia*, in *Scritti inediti e rari*, ed. B. Nogara (Rome, 1927), and *De Roma triumphante* (Basel, 1531), especially books III, IV, and V; Fiocchi, *De Potestate Romanorum libri II* (Antwerp, 1561); and Leto, *De Potestate Romanorum magistratibus, sacerdotiis, jurisperitis, et legibus*, in *Opera varia* (Mainz, 1521). The standard introduction is Domenico Maffei, *Gli Inizi dell'umanesimo giuridico* (Milan, 1956).

6. *Elegantiarum Latinae linguae libri sex*, book III, and "Epistola in Bartoli de insigniis et armis libellum," in *Opera omnia*, ed. Eugenio Garin (Turin, 1962), I, 79 ff and 460 ff. Vegio's commentary in "De Verborum significatione" was first published by Sassi, *Historia literario-typographia mediolanensis* (Milan, 1745).

established came to turn against him — and unfortunately he did not have an Erasmus to defend his work on civil law.

For most sixteenth-century scholars, in fact, the father-figure of legal humanism was not the *orator* Valla but the *grammaticus* Angelo Poliziano, who began the critical study of the *Digest* on the basis of the famous Florentine manuscript and a superior knowledge of Greek. In the early sixteenth century his work was continued by such men as Pietro Crinito, Lodovico Bolognini, Alexander ab Alexandro, Claudio Tolomei, and in some respects by Andrea Alciato, none of whom had much use for Valla.[7] As the manifesto of this grammatical school, we may take Tolomei's little-known treatise of 1517 on the *Corrupted Words of Civil Law,* which argued the case for the new jurisprudence in the form of a dialogue between the grammarian Poliziano and the jurist Giasone del Maino. Such was the Italian tradition that carried on Petrarch's conviction that history was nothing else than the "praise of Rome." As a poet Poliziano himself had celebrated

> the wonderful faith of history reborn,
> the wonderful second dawning of Rome,[8]

and from the standpoint of legal history, none had done more than he and his disciples to bring about this rebirth.

Yet this period of Italian dominance was waning. Before his death in 1505 Crinito detected a "secession of the muses," and transalpine scholars were already proclaiming a "translation of studies" to the north. It is worth mentioning that the term "mos italicus" was applied not to the humanists but to the Bartolist school, which still kept its hold on the universities. What is more, it seems to me that northern scholars were able to achieve not only a wider perspective and a more critical view of the Roman tradition but a deeper understanding of the relations between law and society. For legal history at least, the work of Italians was surpassed by the Germans Ulrich Zasius and Johannes Oldendorp and above all by the scholars of France, which became,

7. Poliziano's emendations appear in his *Miscellaneae*, ch. 41, 78, 82, 95, in *Opera omnia* (Basel, 1553), and in A. Bandini, *Ragionamento istorico* . . . (Leghorn, 1762). For the rest: Crinito, *De Honesta disciplina*, ed. C. Angeleri (Rome, 1955), especially book XV; Alexandro, *Genialium dierum libri sex* (Leiden, 1673); Tolomei, *De Corruptis verbis juris civilis* (Siena, 1517); and on Bolognini, the articles of L. Sighinolfi in *La Bibliofilia* 24 (1922), 165-202, and in *Studie e memorie per la storia dell'Università di Bologna* 6 (1921), 187-308.

8. *Opera omnia,* 621:

> "Felix historiae fides renatae,
> Felix exoriente luca tanta
> Olim publica res Latina surget . . ."

For Petrarch's "Quis est enim aliud omnis historia quam Romana laus?" see T. E. Mommsen, *Medieval and Renaissance Studies,* ed. Eugene Rice (Ithaca, 1959), 122.

as Pasquier proudly declared, "the true center of the new jurisprudence."[9] The reason for this circumstance was not merely the effects of Guillaume Budé's treatise on the *Digest* in 1508, epoch-making as that book was, because Budé was in no position to establish a school and because, to be honest about it, his work was more impressive to literary than to legal scholars. In fact, the man who did most to promote legal humanism and to give it an institutional basis was Budé's rival and sometime protégé Andrea Alciato. He wrote important works on legal history as well as further criticism of the *Digest,* but in France his claim to fame was that he restored philology to the classroom.[10] We may dispute his boast that he was the first to do this in a thousand years; but we cannot deny that it was largely his intellectual progeny at the University of Bourges — especially Eguinaire Baron, François le Douaren, François Connan, François Baudouin, François Hotman, and Jacques Cujas — who made up the "first historical school of law" and, though they were all professional lawyers, who provide the most conspicuous link between legal humanism and history.

Like Gibbon, these men were inspired to their life work through reflection upon Roman ruins — the ruins in their case being the defaced and fragmentary monument of Roman jurisprudence, the *Digest.* Two titles in particular fascinated them and at the same time indicate the two principal facets of their historical method. The first one, on the meaning of terms ("De verborum significatione") provided an occasion for showing off the uses of philology, which in general was focused on the literal meaning (*sensus historicus*), the later changes in meaning, and the historical context of words. Vegio, Valla, Alciato, Barnabé Brisson, and others wrote commentaries on this title. Second was the fragment on the origin of law ("De origine juris civilis") attributed to Pomponius, which traced the course of public law from Romulus down to imperial times. This title, it seems to me, marks the true beginning of legal history. It inspired not only a number of commentaries by humanists but also the *History of Civil Law* published by Aymar du Rivail in 1515.[11] Du Rivail corrected Pomponius' account with the help of Livy and organized it with the help of Aristotle's three-fold division of governmental forms, which he arranged to parallel the major sources of law, that is, the regal laws, the laws

9. *Recherches,* IX, 39. I have discussed the French school from another point of view in "Guillaume Budé and the First Historical School of Law," *American Historical Review* 72 (1967), 807-834, with fuller documentation, which I shall not repeat.

10. *Paradoxa juris civilis,* "prooemium," in *Opera omnia* (Frankfurt, 1617), IV, col. 1.

11. *Historia juris civilis,* in *Tractatus universi juris,* duce et auspice Gregorio XIII (Venice, 1584), I, fol. 3 ff, followed by a *Historia juris pontificalis.* The best of the humanist commentaries on this title (*Digest,* 1, 2, 2) is that of Zasius, *Opera omnia* (Lyon, 1550), I, 270 ff. The characterization of Du Rivail is that of Ernst von Moeller, *Aymar du Rivail, der erste Rechtshistoriker* (Berlin, 1907).

of the people, the *plebiscita,* the *senatusconsulta,* and the pretorian edicts. This book is, if only nominally, the first history of law.

In the next fifty years legal humanism became a coherent and self-conscious movement and, as the "mos gallicus juris docendi," was increasingly confined to the legal profession. In 1565 one of Le Douaren's students, Valentinus Foster, published another *History of Civil Law,* this one including an account of the historical school of law assembled at the University of Bourges, which one hostile critic, Alberico Gentili, was later to identify as the "Alciatei" or the "Cujacii," and another, Etienne Forcadel, as the "plebeians," in contrast to the "patrician" Bartolists.[12] Meanwhile, the field of legal history had been explored from several angles. Among Alciato's first followers Antonio Agustín "far out-rivalled his contemporaries," in Mommsen's opinion, as an investigator of the sources. Besides making many corrections in the first humanist edition of Justinian, which Gregory Haloander had begun to publish in 1529, he was the first to show that the Florentine manuscript could not be a Byzantine original. In 1553 Lelio Torelli finally published an edition of this manuscript, just in time to serve Cujas and his generation. Extended researches were carried out into pre-Justinianian sources, such as the works of Ulpian and Paulus and the Theodosian Code, which numbered among Cujas' own significant contributions; and attempts were made by others, including Baudouin, Louis le Caron, Hotman, and Oldendorp, to reconstruct the law of the Twelve Tables from classical sources.[13] Add to this countless monographs on all aspects of civil law, and it is easy to see why defenders of the old jurisprudence like Gentili and Etienne Forcadel felt threatened by the historical school.

The first purpose — and greatest joy — of this school was to rescue civil law from the clutches of the medieval commentators, "la chambre de Bartole italien" as Pasquier referred to them, and from Accursius, whose *Gloss* constituted both a vulgate text and an authoritative *Summa* of the legal profession. As everyone knew, Justinian had specifically forbidden further "interpretation" of his collection, and the endless *opiniones* of the scholastic doctors violated this directive as well as humanist sensibilities.[14] The tone of humanist

12. Fosterus, *De Historia juris civilis Romani* (Basel, 1565); Gentili, *De Juris interpretibus libri sex* (London, 1582); and Forcadel, *Sphaera legalis* (Lyon, 1569), 71.

13. Baudouin, *Commentarius de legibus XII tabularum,* and Le Caron, *Ad Leges duodecem tabularum,* in *Tractatus universi juris,* I, fol. 225 ff; Hotman, *De Legibus XII tabularum . . . commentatio* (Lyon, 1564); and Oldendorp, *Juris naturalis gentium* ἑισαγογή (Antwerp, 1539). A study of such works would furnish an interesting test of humanist scholarship, it seems to me. Agustín's contributions have been published in *Thesaurus juris Romani* (Basel, 1741), I; see also the critical study by F. de Zulueta (Glasgow, 1939).

14. In his "Tanta," Justinian had made provision only for literal interpretation and paratitles, as Cujas recalled in the introduction to his own *Paratitla* (Paris, 1569).

complaints is well illustrated by a remark supposedly made by Eguinaire Baron, Alciato's first successor at the University of Bourges, during an official visitation to one of his classes by Michel de l'Hôpital. "When a dog has pissed somewhere," Baron said, "there is no cur . . . that will not come to raise his leg and do likewise; so when Bartolus, Baldus, and such pettifoggers discuss a point in some passage, no matter how long or irrelevant, the whole pack of doctors will come to befoul the same passage with conclusions, conditions, reasons pro and con . . . and other apparatus."[15] This outburst is perhaps more than usually colorful, but it is wholly typical of the humanist position, especially in its imagery. The aim of the legal humanists was indeed, according to one of their favorite conceits, to cleanse the Augean Stables of law.

But removing the outer crust of scholastic interpretation was only a first step. Much more difficult was detecting the interpolations introduced by Justinian himself, or rather by his editor Tribonian. This "anti-Tribonianist" theme, first sounded by Valla, echoes most resonantly in the famous discourse of Hotman. "Since good letters opened the eyes and minds of men," he wrote in 1567, "it has been discovered that Tribonian falsely included not merely three or four words but even whole sections, such as the 'de origine juris,' which is obviously fables added by Tribonian and ascribed to Pomponius." Hotman had come to this conclusion twelve years before, and his reasons were "based on style," as he put it, "as well as historical truth."[16] As usual, Hotman was hypercritical, but his general line of argument was not disputed. In order to make classical jurisprudence conform to Byzantine custom, Tribonian had introduced various anachronisms (*Tribonianismi*) and contradictions (*antinomiae*), which could be corrected only through historical research or, more precariously, conjectural emendation. In this way the *Digest* became a vehicle for the most sophisticated methods of historical scholarship as well as a prize exhibit of the process of historical change.

Gibbon has honored Hotman as the leader of the anti-Tribonianist "sect," and most students recognize Cujas as the most successful hunter of "Tribonianisms," but no one has ever given much credit to Baudouin, although in many ways he was the most original scholar of the group. To begin with, his *Justinian, or the New Law* of 1559 was the first comprehensive treatment of the anti-Tribonianist theme. "Many laws pertain to the history of the times rather than to civil law as we know it," he noted, and his conclusion was

15. Noel du Fail, *Contes et discours d'Eutrapel,* in *Oeuvres facétieuses* (Paris, 1874), I, 263.

16. *Antitribonian* (Paris, 1603), 96, and *Africanus* (Strasbourg, 1555), unpaginated. In general, see J. Heineccius, "De Secta Tribonianomastigum," in *Opera* (Geneva, 1748), III, 171 ff, and the richly documented book of L. Palazzini Finetti, *Storia delle interpolazioni nel corpus juris giustinianeo* (Milan, 1953).

that "the memory of ancient law is necessary for a knowledge of new law."[17] It was this train of thought that led Baudouin to his program for a permanent alliance between law and history. Such was the aim of his major work, the *Method of Universal History and its Conjunction with Jurisprudence* of 1561, which was at once a handbook of historical method and a manifesto of the historical school of law. The striking thing is that Baudouin had already become less interested in "civil law as we know it" than in law that was technically obsolete (*obsoletus, antiquitatus, in desuetudinem*). His studies of the Twelve Tables, various republican laws, and the jurisprudence of the Scaevola family gave him priority even over Cujas, "my successor in France," as Baudouin referred to him,[18] in the attempt to reconstruct the history of law before Justinian. It is perhaps not too surprising that in effect Baudouin abandoned the legal profession for the study of history. For whatever reason, the development of Baudouin's thought seems to recapitulate the rise of legal history as I have been describing it.

But there is another dimension to legal humanism which has never been appreciated, namely professional conservatism. Contrary to the views of many scholars, the method of the historical school of law was not simply an adaptation of classical philology, nor does it quite fit the definition of humanism offered by Paul Kristeller. The main reason for this was that the Alciatei, however heatedly they might talk of "reforming" jurisprudence, were intensely loyal to their profession, and they had no intention of allowing the science of law to be governed by the liberal arts. In the law schools "grammaticus" was a derogatory term that still implied an inferior rank in the hierarchy of learning, and if Cujas accepted the epithet, as one of his students reported, it was purely in a spirit of defiance.[19] Alciato himself gloried in his academic status and could not refrain from contrasting it to that of Budé, a mere "master of arts" who never finished his doctor's degree. Such conservativism is evident in the systematizing treatises of Le Douaren, Connan, and others, and especially in the pedagogical works ("De ratione docendi juris") which almost all of Alciato's followers wrote.[20] They agreed in favoring the use of a dialectical method, and Cujas went so far as to recommend, at least for beginning stu-

17. *Justinianus, sive de jure novo* (Halle, 1728), 273 and 379. The subject is discussed in another context, though without sufficient attention to legal scholarship, in my "Francois Baudouin's Conception of History," *Journal of the History of Ideas* 25 (1964), 35-57.

18. *Commentarius de legibus XII tabularum*, fol. 228^r.

19. François Pithou, in *Scaligerana . . .* (Amsterdam, 1740), II, 285, remarked, "When people wanted to offend M. Cujas, they called him 'grammarian,' but he did not mind and said they were irritated because they were not."

20. The "methods" of Le Douaren, Baron, Baudouin, Hotman, and others are in Nicolas Reusner, *Cynosura juris* (Spires, 1588), Cujas', published by J. Flach in *Nouvelle revue historique de droit français et étranger*, sér. 3, 7 (1883), 205 ff.

dents, the much maligned *Gloss* of Accursius. Here is the basis for what some modern scholars have termed "neo-Bartolism."

For legal historians there was one important lesson to be learned: a truly historical view of law required not only a knowledge of the sources and a philological method but a systematic understanding of jurisprudence. Ignorance of this is precisely what made Valla's method — "juristic classicism" one modern critic has scornfully called it[21] — intolerably rigid and anachronistic, and what prompted Alciato's critique. Like his friend Erasmus, Alciato believed that a scholar had to reveal the spirit as well as the letter of a text, the *voluntas* as well as the *verba* of a law.[22] Likewise, a scholar had to consider not only the historicity of an act — say, the donation of Constantine — but its legality, that is, the later tradition accepted by custom or prescription. In a more general fashion, Baudouin came to believe that the purpose of the historian was not simply the restoration of an ideal antiquity but the reconstruction of a long tradition; and as some jurists were coming around to acknowledge, this might mean reading the commentators as well as the sources of law.[23] In short, I would submit, the method of the historical school of law was a hybrid: a compromise between the legalistic approach of Bartolism, without his pragmatism and present-mindedness, and the grammatical approach of Valla, without his rabid classicism. It was, in Baudouin's phrase, a "conjunction of grammar and jurisprudence."

II. CANON LAW

This conservative attitude served not only to restrain the excesses of philology; it helped to broaden the horizons of legal history. In order to set Roman law in its proper perspective it was necessary to examine post- as well as pre-Justinianian traditions, and this meant looking into canon and feudal law. Despite a lingering prejudice against these "barbaric" subjects, which critics attacked in even more scatological terms than they did civil law, every one of Alciato's disciples was enticed into these fields in one way or another. As with civil law, they applied the techniques of philology, tried to extricate old from new law, labored to produce critical editions, and began to reconstruct

21. Fritz Schulz, *History of Roman Legal Science* (Oxford, 1953), 278 ff.

22. *De Verborum significatione* and *Dispunctiones*, in *Opera omnia*, I, 1025, and IV, 7. Alciato's attacks on Valla's criticism of the donation of Constantine appears in his *Praetermissa*, VII, 19, in I, 403.

23. According to Jacques Brejon, *André Tiraqueau (1488-1558)* (Paris, 1937), iii: "Tiraqueau teaches us that the historical school has been largely prefaced by Bartolus and his disciples" and that "it is necessary to investigate law in its monuments but also in its interpreters." See also the works of Guido Kisch, particularly *Humanismus und Jurisprudenz* (Basel, 1955), and the enlightening remarks of Myron Gilmore, *Humanists and Jurists* (Cambridge, 1963), 168, concerning Bonifacius Amerbach.

historical development. In the study of ecclesiastical and feudal law, however, they encountered new obstacles, namely, the modern descendants of these traditions. Civil law, since it was the "emperor's law," still constituted a political threat in France, but legal humanists could for the most part ignore the conventional issues of the imperialists. With canon and feudal law, on the other hand, they could not avoid calling living traditions and vested interests to account. In the attempt to throw light upon the organization of the early church or the ancient constitution of France, scholars ran a serious risk of igniting explosive religious or political controversies. Inevitably, these branches of legal history were shaped by such controversies and by the commitments of professional canonists and feudists.

The roots of the history of canon law are not quite so easily traced as those of civil law. Nominally, the first book was Aymar du Rivail's *Historia juris pontificalis,* appended to his *History of Civil Law* of 1515, but it was a brief and insignificant sketch. Once again, it seems most proper to begin with the work of the philologists, who transformed, if they did not originate, the study of the sources. And once again the man who blazed the first trail was Lorenzo Valla, whose notorious declamation on the donation of Constantine was among other things a grammatical assault on the *Decretum* of Gratian. From other of Valla's works, too, it is evident that he had looked over the "scriptura corrupta" and the misattributions of Gratian with a critical eye; but since it was "for the most part Gothic" in character, as he put it, he did not pursue this line of research very far.[24] Neither did Erasmus, but his awareness of the deficiencies of the *Decretum,* referring in particular to the spurious decretals of Isidore, did move him to call for a critical edition of Gratian. This was the task of the next two generations, and the stages included the pioneering editions of Antoine de Mouchy in 1547, of Baudouin's old friend Charles Dumoulin in 1554, and finally that of the official Roman "Correctores" in 1582. But again some of the most important contributions were made by legal humanists. By the time Agustín's emendations of civil law appeared in 1543, he was already immersed in the sources of canon law, and he published his results in 1587. Editions were prepared also by Cujas' colleague at Bourges, Antoine le Conte, and by his two favorite pupils, François and Pierre Pithou, who provided a critical history of the sources of canon law as well.[25] As in so many other branches of scholarship, the foundations of

24. "Pro se et contra calumniators ad Eugenium IIII. Pont. Max. apologia," and *Elegantiae,* III, "praefatio," *Opera omnia,* I, 800 and 80.

25. *Corpus juris canonici,* ed. Pierre and François Pithou (Paris, 1687), "Synopsis historica . . . Petri Pithoei." There are no studies of canonist scholarship comparable to those of Maffei, Dante dal Re, P. F. Girard, and others on legal humanism, but one may find some leads in the histories of the sources of canon law by Schultz and Maassen. For French scholars, see also Michel Reulos, "Le Décret de Gratien chez les humanistes, les Gallicans et les réformés français du XVIe siècle," and René Metz, "La

canonist studies had been laid before the seventeenth century, although they are not easy to perceive beneath the more imposing constructions of that learned age.

There is another reason why the work of these pioneering critics and collators has been obscured, and this is because, as I have suggested, the controversial nature of the material attracted bolder men with deeper commitments — and louder voices. In the sixteenth century it was impossible to separate the investigation of canon law from the general reevaluation — or perhaps we should say transvaluation — of ecclesiastical history inspired by the Reformation. It is not surprising, then, that Valla's most direct descendants were men like Luther, Melanchthon, and Calvin, men who, despite their sympathy for certain humanist ideals, placed what might be called ideological goals above scholarly standards. Luther literally brought more heat than light to the problem of canon law. In 1520, a few months after he had discovered Valla's treatise, he wrote a pamphlet explaining "Why the books of the popes and their disciples must be burned."[26] His reason was simply that it was from the canonist tradition that "all misfortune had come into the world." Calvin's position was substantially the same, but he was more specific about the falsities and forgeries of canon law which had caused the break with true ecclesiastical tradition and the emergence of Antichrist. "In today's bright light," he wrote of the canonists, "they still wish to peddle the same smoke with which in an age of darkness they formerly deluded the simple-minded."[27] Calvin himself had to return once more to an attack on the donation of Constantine, which as late as 1548 had been defended in a treatise by Agostino Steuco.

Protestant historical writing in general, and the history of canon law in particular, revolved about two conceptual, or rather mythical, poles. One was the *ecclesia primitiva,* a notion which referred to an almost prehistorical age of pure religion and uncorrupted and essentially unwritten custom. The other was *traditio humana,* which included practically the whole legal and institutional history of the church. These ideas were obviously analogous to the humanist idealization of antiquity and lamentation about later "degeneration." Again, however, there was a shift of interest toward that very process of degeneration; indeed, the rise of legal history was itself the product of a kind of

---

Contribution de la France à l'étude du décret de Gratien depuis le XVIe siècle jusqu'à nos jours" in *Studia Gratiana,* II (Bologna, 1954), 679-696 and 495-518.

26. Translated by Lewis Spitz in Luther's *Works,* ed. H. J. Grimm (Philadelphia, 1957), XXXI, 383-395. Ernst Schäfer, *Luther als Kirchenhistoriker* (Gütersloh, 1897), 203, has pointed to "canon law as one of the most important sources for Luther's historical knowledge."

27. *Institution de la religion chrétienne,* IV, 7, 1. Steuco's book is *De Falso donatione Constantini libri duo* (Lyon, 1547). In general, see the informative work of Maffei, *La Donazione di Costantino nei giuristi medievali* (Milan, 1964), 297 ff.

secularization of ecclesiastical history. And again, it should be noted that the legal profession left its mark upon this subject. Not only did many authors, including Luther and Calvin, derive much of their knowledge of church history from the study of canon law, but there were in the canonist tradition certain conventions of importance for legal history.[28] These include the fundamental distinction, like that made by civilians, between old and new law, that is, between the *Decretum* and the later additions; the recognition of the profound mutability of human law in terms of time, place, and circumstance; and several canonist procedures, such as the insistence on firsthand evidence, argument from history, judging the relative weight of authorities, and determining the authenticity of documents. This is another subject that has not been fully investigated, but it seems to me that these features of medieval scholarship helped to reinforce and in some ways supplemented the historical methods created by Renaissance philology.

The medieval roots of canonist scholarship are especially obvious in France. There the Gallican doctrine had developed a perspective from which the Romanist interpretation of ecclesiastical history could be reassessed more critically. Even before the emergence of Luther, Frenchmen had begun to look at their church with new eyes, to see it not simply as a legal structure but as the product of a long historical development. This was implicit in the ideological wars of the conciliar period and of the time of Philip IV, when the "ancient liberties of the Gallican church" were being assembled and given, with more ingenuity than respect for history, an honorable ancestry. In the sixteenth century this historical attitude became distinctly more conscious, although again it was the product of political conflict rather than humanism. Such was the case with Jean Lemaire de Belges' *Treatise on Schisms and Councils,* which was a byproduct of the Gallican crisis of 1511;[29] and such, more spectacularly, was the case with the literature produced by the Gallican crisis of 1551, which was of crucial importance for the historical study of canon law.

The remarkable thing about this polemical outburst was that, while it was clearly inspired by problems of religious reform and a national church, it was written entirely by members of the historical school of law who in every case were professed or fellow-travelling Calvinists. The discussion was opened in

28. Especially, *Corpus juris canonici*, Extravagantes Joann. XXII, T. 14, "De verborum significatione." See also the interesting discussion of J. M. Salgado, "La Méthode d'interprétation du droit en usage chez les canonistes," *Revue de l'Université d'Ottawa* 21 (1951), 201-213, and in general S. Mochi Onory, *Fonti canonistiche dell'idea moderno dello stato* (Milan, 1951).

29. *Le Traicté de la difference des schismes et des conciles de l'église*, in *Oeuvres*, ed. J. Stecher (Louvain, 1885), III, 232 ff. The best study of the Gallican tradition for my purpose is still Joseph Lecler, "Qu'est-ce les libertés de l'église gallicane," *Recherches de science religieuse* 23 (1933), 385-410.

1551 by Le Douaren, who was then, since Alciato and Baron had died the year before, the acknowledged dean of legal humanists. In his book, entitled *The Ministers and Benefices of the Holy Church*, Le Douaren addressed himself from a more specifically legal point of view to the questions posed by Calvin eight years before: "What was the world like in the time of Christ and the apostles?" and how was this innocence lost? He began with a sketch of the history of canon law and its "degeneration" after Gratian, who played much the same role as Tribonian had for civil law, and then went on to explain the philological basis for his critique of ecclesiastical tradition.[30] Briefly, his assumption was that changes in law were accompanied by changes in vocabulary, and so in effect he rejected the conventional view that canon law was the elaboration of divine principles transcending time and the human condition. Just as certain Latin terms were evidence of the vital links between canon and civil law, he argued, so the appearance of modern or "barbaric" terms signalized a departure from the ways of the primitive church, which is to say scripture. He applied this test not only to specific institutions, such as the benefice, to which he attributed a lay character as well as a late origin, but to the whole hierarchy of the church, which was a creation of "human tradition." In short, he rejected Romanist claims to universality in both a temporal and a geographic sense. As a Gallican he looked upon papal government as an Italian establishment of recent centuries, and as a humanist he construed the history of canon law as a secular process varying according to times and circumstances.

Le Douaren's book not only stoked the fires of religious controversy in France (and incidentally forced him to make a public apology to the *parlement* of Paris), but it also set off a whole train of canonist studies. The best known of these were Charles Dumoulin's commentary on Henry II's edict against the "little dates," of 1552; Hotman's *State of the Primitive Church,* written the following year in Dumoulin's defense; and Baudouin's *Response of Christian Jurists* of 1556, which summed up the course of the debate.[31] Baudouin himself was more radical than Le Douaren and took him to task for relying too much on Gratian's authority, but in later years Baudouin came to hold a more moderate view of ecclesiastical tradition. Interest in canon law became still more intense in the next few years with the appearance of various explosive issues, including the establishment of the Jesuits in France, the reception of the Tridentine decrees, and finally the division between

30. *De Sacris ecclesiae ministeriis ac beneficiis libri octo* in *Opera omnia* (Lucca, 1768), IV, 191 ff. This whole subject is treated more fully in my "Fides Historiae: Charles Dumoulin and the Gallican View of History," *Traditio* 22 (1966), 347-402.

31. *Responsio Christianorum jurisconsultorum ad Fr. Duareni commentarios . . .* (Strasbourg, 1556), anticipated by his *Juris civilis Argentinensis* (Strasbourg, 1555). Hotman's *De Statu primitivae ecclesiae ejusque sacerdotiis* and Dumoulin's commentary are published in the latter's *Opera omnia* (Paris, 1681), IV.

Catholics and Huguenots that led to civil war. At the same time these issues were spilling over into the more general study of church history, which was in the process of becoming a major scholarly industry. These tendencies were noticed by Baudouin, and indeed they provided part of the foundation for his ideal of historical scholarship. Just as a jurist should be learned in both laws and take his degree *utriusque juris,* he argued, so an historian should study both sacred and profane traditions and view the past *utriusque historiae*.[32] And just as the student of civil history should depend upon legal records, so the student of ecclesiastical history should make full use of the sources of canon law. Here was another lesson for Pasquier and the historians of his generation, and they did not fail to profit from it.

III. FEUDAL LAW

In Baudouin's imposing *universitas* of history there is one more ingredient that must be analyzed briefly. In his pioneering sketch of legal history published in 1545, Baudouin had remarked that, after the fall of the empire, "there arose in the place of Roman law those customs which today we call *feuda*"; and in 1561 he declared that the coherence (*individuitas*) of history required the consideration of these national traditions.[33] In civil law *consuetudo* referred to unwritten and particularized usages, but by the fourteenth century jurists did not hesitate to apply the term to the written and fairly general custumals of Europe. The assumption was that these customs developed in much the same way as Roman law had done, that is, emerging gradually from *boni mores* and taking at once a written, more generalized, and more litigious form. Not everyone liked this process of "civilization," but for legal historians the main problem was how it came about. Was it the product of outside influence, or was it indigenous and self-generating? To put it in sixteenth-century terms, was it the result of "imitation" of one nation by another, as the Romans had, according to the account in Pomponius, imitated the Greeks? Or did it simply accompany the growing complexity of a society and its need for written rules and records, as the usual understanding of *consuetudo* seemed to suggest? Or was it perhaps a combination of the two? For European customs, of course, this boiled down to one fundamental question: precisely what role, if any, did civil law play in the emergence of feudalism?

Once again it was the lawyers who began serious investigation of this

32. *De Institutione historiae universae et ejus cum jurisprudentia conjunctione* (Strasbourg, 1608), 45.

33. *Commentarii in libros quatuor Institutionum juris civilis* (Paris, 1554), "prolegomena," and *De Institutione historiae,* 55-56.

problem. Naturally, they started with the most authoritative collection, the so-called *Libri feudorum,* a twelfth-century mélange of imperial legislation and northern Italian jurisprudence that was normally taken as an integral part of civil law. From the fourteenth to sixteenth century this book was the subject of scores of commentaries, and it became the core of the feudist tradition. It was one of the conventional rubrics of these commentaries, I believe, that provided the true point of departure for the historical study of feudalism. This was the much-debated *quaestio* on the origin of fiefs, "De origine feudorum" or "De origine juris feudorum," established on the analogy of the *Digest* title discussed earlier.

On this question there was — as indeed there still is — a division of opinion. A few medieval jurists, including Jacopo di Ardizone and Andrea de Isernia, admitted that the terminology of feudal law was modern (*recentissimum*) and unrelated to that of ancient Rome, and others argued that even in Justinian's time the empire never included all parts of feudal Europe.[34] But this was the view of an anti-imperialist minority. The accepted interpretation, the *communis opinio,* insisted that the *Libri feudorum* was an "authentic" part of imperial tradition, that the word *feudum* was derived from *fides* or *fidelitas,* and that the institution itself was *antiquissimum.*[35] The curious thing was that the humanist reaction, although it was determined by aesthetic rather than political considerations, tended to reinforce the Romanist thesis. It is true that Petrarch himself was horrified at the idea of connecting classical jurisprudence with that barbarous deformity (*labes germanica*), the *Libri feudorum*; but the first generation of legal humanists tried to establish just such a connection. In order to adorn feudal law with an elegant pedigree, or so later critics charge, Budé and Alciato traced the feudal contract to the ancient clientele, while Zasius opted for the military land grants of the later empire.[36]

By the latter half of the sixteenth century, however, scholars were beginning to react both against the naive classicism of humanists as well as against the rigid legalism of imperialists. Alciato had already warned against the fallacy of ascribing Latin roots to foreign terms. Since then the work of Beatus Rhenanus and others had revealed clearly the Germanic etymology of the *feudum,* and

34. Isernia, *In Usu feudorum commentaria* (Naples, 1571), fol. 6r, and Ardizone, *Summa feudorum* in *Tractatus universi juris,* X (I), fol. 225v. The field of feudist scholarship was opened up by Savigny's student Ernst Adolph Laspeyres, *Ueber die Entstehung und älteste Bearbeitung der Libri Feudorum* (Berlin, 1830), but little more has been done since then, except for the few soundings I have taken in "De Origine Feudorum: the Beginnings of an Historical Problem," *Speculum* 39 (1964), 207-228.

35. Pierre Rebuffi, *Feudorum declaratio* in *Tractatus universi juris,* X (I), fol. 300v, citing *Consuetudines feudorum,* II, 3.

36. Budé, *Annotationes in quattuor et viginti Pandectarum libros* (Paris, 1535), fol. 146r, and Zasius, *Commentaria de origine juris civilis* in *Opera omnia,* I, 273.

such philological arguments made their way into the first critical edition of the *Libri feudorum,* published in 1566 by none other than Jacques Cujas.[37] Even before this Le Douaren had rejected the view of his old patron Budé. On principle he assumed that "public law arises from custom and private law from prescription," and it was only natural that he should come to accept feudal law as Lombard in origin.[38] But once again the crucial impulse came from within the legal profession. In 1539 Charles Dumoulin published what in fact was the first comprehensive history of feudalism. In form it was a commentary on the Parisian *coutume*, and it was the product of many years' experience practicing in the *châtelet,* the municipal government of Paris, as well as in the *parlement.* On the basis of this experience Dumoulin was able to add a much greater range of sources and a wider perspective to the conventional legal and linguistic treatment by the feudists.[39] Not only did he revive the old positions that feudal vocabulary was modern and that much of Europe, especially the French monarchy, was historically independent of the Roman empire; he argued that for the history of European feudalism the *Libri feudorum* was much less relevant and representative than the customs of France and Germany, that is, the Carolingian Franks. It was on the basis of this hypothesis that the major accomplishments in the history of feudal society would be made in the following generations.

It should be admitted that this aspect of legal history was swayed as much as the study of canon law by the winds of doctrine. In the sixteenth century every national group was eager to show the indigenous, independent, and if possible superior character of its traditions. In France, for example, there was a kind of "Celtic renaissance" in the 1550's, promoted largely by literary men, including Pasquier; and one legal humanist, François Connan, suggested, on the grounds of the Celtic etymology of the term "vassal" and the testimony of Caesar, that feudal law should be seen as a legacy of the ancient Gauls.[40] Although it survived until the nineteenth century, this *gaulois* theory was never a serious competitor of the Germanist thesis, which came into its own because

37. *In Libros quinque feudorum* in *Opera omnia* (Prato, 1840), X, 829 ff. The best "historiographical" survey of the problem is Marino Freccia, *De Subfeudis baronum et investituris feudorum* (Venice, 1579), 3-8, mentioning the *opiniones* of Isernia, Lucas de Penna, and such contemporaries (*moderniores*) as Budé, Alciato, Zasius, Baudouin, Oldendorp, Torelli, Connan, Jean Pyrrhus d'Angleberme, and above all Dumoulin. Cf. Beatus Rhenanus, *Rerum Germanicarum libri tres* (Basel, 1551), 95.

38. *Commentarius in consuetudines feudorum* and *In Primam partem Pandectarum sive Digestorum, methodica enarratio* in *Opera omnia,* I, 310 ff and 14.

39. *Commentarii in parisiensis . . . parlamenti consuetudines,* in *Opera omnia,* I, 1 ff. A recent book of interest is Vincenzo Piano Mortari, *Diritto romano e diritto nazionale in Francia nel secolo XVI* (Milan, 1962).

40. *Commentariorum juris civilis libri X* (Naples, 1724), II, 9. See now C. Bergfeld, *Franciscus Connanus (1508-1551)* (Cologne, 1968), and the interesting remarks in what is still the best book on Bodin, Jean Moreau-Reibel, *Jean Bodin et le droit public comparé dans ses rapports avec la philosophie de l'histoire* (Paris, 1933).

of the explosive anti-Romanist pressures of the wars of religion. The most conspicuous illustration of this tendency is the work of Hotman. Between 1558, when he edited the commentaries of Connan, and 1560, when he published the first book of his own *Observations and Emendations,* Hotman had rejected the *gaulois* thesis and had come around to the views of his old friend Dumoulin. At least he was defying legal convention by urging the Germanic etymology of the term *feudum.* But it was not until after a decade of bitter fighting that Hotman set down, in his *De Feudis* of 1573, the Germanist thesis in its classic form.[41] Not only did he present the arguments for the Carolingian origin of the fief; he also suggested that vassalage itself should be traced back to the *comitatus* described by Tacitus. Such was one of the ingredients of Hotman's "Franco-Gallic" view of history.

Undeniably, this Germanist thesis was distorted by ideological bias. Hotman in particular showed an almost racialist desire to exalt the liberties and virtues of the Germans (by inference the Protestants) above the perfidious Romanists, or "Italo-Gauls" as he called them. But the idea did offer a timely corrective to the excess of Romanism, which had intimidated professional jurists for so many generations; and, more important, it provoked further investigations into the sensitive problems of this area of legal history. By the last quarter of the century scholars could take a more balanced — or a more eclectic — view. Why, for example, could one not accept the fact that "fief" was a modern term and the product of native custom and still dig a bit deeper to see if it might not owe something to the "benefices" of the empire? Such was the attitude of Pasquier's friend Jean de Basmaison, who published his *Origins of Fiefs* in 1579.[42] Yet in the final analysis what counted about these researches was not the particular theses defended but rather the growth of knowledge about the variety and complexity of feudal traditions. In fact, the debates about the pedigree of the fief led many historians to the suspicion that questions of ultimate origins, since they were prehistoric and without documentary foundations, were not really the historian's business anyway.

IV. FROM THE PROFESSION OF LAW TO THE ART OF HISTORY

This is by no means the end of the story, but it is a convenient place to conclude. By the second half of the sixteenth century a group of jurists, mainly

41. *Observationum liber secundus* (Basel, 1561), 12-19, and *Ad Disputationum de feudis* in *Opera* (Geneva, 1599), I, col. 801 ff. The importance of this, as well as of the *Anti-Tribonian,* for Hotman's notorious *Franco-Gallia* has been well described by Ralph Giesey, "When and Why Hotman Wrote the *Francogallia,*" *Bibliothèque d'humanisme et renaissance* 29 (1967), 581-611.

42. *De l'Origine des fiefs et rierefiefs* (Paris, 1611), originally entitled *Sommaire discours des fiefs et rierefiefs* (Paris, 1579).

French jurists, had laid the foundations for a new branch of scholarship, the history of laws and institutions, and had made some forays into the more obscure field of social history. This they had done not only through the critical reading or original sources following humanist methods but also by the discriminating use of certain medieval, scholarly traditions. Within the legal profession this tendency was noticed and deplored by such old fashioned jurists as Gentili, who charged that the "Cujacians" were not lawyers but philologists and historians. This was unjust, but in one sense he was right. The truth is that the best of Cujas' disciples, men like Pasquier, Loisel, and the brothers Pithou, did not follow their master into university chairs; instead, they became antiquaries, editors, and historians. Their purpose was not to further the reform of the legal profession; it was to import the values and methods of legal humanism into the study of the European past. In short, the accomplishment of these alumni of the historical school of law was to professionalize the study of legal history and so to reshape historical scholarship in general.

In this circuitous fashion I come back at last to my point of departure. Etienne Pasquier's *Recherches de la France* is, among other things, one of the best illustrations of that "conjunction of history and jurisprudence" proclaimed by Baudouin in 1561. It was not the work of an amateur. Fifteen years before Pasquier had heard both Baudouin and Hotman lecture on civil law in Paris, and later he also attended classes of Cujas and Alciato.[43] He was not only a practicing lawyer but also an able enough civilian to compose a commentary on the *Institutes* of Justinian. This background, coupled with the interest stimulated by the controversies over France's political and cultural heritage, led Pasquier into many expeditions into the fields of civil, ecclesiastical, and feudal law. Indeed, his book represents the convergence of all of the themes I have discussed in this paper.

Like Baudouin and Hotman, but much more comprehensively, Pasquier tried to see the development of modern jurisprudence in a broad perspective. And like contemporary scholars, he recognized in general three stages.[44] First came "les glossateurs," including Irnerius, reputedly the founding father, and Placentinus, who introduced the study of civil law into France. Then there appeared "les docteurs en droit," or "scribentes" (so called because of their great productivity), including Placentinus' disciple Accursius, Guillaume Durandus, Bartolus, and a whole school of "Italian doctors," whose output staggered Pasquier. He marvelled, for example, at the famous collection published in Venice in 1584, containing twenty-five volumes, each larger than the *Code* with its accompanying *Gloss*. The methods of these "Bartholistes"

43. *Lettres*, XIX, 13; cf. IX, 6, for Pasquier's exalted view of the legal profession.
44. *Recherches*, IX, 34-41, referring to *Tractatus universi juris*.

were adopted by all the law faculties of France, which Pasquier surveyed one by one. Pasquier repeated the old legend, not discredited until the seventeenth century, about the miraculous recovery of the unique manuscript of the *Digest* in the capture of Malfi by the Pisans, who themselves surrendered it to the Florentines in 1406. It was the study of this monument that brought about the "third age of jurisprudence," dominated by "les docteurs humanistes." Of the scholars who "followed with great honor the trail of our Budé," Pasquier added, the most distinguished was Cujas. In the course of his work Pasquier also reviewed many of the themes of legal humanism, including the importance of stylistics and ability to detect anachronisms and the old anti-Tribonianist complaint that "the Digest is a pesle-mesle of jurists . . . , the Code a pesle-mesle of unrelated ordinances."[45]

What interested Pasquier most about Roman law, however, was not its value as a source for ancient history but its afterlife, especially its posthumous impact upon French society. Like Hotman, he believed that the influence of written law, by which he meant canon as well as civil law, was as pernicious as it was profound. Romanist tyranny was reflected not only in public law, where it was advertised by such popular formulas as the "princeps legibus solutus" and the "plenitudo potestatis," but in private law, as shown by the "patria potestas" and the preference for testamentary succession, which always operated to the detriment of the *grandes familles*. The worst effects of Romanism appeared in the form of judicial corruption and "chicanery," which he condemned in the same moral tones as Dumoulin, Hotman, and for that matter Rabelais, contrasting it with the fond memory of St. Louis, dispensing justice personally under the oaks in Vincennes. The universities bore some of the responsibility for this, but the real culprit, "la source première de tous maux," was the Avignonese papacy. Still worse was its ultramontane descendant of the sixteenth century, especially as represented by the Jesuits; and Pasquier, though he remained a Catholic, did not hesitate to place more blame for the wars of religion upon this "sect" of Loyola than he did upon the sect of Luther.[46] In this spirit Pasquier traced in detail the Gallican liberties from Merovingian times, "the middle age of our church" as he put it, through the seminal conciliar period down to his own day. It was largely in response to canonist usurpation, he concluded, that "the Gallican church was built up during a long succession of time."[47]

In his discussions of feudalism, too, Pasquier's purpose was, to paraphrase the title of a still more famous book by his friend and fellow propagandist Joachim du Bellay, "the defense and illustration" of the French monarchy.

45. *Lettres*, XIX, 14, and cf. *Interprétation des institutes de Justinian*, ed. M. le duc Pasquier (Paris, 1847), I, 26 ff.

46. *Recherches*, III, 44.

47. *Recherches*, III. 26.

The feudal customs of France may have been chaotic and contradictory but not more so than civil law, and in any case they had the merit of being "formed gradually in each province according to the diversity of our characters."[48] He assumed, in other words, that laws were expressions of a particular social context and historical experience, and the same went for the other institutions he analyzed, including the *parlement* of Paris and the sovereign courts and the principal offices of the crown. But in a more ultimate sense, Pasquier admitted that "we in France fashion [our laws] in a generally Roman spirit." Once again he rehearsed the question of feudal origins and listed the three main theories. "Some have attributed the first source of fiefs . . . to the peoples of Germany"; he wrote, "others, to banish barbarism from their discourse [he meant Budé], to the ancient Romans . . . ; still others [referring to Connan], to gratify our nation, to the Gauls."[49] As for himself, Pasquier agreed with Cujas in preferring a moderate Romanist thesis, linking fiefs with the frontier lands given to Roman mercenaries. Pasquier had himself gone through a "gaulois" phase, and he never overcame his anti-Romanist prejudice. But on the whole, in this lifelong pilgrimage in search of France's cultural identity, Pasquier took a balanced and broad-minded view of the various traditions — Roman, Greek, German, and Gallic — that went into the making of French society; and for legal and institutional history, at least, his book represents the best that Renaissance scholarship has to offer.

This is far from all there is to say about Pasquier's work — or about the convergence of law and history in the sixteenth century. But it does throw some light, I hope, upon one of the more obscure corners of modern historical thought. The legal scholarship of the later Middle Ages and Renaissance, lying as it does at the roots of modern social science as well as of historical studies, is still a largely unexplored area of intellectual history; and many more such expeditions must be made into this wilderness before it can be charted and its riches made known. In my view this territory promises to be as fruitful as the history of medieval science — and the history of Renaissance philosophy — have been in the past two generations. One lesson in particular has been impressed upon me: that however difficult interdisciplinary investigation may be, it is essential for a more refined understanding of the development of modern thought, which may be distributed into professional pigeon holes and dispensed from them, but which certainly did not appear that way in the first place. "All decisive advances in the history of scientific thought,"[50] Arthur Koestler has declared, "can be described in terms of mental cross-fertilization between different disciplines." It seems to me that a similar suggestion might be made about historical thought. Pasquier's work

48. *Lettres*, IX, 1.
49. *Recherches*, II, 15.
50. *The Act of Creation* (New York, 1964), 230.

bears this out, and so does that of Cujas and the legal humanists considered here. There is no reason to suppose that contemporary scholars are exempt from the rule. Without such interdisciplinary experience, we may well have — in the words Pasquier himself used to justify his break with conventional historiography — "rather the darkness of the schools than the light of history."[51]

State University of New York
Binghamton

51. *Recherches,* introduction.

VI

CIVIL SCIENCE IN THE RENAISSANCE: JURISPRUDENCE ITALIAN STYLE

In the history of Renaissance thought and learning jurisprudence seems to be a missing term. Not that the scholarship of civil, canon and customary law is itself lacking, or lagging, but it has not been sufficiently integrated with that of other fields, and even in the modern history of the Renaissance 'encyclopedia' it does not hold high priority. In some modern views of the *studium*, in fact, law seems to stand not only below the *trivium* and *quadrivium* but even, since it lacks utility as well as liberality, below the mechanical arts. Petrarch and other humanists would no doubt be pleased at this turnabout; and others may find justice (in a historian's if not a lawyer's sense) at the fall of the profession of law from academic grace. For present purposes, however, we must try to lay aside the prejudice which many of us may feel toward lawyers, modern counterparts of the pedants derided by Petrarch and the 'mean and mercenary' pettifoggers denounced by Cicero. It is not the purpose here to plead the cause of Renaissance jurists; but it may be possible, by attending to some of their less celebrated (or lamented) achievements, to do some justice to their place in the history of learning.

I

Much, perhaps too much, has been made of the sixteenth-century battle between the Italian and the French methods of law (*mores italicus* and *gallicus*), that is, between the scholastic jurisprudence associated with Bartolus and his professional colleagues and the new wave of humanist studies of the law.[1] The popular view of this controversy is illustrated by a little-known treatise *On the corrupted words of civil law* published by Claudio Tolomei in 1517. In this dialogue Giason del Maino appears as spokesman for the professional lawyers and Angelo Poliziano for the usurping 'grammarians'. Invoking the names of Pico, Ermolao Barbaro

[1] From different point of view there are discussions of 'legal humanism' (an unfortunate coinage since it suggests a counterpart 'illegal humanism') in D. Maffei, *Gli inizi dell'umanesimo giuridico* (Milan, 1956); D. R. Kelley, *Foundations of modern historical scholarship* (New York, 1970); and H. Troje, *Graeca leguntur* (Cologne, 1971).

and other men of eloquence, Poliziano ridicules Giason for his ties with Bartolus, Baldus and such barbarians, whom he taxes with ignorance of history and bad taste in language (practically equivalent faults).[2] Giason's endorsement of such neologisms as *bastardum* and *guerra* (for *bellum*) could only corrupt the pure sources of law, as Lorenzo Valla had pointed out, and indeed Petrarch before him. Against such charges Giason seemed defenceless, and his weak responses typify the generally bad press enjoyed by Bartolists in the Renaissance, at least in texts likely to be read by historians.

Yet the notion that the conflict between humanist and scholastic jurisprudence was a gradual victory of the children of the light against the forces of medieval darkness is in no way historically tenable. To characterize the relationship in general one can hardly do better than to quote the conclusions of P. O. Kristeller about the analogous relationship between philosophy and humanism. 'The common notion that scholasticism as an old philosophy was superseded by the new philosophy of humanism is . . . disproved by plain facts,' writes Kristeller, 'for Italian scholasticism [here read: the *mos italicus*] originated toward the end of the thirteenth century, that is, about the same time as did Italian humanism, and both traditions developed side by side throughout the period of the Renaissance and even thereafter.'[3] Contacts there surely were, but no conquest of one by the other. So it was, too, with *l'umanesimo giuridico*, a movement that belongs rather to the history of literature, scholarship and education than to the law. The iconoclasm of Valla and the 'grammatical' method of Poliziano were certainly essential for the restoration and interpretation of legal texts, but they had no closer relation to jurisprudence than the higher criticism of the Bible has to theology – which is to say, not necessarily any at all. In order to understand the significance of Renaissance jurisprudence attention must shift from this noisy but peripheral logomachy – another of the interminable and inconclusive *dispute delle arti* – to the proper intellectual concerns of the jurists. So the focus here is not on the amateurs of the *mos gallicus*, who would subordinate law to the *studia humanitatis*, but rather on the 'pros', the advocates of the *mos italicus* – that is, so to say, on 'jurisprudence Italian style'.[4]

The starting point for the modern science of law is the authoritative corpus of Romano-Byzantine law assembled by the editors of the Emperor Justinian in the sixth century. These texts, together with the sources of older Greek and especially Aristotelian science, formed the

[2] Claudii Ptolemaei Senen., *De corruptis verbis iuris civilis dialogus* (Siena, 1517?), sig. Bi ff. Cf. P. Rossi in *Studi Senesi*, XXIX (1912), 358–72.

[3] *Studies in Renaissance thought and letters* (Rome, 1956), p. 576.

[4] G. Kisch, *Humanismus und Jurisprudenz, Der Kampf zwischen mos italicus und mos gallicus an der Universität Basel* (Basel, 1955), and G. Astuti, *Mos italicus e mos gallicus nei dialoghi 'de iuris interpretibus' di Alberico Gentili* (Bologna, 1937), are fundamental studies.

basis for the first great revival of ancient learning in the twelfth century.[5] One striking but not always noticed characteristic of this antique legacy is its conceptual duality, a duality which reflected and preserved the ancient polarity between *physis* and *nomos*, between nature and convention, or law. On the one hand there was the natural, and naturalistic, science of Aristotle and attendant works; on the other hand the systematic doctrine of social rules, customs, procedures and institutions which medieval jurists came to call *legitima, legalis* or *civilis scientia*; and the two have never been entirely at ease with one another. Jurists defiantly represented their self-sufficient and self-generating 'civil science' as 'true philosophy' and, even when resorting to Aristotelian devices, set it apart as a rival and even a superior system. In a way this opposition represents the original confrontation of the 'two cultures'.

The story of this first legal renaissance is shrouded in legend; but the advancement of formal legal study from a rudimentary art (based on the literal and sometimes mistaken reading of the texts of the Digest, Institutes and Code) to a full-fledged science is well documented and well known, at least to legal historians. Ironically, this process began with a transgression of the law. Justinian, declaring that his collection would be unchanged 'for all time', officially prohibited any 'interpretation'; and it was in direct violation of this ban that civil science was established.[6] The first jurist to take this crucial step, according to Giason's colleague Andrea Alciato, was Azo; and the first stage of modern legal science, that of the 'glossators', was completed in the later thirteenth century with the assembling of the great Gloss of Accursius.

The second stage, and the one being considered here, is that of the Commentators; and it extends from that time not only through the Renaissance but well into the nineteenth century.[7] At the beginning of this tradition stand the philosophically inclined critics of the Gloss, including such French masters as Jacques de Révigny and Pierre de Belleperche, and at the other end such modern systematizers of civil law as Savigny and Rudolph von Ihering. However, the major phase, the great age of Italian legal science, extends from the time of Cino da Pistoia, contemporary and comrade of Dante, down to that of Alicato,

[5] See my 'Vera philosophia: the philosophical significance of Renaissance jurisprudence', *Journal of the History of Philosophy*, XIV (1976), 267–79; and for background E. Cortese, *La norma giuridica* (2 vols., Milan, 1962–4); F. Calasso, *Medio evo del diritto*, I (Milan, 1954); P. Koschaker, *Europa und das römische Recht* (Berlin, 1958); F. Wieacker, *Privatrechtsgeschichte der Neuzeit* (Göttingen, 1967); *La formazione storica del diritto moderno in Europa* (*Atti del terzo Congresso internaz, della società italiana di storia del diritto*) (3 vols., Florence, 1977); and for bibliography W. Ullmann, *Law and politics in the middle ages* (Ithaca, 1975).

[6] Justinian, constitution *Omnem*, and Alciato, *Parerga*, IX, 25, in *Lucubrationum in ius civile*, II (Basel, 1557), 86 ff. Cf. F. Pringelsheim, 'Justinian's prohibition of commentaries to the Digest', in his *Gesammelte Schriften*, II (Heidelberg, 1961), 438.

[7] Classic survey by W. Engelmann, *Die Wiedergeburt der Rechtskultur in Italien durch die wissenschaftliche Lehre* (Leipzig, 1938).

contemporary and comrade of Erasmus. The focus here is on this period, roughly from 1300, when Cino began to part company with his French masters, to 1550, when Alciato died and was already being superseded by his (also French) disciples. If this discussion does not always respect chronology, this is quite in keeping with the style of the jurists themselves, who collaborated and debated over many generations: indeed such transcendant 'cooperative scholarship' was essential to civil science.

Yet if lawyers continued to live in their own world, this does not mean that they did not keep up with the times. Recent attention has been given to 'the role of the lawyers in starting the Renaissance' (in the words of Roberto Weiss),[8] and much more remains to be said about their role in continuing it. Not only defectors like Petrarch and iconoclasts like Valla but also humdrum professionals like Bartolus and Giason contributed to the transmission and transformation of ancient learning. If the opposition between scholasticism and humanism has been overdrawn, so has that between the mindless 'apes of Cicero' and the barbaric worshippers of novelty, the first stage of the notorious quarrel between ancients and moderns. Cino da Pistoia, one of the founders of the *mos italicus* – *conditor iuris*, Bartolus calls him – is an excellent example of a Renaissance scholar whose method was based on a balance and synthesis of ancient and modern learning. On the one hand he was an accomplished classicist who cited in his commentaries not only jurists and orators but also poets (such as Juvenal and Ovid) and historians (such as Valerius Maximus and that *princeps historiographorum* Sallust). On the other hand he did not overlook what he called the 'novelties of modern scholars' (*novitates modernorum doctorum*), and in fact at the beginning of his famous lectures on the Code he took as his motto the principle that 'all novelty is pleasing' (*omnia nova placent*).[9] In this progressivist sense the Bartolist school belonged almost by definition to the party of the Moderns.

Cino's formula was hyperbole, of course. What he meant to express was not a celebration of all change but only the view that neither knowledge nor the process of thought was exhausted, or indeed exhaustible. Justinian's corpus was not the end of legal science, and neither was the Accursian Gloss. Some modern scholarship was nonsense, no doubt; and like his friend Dante, Cino rejected in particular the modernizing errors of the canonists (*decretistae*), whom he dismissed as politically corrupt as well as legally amateurish (*idiotae*); but ancient doctrine, he realized, could not be recovered or applied without modern analysis and adaptation. Politically, this procedure was illustrated by the

[8] *The dawn of humanism in Italy* (London, 1947), p. 5.

[9] *Lectura in Codicem, ad tit.* (Paris, 1528). In general, see G. Monti, *Cino da Pistoia giurista* (Città di Castello, 1924); G. Zaccagnini, *Cino da Pistoia* (Pistoia, 1918); and the collaborative volume, *Cino da Pistoia nei VI centenario della morte* (Pistoia, 1937).

attempt to justify the modern Ghibelline programme (which Cino shared with Dante) through the ancient imperial ideal.[10] In juridical and academic terms it meant moving from the specificity of ancient experience, that is, the letter of civil law, to a more general or equitable meaning which could serve and enhance modern society, in particular the Italian city states. Here we can see one of the perennial themes of civil science over many centuries: the pursuit of the 'reason' or 'spirit of the law' (*mens, ratio, intellectus, sententia* or *voluntas legis*).

Modernization through rationalization: this was the central aim of civil science as it was established by Cino and his successors. It is important to understand, however, that jurisprudence Italian style was by no means limited to the theory and practice of law narrowly, or pragmatically understood. Jurists had to evaluate questions both of fact and of law; they had in other words to be both experienced social critics and learned masters of a systematic science. What is more, the nature of their science and their method required them also to be in some ways historians and (in the old philosophical sense) anthropologists; and so at least inadvertently, and by the time of Alciato deliberately, they had begun to investigate aspects of the human condition that went far beyond legal pedagogy and normative practice. In at least one line of development the result was the transformation of legal science in one of its modes into what amounts to social science.

II

These goals of rationalization and anthropological enquiry unavoidably required attention to philosophy; and here, since the Glossators had scant interest in the subject, the French connexion was of prime importance. This includes not only the Aristotelianism of the university of Paris but also the methods of the jurists at the university of Orleans, most notably Jacques de Révigny, whom Cino called *magister omnium philosophorum*. Among the results of this was the introduction of the Aristotelian system of four causes and an adaptation of the scholastic method developed within the arts faculty. This is the way Cino described his method of teaching: 'First I shall make divisions, second give an account of the case, third offer comparisons, fourth objections, and fifth pose questions.'[11] In this dialectical scheme authority seems conspicuously inferior to reason; and so, for example, Cino declared on one point of law that 'no matter how many doctors agree, even if there are a thousand, they are all wrong'. The criterion was reasonableness; and the bottom line, the ultimate expression of the *ratio legis*, was (in Cino's words) 'my interpretation' (*doctrina mea*).

In the fourteenth century the philosophical interpretation of law was

[10] Zaccagnini, *Cino da Pistoia*, p. 200; cf. C. Davis, *Dante and the Empire* (Oxford, 1957), p. 141.

[11] Calasso, *Medio evo del diritto*, I, 571.

carried on and much elaborated by Cino's followers, especially his disciple Bartolo de Sassoferrato and his grand-disciple Baldo degli Ubaldi, who in later generations became the eponymous heroes of the *mos italicus* and villains of the *mos gallicus*.[12] In the sixteenth century students with humanist inclinations were still complaining about the excessive professionalism of 'Bartolo-Baldizing' professors, while conservatives like Alberico Gentili were still singing (in their prosiac way) the praises of these authors.[13] In fact the ill repute of conventional jurisprudence derived less from the founders themselves than from their deferential disciples – the proliferating academic progeny who in the intervening generations canonized Bartolus and Baldus, transforming them literally into '-isms', as philosophers had done to Thomas, Scotus and many others. In most quarters Bartolus and Baldus themselves continued to be respected; and even for Alciato, reputed founder of the *mos gallicus* (during his tenure at the university of Bourges) they remained the most authoritiative of all jurists. Bartolus was pre-eminent, the only jurist whose words had statutory weight, but Baldus was perhaps the more philosophical minded (φιλοσοφότατος was one of his titles) and the most often cited on political questions.[14] He is also one of the major Renaissance scholars still lacking a modern critical study.

Philosophy is undoubtedly one of the cornerstones of 'jurisprudence Italian style', but at this point it is essential to avoid one common misunderstanding. Methodologically civil law was in no way, according to its own lights, subordinate to formal philosophy. In a general way Baldus might acknowledge that 'moral philosophy is the mother of laws', but this was no more than to say that law was the product of justice.[15] In other words the civil science of the Renaissance was created not simply by infusion of Aristotelian categories and 'scholastic' method. More fundamentally it was the product of philosophical ideas and constructs embedded in its own tradition. Aristotelianism supplied some of the style, but the substance and structure of civil science were largely inherent – or more precisely the result of a much earlier, pre-Christian invasion of Greek ideas.[16] The notion of the 'four causes' was a feature of Cino's and especially of Baldus' thought, for example, but these categories merely imposed a general teleology on the legal process and did not even require a naturalistic interpretation.[17] The efficient cause referred to the original law-giver, the emperor or magistrate, corresponding to God or

[12] *L'Opera di Baldo, per cura dell'Università di Perugia nel V centenario dela morte del grande giureconsulto* (Perugia, 1901). There is a comparable *Bartolo da Sassoferrato: Studie e documenti per VI centenario* (2 vols., Perugia, 1962–3).

[13] Th. Beza, *Correspondance*, ed. H. Aubert et al., I (Geneva, 1960), 35.

[14] Calasso, *Medio evo del diritto*, I, 571.

[15] *Commentariorum iuris utriusque interpretis doctissimi Baldi de Ubaldis Perissimi Prima pars in Digestum vetus* (s.l., 1535), fo. 5.

[16] F. Schulz, *A history of Roman legal science* (Oxford, 1953), pp. 62 ff.

[17] *Commentarii*, fo. 3 ff; cf. C. de Seyssel, *Speculum feudorum* (Basle, 1566), p. 14.

the first mover; the material cause to the facts (to particular case or, more generally, to history as a whole), according to the old rule that law emerges from fact (*lex ex facto oritur*); the formal cause to particular laws and statutes; and the final cause to the public good of a community. A 'scholastic' form of argument was employed, but in detail it proceeded from cases and according to legal authorities and legal rules. Much the same can be said of the *quaestiones* and *divisiones juris*, which likewise depended on legal convention. In general, when Renaissance jurists called their discipline 'true philosophy' (*vera philosophia*), they meant that it was independent of other sciences, so of course of other academic faculties, and had its own traditions, methods and purposes. This was one of the first lessons taught by Bartolus and Baldus – and also, of course, one of the first targets of alien critics, whether philosophers, theologians, doctors of medicine or the lowly humanists.

The most philosophical of jurists, Baldus was also the most ingenious in developing the conceptual resources of civil law. One perennial problem was the contradictions or 'antinomies' which Justinian's editors were unable to purge from the millennium of accumulated legal experience and legislation on which the Digest was based. Like the Byzantine compilers, the Glossators had tended to deny the existence of such *antinomiae*, while most commentators tried to argue them away; but Baldus' reaction was quite different. He went so far as to welcome *contraria* on the grounds that they opened up new possibilities of interpretation and of resolving difficult cases.[18] Like Cino, whose 'golden work' he much admired, Baldus was attracted and influenced by 'novelty'. His views constitute a reminder that it was not only the humanists who looked forward to a new age, to new cultural achievements and so, in a sense, to the advancement of learning. This dimension of the legal tradition has been recognized by Ernst Kantorowicz and others, but the difficulty of accommodating it to the stereotype of the Renaissance has restricted its appreciation too narrowly to medievalists.

Fundamental to Baldus' conception of civil science was the attempt to bridge the gap between nature and will. The connecting link between these opposed forces was human – or what from the twelfth century has been called 'positive' – law. 'Nature is ruled by the heavens...,' wrote Baldus of the *jus naturale*; 'the will, however, is free, and the law renders the latter so that it is not reduced to the former, and so free will is limited for the sake of justice' (*ad bonum et aequum*).[19] Though excluded by natural philosophy, the factor of free will was central to jurisprudence. 'The science of law cannot exist without the acts of men,' said Baldus, and elsewhere, 'jurisprudence is the science of accidents'. Human will not only created the need for legal science but also established its tie with

[18] *Commentarii*, fo. 4.

[19] Ibid. fo. 6; see also Tarducci in *L'opera di Baldo*, pp. 415 ff., and E. Kantorowicz, *The king's two bodies* (Princeton, 1957), pp. 298 ff.

the *vita activa* and the demands of communal life. 'New cases require new remedies,' declared Baldus; 'so new material arises, and so it is necessary to have recourse to the legislator.' It is the jurist, we may infer, who first encounters, judges and reacts to social novelty, one of the most concrete and immediate forms of historical change. Such attitudes constituted not only a challenge but also a duty to contribute to a growing body of theoretical and practical judgments to be fitted into a consistent philosophic framework. Indeed it was this combination of *theoria* and *praxis* that established the claim of jurisprudence to be 'true philosophy'.

III

If civil science did not take humanism very seriously in a conceptual way, this is by no means to imply that it did not in its own way depend upon classical models and precedents. The difference is that the *mos italicus* was concerned to preserve the spirit of classical forms rather than the letter of classical texts. This is a vast but, surprisingly enough, largely neglected question, even among legal historians. The formal connexions between the legal science of antiquity and that of the Renaissance are a function of that scholarly syndrome which I have called 'Gaianism', after the second century (A.D.) jurist commonly referred to (by medieval and modern civilians as well as by Justinian) as *Gaius noster*, 'our Gaius'.[20] The argument addresses itself to four aspects of the great tradition of Roman, or Romanoid, jurisprudence: legal methodology and hermeneutics, the form of social thought, the search for an 'intelligible field of study' for mankind as a whole, and finally the values and goals of human society. These four themes, corresponding to central issues in jurisprudence 'Italian style', also form some of the major links between ancient learning and modern legal science.

The methods of civil science have been deeply indebted to Gaius, and Renaissance jurists in particular remained faithful to the twofold approach that he exemplified. On the one hand Gaius placed the most fundamental reliance on history – not only on the accumulated Roman experience on which his *Institutes* was based but also on the conviction that jurists were professionally obliged to inquire into origins and causes in matters great and small. 'The most important part of anything is the beginning,' Gaius declared (*rei potissima pars principium est*).[21] This axiom served as the justification for the famous title 'On the origin of law', which constituted the historical introduction to the Digest (and incidentally the

[20] Pursued further in my '*Gaius Noster:* substructures of Western social thought', *American Historical Review*, LXXXIV, (1979), 619–48.

[21] Cf. my '*De origine feudorum:* the beginnings of an historical problem', *Speculum*, XXXIX (1964), 27–68, and 'The rise of legal history in the Renaissance', *History and Theory*, IX (1970), 174–94.

classical model for one genre of legal history). It also defined the strategy for the examination of any particular *quaestio*. 'The jurisconsult...', according to Baldus, 'begins at the origin of law with the investigation of first principles' (*Jurisconsultus... incipit ab origine iuris ab investigatione principiorum*).[22] Joined to this concern for the *causa, fons et origo* was Gaius' equally characteristic dialectical method, derived from Greek philosophy and the basis for various essential distinctions, divisions and modes of explanation. In view of the persistence of these two defining features of Gaianism throughout the whole career of Roman legal science, it is not surprising that jurisprudence Italian style, possessing its own sources of rational and historical method, should be understood as independent both of scholasticism and Renaissance humanism.

IV

Within this general methodological strategy Renaissance jurists developed their own particular tactics, and in fact their conception of interpretation represents a significant (though again largely neglected) phase in the history of hermeneutics. Starting with the classic essay of Dilthey, 'Die Entstehung der Hermeneutik', this field has been understood mostly in terms of literary, biblical and philosophical criticism; but in some ways the juristic counterpart of these more recognizable traditions was developed in a more sophisticated and certainly more socially relevant fashion.[23] Despite Justinian's ban, the practice of *interpretatio* was unavoidable; and from the fourteenth century there arose a massive literature, indeed a new literary genre, devoted to the interpretation of law. The focus was on the very last title of the Digest, 'On the meaning of words' (*De verborum significatione* or *significationibus*), a topic which attracted a flood of commentary down to the classic, though in many ways derivative, treatise published by Alciato in 1522.[24]

In this connexion it is desirable to clear up a common misunderstanding about the alleged historical and philological incompetence of the Bartolists. In general, legal methods forbade alleging an error in the law on such grounds, but in all cases jurists were professionally bound to subordinate literary accuracy and even historical fact to legal principle. 'Grammarians will not fight with jurists if they understand them aright,' wrote the sixteenth-century legist Rebuffi, 'for justice must have priority.'[25] Baldus was well aware, for example, that deriving law from justice (*jus a justitia*) was grammatically and etymologically incorrect; and

[22] Cited by V. Piano Mortari, *Ricerche sulla teoria dell'interpretazione del diritto nel secolo XVI* (Milan, 1956), p. 27.

[23] 'Die Entstehung der Hermeneutik', *Gesammelte Schriften*, v (Munich, 1927), 334. A qualified exception to this is the work of Emilio Betti, who wrote on law as well as legal hermeneutics.

[24] 'De verborum significatione' (on Digest, 50), in *Opera omnia*, I (Frankfurt, 1617).

[25] P. Rebuffi, *Explicatio ad quatuor primos Pandectarum libros* (Lyon, 1589), p. 1.

he duly noted the *oppositio* according to which, and properly, '*jus* is included in the definition of *justitia*'.[26] But justice had to be prior to the law in two ways, he responded, first with regard to actions at law and second with regard to jurisdiction; and at this point he appealed to the authority of Aristotle as well as to reason, arguing that in causal terms law was the product of justice: *Jus causale finis est justitia; jus formale nascitur ex justitia.* This allegation, like many others in civil law, might not be acceptable in the rules of grammar, but it did serve the higher science of law, the 'art of the good and the just'.

As jurists might have to offend grammatical propriety, so they might also have to violate historical accuracy. A classic example was the problem of the donation of Constantine, a burning issue among jurists from Cino's time onwards. It so happened that Baldus was highly critical of this alienation of imperial authority, as indeed were Cino, Dante and most imperialists, in contrast with their canonist rivals. The authenticity of the document, however, or even the historicity of the act, was not at issue. Even if such a donation had not been made in the fourth century, the principle could be justified quite properly on grounds of prescription. In fact canonists did argue from this most useful civilian formula (the *praescriptio longae temporis*) and were still so arguing in the sixteenth century, long after the exposure of the donation as a forgery by Cusanus, Valla and others.[27] Similar reasoning underlay orthodox defences of the scriptural Vulgate.

Here we can see the major conceptual grounds for the conflict between humanism and Bartolism, a conflict which found classic expression in the invectives of Valla against Bartolus. Included in Valla's indictment were also Baldus, Accursius, Dinus and other barbarians (*idque genus hominum, qui non Romana lingua loquantur, sed barbara*).[28] In this polemic and in his criticisms of the Digest included in his best-selling *Elegancies of the Latin language* (even more than in his assault on the donation of Constantine) Valla fell afoul of the jurists because of his subversive appeal to the authority of grammar and rhetoric over that of law. The true issue, moreover, was not elegance but anachronism, that is, the appropriateness of antiquated language in the modern world. So the Bartolist Gentili, attacking the literary affectations of the humanists – 'Vallenses' – criticized the ancient jurist Tubero for his use of outmoded language instead of accommodating himself to his own time, 'as did Bartolus'.[29] On a less controversial level Valla also offended jurists by his grammatical criticisms of the Aristotelian *praedicamenta* (time, place,

[26] *Commentarii*, fo. 1.

[27] D. Maffei, *La Donazione di Costantino nei giuristi medievali* (Milan, 1964).

[28] Invective against Bartolus in Valla's letter to Pier Candido Decembrio in *Opera omnia* (Turin, 1962), 1, 633.

[29] *De iuris interpretibus dialogi sex* (London, 1582), p. 58. See the discussion of Valla's *Elegantiae* and *Dialecticae disputationes* in my *Foundations*, ch. 11.

quality and the like) on which Bartolists relied so heavily. Without such apparatus no interpretation except the most literal – and so in many cases the most irrational and unjust – would be possible.

It was on such professional grounds that even Alciato, otherwise so supportive of the *studia humanitatis* and the ancillary value of philology, launched his attack on the 'folly' (consciously using the Erasmian term *Moria*) of the 'contentious grammarians', and above all of their 'emperor' Lorenzo Valla.[30] Yet at the same time Alciato took a more complicated view of the task of preserving and restoring ancient jurisprudence. Alciato never denied the value of the commentators and in fact one remarked that 'Without Bartolus and other such interpreters we would have no science'; but he believed that such secondary wisdom could be presented in more economical and elegant form than the 'multiplicity of opinions' that dominated the margins of texts and intimidated students; and in fact he praised his teacher Giason del Maino for doing just that.[31] In turning to classical antiquity Alciato was furthering this hermeneutical goal by seeking out the primal meaning of civil law – by drinking from the fountain, as he put it, and not from the secondary streams (*a fonte ipso, non a rivulis*). The problem was still one of anachronism – to get behind modern usage (*novus sensus, novus intellectus*) and back to the words of classical authors like Ulpian (*Ulpiani immaculata verba*); and this in turn had to be accomplished not through the 'interpretation of Accursius' but only through 'erudition and the elegance of the Latin language'.[32] Yet it must be said about Alciato – as it cannot be said about Valla, Poliziano, Pietro Crinito or even Guillaume Budé – that his efforts were carried out within the guidelines of professional jurisprudence.

Despite the encroachments of liberal arts and philosophy, then, the hermeneutics of civil science had its own authorities, its own rationale and its own line of development. The basis principles of juridical interpretation were described by Alciato in his commentary 'On the meaning of words', but he was doing little more than giving more literary expression to the rules set down by Baldus a century and a half before. In the first place, according to the conventional formulation of Baldus, 'Interpretation should not be literal (*ad literam*) but meaningful (*ad sensum*), for the sense of words should prevail.'[33] In elaboration Baldus identified two modes of *interpretatio* besides the literal *expositio vocabuli*. One he referred to as 'the explanation of true meaning (*ad verum intellectum*), understood according to the reason rather than the shell and exterior of words...'. The basis for this sort of interpretation was that

30 *Dispunctiones*, III, 1, in *Lucubrationes*, II, 78. Cf. Alexander ab Alexandro, *Genialium dierum libri sex* (Leiden, 1673), I, 19; II, 28; III, 19, etc.

31 'De verborum significatione', *Opera*, I, 461.

32 *Dispunctiones*, I, and *Parerga*, I, 31, in *Lucubrationes*, II, I, 199.

33 Piano Mortari, *Ricerche*, p. 68.

'natural reason' which Gaius himself had proclaimed to be the major source of human law next to custom, and which in turn was derived from natural law. For Baldus, of course, there was an additional implication that Christian faith would lead beyond the deadening letter to the life-giving spirit of the law, and he expressly warned against interpreting the law 'Jewishly' (*judaice* or *more Judaeorum*), implying a literalism untouched by grace or reason.[34]

Essential as it was to determine the spirit of the law, it was not always sufficient. Following the lead of Cino, Bartolus and Alberico de Rosate, Baldus also conceded to the jurist discretion in applying interpreted law to particular cases. Here arose, according to Baldus, the problem of 'discussing the subtleties created by the authority of experts...' and more particularly the endlessly debated question of strict as against liberal interpretation (*restrictiva* and *extensiva interpretatio*).[35] The distinction between a 'rigorous' and a 'more benign' judgment constitutes a central theme not only of the *mos italicus* but of European jurisprudence as a whole. The consensus (the *communis opinio*) seemed to be on the side of liberal interpretation, which is to say judicial discretion; but the limits and guidelines of this professional principle became almost unmanageably complicated in the crush of monographs devoted to legal *interpretatio* and *extensiones*. What extended juridical liberalism still further was the ever present assumption that judgments had to be in accord with 'equity'. According to a much repeated formula, *aequitas* or *epieikeia* was the basis of interpreting laws and treaties (*fundamentum interpretandi leges et pacta*); and the final goal, the *jus aequissimum*, was natural law, which in its primary form was usually identified with divine law.[36] This premise, too, takes us back to Gaius.

V

Though less conspicuous, there is an aspect of civil law even more basic than inherent methodology and the expanding theory of interpretation, and this is its structure. Here again the influence of Gaius is obvious, pervasive and virtually unquestioned before the sixteenth century. The full text of Gaius' *Institutes* was not known until the nineteenth-century discovery by Niebuhr, but many fragments had been preserved in the Digest, and perhaps more important the form of his system was carried over intact into the *Institutes* of Justinian. This work remained the standard textbook of civil law for many centuries and indeed continues to be the model in Italy, Germany and France. The heart of the Gaian

[34] See Engelmann, *Die Wiedergeburt*, pp. 152 ff.

[35] See especially Piano Mortari, 'Il problema dell'interpretatio iuris nei commentatori', *Annali di storia del diritto*, II (1958), 29–109, and Cortese, *La norma giuridica*, I, chs. VI–VII.

[36] N. Horn, *Aequitas in den Lehre des Baldus* (Cologne, 1968), and G. Kisch, *Erasmus und die Jurisprudenz seiner Zeit* (Basel, 1960).

system – or as medieval jurists would prefer to say, its soul – lay in the celebrated tripartite classification of law. 'All our law', Gaius declared, 'pertains either to persons or to things or to actions'; and this secular trinity represents in effect the metaphysical foundations of legal science, and to some extent of social thought, down to the nineteenth century.[37] Renaissance jurists never tired of discussing this arrangement and of explaining how broad and adaptable the categories were. Persons could be collective as well as individual, for example, and it was commonplace that the notion of 'thing' had to be understood in an abstract as well as a concrete sense (*res incorporeales* as well as *corporales*). But none of Gaius' successors were tempted to suggest any alternative.

What is important to notice in this context is that the Gaian triad had philosophical, and especially epistemological, as well as legal implications. The essential point – the *sine quo non* – is that 'personality' was situated at the very centre of civil science; for as Justinian wrote in justification of the Gaian arrangement, 'It is of little purpose to know the law if we do not know the persons for whom the law was made.' Only after determining the status of persons, that is, the degree of liberty, kinship and other social attributes, could attention be turned to the world of reality (*res*), that is, to material objects and how to acquire, retain, retrieve, exchange and pass on the same, and finally to the relationship between subjects and objects, that is, to 'actions' in a general sense.[38] First subject and then object was the proper sequence: first humanity and then its worldly concerns, which was above all to say property.

In keeping with this anthropocentric orientation, with this premise of legal 'subjectivity', as lawyers called it, one of the prime rubrics of Roman jurisprudence (Digest 1, 5, 3, and Institutes 1, 8) dealt with the quality of the 'human condition'. In legal terms the Ciceronian notion of *conditio humana* corresponded to Gaius' *condicio hominum* and to Justinian's *status hominum*. This rubric not only formed a locus for the discussion of human liberty and servitude in political terms but also, for more philosophical jurists, an occasion to digress and offer obiter dicta on that famous humanist topic, 'the dignity of man', sometimes in the style of and with reference to the famous oration by Pico.[39] Indirectly at least, this title represents a link between an old humanist topos and modern formulations of 'the rights of man', most notably in the Napoleonic Code, whose form was also Gaian and whose interpretation has in many ways followed the pattern of the *mos italicus*.[40] The Roman

[37] Gaius, *Institutes*, I, 8, and Justinian, *Institutes*, I, 2, 12. See G. Pugliese, '"Res corporeales", "res incorporeales" e il problema del diritto soggetivo', *Studi in onore de Vicenzo Arangio-Ruiz*, III (Naples, 1953), 223–60.

[38] Relevant discussions include P. Zatti, *Persona giuridica e soggetività* (Padua, 1975), and C. Maiorca, *La cosa in senso giuridico* (Turin, 1937).

[39] B. Chasseneux, *Catalogus gloriae mundi* (Paris, 1529), x, 18 ff.

[40] See the classic survey of F. Geny, *Méthode d'interprétation et sources en droit privé positif* (Paris, 1899).

Empire has been lost, as Lorenzo Valla lamented; and so, as a living force, has the Roman tongue, despite the efforts of Valla and other Renaissance humanists. Still remaining, however, is the spirit of Roman law: *mens legum non moritur.*

VI

In its broadest and most philosophical sense civil science may indeed be understood as a systematic attempt to comprehend and to order the human condition; but of course even Italian jurists did not expect to pursue this in exclusively Roman terms, even in the symmetrical terms of the Gaian system. Nevertheless, it was in civil law that the enterprise of empirical and transcultural investigation found what Toynbee called an 'intelligible field of historical study'. This oecumenical Roman construct was the *jus gentium*, that 'law of nations' which, according to the definition of Gaius, included the customs and institutions of non-Roman peoples who had been drawn into Roman jurisdiction. The line between the *jus gentium* and the *jus naturale* was often hard to draw, but it was generally agreed that such conventional institutions as war, slavery and property belonged to the law of nations. In this widest field of human law (*jus communissimum*, as Baldus called it)[41] the continuing search for equity and 'extensive interpretation' was carried on; and so, more significantly, was the cultivation of comparative legal and institutional studies. One special task was the adaptation of civil law to municipal statutes, and according to Walter Ullmann, Cino's efforts in this task entitle him to be listed among the founders of comparative law.[42] This modern projection of the *jus gentium* was carried on by Bartolus and Baldus, who extended it into the still newer field of international law, another area where the spirit of Roman law has been preserved.

The civil science of the Renaissance, expanding within the framework of the *jus gentium*, or *jus naturale gentium* as it was later called, had to be elaborated and adapted in later times along lines unforeseen even to Bartolus and Baldus. Demanding to be accommodated to modern legal and social thought were not only the feudal monarchies that denied any affiliation with the old Roman *imperium* and the Italian city states that were struggling to act independently of it, but also, with the widening horizons and great discoveries of the later middle ages, the strange peoples who had never heard of it. Investigations in both space and time made the human condition appear 'curioser and curioser', and classical assumptions and norms were stretched badly out of shape. Yet conceptually all had to be related to the 'law of nations', since according to highest authority (that of Justinian and Gaius) it applied to 'all peoples' (*omnes gentes*). This modernized form of an ancient category Baldus designated the 'newest law of nations' (*novissimum jus gentium, quo omnes*

[41] E. Besta, *Introduzione al diritto commune* (Milan, 1938), p. 43.

[42] *The medieval idea of law as represented by Lucas de Penna* (London, 1946), p. 107.

gentes utuntur),[43] and its content was drastically changed in the century and a half between his time and that of Alciato. Of course it was changed still more in the two centuries between Alciato's time and that of Giambattista Vico, whose *scienza nuova* was explicitly defined as a modern version of the *jus naturale gentium* and may be regarded as one of the last and certainly most famous transmutations of Italian 'civil science'.[44]

This expansion of legal horizons was reflected not only in the discovery of the variety but also in the appreciation of the mutability of the human condition. The notion that Bartolism was lacking a sense of history is merely a more recent (but no more tenable) version of the self-congratulatory humanist hyperbole that claimed a monopoly over classical learning. In fact these professional jurists understood very well the character and irreversibility of historical change (more realistically, perhaps, than many of their humanist critics), but they were little interested in its emotional or antiquarian implications.[45] Though devoted to the ideal, they had to understand the real, or more precisely the interplay between the two; and this preoccupation led to an extensive and historically fruitful discussion of human customs in both a positive and a negative sense (both *consuetudo* and *disuetudo*). Formerly the custom or law was so, went the formula, but today (*hodie*) something quite different. Even the allegedly immortal corporations (*universitates*) sometimes perished. According to Baldus, for example, the Roman senate could not be restored by the meeting of a couple of senators 'because there is no hope of the formal revival (*reintegratio*) of the number and order of senators'. It was on the basis not only of humanist scholarship but also of such professional considerations that Roman history, especially legal, institutional and social history, was reconstructed. This was the background of Alciato's work on the *Form of the Roman Empire* and other more technical contributions to Roman history.[46] No doubt it would be too paradoxical to press further the claims of scholastic jurisprudence to be a major factor in the reconstruction of western history – and yet paradox has always troubled logicians more than humanists and historians.

VII

Perhaps the most familiar question about civil science is its ideological significance, and here again interpretations have tended to be distorted or partial at best. Politically the main party line within academic

[43] Horn, *Aequitas*, p. 74. Cf. J. A. Wahl, 'Baldus de Ubaldis and the foundations of the nation state', *Manuscripta*, XXI (1977), 80–96.

[44] See my 'Vico's road', in *Giambattista Vico's Science of Humanity*, ed. G. Tagliacozzo and D. Verene (Baltimore, 1976), pp. 15–29.

[45] Further discussion in my 'Clio and the lawyers: forms of historical consciousness in medieval jurisprudence', *Medievalia et Humanistica*, n.s., V (1974), 25–49.

[46] *De formula Romani imperii libellus* (Basel, 1559), and see note 21.

jurisprudence (aside from the differences between canonists and civilians) was that marking off the 'ultramontanes' from the 'citramontanes'. The latter, Italian for the most part, looked more respectfully on Romanist tradition; and Cino in particular complained about the irreverent *ultramontani* who were continually carping at the Accursian Gloss.[47] More subversively, this group were not inclined to accept the 'Emperor's law' on grounds of authority but only of reason. While Bartolus argued that Italian cities were *de facto* independent of the Empire, the Ultramontanes denied a *de jure* relationship – or indeed that the northern European nations had even historically been subject to Roman rule. In general, the Citramontane position was universalist. Whether their sympathies were imperial or republican, lay or ecclesiastical, their motto was summed up in the civilian formula which declared Rome to be the 'common fatherland' of nations: *Roma communis patria.*[48]

Once again this Romanist orientation suggests a congruence between civil law and Renaissance humanism, but once again the relationship is neither causal nor even sequential. Mutually reinforcing is perhaps a better way of expressing it, despite conspicuous methodological and linguistic divergences. Roman law, as Walter Ullmann has written, 'was perhaps the strongest bond holding together the ancient, medieval and modern worlds'.[49] It was also a vehicle of certain humane values conceptually associated with the humanist movement – and with the easy classicist assumption that *Romanitas* was the moral equivalent of *humanitas.* Conversely, of course, there was the mutual scorn of 'barbarism'. In more historical terms the symbiotic relationship between civil law and humanism was preserved through a mutual dependence on that key member of the *studia humanitatis,* the art of rhetoric.[50] This dependence is apparent not only in the medieval *ars dictaminis,* which involved both a rudimentary legal expertise and public speaking, but also in the teaching of law, pleading and the law of evidence. The continuing connexion is apparent in the importance that legal training and scholarship had for many leading humanists. Classical jurisprudence, if not the academic variety, was prized by Petrarch, Salutati, Bruni and Valla, among others on political as well as literary grounds.

On these same political grounds the public image of civil law has often

[47] *L'opera di Baldo,* p. 78.

[48] Alciato, *Dispunctiones,* II, 21, in *Lucubrationes,* II, 30; cf. Digest, L, 1, 33; XLVIII, 22, 7, 15; I, 12, 1, 13.

[49] *Medieval foundations of Renaissance humanism* (London, 1977), pp. 156–7.

[50] Good discussion in Q. Skinner, *The foundations of modern political thought* (2 vols., Cambridge, 1978), I, 28 ff. Cf. P. Stein, 'The relations between grammar and law in the early Principate: the beginning of analogy', *La critica del testo,* II (Florence, 1971), 757–69; F. Lanfranchi, *Il diritto nei retori romani* (Milan, 1938); A. Giuliani, 'The influence of rhetoric on the law of evidence and pleading', *The Juridical Review* (1962), pp. 216–51; and C. Vasoli, 'La dialettica umanistica e la metodologia giuridica nel secolo XVI', *La formazione storica del diritto moderno in Europa,* I, 237–79.

been something of a caricature, portraying a monolithic doctrine of authoritarianism and absolutism. The inadequacy of this view has become increasingly apparent with recent investigations into the contributions of civil law to conceptions of representation, popular government, individual rights and even political resistance.[51] What adds further weight to this line of interpretation is the not always appreciated fact that civil law was technically restricted to the domestic, moral or private sphere: that the *jus privatum* was carefully marked off from the *jus publicum*, in other words, implied that individual relations were generally immune, theoretically at least, from political interference. In a sense, then, civil science represented an asylum for a variety of rights, especially those of life, liberty and property.

Recent enthusiasm for the Renaissance epiphenomenon known as 'civic humanism' has been restricted all too narrowly to the more popular Florentine ideologues associated with Machiavelli and what a recent historian has identified as the 'Machiavellian moment'.[52] Unfortunately excluded from this perspective is recognition of the fact that civil law was also a major repository – it is hardly too much to say a locus classicus – of a kind of political, social and historical consciousness that self consciously appealed to a distinction between antiquity and modernity. This cast of mind, or scholarly syndrome, which for convenience might be called 'civil humanism', involved commitments to 'liberty', civic spirit, republicanism and a critical view of Italian history; and while it may not be located so precisely in time or tied to social context, it surely has a more coherent and continuous professional basis; and in doctrinal terms it may be identified more easily and traced more directly than the 'civic humanism' which has been stretched over three centuries and more. The juridical *civilità* of Cino and his successors comes much closer than the *vivere civile* of Bruni and his successors to representing a political 'paradigm' in Thomas Kuhn's much used and abused sense of this term.

Beyond the legal profession the social and institutional base of civil humanism was provided by the Italian city state. Conceptions of citizenship and the rights thereof and active political life in general gave new life to Roman jurisprudence. So Bartolus, one of the pioneers in adapting ancient patterns to modern civic life, not only gave legitimacy to the Italian *civitas* by identifying it with the Roman *princeps* but also, from his knowledge of ancient law and philosophy, drew up a classic indictment of political tyranny.[53] Baldus followed suit by posing funda-

[51] Beginning with the fundamental work of G. Post, *Studies in medieval legal and political thought* (Princeton, 1962); and see J. Kirshner, 'Civitas sibi facit civem: Bartolus de Sassoferrato's doctrine on the making of a citizen', *Speculum*, XLVIII (1973), 694, and '*Ars imitatur naturam: a consilium* of Baldus on Naturalization in Florence', *Viator*, V (1974), 289.

[52] J. Pocock, *The Machiavellian moment* (Princeton, 1975), building, as so many others, on the work of Hans Baron and Eugenio Garin.

[53] See F. Ercole, *Da Bartolo all'Althusio* (Florence, 1932) and the classic work of C. Woolf, *Bartolus of Sassoferrato* (Cambridge, 1913).

mental questions about political authority and legitimacy, such as 'whether tyrants are recognized by the *jus gentium*', 'whether a ruler may be expelled by reason of tyrannicide', and 'whether governments are continued by election or succession'.[54] With customary professional 'duplicity', jurists could argue these and other questions in the most rational and radical terms; and both the style of argument and particular formulations can be traced over several centuries and through several social contexts. More generally, civil science was associated by its practitioners with the highest moral and political qualities of free men. What Valla claimed for rhetoric and Poliziano for grammar, Renaissance jurists claimed for their discipline: it represented the highest product and agency of the civilizing process.

These are only a few of the more prominent features of civil science that establish ties between ancient and modern learning and that, despite an almost institutionalized neglect, deserve recognition as a vital part of Renaissance thought. We can no longer conceive of jurisprudence as 'true philosophy', perhaps, or even as a plausible model of social science, but with a little imaginative effort we may be able to appreciate some of its cultural significance in a pre-scientific and pre-technological age. Jurisprudence Italian style offered a sophisticated hermeneutical theory applicable to various levels of social and textual criticism; it suggested a conceptual system to rival Aristotle's and a way for social thought to maintain its independence from natural philosophy; it provided a vehicle for historical, social and anthropological investigation beyond its original normative function; and through the millennium, or rather two millennia, of thought and experience reflected in its sources, it offered insights into the human condition and a range of cultural ideals which, on a higher level, might extend that normative function. In a long perspective what Ernst Curtius remarked about Latin literature might apply also to civil science: it constitutes a 'crumbling road from the antique to the modern world'.[55] And of this *via* both *antiqua* and *moderna* 'jurisprudence Italian style' constitutes one of the most direct and best constructed, if not most scenic, stretches. It should be travelled more often.

[54] *Commentarii*, fo. 1.

[55] *European literature and the Latin middle Ages*, trans. W. Trask (New York, 1953), p. 19.

VII

CIVIL SCIENCE IN THE RENAISSANCE: JURISPRUDENCE IN THE FRENCH MANNER*

The sixteenth century was the golden age of 'civil science', which is to say that scholarly and systematic form of jurisprudence produced by Roman law and the tradition of commentaries and interpretations arising in the universities and courts of thirteenth-century Europe. According to Claude de Seyssel, writing two centuries later, *civilis scientia* was superior to all other sciences because it was practical as well as theoretical, hence in Platonic terms 'true philosophy'.[1] This grand tradition of legal and social thought Seyssel divided into three stages: the ancients (*antiqui*), including Byzantine as well as classical jurisprudence; more recent interpretations (*noviores*), referring to the medieval glossators of the thirteenth century; and finally the moderns (*moderni*), which was to say the so-called 'Bartolist' commentators, among whom Seyssel himself, then teaching at Turin, was numbered.[2] If he had not left his first profession to enter into the service of the French monarchy, Seyssel might have seen signs of another phase, that 'humanistic jurisprudence' which emerged in the sixteenth century to challenge Bartolism, at least in terms of scholarship and teaching. The intellectual ferment caused by the interaction of humanism and scholasticism was evident in several branches of learning, but nowhere so strikingly as in that jealously guarded domain which called itself 'civil science'.

In the golden age of this discipline, starting in the second quarter of the sixteenth century, the dominant, or at least most publicised school was the so-called 'French manner of teaching law' (*mos gallicus juris docendi*), contrasted with the older scholastic method (*mos italicus*) associated with Bartolus, which seemed to prefer Aristotelian dialectic to classical elegance and practical application to historical understanding. In 1517 the conflict between these two schools was dramatised in a dialogue published by Claudio Tolomei, who introduced the late great Angelo Poliziano as spokesman for the amateur and usurping humanists ('grammarians' was Poliziano's term) and Seyssel's old mentor Giason del Maino as advocate of the *Bartolisti*.[3] This colourful debate was carried on in various contexts over the rest of the century, perhaps most famously in the anti-humanist dialogues published in 1582 by Alberico Gentili, who lamented the pedantry and professional irrelevance of the upstart humanist school.[4]

Yet in many ways the significance of this celebrated *Methodenstreit* has been exaggerated, or rather it has been allowed to obscure the true character of the French approach to legal science and perhaps more fundamental contrasts with Italian methods. In fact philosophical and 'scholastic' jurisprudence had been

*An early version of this paper was given at Smith College in October 1979 for a Renaissance conference on 'the lessons of history' held in honour of Myron Piper Gilmore.

established in France in the first place, most notably by Jacques de Révigny, 'master of all philosophers', as he was called by Cino de Pastoia, teacher of Bartolus and a founder of the presumed 'Italian method'.[5] On the other hand Italian jurists, including especially the said Cino, were themselves receptive in many ways to classical learning. It was Italian scholarship, especially as represented by Lorenzo Valla and Poliziano, which created the tools of legal humanism and which imported them into the legal profession, especially through the work of Andrea Alciato, nominal founder, during his tenure at the university of Bourges, of the 'French method'. The fact is that the defining features of French jurisprudence in the sixteenth century had a different nature and provenance than the methods, attitudes and prejudices of humanism. Elsewhere, in a complementary discussion of 'jurisprudence Italian style', I have tried to assess the contribution of Italian thought from about 1300, when Cino broke with his French masters, to 1550, when Alciato died and was already being superseded by his French disciples at the University of Bourges.[6] Here I should like to consider the national heritage and intellectual direction taken by civil science when taken over — practiced as well as preached — by virtuosi of the 'French manner'.

What should be observed first of all is the peculiar professional context in which French jurisprudence developed, including not only the law faculties of Bourges, Orleans, Toulouse and other universities (though not Paris) but also a highly developed and self-conscious legal profession. A royal ordinance of 1274 established the 'Confraternity of St. Nicolas and community of advocates and procurers', a quasi-religious corporation whose members swore a life-long oath to uphold truth, to remain orthodox and never to cheat or to overcharge clients, though it was a moot point whether or not they might defend 'bad causes' (*causae iniustae*).[7] They took this oath on tablets bearing images of Jesus and John and the text, appropriately enough, of John 1: 1, 'In the beginning was the Word'. Prerequisite for admission to the guild was a *lettre de licence*, given after five years of formal legal study; but by the sixteenth century the Parlement of Paris, which was the capstone of the legal profession, policed the curriculum as well as the discipline of the French law schools and even required their graduates to plead before it. By the sixteenth century the academic corporation of legists had built up not only a professional monopoly but also a formidable legend, pretending to a tradition of eloquence and service going back to the Carolingian *missi dominici*, associating themselves as well with the revived splendour of classical oratory, and even claiming inherent nobility through their office and their 'science'.[8] They constituted not only an intellectual élite but in effect the ideological shock troops of the 'grand monarchy of France'. They were the original 'fourth estate'.

From the beginning the French legists were suspicious of their 'citramontane' Italian colleagues; and in the early fourteenth century Cino complained about the 'ultramontanes', including his own French mentors, for their continual carping at the Gloss of Accursius. The basic issue separating the *citramontani* and *ultramontani*, however, was political, and specifically the old rivalry between Emperor and King. No one formulated the question better than Alciato.[9] 'The point is to determine whether [the King of France] recognises the Emperor as superior' he wrote, and his answer was taken from the most authoritative of his 'citramontane' predecessors. 'Bartolus says yes [*quod sic*]. . .' he continued 'for the Emperor is lord of the whole world'. About this famous civilian formula (*dominus totius orbium*), of course, the ultramontanes violently disagreed, especially during the sixteenth-century conflict of Habsburg and Valois, re-ignited by the imperial election campaign of 1519. Indeed the complementary formulas, that 'the Emperor was never lord of the world' (*imperator numquam dominus mundi*) and that the King himself was 'emperor in his kingdom' (*rex imperator in regno suo*), became the cornerstones of royalist ideology in France — and an inarticulate major premise of French jurisprudence. One classic formulation of this is that of Barthélemy de Chasseneux, whose *Catalogue of the Glories of the World* (1529) invoked Pico della Mirandola's 'Oration on the Dignity of Man' to establish the proper political as well as natural rankings.[10] As jurists stood at the apex of the intellectual hierarchy, according to Chasseneux, so the French monarch preceded all other European rulers.

What fundamentally distinguished French jurisprudence from Italian was the complex of legal traditions and enactments which Seyssel grouped under the rubric of '*la justice*'.[11] These included above all the provincial customs of France, in the course of being 'reformed' in the sixteenth century and the accumulation of royal ordinances and parlementary *arrêts*, which incorporated the private as well as the public law of the monarchy. In this ideological context neither civil nor canon law could have any legal authority. If 'the Emperor's law' had been put in question by the critical attitudes of legal humanism, the *mos gallicus*, it was more fundamentally undermined by the nationalist and anti-Romanist thrust of French jurisprudence. In France the 'reception' of Roman law was accomplished 'not by reason of empire but by the empire of reason', according to the famous formula (*non ratione imperii sed rationis imperio*). Whence the tendency of French jurists to seek not the letter but the 'reason' or 'spirit' of civil law (*ratio legis, mens legum*) — not to reject the rich Romanist legacy but to adapt, to rationalise and finally to transform it for national purposes.[12] Among the later products of this effort, it seems to me, are both Montesquieu's *Spirit of the Laws* and the *Code Napoléon*.

In France Roman law was technically common law only in the so-called 'provinces of written law' in the south, while customary law reigned in the provinces of the north. Custom (*consuetudo*) was itself a concept of Roman law, implying unwritten usage, but from the thirteenth century it began to acquire more formal status. As Philippe de Beaumanoir wrote at that time, 'It is good and profitable to write down and enregister customs'.[13] 'Law is either natural or positive' we are told in the oldest of French *coutume*: natural law comes from God, but positive law (*jus positivum*, that is, posited law) is 'established by men for the good of the community and differs from province to province according to its different sources'.[14] If custom could be regarded as the prehistorical and natural source of law (*altera natura*, Azo called it),[15] it was also a legal factor of continuing force; for as jurists like to repeat, 'custom is the best interpreter of law' (*consuetudo legum interpretatur*). This civilian formula was used by practitioners of the French method to justify the glorification of their own feudal canon, for example in the edition of Jacques d'Ableiges' *Grand Coutumier de France* published by Louis Le Caron in 1598.[16] 'Usage is the corrector of law', (*usus legum corrector*), Le Caron remarked in his preface. In general, by the sixteenth-century customary law had acquired not only scientific and even philosophical status in the work of feudists, but also national authority through the redaction and contemporary 'reformation' of customs and especially through incorporation into royal edicts.

It has often been said that 'feudalism' (or *féodalité*) was an invention of the eighteenth century, but in fact 'feudal law' (*ius feudale* or *feudisticum*) had achieved a certain conceptual coherence by this period.[17] This was due in part to Romanist commentaries on the most authoritative of feudal texts, the northern Italian collection called the Book of Fiefs (*Libri* or *Consuetudines Feudorum*), in part also to commentaries on French provincial customs in the early sixteenth century, most notably those of Chasseneux, Tiraqueau and Angleberme, who likewise applied the standards and terminology of civil law to feudal concepts. Most important of all was Angleberme's student Charles Dumoulin, who prepared a pioneering commentary on the most authoritative of French *coutumes*, that of Paris, and who later made notes on all the provincial customs making up what he called the 'feudal complex' (*complexus feudale*) of France.[18] Feudal law was also taught in French universities, especially in the law faculty of Bourges, to which many German as well as French students came. French and German jurists, as I have pointed out elsewhere, were especially concerned to demonstrate the native and non-Roman provenance of feudal institutions.[19] Dumoulin was the most famous of these early 'Germanists', but his opinion was shared as well by academic jurists like François Le Douaren. Practical and theoretical jurists stood together in their defense of national tradition, which provided the ideological context of the *mos gallicus*.

The great centre of the 'French method' was the University of Bourges, where the progeny of Alciato (*Alciatei* is the term applied in later legend) emerged in the 1540s to establish their faculty as perhaps the most distinguished in Europe as well as in France.[20] The two leading figures — and bitter rivals — were Eguinaire Baron and François Le Douaren, whose respective followings in the latter half of the sixteenth century developed into academic factions and eventually confessional 'parties'. The falling out between these two scholars resulted in the temporary exile of Le Douaren until Baron's death in 1550 (the same year that Alciato died). Among the disciples of Baron were François Baudouin and, indirectly, Jacques Cujas, who succeeded Le Douaren upon his death in 1559. On the side of Le Douaren were François Hotman, Hugues Doneau and others. Although irreconcilable on religious and political issues, all of these scholars contributed to the 'French method' of civil law and to the rationalisation of the French legal tradition. The ideological extremes of Romanism and Germanism, reached especially during the crisis of the civil wars, were expressed in the works, respectively, of Cujas and Hotman; but the previous generation of jurists took a more balanced view of the variegated cultural tradition of French society — accommodating Celtic as well as Roman and Germanic factors in their attempt to interpret the richness of their juridical inheritance.[21]

For the most part, however, the conceptual basis of the 'French method' remained the tradition of Roman law, and it was developed almost exclusively within an academic setting. Both Baron and Le Douaren were theoretical rather than practical jurists, remarked a later critic (*sapientes potius quam jurisconsulti*).[22] And yet both dealt with current issues as well as antiquarian problems, one of them being the problem of sovereignty (*merum et mixtum imperium* was the scholastic formula).[23] But while they disagreed on this and other ideological issues, Baron and Le Douaren were in perfect agreement on the question of methodology. From the second quarter of the sixteenth century '*methodus*' became a word to conjure with, and it provided the title for many manifestos of scholarly interpretation, including Baron's introductory statements to both civil and feudal law and a famous essay by Le Douaren.[24] What was reflected in such treatises was not only a new scholarly genre, 'methods' of legal study comparable to the 'methods' of history, philosophy and other disciplines, but also a crucial stage in the development of modern legal hermeneutics. The method of interpretation of the school of Bourges was expressed not only in such manifestos but also in a formal decree of 1548 by the whole faculty on 'the order, way and rationale of interpreting laws' (*de ordere, via et ratione interpretandi iures*).[25] The city fathers complained at this pedagogical indulgence, so contrary, they added, to the approach sanctioned by the Parlement of Paris; but Marguerite of Navarre, Duchess of Berry and her Chancellor Michel de l'Hôpital, supported these and other intellectual innovations.

Until his death in 1550 Eguinaire Baron, first professor of Law, was the leader of the 'French method'. This 'great and noble lord of the law', remarked one observer, 'lectured at the university with such majesty, dignity and learning that you might have mistaken him for Scaevola'.[26] With his 'companion Douaren, likewise a Breton, [he] wanted to understand the law in its purity and splendour'; and both scholars 'bitterly pursued those who had obscured the beauty of the law with their interminable commentaries'. With his long grey beard and in his red robes he denounced in scatalogical terms the defilement of Roman law committed by practitioners of jurisprudence Italian-style.

What must be kept in mind is that, despite the hyperbole about the splendours of Roman law, Baron and his colleagues did not, any more than their professional brethren in the Parlement of Paris, accept the authority of Roman law, especially in its modern Italian form. The historical perspective encouraged by the French method was not only a necessary part of modern philosophy, it was also a way for French scholars to deprive their citramontane rivals of the reflected glory of classical tradition and also to proclaim the independence and parity of their own national tradition. For both reasons they denied all connections between the *Book of Fiefs*, Accursian glosses and Bartolist commentaries and 'the purity and splendour of ancient law'. That pristine law was to be respected not for its authority, which was wholly obsolete, but for its rationality and for its historical illumination. The first of these derived from the proximity of Roman to natural law, the second from the historical instruction embedded in Roman jurisprudence, most systematically expressed in the Digest title 'On the origin of law'.[27] The lesson was not (as dogmatic Romanists would have it) that European legal traditions were imitations of Roman institutions but rather, as Le Douaren summed it up, 'that public law is born of custom, private law of prescription'.[28] And this was a pattern common to all nations.

The common preoccupation of jurists in the sixteenth century was to perfect and give order to existing laws and institutions. In practical jurisprudence the most direct expression of this ideal was the movement, headed by Christofle de Thou, first president of the Parlement of Paris, to 'reform' the disparate customs of France.[29] The foremost spokesman for this project, envisioned in royal edicts since the fifteenth century, was Charles Dumoulin, whose call for the 'union and concord of the customs of France' was published in 1546.[30] On the academic side were the Romanist, or rather Romanoid, systematisers, who tried to rationalise civil law through philosophy and natural law ideas (law as *recta ratio*) — a more or less identifiable tradition extending from Le Douaren and his disciple Doneau down to the more doctrinaire 'jusnaturalists' of the seventeenth century, such as Jean Domat.[31] But there was a third way of viewing modern jurisprudence which in a sense mediated between the extremes of nationalism and rationalism; and that was in terms of the 'law of nations' (*jus gentium*), a legal framework designed originally to accomodate the 'barbarian' customs of peoples conquered or absorbed into the Roman empire but in modern times expanded to include other peoples and even stranger customs. The comparative way was the one chosen by Eguinaire Baron, who was at once the eldest and, in modern scholarship, most neglected of the pioneers of the 'French method'.

Baron was a seminal figure in the development of comparative law (as Jean Moreau-Reibel recognised many years ago).[32] In a sense such an approach was inherent in modern jurisprudence, 'ultra-' as well as 'citramontane'. Scholastic commentators were acutely aware of the differences not only between national traditions but also between ancient practices and modern ones ('*Hodie*', the formula was, we do things differently),[33] and interpreters of feudal law were even more struck by such disparities. A minority opinion, argued from a nominalist position, insisted as early as the fourteenth century that the *jus feudale* was indigenous and post-Roman; and humanist scholarship reinforced this view. These were some of the assumptions made by Baron in his excursions into comparative law.

In one way the connections between French and Roman jurisprudence were quite direct, and that was the common attitude toward the philosophy of law. Baron shared the same intellectual continuum with Ulpian and other classical jurists — the *doctores legum* as distinguished from the *pragmatici*, or *practiciens* — and invoked the same formulas identifying jurisprudence with 'true philosophy' and wisdom and regarding jurists as a secular priesthood. Ultimately, Baron wrote, Ulpian's conception of legal philosophy derived from Cicero, Aristotle and especially Plato; and the difficulties and contradictions arose not from the laws but from the private and public controversies created by the clash of human wills.[34] Jurisprudence transcended such human instability and yet adapted itself to social change, producing new forms to suit the times and making some customs obsolete (*antiquata*) in the course of time. Although laws were produced by human dilemmas, and specifically by the legal actions initiated to resolve these dilemmas, their final formulation produced a wholly rational and indeed 'divine science', and French customs had no less a claim than civil law to this science.

From the mid-1520s Baron had been at least inadvertently involved in a comparative approach within this philosophical framework. His investigations of what he called 'that divine legal wisdom of Roman and Gallic law' (*divina illa iuris sapientia ius Romanum et Gallicum*) was no doubt reinforced by the contemporary political rivalry between the Emperor and the French king; but conceptually his concern was with a more difficult and longer standing issue, namely, the pivotal concept of legal interpretation.[35] Unlike their Italian and German rivals French jurists like Baron were not intimidated by Justinian's formal prohibition of such interpretation; but Baron in any case addressed himself to a larger question, which was that of translation (also rendered in Latin as *interpretatio*). From at least the time of Leonardo Bruni's *De Recta Interpretatione* in the early fifteenth century students of antiquity were concerned with rendering the thoughts of one culture in the language of another; and by extension, questions arose about the translatability, that is, comparability, of laws, customs and institutions as well as political traditions.[36] This humanist and in a sense extra-legal sort of 'interpretation' appeared in the philosophical tradition, most famously represented in France by Guillaume Budé's *Annotations on the Digest* published in 1508, a work at least indirectly significant for the 'French method'.

Such was the starting point of Barons' so-called 'bipartite commentaries' (*commentarii bipartiti*) on the Institutes and Digest of Justinian. In general his procedure was to discuss successively the rubrics of civil law and to suggest French counterparts: '*accommodata huius tituli ad mores Galliarum et leges Regias*' was his formula.[37] For the Roman concept of equity (*bonum et aequum*), for example, French jurists spoke of what is '*profitable et raisonnable, ou utile et iuste*'. Corresponding to the *interpretatio prudentium* was application of the laws (*practiquer les loix*), to the *Senatusconsulta* the '*Ordonnances de la cour de Parlement*', to the *praefectus urbi 'le prevost de Paris*', to the *plebs 'le tiers estat*', and so on. In these juxtapositions Baron pointed out differences as well as similarities, normally to the advantage of the French monarchy; and to this extent he was following the patriotic pattern established by earlier political observers, among them Seyssel, whose *Monarchy of France* also began with an invidious comparison with the Roman empire, and the great humanist Guillaume Budé, whose commentaries on the Digest included a digression on the superiority of the French Parlement to the Roman senate.[38] But Baron pursued these parallels down into lower levels of government and society.

For Baron, as for all French legal scholars, amateurs and professionals alike, Roman law provided not an authoritative system but rather a conceptual model, with attendant philosophical, political, legal and social categories and standards of judgment. So it demanded not to be adapted and modernised but rather to be understood in its own historical terms. More severely than Alciato, then, and more philosophically than Budé, Baron denounced the ways in which Accursius and Bartolus and their colleagues had muddied the pure waters of Roman tradition. Bartolist misconstructions were notorious; but even the Accursians, although they affected to observe Justinian's ban on 'interpretation', had been guilty of distortions. 'This law' Accursius had declared of the Digest title of Roman magistrates, 'is not to be considered' (*non legitur*).

> And why it is not to be considered, Accursius? [asked Baron]. Because it has been revoked by a new law? Or it is because what you need cannot be supplied by the magistrates of that age? For the same reason I do not identify the great offices of the Roman empire with those of the kingdom of France, for instance the *seneschaux* and *baillis* with the proconsuls; but the mode of jurisdiction is virtually the same.[39]

And Baron proceeded to suggest the parallels, structural and historical if not legal, between the Roman and French administrative and judicial offices.

On the subjects of legislation and jurisdiction Baron took a similarly critical and discriminating view. The earliest laws of both Rome and France, that is, the Twelve Tables and the Salian Law, had both been established by popular consent; but in a later and more mature age the law-making power had passed wholly into the hands of the prince. Customs, arising from popular usage, continued indeed to be produced; but in later times these also needed royal endorsement. In France, Baron remarked, 'customs have no force [*ratio*] unless written down in an edict. . . .'[40] In a general sense, too, French jurists accepted the 'absolutist' principle that the prince's will was law; and Baron regarded the royal edicts (*leges Regias*) as virtually equivalent to imperial constitutions, the main difference being that in France the Parlement had to review and enregister legislation. This 'sovereign court', modelled self-consciously on the Roman senate (to the extent indeed that its numbers totalled theoretically one hundred), thus preserved some of the authority which its Roman counterpart had lost by the time of Justinian. 'To the Roman *princeps* we oppose the French *rex*, [Baron wrote] for in establishing and promulgating law he follows reason more closely than the Emperor'.[41] The rendering of justice was also more complex in France, since it possessed 'three pillars': 'high', 'medium' and 'low' justice (*haute, moyenne et basse justice*), the first two levels corresponding to the *merum et mixtum imperium* which Baron had debated with Le Douaren and others.[42] In a number of ways political and legal authority in France seemed more dispersed and, in Seyssel's words, 'bridled', than in Roman tradition.

In private law, differences were even more striking. As political absolutism was moderated in France, so the old Roman 'tyranny' of paternal power (*patria potestas*) had never been accepted in French society. In the matter of personal status, too (*De Statu hominum* was the rubric), French law was more complex and less rigid than that of the Romans, which recognised only the distinction of slave and free. Baron pointed out in particular the position of 'naturalised' foreigners, on which he compiled a brief (*consilium*), and especially that of women, which was inferior and yet not negligible.[43] The moderating effect of French and Gallic ideas was conspicuous in this last area, at least in the interpretations of Baron and another of Alciato's disciples, François Connan. Like Germanism the influence of the mid-sixteenth century 'Celtic renaissance' tended to moderate the presumed rigidity of Roman convention.

More generally, Roman law provided not only a standard of comparison but also the makings of a larger framework of social thought, suggested specially in the *jus gentium*. This law of nations, produced by military and then commercial exchange between Rome and 'barbarian' peoples, consisted both of a general law common to all the *gentes* and, as Baron repeated from medieval jurists, a particular law (*jus proprium*) for each nation; and this is what accommodated the wide range of social behaviour in different cultural traditions. Baron distinguished between two kinds of *jus gentium*, as usual following medieval convention, one primary and the other secondary.[44] 'The primary [law of nations] means what is in accord with natural reason' Baron explained; the secondary what in fact (*de facto*) was reflected in the collective behaviour of people. Implied in the distinction between the law of nature and the law of nations was the (now) familiar historical movement from a natural to a social state; for by nature, Baron repeated, men were free and equal, while laws were accompanied not only by social restraints and divisions but also by slavery and war. Roman tradition itself had reflected such a pattern of development in its own *ius civile*, and the experience of the expanding *jus gentium* suggested that each nation traced a similar pattern, similarly reflected in its own *ius proprium*.

In his comparative approach to modern law Baron was in some ways following the procedures of medieval commentators, except that he was concerned rather to discriminate than to accommodate ancient and modern law. In other ways he was carrying on the work of the feudists, except again he was concerned not with assimilating one to the other but with comparing one with the other. The path to legal science, that is, in a sense, social science, chosen by Baron was not that of pure reason but rather that of empirical, historical and comparative studies. The significance of Baron's work is that he helped to open further the 'world of nations' (in Vico's famous phrase) charted more fully later by a distinguished sixteenth-century progeny who, though in some way epigones, overshadowed their master.

The comparative approach and 'comparatist' mentality were common among jurists in the generation or two following Baron, whose collected works were published in 1562 by his protégé François Baudouin. Two facts gave practical and social reinforcement to this academic way of looking at law. One was the mounting campaign for the 'reformation of customs' beginning in 1555, carried on over the next thirty years and reflected in private scholarship as well as in the public efforts led by the Parlement of Paris.[45] Like Dumoulin, Premier Président Christofle de Thou hoped to bring about this reformation by decreasing and even excising the influence of Roman Law. The other factor was the partisan concern for the mixed provenance — Roman, German and Celtic — of French society, which was called into question by the political and national crisis of the wars of religion. The epigones of Baron and Le Douaren, practitioners all of the 'French method', were all engaged at least marginally in both of these movements, and above all in the re-evaluation of the national past which constituted one aspect of the ideological controversies underlying the civil wars. It was in this context that the extremes of Romanism and Germanism, or rather 'Francogallism', were reached, and that the comparative approach was tested and elaborated as well as distorted.

The convergence of these factors with academic jurisprudence began in the first decade of civil war; and to illustrate some of the consequences of this new and in a sense socialised stage of the French method I will mention five young scholars, all associated with the 'new jurisprudence' of Bourges, who were beginning to extend the doctrines of this school into areas beyond the academic study of law.[46] In 1566 Jean Bodin, who had studied with Baron at Angers, published his famous *Method for the Easy Comprehension of History*, including a very self-conscious effort to apply a comparative method to public law. The next year the Huguenot jurist François Hotman, who had taught at Bourges, was commissioned to write a comparative study of French and Roman law, published eventually as the *Antitribonian,* in support of the contemporary 'reformation' of French legal education and practice. By this time Etienne Pasquier, likewise under the influence of legal humanism, had already begun to publish his *Researches of France*, including (in the 1565 edition) historical studies of the Parlement and the legal profession, with particular attention to the intermixture of Roman and native institutions. A friend and collaborator of Pasquier in the resurrection and defense of national culture and legal traditions, Louis le Caron was also a recent graduate of the law faculty of the University of Bourges; and in 1567 he began his own comparative study of Roman and French law, conceived of first as a translation of the Digest but including also, and finally (when published twenty years later) being overwhelmed by, commentaries on parallel French institutions. An even closer friend and collaborator of Pasquier, Antoine Loisel was beginning a scholarly and professional career which was to culminate in the publication of a study of French legal traditions called *The Customary Institutes*. Emerging from the same professional and intellectual milieu, these members of the second generation of the French method each produced a classic work of comparative jurisprudence, and each illustrates, in his own way, the richness, variety and potential of a comparative approach to civil science.

Bodin's *Methodus* has attracted a large amount of commentary in connection both with political theory and with historiography; and I will not attempt to survey all the meanings, real and imaginary, attributed to his work by later interpreters. For present purposes suffice it to recall one vital contribution summed up in the often-quoted formula, 'The better part of law may be found in universal history' (*In historia iuris universi pars optima latet*).[47] What Bodin provides in this observation is a theoretical justification for the juridical practice of Baron and his colleagues, for the implication is that the old *ius gentium* ought to be expanded through historical investigation to include extra- and especially post-Roman cultural traditions and the new and unheard of customs and patterns revealed by such investigations. As earlier practitioners of the French method had objected, on national as well as historical grounds, to arrogant Romanist claims of priority and superiority, so Bodin more generally and more methodologically objected to Roman universalism, substituting for the old 'translation of empire' thesis a conception of a plurality of national traditions — Vico's 'world of nations'. Human history 'flows from the will of mankind, which ever vacillates and has no objective', Bodin remarked. If it was the task of the historian to retrace the patterns produced by this vacillating will, it was the task of the jurist to regulate and to rectify it. Such was Bodin's conception of civil science, a conception which he realised as he moved from the descriptive and interpretative effort of the *Methodus* to the normative and prescriptive achievement of the *Republic*, published a decade later. Establishing a general framework for the comparative and historical study of society and culture, Bodin's work leads more or less directly to Grotius' development of modern international law, to Vico's 'new science' and to Montesquieu's 'spirit of the laws'.

Despite the most fundamental ideological differences, Hotman also inclined to this national orientation and rejected even more decisively the intellectual — as well as the political and ecclesiastical — hegemony of Rome. Like Bodin, too, Hotman began with the Aristotelian premise that all laws had to be accommodated to the republic and not the reverse; and the inference he drew was that Roman law itself was irrelevant and even harmful to every state except that of its original Roman context.[48] The first error was that of Tribonian, who tried to accommodate the old *ius civile* to an alien Byzantine society: how much less appropriate, Hotman asked, was this Romano-Byzantine mélange to modern French society? Such was the two-fold, historical and ideological, thrust to the 'anti-Tribonianist' thesis — 'sect', Gibbon called it — established by Hotman. The evils of this corrupt Romanism had been introduced into France mainly through the universities from the thirteenth century, and Hotman deplored the consequences both for education and for legal and political institutions. In particular he objected to the 'stupid practice' of drawing up legal documents in Latin, the irrelevant antiquarianism of Roman legal studies, and more generally the rigidity, 'chicannery', 'tyranny' and (implicitly) idolatry of the Italianate legal tradition, which had been worsened by associations with canon law and popery. Yet in the midst of this xenophobic project of educational and institutional reform Hotman also took care to detail in expert fashion the parallels as well as the divergences between Roman and French customs, especially in the important areas of private law — law of persons, family, property, succession, paternal power and procedure. Hotman's brand of civil science, establishing a design for legal reform, belongs in the series of plans for legal unification culminating (after a revolution profounder than that contemplated by Hotman) in the Civil Code.

Worlds apart ideologically but in agreement with both Hotman and Bodin about the necessity of a national and comparative perspective, Louis Le Caron had studied with Hotman's elder colleague Le Douaren and had an even more exalted conception of 'civil science' as, in Platonic terms, the ultimate form of wisdom.[49] Le Caron followed the general line of Baron, though more critically and invidiously. While dismissing the legend accepted by Baron about Pharamond's authorship of the Salian law and the notion of any connection between this and the fundamental law excluding women from royal succession, Le Caron also laboured to restore authentic native traditions, not only through continuing investigation of feudal institutions but also through his edition of Jacques d'Ableiges' *Grand Coustumier de France*. Le Caron's 'juridical nationalism' was analogous to the linguistic nationalism of the Pléiade (of which he was indeed a fellow traveller) and pursued under the same impulse, which was to assert the superiority of the moderns. 'Thus it is not all necessary to relate French magistrates and their jurisdictions to those of the Romans. . . [he wrote] nor are the judgments and responses of the [Roman] jurists accepted as law in France'. Yet Le Caron also saw the merits of a comparative approach; and indeed his *Pandects of French Law*, published in 1587, represents one of the most learned and comprehensive enterprises of comparative law and legal history. Though French in substance, the work was Roman in form and, in the eyes of its ambitious author, virtually a system of Platonic philosophy; for Le Caron, too, envisaged a unified code of law for France. From his comparative perspective he surveyed, much more exhaustively than Hotman, the chief topics of private as well as public law, proposing to give form and rationality to French tradition, and so modern philosophic status to French civil science.

Pasquier, a longtime friend of Le Caron, joined him in championing French literature and language and carried the programme of 'vernacular humanism' over into the study of history. His attraction to comparative legal studies, though apparent in parts of his *Researches* (especially book IX, which contains a history of civil law in France), did not become central to his interests until his last years, when he composed his *Interpretation of the Institutes of Justinian*, which is, like Le Caron's work, a commentary on French law following the order and rubrics of Roman law.[50] Like all of his French colleagues Pasquier tended to judge Roman law invidiously and to point up the distinctiveness and alleged superiority of the hybrid culture produced in Roman Gaul. In public law this meant for Pasquier that, while the Roman formula 'the prince's will is law' had currency in France, it was 'not to be taken cruelly', which is to say that it had institutional limits; in private law it meant that, in keeping with the original 'free and frank' character of the Germanic inhabitants of France and with the more liberal treatment of women and children, the status of persons was less restricted. For example: 'Paternal power as practiced by the Romans', Pasquier observed (the notorious *patria potestas*), 'has no place among us'. True, there was class division, notably that between noble and roturier, but even this barrier — as Syessel had also argued — could be passed without political difficulty. In general and even more systematically comparative, Pasquier's work followed the trail blazed by Baron and pursued further by Hotman and Le Caron. He followed their 'anti-Tribonianist' attitude, too, and continued the undertaking of restoring civil science in modern French terms.

Antoine Loisel was Pasquier's lifelong friend and correspondent and ended his public career as Henry IV's Advocate General. In retirement an exchange of letters between the two legists opened up the question of judicial authority, so essential to the legal profession; and both agreed in deploring Justinian's action in denying the force of law to judicial decision (the *responsa prudentium* of classical jurisprudence).[51] It was in this connection that Loisel wrote a laudatory history of French advocates and entitled it *Pasquier*. Like Pasquier, Loisel inclined to the view that law was a social and historical product, not merely the expression of sovereign will; but Loisel went much further in suggesting the range of legal sources. Not only royal and parlementary legislation and 'approved custom' but also literature, proverbs and folklore served Loisel as material for his pioneering attempt to compile an 'Institutes' of French custom and in effect to capture what Pasquier also called the 'spirit' of French culture, another way in effect to find a basis for legal unification. In his discussion of the complex problem of personality Loisel dropped the Roman distinction between public and private to consider the whole range of political and social types — from the king, who 'never dies', to the bastard, who 'never succeeds' (unless legitimated by the king). As for things, or property, and succession thereto, Loisel drew upon feudal sources, especially the provincial *coutumes*, for his rules, as he did for actions and procedure. He preserved Baron's comparative strategy at least to the extent of utilising the basic Romanoid form of civil law, but otherwise he diverted attention entirely to the folk wisdom of France's feudal past. More than any other practitioner of the French method Loisel contributed to the naturalisation — or nationalisation — of Renaissance civil science.

The judgment that the sixteenth century was the golden age of jurisprudence refers usually to the accomplishments of legal humanism — of what later scholars called *Jurisprudentia Cujaciana*, which was concerned above all with the restoration of ancient Roman law in form as well as content. It may include as well that 'systematic jurisprudence' of Cujas' elder colleagues, François Connan, Le Douaren and Hugues Doneau, whose attempts to reform civil law and improve it conceptually led to the more radical rationalism of Jean Domat and other philosophers of natural law. Both of these interrelated traditions and their respective founders grew out of the 'French method' established at the University of Bourges, and both contributed to the preservation and in a sense transformation of Roman law. But there was another impulse produced by French academic jurisprudence leading away from Romanism and transferring the methods and insights derived from civil law into vernacular and feudal channels. This direction, suggested by Baron's work, was followed by a number of the more practical-minded jurists of the later sixteenth century; and in some ways their accomplishments were even more significant for civil science — in the sense both of the systematic understanding of human society and of the creation of a modern system of law.

It is curious but perhaps not altogether surprising that the great achievements of jurisprudence in the French manner reached their highest level during the bloodiest and most violent generation in French history. The academic 'partisans' of Baron and Le Douaren came to divide along confessional as well as professional lines, Baudouin and Cujas turning their legal talents to the aid of the Catholic party, while Doneau and Hotman became propagandists for the Huguenots.[52] Recalling Cujas' legendary determination to ignore everything outside the bounds of Roman law (*Nihil hoc ad edictum praetoris*), one tends to forget that he also wrote a defense of the royal policy in part responsible for the massacres of St. Bartholomew. So, on the other side, did Hotman and Doneau, whom those massacres had sent into exile; and of course Bodin's defence of political absolutism in his *Republic* was itself an indirect commentary on these disorders. The work of Pasquier, Loisel, Le Caron and others also reflected, in the midst of their professional and scholarly concerns, the political and social controversies of the civil war years, although many of these Gallican jurists tried to maintain a balance between the ideological extremes of Roman and German — or Catholic and Protestant. It is important to keep in mind that expansion and elaboration of civil science occurred in this incandescent atmosphere.

It is no less important to recall, however, that civil science in the French manner outlived these political and religious controversies — methodology, in a sense, surviving ideology. Not only legal humanism and legal systematics but also comparative jurisprudence continued to be cultivated; and the alliance between practical and scholarly legal study, celebrated by and symbolised in Loisel's *Pasquier*, was also preserved in the old regime. French civil science in this broadest sense was central not only to the legal profession and legal education but also to the 'doctrinal origins' of the French Civil Code and to the revival of jurisprudence in the nineteenth century, especially the 'historical school of law'. This is another story, but to tell it completely one must look back to Renaissance jurisprudence as practiced in the French manner.

University of Rochester

NOTES

1. *Commentaria in sex partes Digestorum et Codicis* (n. p., 1508), fol. 1.
2. *Speculum Feudorum* (Basel, 1566), p. 4.
3. *De Corruptis verbis iuris civilis dialogus* (Siena, 1517), sig. Aiii.
4. *De Iuris Interpretibus dialogi sex* (London, 1582).
5. *Lectura in Codicem* (Paris, 1528), *ad tit.*
6. 'Civil Science in the Renaissance: Jurisprudence Italian Style', *Historical Journal* **XXII** (1979), 777–794, with further bibliography.
7. R. Delachenal, *Histoire des avocats au Parlement de Paris 1300–1600* (Paris, 1885), 29ff; and see Bimbenet, *Histoire de la ville d'Orléans* (Orleans, 1887) **III**, 149.
8. The classic work is Antoine Loisel, *Pasquier, ou Dialogue des advocats du Parlement de Paris,* ed. A. Dupin (Paris, 1844).
9. Commentary on Digest I(1), 1, in *Opera omnia* (Basel, 1582) **I**, col. 9; and see S. Mochi Onory, *Fonti canonistiche dell'idea moderno dello stato* (Milan, 1951), 96ff and Gaines Post, *Studies in Medieval Legal Thought* (Princeton, 1964), 453ff.
10. *Catalogus Gloriae Mundi* (Geneva, 1617), 240ff.

11. *The Monarchy of France,* trans. J.H. Hexter, ed. D.R. Kelley (New Haven, 1981), p. 54.
12. See D.R. Kelley, 'Vera Philosophia: The Philosophical Significance of Renaissance Jurisprudence', *Journal of the History of Philosophy* **XIV** (1976), 267–279; and 'The Prehistory of Sociology', *Journal of the History of the Behavioral Sciences* **XVI** (1980), 133–144.
13. *Les Coutumes de Beauvoisis,* ed. le Comte Beugnot (Paris, 1842) **I**, 14; and see A. Lubrun, *La Coutume* (Paris, 1932).
14. *Le Très ancien Coutume de Normandie*, ed. E.J. Tardif (Rouen, 1882), p. 5.
15. *In Ius Civile Summa* (Lyon, 1564), fol. 233^{v}.
16. *Le Grand Coutumier de France,* ed. Le Caron (Paris, 1598); cf. *Pandectes ou Digestes du droit françois*, ed. Le Caron (Lyon, 1596), 396ff, citing Digest I(3), 37; and below (note 49).
17. See the old work by Savigny's student, E.A. Laspeyres, *Ueber die Entstehung und älteste Bearbeitung der Libri Feudorum* (Berlin, 1830), and especially F. Olivier-Martin, *Histoire de la Coutume de la Prévôté et Vicomté de Paris* (Paris, 1922), as well as a host of synthetic and comparative works such as the customary 'Institutes' of Loisel (see below note 51), Claude de Ferrières and the commentary on Loisel by Fr. de Launay.
18. See now the recent work of Jean-Louis Thireau, *Charles Dumoulin (1550–1566)* (Geneva, 1980).
19. 'De Origine Feudorum: The Beginnings of an Historical Problem', *Speculum* **XXXIX** (1964), 207–228.
20. Discussion in D.R. Kelley, *Foundations of Modern Historical Scholarship* (New York, 1970), ch. 4 and *passim*, with further bibliography.
21. See R.E. Asher, 'Myths, Legends and History in Renaissance France', *Studi Francesi* **39** (1969), 408–419.
22. Gentili, *De Iuris Interpretibus*, p. 27.
23. Discussion in Myron P. Gilmore, *Argument from Roman Law in Political Thought 1200–1600* (Cambridge, Massachussetts, 1941), 80ff.
24. 'Epistola Francisci Duareni ad Andream Guillartum. . . De ratione docendi discendique Iuris conscripta', *Opera omnia* (Geneva, 1608), pp. 288–293, and Baron, 'De Ratione docendi, discendique iuris civilis, Ad iuventutum', *Opera omnia*, ed. Fr. Baudouin (Paris, 1562), p. 1; both reprinted in Nicolas Reusner, *ΧΕΙΡΑΓΩΓΙΑ, Sive Cynosura Iuris* (Speier, 1588), pp. 11–37, 37–40.
25. Baron, *Opera omnia* **III**, 48.
26. *Contes et discours d'Eutrapel*, in N. du Fail, *Oeuvres facétieuses* (Paris, 1874) **I**, 263. See E. Durtelle de Saint-Sauveur, 'Eguiner Baron et l'Ecole de Bourges avant Cujas', *Travaux juridiques et économiques de l'université de Rennes* **XV** (1936), pp. 69–114; but there is no adequate study of Baron's career comparable to W. Vogt, *Franciscus Duarenus (1509–1559)* (Stuttgart, 1970).
27. See D.R. Kelley, 'The Rise of Legal History in the Renaissance', *History and Theory* **IX** (1970), 174–194, and literature there cited.
28. On Digest I(3), in *Opera omnia* (Lucca, 1765) **I**, 14.
29. René Filhol, *Le Premier Président Christofle de Thou et la réformation des coutumes* (Paris, 1937).
30. 'Oratio de concordia et unione consuetudinum Franciae', in *Tractatus commerciorum. . .* (Paris, 1546), pp. 807–816.
31. On which see A.-J. Arnaud, *Les Origines doctrinales du code civil français* (Paris, 1969).
32. Jean Moreau-Reibel, *Jean Bodin et le droit public comparé dans ses rapports avec la philosophie de l'histoire* (Paris, 1933).

33. See D.R. Kelley, 'Clio and the Lawyers: Forms of Historical Consciousness in Medieval Jurisprudence', *Medievalia et Humanistica*, n. s., 5 (1974), p. 34, and article cited above, note 19.
34. Commentary on Digest I(1), 1, in *Opera omnia* **I**, 28.
35. Letter to Marguerite de Navarre, 1546, in *Institutionum civilium ab Iustiniano Caesare editarum libri III* (Poitou, 1550). In general see V. Piano Mortari, *Ricerche sulla teoria dell'interpretazione del diritto del secolo XVI* (Milan, 1956), and *Diritto romano e diritto nazionale in Francia nel secolo XVI* (Milan, 1962), esp. 70ff.
36. *Humanistisch–Philosophische Schriften*, ed. H. Baron (Leipzig, 1928), pp. 88–96.
37. *Opera omnia* **I**, 27, 38, *passim*; 52 etc.
38. *The Monarchy of France*, 39ff; and Budé, *Annotationes . . . in quatuor et viginti Pandectarum libros* (Paris, 1535), fol. 40ff (on Digest I(9), 12); and cf. D.R. Kelley, *Foundations of Modern Historical Scholarship*, p. 79.
39. *Opera omnia* **I**, 164.
40. *Ibid.*, p. 67.
41. *Institutionum civilium . . . libri III*, p. 5.
42. *Opera omnia* **I**, 38, and see above, note 23.
43. *Ibid.*, pp. 92–96. Cf. Connan, *Commentariorum iuris civilis libri X* (Paris, 1558), p. 29; and cf. Christoph Bergfeld, *Franciscus Connanus 1508–1551* (Cologne, 1968).
44. *Opera omnia* **I**, 29. And cf. Ennio Cortese, *La Norma giuridica* **I** (Milan, 1962), 55ff.
45. See above, note 29.
46. The best scholarly introduction is Hans Troje, *Graeca Leguntur* (Cologne, 1971), and see also his bibliographical section in *Handbuch der Quellen und Literatur der neueren europäischen Privatrechtsgeschichte* **II**, ed. Helmut Coing (Munich, 1977).
47. Further discussion in D.R. Kelley, 'The Development and Context of Bodin's Method', in *Jean Bodin: Verhandlungen der internationalen Bodin Tagung in München*, ed. Horst Denzer (Munich, 1973), pp. 123–150; this volume also has the best bibliography of Bodiniana.
48. The *Antitribonian* has been reproduced with commentary in the Paris law thesis of Mme A.H. Saint-Charmaran; and see D.R. Kelley, *François Hotman* (Princeton, 1973), 191ff.
49. Further discussion in D.R. Kelley 'Louis Le Caron Philosophe', in *Philosophy and Humanism: Renaissance Essays in Honor of Paul Oskar Kristeller*, ed. Edward P. Mahoney (Leiden, 1976), pp. 30–49; a comprehensive study is still needed.
50. *L'Interprétation des Institutes de Justinian, avec la conférence de chasque paragraphe aux ordonnances royaux, arrests de Parlement et coustumes générales de la France*, ed. M. le duc Pasquier (Paris, 1847). See also D.R. Kelley, discussion in *Foundations of Modern Historical Scholarship*, ch. X, and the recent biography by Dorothy Thickett. Other works of this type are listed in the *Handbuch* (cited above, note 46) **II**, 297–299.
51. *Institutes coutumieres*, ed. Michel Reulos (Paris, 1935), and Reulos, *Etude sur l'esprit, les sources et la méthode des Institutes coutumières d'Antoine Loisel* (Paris, 1935). Cf. Pasquier, *Les Lettres* (Paris, 1619), bk. XIX, letters 8–14, and Loisel, *Divers opuscules* (Paris, 1652), 95ff; also Loisel, work cited above, note 8.
52. See D.R. Kelley, *The Beginning of Ideology: Consciousness and Society in the French Reformation* (Cambridge, 1981), ch. 5.

VIII

The Development and Context of Bodin's Method

I. Bodin: Quid et Quotuplex

Jean Bodin is a many-sided figure who has been in recent years the subject of proliferating and increasingly specialized studies. The one persistent habit of Bodin scholars, it seems to me, has been to restrict themselves to one of two of these sides, which moreover are defined in terms of rather formal categories of political thought, historical method, law, geography, and the like. This habit is well illustrated by the agenda (though perhaps not the purpose) of the present conference, and I must confess that it has affected my own work. But I have for a long time been uncomfortably aware that Bodin's «method», like his «republic», is like no other, and that approaching him through modern compartments of knowledge is not only anachronistic but also somewhat distorting. In any case it is these convictions, which have proved stronger than my sense of scholarly caution, which have led to this experimental attempt to see Bodin in a somewhat broader perspective and more philosophic context.[1]

Bodin seems to present a historical paradox. On the one hand he was almost too typical of his age. «Humanist, jurist, astrologist», Etienne Fournol remarked, «here indeed is a man of the 16th century». On the other hand, and in a longer perspective, he was a man for many ages. «If he was one of the last of the legists», Fournol added, «he was also the first of the philosophes.»[2] Yet there is no real contradiction here, except to the extent that Bodin himself entertained extreme and conflicting views. For if he displayed the spirit, methods, and some of the substance of scholastic learning, he also rebelled against the restraints of conventional «authority» and set out quite deliberately to create a science of society that was, according to his lights, empirical as well as rational. Drawing

[1] In general this essay is a byproduct of my Foundations of Modern Historical Scholarship, New York 1970 and, in part, a justification for not including Bodin, except peripherally, in the constellation of érudits discussed there (though I confess that it was an interest in Bodin's work that provoked this book in the first place).

[2] Fournol [51] Bodin prédécesseur de Montesquieu, Paris 1896, 21, 27; cf. Fournol Sur quelques traités de droit public du XVI. siècle, *Nouvelle revue historique de droit français et étranger* 21 (1897), 298–325 [54].

upon the wisdom of the past, he tried to build a system for the future. «The republic never dies», ran the old maxim, and Bodin wanted to insure that his own *Republic* had a comparable longevity.

A man with a passion for the past and designs upon the future, Bodin does not seem to have been much at home in his own time; he might well have preferred to be a contemporary of St Thomas or of Descartes. For in an age of academic inhibition he was a boldly speculative thinker, in an age of doctrinal faction a philosophical syncretist, in an age of discriminating criticism a compulsive and rather credulous eclectic. Not satisfied merely with investigating the past, he sought to extract from it principles of universal and eternal import; not satisfied with determining rules of human behavior, he wanted to arrange them into a coherent system; not satisfied with analysing society in rational terms, he wanted to uncover the *arcana* of nature as well as of the imperium. These overreaching philosophical ambitions led him down strange and even forbidden paths and gave him an almost Faustian reputation. Small wonder that he inspired distrust among such careful scholars as Cujas and Scaliger. Several contemporaries suspected that Bodin literally did not quite belong to their world. According to François Pithou (who heard it from Claude Fauchet), «Bodin was a sorcerer».[3]

Bodin accepted no man as his master, though he learned from many; he belonged to no school of thought, though he attended several. His first intellectual allegiance was clearly to the legal profession, with all of its totems, taboos, and traditions. From the beginning, too, Bodin was attracted by the humanist movement and its concern for educational reform. Yet he submitted to the standards neither of the professional lawyer nor of the professional humanist. He shared neither the arrogance of the first, who insisted that his «science» was superior *(nobilior et dignior)* to all others, nor to the snobbery of the second, who seemed prize eloquence above doctrine.[4] On the contrary, to Bodin nothing human – or superhuman – was alien, and in effect he assumed the unity

---

[3] *Scaligerana, Pithoeana . .*, Amsterdam 1740, I, 500. That Bodin shared some of Machiavelli's diabolical reputation is shown, e.g., by Antonio Possevino's *Judicium de Nicola Machiavelli et Joannis Bodini scriptis* in his translation of the former's *Princeps*, Ursel 1600, 197. See also Mr. Baxter's paper on Bodin's «demon.» With all the books on Bodin there has been no satisfactory attempt to treat him as a philosopher.

[4] Two classic but seldom cited panegyrics of the «science» of law appear in Chasseneux, *Catalogus gloriae mundi*, Paris 1529, pars X, passim, and Jean Corras, *De Jure civili, in artem redigendo*, in the fundamental collection, *Tractatus universi juris*, Venice 1584, I, f. 62v. The various (sometimes «interdisciplinary») attempts of 16th century jurists to place law in the encyclopedia of arts and sciences deserve further investigation.

of all learning. If he preferred, in humanist fashion, to arrange this learning in a circular way *(encyclopaedia)* rather than according to a hierarchy, he did not hesitate to open this classical preserve to «barbarian» ideas. His attitude was at once inter-disciplinary and inter-cultural.

In general the pattern of Bodin's intellectual growth was one of exploring and charting large and distant fields of thought, but seldom of settling and cultivating them carefully. In particular his route led from a wide-ranging study of history, law, and philosophy to a system that embraced, while at the same time it transcended, all three. But Bodin rarely adopted other mens' views without transmuting them to suit his own goals, and so some of the most interesting features of his thought are not fully accessible through simple exegesis, conventional biography, or piecemeal *Quellenforschung*.[5] What I propose here is to supplement such studies (of which we have an abundance) by means of two related lines of inquiry: first to suggest, by comparison with views of contemporaries, certain features of his intellectual environment and certain scholarly traditions which helped to shape his historical and political philosophy; and second to reveal, by a kind of structural analysis, some of the changing configurations of his thought leading up to the *Republic*. What ever the merits of this approach, it seems to be in keeping with and perhaps even invited by Bodin's own «method», which likewise depended upon comparisons to locate essential, underlying principles, which likewise used logical rather than literal analysis to show these relationships, and which in general exhibited an *esprit de système* that seems to soar uncomfortably high above its alleged sources.

II. Bodin: Grammaticus

If Bodin had any single point of departure, it was the «new learning» of the Renaissance, for which his Toulouse oration of 1559 was an advertisement.[6] Here he rehearsed the story of the «translation of studies» from Italy to France, sponsored by that «father of letters», Francis I, with the help of Guillaume Budé, and given institutional embodiment in the royal

---

[5] So it would not be appropriate, even if it were possible, to cite here the vast and growing quantity of Bodiniana bearing upon such questions, though I should record my special debts to the work of MOREAU-REIBEL, BROWN, REYNOLDS, MESNARD, and CHURCH.

[6] *Oratio de instituenda in repub. juventute ad senatum populumque Tolosatem*, in *Œuvres philosophiques*, ed. PIERRE MESNARD, Paris 1951 [4.20], 9 ff; cf. LE ROY, *G. Budaei vita*, Paris 1540, 46 ff. The later parallels between the thought of these two is well known, having been discussed by J. B. BURY, ROGER CHAUVIRÉ, and others.

«College of Three Languages» established during the 1530's. This often told tale was sanctioned by Budé himself and by his first biographer, Louis Le Roy (who like Bodin was a graduate of the Toulouse law school and later a professor in this same royal college), and by the time Bodin gave his oration it had become quasi-official doctrine. But for Bodin and Le Roy and indeed most scholars of their generation the «studies» thus celebrated were exclusively neither ancient nor Italian; they were perforce joined to and colored by the whole glorious tradition of the French monarchy, barbarous and vernacular as it was. As a result the humanist «encyclopedia» was expanded to include the entire cultural past of Europe and came to resemble the usage of D'Alembert more closely than that of Budé.[7] Being heir to such eclecticism, Bodin could hardly help breaking out of the humanist mold.

Within the new learning Bodin attached special importance to the «new jurisprudence», which was one of its byproducts and which had flourished especially in France. This so-called *mos gallicus* had been pioneered by Budé, had been introduced into the universities by Andrea Alciato, and had been developed further by such «Alciatei» as François Connan, to mention the three jurists specifically named by Bodin at this time. The story of this phase of the humanist movement, a sort of companionpiece to the Budé legend just referred to, was also told by Le Roy, this time in his biography (again the first) of Connan.[8] Toulouse was not particularly cordial to «legal humanism», but it was here nonetheless that Bodin, like Cujas and Le Roy, became a devotee of this new school which, as he now thought, had enriched the study of law with philosophy as well as with classical learning. It is perhaps significant that already Bodin emphasized the philosophical rather than the philological aspect of the «reformed jurisprudence», that he gave no credit to the real founders of the school (Lorenzo Valla and Angelo Poliziano), and that of all the distinguished disciples of Alciato he singled out not one of the university jurists but a practicing advocate interested in legal reform. Connan did repeat certain humanist commonplaces, including strictures against a servile imitation of Aristotle and the neglect of history and philology, but of all the pro-

---

[7] BUDÉ himself, who helped to promote the Italianate «encyclopaedia», notably in his *Annotationes in Pandectas* of 1508 and his *De Philologia* of 1532, spoke of a «Minerva Franciae» in the preface to his *De Asse* of 1515, where he also celebrated the «translation of studies». Such naturalization of the classical idea of culture is even more conspicuous in such vernacular works as LE ROY'S *De la vicissitude ou varieté des choses*, Paris 1575, and ETIENNE PASQUIER'S *Recherches de la France*, Paris 1621, esp. book IX.

[8] *De Francisco Connano* ... (1553) in CONNAN'S *Commentariorum juris civilis libri X*, Naples 1724; cf. BODIN, *Oratio* [4.20], 17. One of the earliest full versions of this story appears in PASQUIER, *Recherches*, X, 39.

ducts of the *mos gallicus* he was possibly the least typical excepting Bodin himself.[9]

There has been much discussion of «legal humanism» in recent years, but the subject is still in some confusion. The trouble is that we continue to see the movement less in terms of its accomplishments than of its public image, whether through the panegyrics of its friends, such as Cujas, or through the invectives of its enemies, such as Alberico Gentili.[10] By Bodin's time, in fact, the contrast between the *mores gallicus* and *italicus* was not nearly so sharp as contemporary polemic suggests. On the one hand there were many conventional jurists (*Bartolisti, doctores scholastici, doctores italici* as they were variously, and almost always invidiously, called) who not only possessed elegant literary tastes but who, like Charles Dumoulin, «the glory of our profession», as Bodin referred to him, also had impressive philological skills and interests in textual emendation. On the other hand there were humanists (*grammatici, encyclopedei, Vallenses, Alciatei, Cujacii, docteurs humanistes,* and other epithets) who, like François Hotman and indeed Alciato himself, did not hesitate to revert to a basically scholastic method (and indeed for pedagogical purposes even Cujas recommended a conservative approach).[11] What is more significant, methodology was becoming a less divisive issue than ideology, especially as expressed in the conflict between the Italians (also called *doctores italici*, or *ultramontani*, here in a political, though still often derogatory, sense) and the Gallicans *(doctores citamontani)*.[12] This distinction cer-

---

[9] CONNAN, *Commentarii*, Praefatio: «Nec hujus causa mali sunt fuit doctorum penuria (qua enim in scientia plures) sed ignoratio docendi, cum hi nullam artem scirent, neque Latinae linguae essent et historiae periti, quod utrumque fuerat necessarium.»

[10] *De Juris interpretibus dialogi sex*, London 1582, attacking not only the «encyclopedia» and Latin and Greek eloquence but dialectic and especially history («Pomponius. Historia non est cur legat Juris interpretes»). One famous reference to this conflict was made by a man who, like Bodin, rose above it: FRANÇOIS HOTMAN, *Antitribonian,* Paris 1603, ch. 15 (p. 120). distinguishing between «chauffoureurs, Bartholistes et barbares» and «Humanistes purifiez et grammariens desquels aucuns [referring to Bodin?] mettent le docte François Connan», for whose works Hotman himself had written a preface. The best and most relevant recent survey is JULIAN H. FRANKLIN [226], Jean Bodin and the Sixteenth Century Revolution in the Methodology of Law and History, New York 1963, though there are some further qualifications to be made.

[11] JACQUES FLACH, Cujas, les glossateurs et les bartolistes, *Nouvelle revue historique de droit français et étranger* 7 (1883), 205–32. These qualifications have been well brought out by GUIDO KISCH, Humanismus und Jurisprudenz, Basel 1955, 18 ff.

[12] A good example, again, is CHASSENEUX, *Catalogus gloriae mundi,* V, 28, referring to an imperialist view held by «canonistae . . ., Bart. et omnes Itali, et

tainly meant more to Bodin himself, who was interested less in the language than in the concepts – less in making *restitutiones* than in discussing the *opiniones* – of civil law.

Nor was «legal humanism» itself a simple and coherent school of thought. Certain difficulties may be avoided by setting aside particular ideological overtones (such as the incidence and significance of «civic humanism» in legal scholarship, though this is indeed an interesting and almost totally neglected subject worth pursuing) and by regarding this movement in a more neutral fashion; that is, as a combination, in one way or another, of legal scholarship with the *studia humanitatis*, or better with the whole «encyclopedia» of subjects necessary for a proper, which is to say a historical, understanding of law.[13] It is also true that by the latter half of the 16th century there were few amateurs like Valla or Budé who had the temerity to interpret legal texts, and so there was a growing professional uniformity of standards. Nevertheless, within this professionalized tradition of legal humanism there were a number of distinguishable – and increasingly divergent – trends. Three of these were inherent in the civil law itself and were so described by François Baudouin just a year before Bodin's Toulouse oration. Just as the Digest title «de verborum significatione» required the jurist to know some philology, Baudouin wrote, so the title «de origine juris» demanded history and the title «de justitia et jure» demanded philosophy.[14] Each of these tendencies left a certain imprint on Bodin's thought.

In the first place there were the «pure grammarians» like Cujas and Antonio Agustín, whose principal interest was in separating Roman law from the jumbled Byzantine mosaic assembled by Tribonian and

---

ultramontani ...,» in contrast to the «opinio contraria, quam doctores citramontani tenuerunt ...,»

[13] Following here, in other words, the view of humanism taken by P. O. KRISTELLER in his various studies. It may be noticed that a major omission in the many discussions of «civic humanism» made and inspired by HANS BARON is the significance of civil law. As for the formal relations between jurisprudence and the «studia humanitatis», the most direct approach is through the various treatises on the best method of teaching law (see note 21), including those of LE DOUAREN, BARON, BAUDOUIN, HOTMAN, which are all in N. REUSNER, *Cynosura juris*, Spires 1588; also CORRAS (note 4), CUJAS (note 11), and MARIN LIBERGE, *De Artibus et disciplinis, quibus studiorum instructum et ornatum esse oportet*, Anjou 1592, among others; and through such counterattacks as those of GENTILI and GRIBALDI (the latter in Reusner). A study of this topic would be very useful.

[14] *Commentarius de Jurisprudentia Muciana* (1559), Halle 1729, «Epistola auctoris ad lectorem»; cf. LIBERGE, *De Artibus*, 4, attacking «perniciossimae eorum opinioni, qui sine philologia, philosophia, et antiquitatis cognitione juris scientiam et artem intelligi et doceri posse contendunt ....»

Justinian's other editors, or at least in establishing a correct text of the Digest.[15] Their virtues included an often heroic erudition and an acute, indeed an unprecedented, sense of anachronism which permitted them to uncover many «Tribonianisms». Their conspicuous faults were a «trivial» concern with legal and literary vocabulary and a «juristic classicism», as a modern critic (Fritz Schulz) has called it, which not only deprived their work of some relevance but in its own way blocked a clear view of the development of, or changes in, civil law. Now Bodin was properly shocked by «Tribonian's crime» and the corruption of the texts of civil law, and he often relied upon the scholarship of modern critics. Yet he found it increasingly difficult to take seriously «those who would rather be called grammarians than jurists», a description which indeed fits his rival Cujas.[16] Toward the literary and antiquarian excesses of the «Cujacians», as Gentili called them, Bodin took precisely the same critical position as Alciato had taken toward Valla, the «emperor» of the grammarians.[17] Theirs was a game that Bodin would never play, though his understanding of Roman law certainly presupposed their work.

Secondly, there were the legal historians, and in fact it was to this circle – the fifth in Gentili's juridical Hades – that Bodin has often been consigned. More typical of this group were scholars like Baudouin and

---

[15] The symbol and relic as well as chief target of this school was the famous Florentine manuscript of the Digest, whose legendary provenance was repeated by many humanists, including BAUDOUIN, *Praefata de jure civili* (1545), in HEINECCIUS, col. 10; HOTMAN, *Antitribonian*, 124, and *Ex Indice universae historiae* in *Operum, Geneva* 1599, I, col. 1086; LIBERGE, *Universae juris historiae descriptio*, Poitou 1567, 95, as well as PASQUIER, *Recherches*, X, 33. The utility of this manuscript was also attacked by GENTILI, *De Juris interpretibus*, f. 92, who rejected it as an object of a kind of philological idolatry.

[16] *Oratio*, 9; cf. *Methodus ad facilem historiarum cognitionem*, prefatory letter to Jean Tessier [4.20], 108, 109, complaining again of the ineptitude of Justinian's editors and, at the same time, of the «pestis grammaticalis, in intimos omnium disciplinarum aditus usque coepit, ut pro philosophis, oratoribus, mathematicis, theologis: minutos de schola grammaticos fere cogamur.» Contrast this with the remark of FRANCOIS PITHOU about his mentor (*Scaligerana*, II 285): «Quand on vouloit mespriser Monsieur Cujas, on l'appeloit Grammarien, mais il s'en riot, et disait que telles gens estoient marris de ne l'estre pas.»

[17] ALCIATO, *Dispunctiones* (1518), III, 13, in *Opera omnia*, Frankfurt 1617, IV, 201. Even BAUDOUIN disassociated himself from the philological school; so in his *Commentarii de Pignoribus et hypothecis*, Basel 1563, 3, on the general usages of these terms, «Sed id grammaticis relinquo». Indeed, the question had been discussed at some length by VALLA, in his *Elegantiarum latinae linguae libri sex*, VI, 57 (on Digest, 20, 5, 1), and had been answered by ALCIATO, among others; the whole controversy has been assembled in C. A. DUKER, *Opuscula varia de Latinitate jurisconsultorum veterum*, Leiden 1711.

his disciple Marin Liberge, who came to regard civil law primarily as source material for the reconstruction of universal history. Baudouin had made important contributions to the study of early Roman law, especially that of the Republic, and to the search for «Tribonianisms»; and by 1559 these researches had led him to his grand design for an alliance between law and history. Moreover, when he published his *Method of History and its Conjunction with Jurisprudence* two years later, it was clear that history was to be the senior member of the partnership.[18] This was even more clearly the case with one of the later «methods» of history, that by Pierre Droit de Gaillard, who likewise proposed an alliance of law and history *(historiae et jurisprudentiae collatio)*. «All the law of the Romans and of other nations», he declared, «is nothing more than that part of history which describes the customs . . . of each nation.»[19] It might be assumed that Bodin's own *Method of History*, which falls formally in this same genre *(artes historicae)*, would be in accord with this program, and indeed there are obvious similarities that have not gone unnoticed. And yet in certain more fundamental ways Bodin's work was irreconcilable with the others. Baudouin and his followers assumed, to take the most conspicuous example, that both law and history had to be understood in strictly chronological order. «Since later law abrogates earlier law», as Liberge explained, «we will commit many errors . . . if we do not study history according to the sequence of times and keep the chronology of laws.»[20] To such scholarly scruples Bodin could not have been more indifferent; he quite deliberately sought a more rational and supra-temporal (which is to say super-human) arrangement in which, on the contrary, the substance of history would be subsumed under the categories of law.

---

[18] One may follow this shift in emphasis from the *Scaevola* of 1558, where, attempting to recover the legal contributions of this family, he remarked («Lectori»), that «Jurisprudentia cum Romana historia, et historia cum Jurisprudentia Romana perpetuam conjunctionem, ut duas unius veluti corporis partes indivisas esse sentirem», to the *De Institutione historiae universae et ejus cum jurispurdentia conjunctione* of 1561, where he remarks (Strasbourg 1608, 189): «Ego quidem nondum satis statuere potui, plusne lucis historia ex Jurisprudentiae libris, an Jurisprudentia ex historicis monumentis accipiat.» I focus more directly on this school in: The Rise of Legal History, *History and Theory* X (1970).

[19] *De Utilitate et ordine historiarum praefatio*, to Bap. Fulgosias, *Factorum dictorumque memorabilem libri IX*, Paris 1578, a little essay «deprompta ex suis institutionibus historicis», that is, from his *Methode qu'on doit tenir en la lecture de l'histoire*, Paris 1579 – from which circumstance I have taken the liberty of translating Baudouin's own *Institutio* as «method».

[20] *De Artibus*, 85, citing and practically paraphrasing Baudouin, *De Institutione*, 227.

This brings us to the third group, which included such philosophical jurists as Connan, Hugues Doneau, and to some extent François le Douaren, who wanted to establish a rational system of jurisprudence on the basis of Roman law as reconstructed by philology. There was much talk about refashioning law into an art *(jus civile in artem redigendo)* or restoring it to the status of a science which it properly enjoyed; almost every jurist devised his own particular «method» in order to make civil law more intelligible; and almost all of the legal humanists of Bodin's generation wrote at least one essay «de ratione docendi juris civilis» (a genre which which may be traced back to Justinian's often cited edicts prefacing the Digest).[21] Such reforming efforts had philosophical as well as pedagogical motives, and nothing was more common for these jurists than to make analogies with such better organized arts as geometry and to introduce Aristotelian terminology. But in general civil law had its own rationale, and most jurists before the time of Domat and Vico contented themselves with adjusting the schemes established by Justinian. In his «methodical interpretation» of the Digest Le Douaren followed roughly the usual sequence of topics but elaborated on and changed the particular rubrics, introducing his own precepts and theory of textual criticism, while his young protégé Doneau did not hesitate to depart from the order of titles in the Digest as well.[22] So, even more radically perhaps,

---

[21] «Discussion about method was in the air» is the appropriately unspecific remark of J. L. Brown in his fundamental study of Bodin's *Methodus*, which is still the best discussion of the subject. It seems to me that the role of Ramus has been much exaggerated in this connection, though it is difficult to disagree with the spezific link with the *Juris universi distributio*, if not the *Methodus*, argued by Kenneth Mc Rae [189, 228] in *Journal of the History of Ideas* 16 (1955), 306–23, and 24 (1963), 569–71. Useful for background is Neal Gilbert, Renaissance Concepts of Method, New York 1956, 137 ff., but the subject of legal method needs to be investigated more thoroughly. Not quite to the point is F. Ebrard, Über Methode, Systeme, Dogmen in der Geschichte des Privatrechts, *Zeitschrifl für Schweizerische Geschichte* 57 (1948), 95–136. There do seem to be some generally agreed-upon requirements for a proper «method». In one of the most extensive discussions Coras (*De Jure civili*, f 59r) argues, among other things, that it must aim at «praecepta universalia», that it begin with «definitiones et divisiones», that it be in accord with «natura», and he goes on to make a very conventional analogy with geometry; see esp. ch. VIII, «De triplici methodo, resolutiva, compositiva, et definitiva», as well as the other works cited in note 13.

[22] *In Primam partem Pandectarum methodica enarratio*, in *Opera omnia*, Lucca 1765, I, 1; cf. *De Pandectarum compositione, ordine as methodo*, in *Opera*, IV, 47. An excellent discussion of these topics may be found ii Eyssell, Doneau, Dijon 1860 and now in Christoph Bergfeld, Franciscus Connanus 1508–1551, Cologne 1968, the first useful treatment of this jurist so admired by Bodin.

did Connan, whose influential commentaries, published in 1557, included, among other things, comparative discussions of law and feudal institutions. Bodin shared the compulsion, common among jurists of his generation, to find a method which, through its mnemonic and logical virtues, would permit the construction of a system of universal law. And as usual Bodin would be satisfied with no one's handiwork but his own.

III. Bodin: Pragmaticus

In the seven years between his Toulouse oration and his *Methodus* Bodin was increasingly impressed by another tradition that was ultimately more significant than any variety of humanist jurisprudence. This was the practice of law and, inescapably, the Bartolist school on which it relied. At first Bodin had had the usual intellectual's contempt for the *pragmatici*, «those whom Cicero called mean and mercenary», as Hotman dismissed them at just this time. But in the course of his own legal career and especially the experiences of the wars of religion Bodin, like Hotman, came to prize the work of «those who have spent their lives serving the republic» above the «frivolities of the grammarians». He would agree with Baudouin's lofty ideal of «homo politicus, hoc est jurisconsultus».[23] Consequently, like Tiraqueau and others, he came to realize that the development of civil law had to be understood in terms of the later commentators as well as of the original sources. This was particularly necessary for public law, which classical jurists tended to avoid on principle. What is more, Bodin took very much the same attitude toward civil law as had the medieval commentators, regarding it as a treasury of accumulated wisdom (*rerum humanarum et divinarum notitia*, as Ulpian had defined it, if not *ratio scripta*) to be applied to contemporary problems. It was not without reason that Pasquier placed Bodin in «la chambre de Bartole italien».[24]

Yet it will not do simply to call Bodin a «neo-Bartolist». Although he had apparently graduated from academic to practical jurisprudence, he had not in fact merely substituted one tradition for another; as usual he tried to combine the best of both. In methodological terms, however, the Bartolists were hardly better off than the humanists. The crucial point

---

[23] BAUDOUIN, *Commentarius*, 20, and HOTMAN, *Jurisconsultus*, Basel 1559, 34. Cf. Bodin, *Methodus*, 134, attacking those «qui leviores Grammaticorum nugas malunt, quam gravissimas corum narrationes qui totum vitae suae tempus in Repub. gerenda consumpserunt». Here is the theme of «civic humanism», which may be traced back to Budé and especially to Valla (and perhaps earlier).

[24] PASQUIER, *Recherches*, 902.

Bodin made, and not for the last time, in his *Distribution of Universal Law*: unlike all other arts and sciences civil law dealt not with a general subject but with the creation of a particular society, and neither the humanist nor the scholastic jurists had escaped this narrow Romanism.[25] If legal humanism was unacceptable because it dealt with trivial (that is, historical) questions and scorned contemporary legal practice, Bartolism was unacceptable because it failed to notice the limitations and mutability of civil law. Bodin valued the work of the humanists for giving a clear picture of Roman law and that of the Bartolists for insights into the nature of society and politics, but neither offered an adequate basis for constructing a system of jurisprudence or even for drawing general conclusions about institutions. In general, he assumed, it was a fallacy to think that the experience of any single national group was sufficient for political philosophy. This was one of the unspoken axioms of Bodin's method – that the universal was never adequately represented in the particular.

Underlying this assumption, however, was a particular bias as well as a general methodological insight; and here Bodin was indebted to another legal tradition, namely, that of the royal legists in France. Beholden as they were to civil and canon law, these French *avocats du roi* had, over some three centuries, fashioned their own ideology and acquired their own scholarly habits. Most significant for Bodin was their practically unanimous rejection of the «authority» of Roman law. While «ultramontane» jurists, including Alciato as well as Bartolus, had to believe that their emperor was lord of the world *(dominus mundi)* and that «his» law was universal, their French critics, including humanists like Cujas as well as Bartolists like Chasseneux, were bound by the contradictory rule that «the king of France has no superior in temporal things».[26] Although the

---

[25] *Juris universi distributio* [4.20], 71, remarking, «cum artes ac scientiae sint universorum: jus autem civile proprium sit unius civitatis», and (p. 73), «Jus civile, quod unius aut alterius civitatis est proprium, nec in arte cadit». He makes the point still more clearly in the *Methodus*, 107: «At illi juris civilis, id est, singularis cuiusdam civitatis artem tradere sunt conati, quam sapienter, non disputo: nihil tamen artis dignitate ac praestantia potuit alienus cogitari. omitto quam sit absurdum, ex Romanis legibus, quae paulo momento mutabiles fuerunt, de universo jure statuere velle».

[26] Chasseneux, *Catalogus gloriae mundi*, V, 28–29 (see note 4). «Habet multa jura et singularia privilegia, quae non habet alii principes» (f. 141r): the 208 *jura* listed, adding to the well known set compiled by Jean Ferrault, constitute a kind of empirical definition of sovereignty that anticipates Bodin's in many ways. (See the discussion in Mr. Franklin's paper.) His key *opiniones*, that «Imperator non est dominus mundi», and that «Rex Franciae [est] Princeps neminens recognoscens, et non subditus Imperatori», were intended directly to

doctrinal basis for this principle was canon law, much historical evidence could also be adduced to show that «the king of France was not subject to the emperor», as Chasseneux argued, and that consequently «the emperor was not lord of the world». Bodin was in agreement both with this and with his further declaration that the French king «has many unique privileges that other princes do not have», and presumably the reverse held as well. It was for precisely this reason that, in order to discuss a topic like «sovereignty» in general and philosophic terms, it was necessary to resort to a comparative method.

In more general terms, too, French legists had rejected the idea that the Roman tradition was universal. «There are many nations that have never been subject to the empire», declared Charles de Grassaille, «whence the most correct conclusion that the emperor was never in possession of the world».[27] This was a position that had been taken not only by generations of commentators but also, as Cosmo Guymier pointed out a century earlier, by many historians. And if Roman law could not claim universal jurisdiction, how much more circumscribed was that feudal law (the *Consuetudines feudorum)* sanctioned by the medieval German emperors? Not only were these customs without authority in civil (as well as French) law, charged Dumoulin, but the empire itself was merely a local institution.[28] This was quite in accord with Bodin's pluralistic views. What he did in his *Methodus*, in effect, was to transform this legal attitude into a methodological principle, that no national tradition could claim to represent humanity as a whole. It was essentially this Gallican view of the empire *(illa monarchia non fuit universalis* was the phrase of Chasseneux and Grassaille) that inspired Bodin to his attack upon the political and cultural imperialism of Rome, notably in his famous refutation of the theory of Four World Monarchies, though

---

contradict those expressed by such Italian jurists as ALCIATO *(In aliquot primae Digestorum ... titulos commentaria*, in *Opera*, I), who held that «Imperator est dominus torius orbis», and that «Rex Francorum recognoscat Imperatorem de jure in superiorem». For the medieval background (centering on Innocent III's *Per venerabilem*) see SERGIO MOCHI ONORY, Fonti canonistiche dell' idea moderno dello stato, Milan 1951, 96 ff.; F. CALASSO, I Glossatori et la teoria della Sovranità, Milan 1951; and GAINES POST, Studies in Medieval Legal Thought, Princeton 1964, 453 ff.

[27] *Regalium Franciae libri duo*, Paris 1545, 82, citing and repeating Chasseneux as well as Ferrault; cf. *Pragmatica sanctio glossata per Cosmam Guymier*, Lyon 1488, f. 1r: «Franci nulli umquam fuerunt subjecti in temporalibus, ut probatur ex antiquis historiis ...»

[28] *Commentarii in parisienses ... consuetudines*, in *Opera omnia*, Paris 1681, I, 22; cf. GRASSAILLE, *Regalium*, 106, «Leges seu consuetudines feudorum non habent locum in Francia.»

as always he provided his own perspective and supported his thesis with evidence of his own choosing.[29]

A most interesting corollary of this anti-universalist (and anti-imperialist) orientation of Gallicans was the common tendency among French jurists to make comparisons between civil law and institutions, ancient and modern, and those of French society. There were several obvious reasons for this: first because French lawyers were in fact trained in one law in the universities (or two, but the distinction between civil and canon laws was increasingly blurred) and obliged to practice another in many courts; second because civil law was the only feasible model for, and alternative or corrective to, French customary law (for which indeed it was *jus commune* in the so-called provinces of written law); third because customary law logically fit into the civilian category of *jus non scriptum* or *consuetudo* and was often discussed in that context; and fourth because of the growing need (and market) for polemic urging the independence and even the superiority of the French monarchy and its traditions. French historiographers had long argued that the «fortune and virtue» of their kings were not inferior to those of the Roman emperors, but this was little more literary convention; in the 16th century this contrast was given substance through the study of legal institutional history.[30] It was just during Bodin's lifetime, in fact, that there arose a new kind of work devoted to the comparison of particular French offices, institutions, and laws with their Roman counterparts, real or supposed. It may be useful to offer a few examples of this literature, which merits further investigation in its own right as well as background for Bodin's thought.

On the one hand, and perhaps on the lowest level, was the work of the French feudists, who naturally had recourse to civil law as a standard of judgment and as a source of terminology and perhaps supplementary illustrations. This was most conspicuously true of that «prince of legists» Dumoulin, who was a master of every sort of law and who interlaced

---

[29] *Methodus*, ch. VII. Another casualty of Bodin's argument was the old medieval notion of the «translation of empire». With regard to Germany this has been treated extensively by W. Goez, Translatio Imperii, Tübingen 1958, but the interesting fortunes of the idea in Renaissance France await investigation.

[30] A striking example of this is the work of Du Haillan, who continued the conventional themes of Gaguin and Paolo Emilio, most conspicuously in his *De la Fortune et vertu de la France*, Paris 1570, which was a kind of advance announcement for his history of France – and whose *De l'Estat et succez des affaires de France*, Paris 1570, the first comprehensive history of French institutions, carried the somewhat invidious comparison of France and Rome into this area.

his commentaries with references to contemporary practice *(hodie, apud nos . . .)*.[31] It was true as well of such lesser lights as Chasseneux and Tiraqueau, who were among the first to bring something of humanist culture (though little of the philological method) to the study of customary law. Tiraqueau showed a particularly broad interest in the customs and institutions of other societies, and his biographer has suggested that, despite his indifference to any kind of system, his attitude not only resembled but even heralded that of Bodin. Still more impressive, it seems to me, is the work of Chasseneux, who brought to bear upon the Burgundian custom a veritable encyclopedia of learning, philosophical and Biblical as well as historical and literary. His purpose was to enrich, perhaps to inflate, this vernacular text through comparisons with alien but logically similar concepts *(droits de justice* with the *jura meri imperii*, for example, and coutume itself with Roman conceptions of unwritten law).[32] He also tried to bring some order into customary law by the introduction (in Bartolist fashion) of Aristotelian categories such as genus and species for purposes of classification and the notion of final cause to explain the prooemium of this customal. Like Bodin, in short. Chasseneux took an «unhistorical» approach, and like Bodin, too, he could claim a certain philosophical justification.

A similar pattern may be seen still more clearly in another, less traditional, kind of legal literature that emerged in the 16th century which may best be described as handbooks of administration. Among the most interesting of these are Vincent de la Loupe's *Origin of Dignities*, Bernard du Haillan's *State and Success of Affairs in France*, Lancelot de la Popelinière's *Admiral of France*, René Choppin's *Treatise on the Domain of France*, and Jean Duret's *Comparison of Roman Magistrates with French Officers*, which may all be located somewhere between the genre of technical legal monographes (like Jean de Montaigne's work on the parliament of Paris) and conventional historiography (like Du Haillan's history of France).[33] For these works reference to the Roman experience was both

---

[31] This point, which also deserves further investigation, was made by Ralph Giesey [211], The Juristic Basis of Dynastic Right to the French Throne, Philadelphia 1961, a book which itself offers a useful study of comparative law (though this is not its main purpose) with respect to one major topic. On Tiraqueau see the remarks of Jacques Brejon, André Tiraqueau (1488–1558), Paris 1937, introduction and p. 345.

[32] *Consuetudines ducatus Burgundiae*, Frankfurt 1572, especially the prooemium. Chasseneux' work, too, would repay further investigation.

[33] The most striking, though by no means most significant, example is Jean Duret, *L'Harmonie et conference des magistrats Romains avec les offices François, tant laiz, que Ecclesiastiques. Ou succinctement est traicté de l'origine, progrez et iurisdiction d'un chacun, selon que les loix Civiles, Romaines, et Fran-*

a literary convention and a professional necessity, if not a conditioned reflex. Use of a «comparative method» ranged from such far-fetched analogies as that of the «Salic law» with the Roman *lex regia* to the most sophisticated discussions of judicial organizations or of fiscal resources or of the influence of foreign institutions.

Finally, there were the works of French civilians, especially the humanists, who strayed from the texts of Roman law into digressions or obiter dicta on French institutions. This tendency, which is already obvious in Budé's seminal *Annotations on the Digest,* is illustrated most clearly in Eguinaire Baron's little known «bipartite commentary» on Justinian's Institutes (1550), which contains parallel discussions of Roman and French laws and offices.[34] «To the Roman *princeps* we compare the king of France, who follows the same general pattern of establishing and promulgating laws», he wrote, going on to compare the imperium with *haute justice,* for example, as well as to point out certain unique institutions, such as the Roman *patria potestas* and French laws of succession. Similar in intention, but considerably more schematic, were the various attempts to shape French law directly into a Roman mold, as in Pasquier's *Interpretation of the Institutes of Justinian* and in Louis le Caron's *Pandects of French Law,* which originated as a plan to translate the Digest but which ended as a treatise on comparative law. The same impulse may be seen in Le Caron's pioneering edition of the *Grand Customal of France.* Perhaps the best illustration of all is Hotman's notorious *Anti-Tribonian,* which revealed at length the fundamental differences between Roman and French society and, in its own invidious fashion, brilliantly applied a comparative method to a set of problems involving both legal reform and the interpretation of history.[35]

Many of the intellectual habits underlying such works were shared by Bodin, but as usual they were transformed and adapted to his more

---

çoises l'ont permis, sans obmission de l'histoire aux lieux propres ..., Lyons 1574, which, despite its patriotic tone does not hesitate to reject the theory of Trojan origins (f. 9v); among the authorities cited are included not only Grassaille and Gaguin, but also Budé, Le Douaren, and (f. 6v) «Cujacius et Hotomanus, duo amplissimo veteris ac novae jurisprudentia lumina».

[34] *Institutionum civilium ab Justiniano Caesare editarum libri IIII,* Poitou 1550, in tit. and IX. (p. 6, 32). Most interesting of all is the work of Louis Le Caron, who was at once a student of Baudouin and, with respect to customary law, of Dumoulin; I am publishing a fuller investigation of this scholar.

[35] It should be remarked that the «comparatist» point of view was inherent in the century old search for «Tribonianisms», which assumed a fundamental disagreement between classical Roman and Byzantine law (and society as well); indispensable for this subject is Luigi Palazzini Finetti, Storia della ricerca della interpolazioni nel corpus iuris giustinianeo, Milan 1953.

transcendent purposes. What he wanted was not simply to make comparisons between French and Roman institutions but to inquire into those of a multitude of societies and eventually to construct a legal system that would encompass them all. Just as one obtained a knowledge of a species through the investigation of individual specimens, so one could attain a knowledge of universal law through positive law – that is, of the *jus naturale* through the *jus gentium*.[36] In other words, just as Pico assumed that every philosophical or religious tradition reflected one aspect of a general and transcendent truth, so Bodin seemed to assume that the customs and laws of particular societies reflected, however imperfectly, one aspect of an ideal jurisprudence. The ultimate aim of Bodin's comparative method, it may be inferred, was likewise to achieve a kind of «perennial philosophy».

This may suggest something of the breadth of Bodin's vision, the profusion of his ideas, and perhaps the flexibility of his standards. Bodin had moved entirely beyond, and evidently lost interest in, the conventional dichotomy of the *mores gallicus* and *italicus* and indeed that between the *grammatici* and the *pragmatici*; and he admired scholars of both humanist and Bartolist persuasion. As examples of the first he commended Baron and Connan, of the second Tiraqueau, Chasseneux, and Dumoulin. In one way or another they all combined formal knowledge with practical experience. But Bodin, needless to say, demanded still more, and no wonder Gentili threw up his hands. According to the composite portrait presented in the *Methodus*, the perfect jurist was a living encyclopedia possessing at once a knowledge of history and philosophy, an understanding of natural law and equity, a familiarity with the commentators, a competence in both Latin and Greek philology, and above all a proper «method» to organize this refractory mass of material.[37] Given such an intellectual appetite and given a special interest in public law, it was obvious that legal sources alone were insufficient and that only an intense investigation of the past would supply information about the *jus gentium* in Bodin's sense of the term. *In historia juris universi pars optima latet:* it was this axiom that, the essence of universal law would be found in history, that led Bodin to formulate his iconoclastic and yet curiously dogmatic *Method of History*.

---

[36] Bodin's statement of the method he wanted to follow in order to rise from the particular to the universal, that is, from history to political science, appears at the beginning of *Methodus*, ch. VI, which is essentially an early draft of the *Republic:* «utile visum mihi est, ad eam quam instituto methodum, philosophorum et historicorum de Republica disputationes inter se et majorum imperia, cum nostris comparare, ut omnibus inter se collatis, universa Rerum publicarum historia planius intelligatur».

[37] *Methodus*, 108–9.

IV. Bodin: Philosophistoricus

In this pivotal work, which looked at once back to his humanist sources of inspiration and forward to his system of political and social philosophy, Bodin set out to redefine the traditional «art of history». Unlike Baudouin he was not much interested in historical method in a modern sense, in *Quellenforschung* and *Quellenkritik*, and he never even distinguished very consistently between history as object *(actio)* and history as subject *(narratio)*. The main reason for this is that he was concerned not with the writing but with the reading of history: how to «pluck the flowers of history» and then arrange them in the best pattern, or in another image, how to extract from history its medicinal value. Although history was itself a form of memory, it could not in Bodin's view be grasped and retained by individuals in chronological order, that is, in its temporal disorder; it had to be arranged not according to the form of human experience *(ordo temporum* or *naturalis* in the conventional medieval formula*)* but rather according to the form of human reason *(ordo artificialis)*.[38] Although history in a sense already held a position «above all sciences» *(supra scientias omnes)*, it had itself to be converted into a science by the imposition of a rigidly logical «method». Although history retained its connection with the trivium in Bodin's view, its partner was not grammar or rhetoric (as for Baudouin and most other humanists) but rather dialectic.

It was inevitable that the form taken by Bodin's method should be pedagogical, or rather, since the principal aim was «to assist the memory», mnemonic. More specifically, he adopted the model of humanist logic, with its emphasis on topical distribution for handy reference for the resolution of particular problems; and his purpose was literally to define historical commonplaces *(loci communes)* and, without much regard for context, to relocate historical evidence in a rational or at least utilitarian way. The almost obsessively analytical character of Bodin's thought may be suggested by one of those diagrams to popular in dialectical, legal, and even historical works of Bodin's age.[39] Although

---

[38] *Methodus*, 116: «Principio adhibeatur praestans illa docendarum artium magistra, quae dicitur analysis: quae universum in partes secare, et partis cujusque particulas rursus dividere, totiusque ac partium cohaerentiam quasi concentum inter ipsa mira facultate docet.» Cf. Baudouin, *De Institutione*, 38; and in general, Marie Schulz, Die Lehre von der historischen Methode, Berlin 1909, 98 ff.

[39] The accompanying diagrams (see p. 148-149) are somewhat simplified analyses of the basic argument of the three principal works discussed here (and of the *Methodus* by itself). The pattern is particularly clear in chapter III («De Locis

Bodin did not here follow the rigidly bifurcating pattern of Ramus in the *Methodus*, he did move from large to small categories by making distinctions and sub-distinctions, with the expectation, at least in theory, of arriving eventually at the smallest units of historical discourse, that is, the plans, works, and deeds of individual men. For Bodin, then, history was to be methodized by rearrangement into parallel and proliferating sets of categories, or rather topics, which would ultimately accomodate not merely arguments (as in humanist logic) but the phenomena of history itself. The result may not have been a «philosophy of history», but it was a very impressive looking conceptual aid.

Like Baudouin, Bodin made a fundamental distriction between universal and particular history. In this he was following not only the Polybian and Eusebian pattern but also the current conviction of Protestant historians that «history was to encompass all ages», as Melanchthon put it, that it should provide a« portrait of the human race».[40] This fashion was introduced into the «arts of history» by Christophe Milieu, who offered what was perhaps the most comprehensive of all descriptions of the *universitas* of history during that century, making room for social, political, and cultural history *(prudentia, principatus,* and *sapientia,* including *historia literaturae)* as well as natural history. Bodin made a similar analysis, but he related these stages of development to various levels of the human will *(voluntas)*, which related first to the problem of sustinence *(necessitas)*, then to comfort *(commoditas)*, and finally to the products of leisure *(splendor* and *voluptas)*.[41] These motives, taken together with the social and political devices for accomplishing them, constituted the general rubrics under which the stories of particular nations could all be fitted.

One of Bodin's principal disciples complained that he «should have thrown more light upon particular history rather than digressing so upon universal history».[42] Yet in a sense the Bodin of the *Methodus* was interested more in the species than in the genera of the historical world, more in the variety than in the uniformity of human nature, and perhaps

---

historiarum recte instituendis»). What follows here is largely a commentary on this teaching aid which I have extraced from Bodin's writings. It may be added that this sort of diagram was very common in Bodin's age, not only in the works of logicians like Ramus, but of jurists like Hotman (*Tabulae de criminibus* of 1543) and of authors of *artes historicae,* notably that of G. J. Vossius, *Ars historica,* Leiden 1623 (diagram C).

[40] Preface to *Chronicon Carionis,* in his *Opera (Corpus Reformatorum,* XII, col. 705 ff.). In general, see Adalbert Klempt, Die Säkularisierung der universalhistorischen Auffassung, Göttingen 1960 [205].

[41] Mylaeus, *De Scribenda universita rerum historia,* Basel 1551.

[42] La Popelinière, *Idee de l'histoire,* Paris 1599, 29.

more in the texture than in the structure of history. For his intelligible unit of study was not humanity but the national group. This was one reason why he was determined to demolish that myth of imperial historians, the theory of Four World Monarchies, which had established both a false universalism and a false uniformity of perspective. At the same time Bodin distrusted the particular national perspectives which arose from pride and ignorance. It was the question of national origins that furnished perhaps the most fertile field for the cultivation of legend and violation of chronology – and also for the exercise of historical criticism. In theory, that is, for in practice Bodin was still under the influence of the Celtic enthusiasm of the mid-16th century, which had touched scholars like Pasquier and moved Connan to suggest that even feudal institutions were by origin Gallic rather than German.[43] But the significant thing about Bodin's work was the continuing plea for a concentrated and controlled reading of the best historians.

Perhaps the most crucial, and certainly the most characteristic, aspect of Bodin's theory of history was his view of causation. Like Baudouin, Milieu, and others, he made a basic distinction between human and natural (leaving aside divine) history, corresponding of course to the three kinds of law. Unlike them he did not mind letting the human and natural spheres overlap, nor did he hesitate to introduce occult factors. There were three ways of accounting for the variety of human nature, Chasseneux declared: that of the orthodox theologians (especially the Sorbonists), who attributed them simply to inherent qualities of the soul; that of the philosopheres and physiologists, who referred them to particular «complexions» which in turn were functions of the humors; and that of the astrologists – which Chasseneux rejected – who traced them to the influence of the climata and location under the celestial sphere.[44] There was of course nothing revolutionary in bringing «natural» explanations into the field of human behavior. On the contrary, as Chasseneux

---

[43] *Methodus*, 247. Cf. Pasquier, *Recherches de la France*, I, 3; and Connan, *Commentarii*, II, 9. There is need for a study of this Celtic movement of the 1550's, noted briefly by Mesnard [4.20], 37, n. 10; there are some remarks in R. E. Asher [186], The Attitude of French Writers of the Renaissance to Early French History (University of London, unpubl. Ph. D. thesis, 1955).

[44] *Catalogus gloriae mundi*, X; «Prima opinio est philosophantium et medicorum, quo complexioni attribuunt excellentiam ingenii ... Secunda ergo opinio, dicentium complexiones insequi climata et diversitatem coeli ... Omissa ergo opinione astrologorum, quae somnia et phantasmata recitat, ad tertiam opinionem veram, quae est theologorum, maxime Parisiensem, qui determinaverunt unam animam in naturalibus esse alia perfectiorem et excellentiorem, cui determinatione standum est.» And X, 18: «Scire est per causas cognoscere ... Legistae et canonistae cognoscunt per causas et rationes.»

and Coras stipulated, one of the basic characteristics of legal science was that it interpreted its subject in such terms, that is, *scire per causas,* which was a standard definition for science. But Bodin's conception of cause took him further and led him indeed into forbidden territory. Using the deterministic concepts of ancient (and medieval) medicine and astrology, Bodin sketched out a «geohistorical» science, which contained elements of anthropology and ethnography as well as sociology, and which seemed to fulfill the demand, made five years earlier by Baudouin, for an alliance between geography and history.[45]

In general Bodin's *Methodus* constituted an attempt to reduce the field of history to a hierarchical and branching set of topics in which historical information could be stored for use. The pattern may be quite simply diagrammed and the ingeniousness as well as the ambiguities this displayed. «History» itself he defined in three ways, or rather on three levels, though neither entirely explicitly nor entirely unequivocally. Most generally it was a true narrative *(vera narratio)*, and it could be pursued, as far as humanity is concerned, either on a universal plane or on a particular plane, that is, the history of nations, *(maximae respublicae)*, of cities *(minimae respublicae)*, or biography *(res gestae virorum)*. Secondly, history had to be understood from the point of view of the reader of the narration *(as cognitio)*, and this of course, as the principle subject of the book, required its own peculiar distribution. This included first the choosing *(delectus)* and classifying *(ordo et collectio)* of historical works in order to establish a basic reading list; and second the criticism *(judicium)* of these authors in terms of the auxiliary sciences of geography and chronology and in the light of what modern scholarship had to say about such problems as the theory of Four World Monarchies and myths of national origins. In these two ways Bodin discussed what may be called the subjective side of «history».

But the problem of historical knowledge was not one which Bodin was interested in pursuing further; and it was history in its third sense, history as «action» not thought (*res non verba*, in the conventional classical topos), that was to preoccupy him. The main thrust of his interest was clearly in the sphere of human action *(res humanae)*;[46] and the train of thought leading to the *Republic* appears unmistakeably in the third and sixth chapters. The mechanism of history is explained here as the drive of human will toward increasingly civilized goals: that of indivi-

---

[45] *De Institutione*, 181. In general, M. J. TOOLEY [183], Bodin and the Mediaeval Theory of Climate, *Speculum* 28 (1953), 64–83; and A. MEUTEN, Bodins Theorie von der Beeinflussung des politischen Lebens der Staaten durch ihre geographische Lage, Bonn 1904 [58].

[46] Cf. BAUDOUIN, *De Institutione,* opening and closing paragraphs.

dual man toward the necessities of life and that of man in communities toward the comforts and pleasures of life, hence toward a political organization *(respublica)* that can insure these. Thence Bodin moved to the question of political power (the *imperium),* its distribution and administration (through *concilium* and *executio),* and the complex social and cultural pattern underlying it. Such were the categories of human action (including *consilia* and *dicta* as well as *acta*) in which historical knowledge, after being analysed, was to be deposited. For Bodin, in short, history was to be transformed into an applied science.

Whatever the source of inspiration for his logical analysis, it seems clear that jurisprudence remained the principal model for Bodin's codification of history. Both history and law were conventionally equated with wisdom («the knowledge of things human and divine»),[47] and it was natural that Bodin, like Baudouin, should want to bring the two into closer alignment. The difference was that Bodin set out to impose his own almost totalitarian format on both. In both cases he began with a general definition and then distinguished its parts (*jus quit sit, ejus divisio; quid historia sit et quotuplex);* in both cases he recognized three principle types (human, natural, and divine) and a particular as well as universal form (corresponding to national and universal history was *jus civile* and *jus gentium*); in both cases he made a fundamental distinction between private and public (in history between man in community and man as citizen); and in both cases he wanted to find a scheme that would exhaust the substance of his subject (individual *leges* and, in a broad sense, individual *actiones*).[48] In general it is hard to disagree with the conclusion of one of Bodin's most devoted disciples that he was a «theoretical historian» *(historien contemplatif)* and that his book was in fact not a method of history at all but rather «method of law».[49]

---

[47] Ulpian in Digest, 1, 1, 10: «Iuris prudentia est divinarum atque humanarum rerum notitia.» The Ciceronian formula was «sapientia est rerum humanarum divinarumque scientia» – on which see Eugene Rice, The Renaissance Idea of Wisdom, Cambridge, Mass. 1958; it was applied to history, e.g., by Baudouin, *De Institutione*, 9.

[48] Cf. *Juris universi distributio* [4.20], 72–73.

[49] La Popelinière, *Histoire des histoires,* Paris 1599, 28, and see note 42. It may be noted that La Popelinière carried on, in several works, Bodin's concern with geo-history.

V. Bodin: Politicus

A «philosophistorian», according to Bodin, was one who combined the narration of facts with precepts of wisdom.»[50] If we add that Bodin ultimately hoped to dissolve narrative history altogether in his philosophic concoction, this prescription more than fits his work. Given his hyper-rationalizing tendencies and his overriding interest in public law (already evident in the *Methodus*), it is not surprising that he should have left behind the earth-bound concerns of historical scholarship (marginal as they were for him in any case) and moved into the higher sphere of political science *(civilis disciplina)*. And so to his collection of models Bodin added that of political philosophy, and especially Aristotle's. He proceeded with his usual idiosyncrasy, refusing either to be bound by Aristotle's conclusions or to discard any of the material he had accumulated previously; as before he simply moved on to a larger set of categories to accomodate his sources. At the same time, needless to say, the events of the 1560's and the early 1570's tended to sharpen his interest in, while modifying his views about, some of the more explosive issues of politics. Such was the path by which Bodin approached his *Republic*, the first comprehensive study of political science, as Bodin saw it, of modern times.

Among modern authors Bodin found few worthy of consideration and only Machiavelli deserving of praise – and even then rather for his pioneering effects that for his actual accomplishments. The similarities between these men have often been pointed out, but as Bodin himself suggested, the divergences may be more fundamental, especially by the time the *Republic* appeared (1576), when Machiavelli's name had become a synonym for hypocrisy, tyranny, and atheism. Yet there was more to Bodin's charge that Machiavelli identified political science with tyrannical and irreligion ruses than simply the fashionable anti-Machiavellianism of the aftermath of St Bartholomew.[51] For Bodin was also, at least implicitly, objecting to the narrowness of Machiavelli's intellectual horizons and to the superficiality of his conception of politics. Although

---

[50] *Methodus*, 138: «Ut autem Geographistorici regiones cum historia: sic Philosophistorici rerum gestarum narrationem cum sapientiae praeceptis cumularent.»

[51] *Methodus*, 167; cf. preface to the first edition of the *Republic*, translated by KENNETH D. MCRAE in the introduction (A 70) to his edition, Cambridge, Mass., 1962 [7.44]. The view that Bodin was a «disciple» of Machiavelli was taken by CHAUVIRÉ [76], 207, among others. The contrast between the two I have elaborated upon in: Murd'rous Machiavel in France, *Political Science Quarterly* 85 (1970), 545–559.

Bodin and Machiavelli agreed upon some of the grand themes of political philosophy, such as the Polybian *anacyclosis*, and certainly shared the goal of constructing an intelligible science of politics, their modes of perceiving political reality were basically different and their respective methods in some ways irreconcilable.

The reasons for this go deeper than Bodin's obsession with system. To begin with there is an obvious contrast between their life situations. While Machiavelli was a political activist always concerned, directly or indirectly, with policy-making questions, Bodin never held comparable responsible office near the center of power, which seemed not only distant but, in keeping with official ideology, almost sacramental in character. While Machiavelli looked instinctively to the psychology of his fellow citizens, Bodin looked to the inherited traditions and the complex of institutions that circumscribed the actions of Frenchmen. It may be suspected, too, that whereas Machiavelli never lost his faith in the efficacy of individual action, Bodin naturally took a more pessimistic view – if not because of the political inertia of a structure as large and complex as the French monarchy, then surely because of the traumatic experiences of the religious wars. Most important of all, while Machiavelli had enjoyed military as well as diplomatic and administrative experience (and never distinguished too sharply between the arts of politics and of war), Bodin was a professional jurist little interested in diplomatic maneuvering and warfare (one of the few subjects, indeed, in which he was content to follow Machiavelli). In general Bodin worked in a much richer – and more inhibiting – context of legal, historical, and philosophical erudition, and he was by training and nature, if not by nationality, unable to separate politics from its legal and social environment.

In terms of method, then, Bodin and Machiavelli were literally worlds apart. As Bodin's most perceptive commentator summed it up. «The *Republic* is the work not so much of a great politique as of a great legist, the work of a successor not of Machiavelli but of Beaumanoir and Bartolus.»[52] Machiavelli's tendency was to concentrate upon individual motives and strategies, on discrete and even interchangeable factors, and on linear causal sequences. He viewed institutions, constitutional as well as religious, in a functional manner. He sought and usually found simple answers to simple questions; if not he could always take refuge in the old notion of fortune. And in applying the lessons of history he was normally content with easy analogies and accepted Roman experience as a sufficient model. By contrast Bodin could not discuss political change

---

[52] Moreau-Reibel [116], Jean Bodin et le droit public comparé, Paris 1933, 135.

without becoming involved in questions of social structure and relationships. Like Machiavelli he was concerned with questions of power, but for him this entailed private as well as public law, which meant the whole web of society from the family through the various corporate groups, social classes, and administrative hierarchy up to the central government. Between the citizen and the prince, in short, there were many gradations which obscured the lines of force and which greatly complicated the analysis of political transformation. Moreover, he assumed that any political situation or institution had to be understood in terms of a total social structure, a specific geographic milieu, a variety of customs, and a particular national tradition, if not (as in the case of France) a multiplicity of traditions.

As Walter Ullmann remarked about the medieval civilians, «By viewing law as a social phenomenon, medieval jurisprudence was forced to elucidate some basic principles about society, and thus was led to consider topics which, under modern conditions, would be dealt with, not by the lawyer, but by the sociologist.»[53] It was this school of thought above all that distinguished Bodin from Machiavelli – and established him as one of the founders of modern social science.

VI. Bodin: Dominus Factotum

In sum, to judge from the three works discussed here, it was Bodin's intention to do for the *jus gentium* in a general sense what medieval commentators had tried to do for the *jus civile,* that is, to rationalize it, to resolve conflicts and inequities, and to adapt it to contemporary problems; and ultimately he hoped thereby to formulate a social ideal that would approximate the *jus naturale.* Clearly, it was such an ideal, rather than any deep sympathy for humanist or legal erudition, that led him to his total attack upon history, to his search for underlying physical and especially geographical, principles underlying history, to his reassessment of Aristotelian political philosophy, and to his renowned «comparative method», if such indeed it was. In fact his method, to judge from the *Republic*, seems designed mainly to keep all restrictions off the riot of learning which he had gathered. Accepting no «law of citations», he was able to combine legal and philosophical «authorities» with historical and geographical evidence and so to disregard any distinction between historical inference and political generalization, which often

---

[53] The Medieval Idea of Law as Represented by Lucas of Penna, London 1946, 163.

meant between descriptive and normative statements.[54] A curious and confused sort of «empiricism», reminiscent rather of a scholastic than a comparative approach. To this extent, indeed, it may be suggested that Bodin did not altogether escape the utopian impulse.

So we return, again and finally, to the somewhat unearthly quality of Bodin's thought. He ignored the standards of established «disciplines». He rejected, too, the temporal limitations of human history and tried to fix the accumulated experience of humanity into a transcendent system. These characteristics may help to explain how, to one trying to assess the historical significance of Bodin's thought, he seems to be a man belonging to several ages. On the one hand he appears to have the scholastic philosopher's unhistorical and indiscriminate attitude toward his authorities and his faith that an ideal system may be assembled merely by the proper arrangement and criticism of these. On the other hand he sometimes seems, as in his discussion of feudal institutions, to be attempting to find the «spirit of the laws» (*mens legum* was a civilian expression which in fact did imply an ideal, since it referred to the intention or spirit as distinct from the letter of the law)[55] through the comparison of the customs of various societies. In this sense Bodin may be regarded as a significant member of that as yet untraced tradition of social thought leading from the legists of the middle ages to the philosophes of the 18th century – a prime mover in that shifting of the Heavenly City (according to Carl Becker's notorious thesis) to its «earthly foundations». The author of a veritable «Summa of political philosophy», as Henri Baudrillart declared over a century ago, Bodin was nevertheless a «Montesquieu of the 16th century».[56]

This has been only a provisional discussion, but perhaps it may suggest ways of bringing together some of the disparate features of Bodin's thought and of resolving some of the contradictions which many commentators (though not Bodin himself) have found in his work. As the papers of this conference (especially those of Messrs. Giesey and Reulos and Mme Isnardi Parente) have made abundantly clear, Bodin had access to a practically unlimited range of sources as well as to the

---

[54] More specifically, I doubt that Bodin's use of legal citations in the *Republic* is any more orthodox than his discussion of the art of history (in the rhetorical tradition) is in the *Methodus*. This seems to me to be a fundamental and unanswered question: not what his sources were, but what he thought (or assumed) their function was in his system.

[55] See NICOLAS VALLA, *De Rebus dubiis* ... (in *Tractatus universi juris*, XVIII, f. 317v): «Mens ergo legis nihil aliud est, quam sententia et ratio ejus manifesta, ex qua vel obscura, vel ambigua ipsius legis dispositio declaratur, aut generalis et indefinitiva expenditur, aut restringitur.»

[56] BAUDRILLART [27], J. Bodin et son temps, Paris 1853, 109.

Diagram A.

Bodin's Method of History

- HISTORIA
  - I. narratio
    - humana
      - universa (communis)
        - origines [II.
        - eluviones
        - initia rerumpub. & religionum
      - singularis
        - maximae respublicae: Caldaei ..., Graeci, Romani, Germani ..., Americani
        - minimae respublicae: Rhodes ..., Venetia, Florentia
        - res gestae virorum
    - naturalis
    - mathematica
      - geographia
      - chorographia
      - topographia
      - geometria
    - divina
  - III. actiones
    - res humanae (voluntas) Civilis disciplina
      - homo singularis
      - societas
        - necessitas
          - ad tuendam vitam: agricultura, aedificatio, etc
        - commoditas
          - istitoria, fabriles artes, etc
        - splendor
          - ad cultum et victum splendiorem ...
        - voluptas
          - pictura, statuaria, etc
      - Respublica
        - imperium
          - magistrati
          - leges
          - bellum
          - poena
            - ars imperatoria
            - jurisprudentia
            - ars oratoria
            - religio
        - concilium
          - de vectigalibus [VI.
          - de exercitu cogendo
          - de legationibus
          - de propugnaculis
        - executio
          - necessitas ...
          - commoditas ...
          - splendor ...
          - munera civiles (7): militia ..., magistrati
    - res naturales (per causas)
    - res divinae
  - cognitio
    - IV. historicorum delectus
      - informatus
        - a natura
        - a doctrina
        - a natura & doctrina
      - veritas
        - oratores
          - laudatio
          - vituperatio
        - historici
          - de aliena recuspub.
          - de sua rebus pub.
      - ordo
        - universalis
          - historici [X.
          - geographistorici
        - ecclesiastica
          - paganae
          - Christianae
          - secta Arabica
        - particularis
          - Caldaei, Graeci, Galli, etc
        - coloni
        - vires singulares
    - V. judicium
      - natura
        - populi
          - loci (& cael.)
            - Africani
            - media regio
            - Scythae
          - corporis forma
          - humores
          - mores
        - loci
          - terrae
          - res sub sensum
          - calor
          - pestes
        - disciplina
          - divina
          - humana
            - humanitas
            - militaris disciplina
            - religio
            - philosophia
            - geometria
            - arithmetica
            - astrologia
        - VII. refutatio IV monarchia
      - VIII. tempus
        - origo, finis
        - series
        - IX. origo populorum
          - argumenta
          - historia
          - lingua
          - geographia

Diagram C

Vossius: SYNOPSIS

- Historiae & historices
  - vox, cap. I
  - res ipsa
    - natura artis
      - an sit
        - ἁπλῶς, cap. II
        - restricte, an ab aliis artibus distincta sit, cap. III
      - quid sit, ubi de materia & forma, cap. IV
      - causae externae
        - finales, cap. V
        - efficientes, sive primi historiae scriptores, cap. VI
      - distributio
        - historiae, cap. VII
        - historices, cap. VIII
    - artis praecepta. Hic exponitur historiae
      - fundamentum: cujus leges
        - nequid falsi dicere audeamus, cap. IX
        - nequid veri non audeamus, cap. X
      - structura: cujus traditur
        - materia quadruplex
          - narratio
            - totius corporis
              - rei gestae unius. Haec consideratur
                - ratione totius, cap. XI
                - secundum partem aliquam: nempe
                  - personam, cap. XII
                  - actionem, cap. XIII
                  - locum & tempus, cap. XIV
                  - occasionem, modum & eventum, cap. XV
              - imperii unius, omnis aevi — cap. XVI
            - unius hominis, cap. XVII
          - judicium: de quo
            - universe, cap. XVIII
            - ratione Sententiarum, cap. XIX
          - conciones, cap. XX & XXI
          - digressiones, cap. XXII
        - dispositio: ubi spectatur
          - prooemium, cap. XXIII
          - ordo in narrando, cap. XXIV
          - divisio in libros, cap. XXV
        - expositio: ubi in considerationem venit
          - an doctrina ejus necessaria sit, cap. XXVI
          - quae virtutes ejus communes: uti sunt
            - puritas & perspicuitas, cap. XXVII
            - ornatus & decorum, cap. XXVIII
          - ut historicae locutio differat
            - ab oratoria, cap. XXIX
            - a poetica, cap. XXX

Corollarium, de virtutibus in historico requisitis, cap. XXXI

Diagram B follows on the next two pages.

VIII

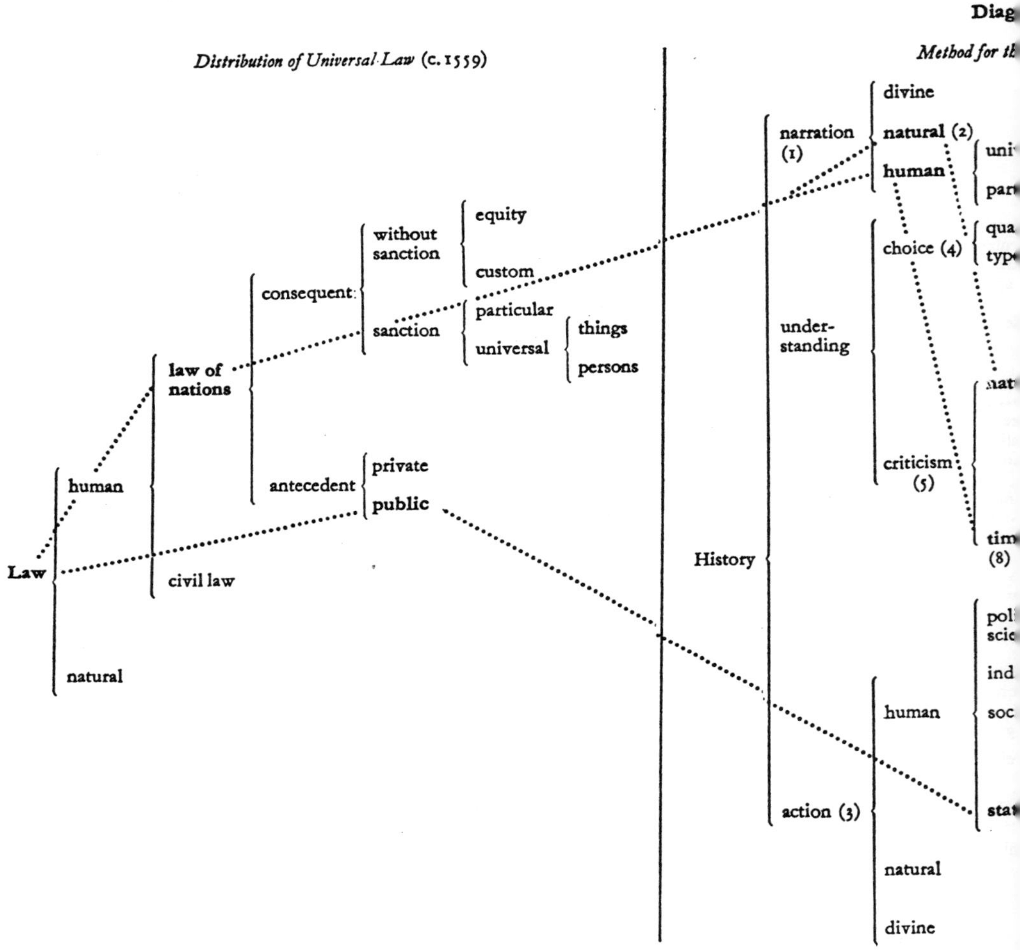
Distribution of Universal Law (c. 1559)
Law
human
natural
law of nations
civil law
consequent
antecedent
without sanction
sanction
equity
custom
particular
universal
things
persons
private
public
History
narration (1)
under-standing
action (3)
divine
natural (2)
human
choice (4)
criticism (5)
human
natural
divine
(8)

VIII

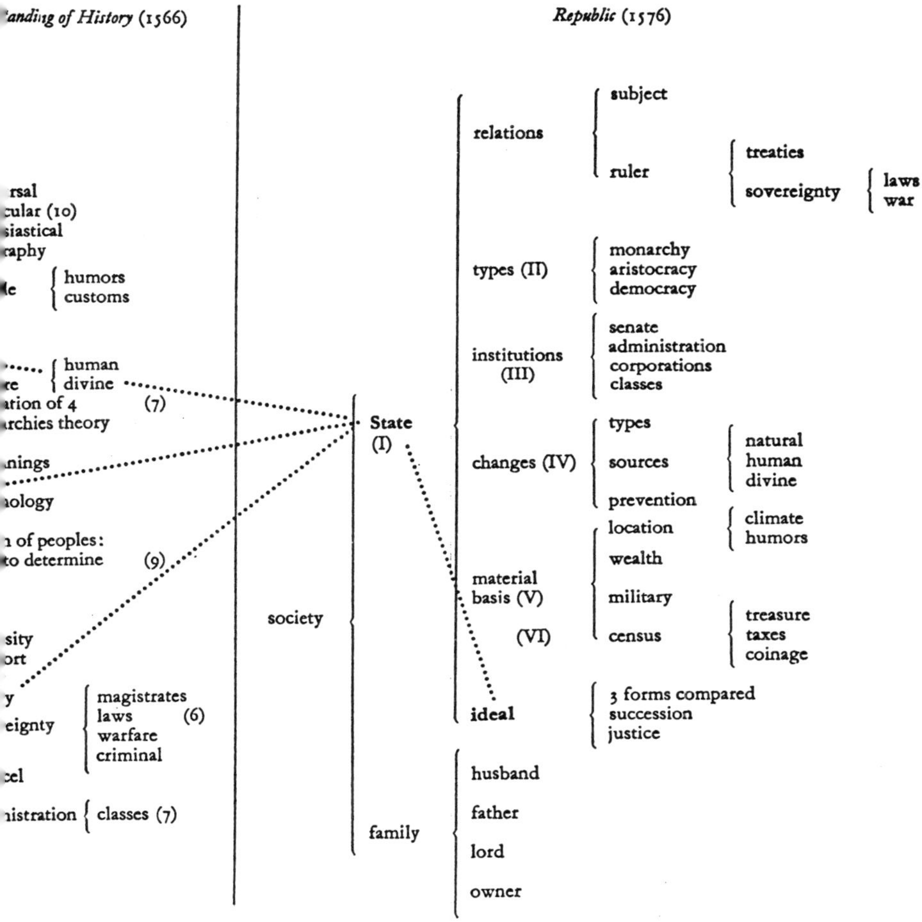

…anding of History (1566)
Republic (1576)
…rsal
…cular (10)
…siastical
…raphy
…le
humors
customs
…
…re
human
divine
…ation of 4
…archies theory
(7)
…nings
…iology
…n of peoples:
…to determine
(9)
…sity
…ort
…y
…eignty
magistrates
laws
warfare
criminal
(6)
…cel
…istration
classes (7)
society
State
(I)
family
relations
subject
ruler
treaties
sovereignty
laws
war
types (II)
monarchy
aristocracy
democracy
institutions
(III)
senate
administration
corporations
classes
changes (IV)
types
sources
prevention
natural
human
divine
material
basis (V)
location
wealth
military
census
climate
humors
treasure
taxes
coinage
(VI)
ideal
3 forms compared
succession
justice
husband
father
lord
owner

most challenging political and social paradoxes of modern times. Yet it is no less obvious that Bodin entertained an almost compulsive monism that drove him to accommodate this personal and vicarious experience in a single and coherent system.

This has been reflected in part by Bodin's fascination with the «old metaphysics of order» (as Mr. Greenleaf put it) and in the new logic of Ramus (as Mr. McRae has shown), with ancient notions of harmony (as Mr. Villey has explained) and with modern notions of tolerance through the reconciliation of opposites (as Mr. Roellenbleck has argued). Above all it has been exemplified by Bodin's struggles to reconcile old ideas of corporate and «constitutional» order with with a new view of absolute sovereignty (as has been indicated in different ways by Messrs. Salmon, Franklin, Polin, Scheuner, and others). To what extent particular works may be reconciled with Bodin's general though changing system may be debated, but (as I myself believe) his last and most neglected work, the *Theater of Universal Nature,* shows that his systematizing urge never deserted him. To set for himself such transcendent goals Bodin must indeed have cast himself in the role of prophet (as Mr. Baxter has suggested) if not of sorcerer. Nor can I think of any more plausible way of accounting for the wonder, suspicious as well as worshipful, which Bodin has inspired in generations of scholars down to the present day, present company included.

IX

LOUIS LE CARON PHILOSOPHE

"To jurisprudence," Giambattista Vico liked to point out, "the Romans gave the same name as the Greeks gave to wisdom, 'the knowledge of things divine and human.' "[1] In this celebrated formula, repeated hundreds of times over the preceding fifteen centuries, we have a statement both of the significance of jurisprudence for the history of thought in general and of the theme of this essay in particular. Too often legal scholarship has been regarded as a forbiddingly technical and professional subject without redeeming intellectual value, but such was by no means always the case, especially not in antiquity and again, at least in some circles, in the Renaissance. As a result largely of the humanist movement and the revival of classical ideals the study of law in many schools became less technical and more immediately meaningful than philosophy. In several senses jurisprudence was "humanized" : it combined with the *studia humanitatis* in the curriculum (and in sixteenth-century France was often little more than a major subject within the liberal arts course), it was normally taken to be a part of moral philosophy, and according to several classifications of learning it was incorporated into the humanist "encyclopedia."[2] It is in such terms that jurisprudence has, from Valla to Vico, had a significant, though not always immediately apparent impact upon history of ideas.

What made this impact especially deep and enduring is the historical fact that the study of law, mainly civil law, provided a major source—perhaps the major source—of secular, higher education for European

---

[1] *De Universi juris uno principio et fine uno,* ed. F. Nicolini (Bari, 1936), "Proloquium." See n. 9.

[2] Budé, *Annotationes ... in quatuor et viginti Pandectarum libros* (Paris, 1535), f. III, "... studium nunc iuris prorsus ab antiquo veroque degenerasse, nisi vero arbitrabimur philosophiam, id est studium sapientiae ..." Alciato, *Praetermissa,* in *Opera omnia* (Basel, 1582), IV, 250 : "Cum enim in jure multa sint quae sine cognitione studiorum humanitatis percipi nequeant ..." Cf. Poliziano, *Panepistemon,* in *Opera omnia* (Basel, 1553), 428. See also diagram of Le Caron.

society as a whole. "The prime role of lawyers in starting humanism in Italy" was pointed out by Roberto Weiss;[3] it should be added that they played a role also in extending and preserving humanism outside of Italy. In sixteenth-century France no other professional group is anywhere near so well represented among publishing authors, and perhaps among readers as well. There was a whole class of lay intellectuals, especially office-holders, who had studied law mainly as a branch of literature or philosophy, but who had little to do with it in a professional way. Through such men law helped to shape the language and the thought of society in general, though again the detection and tracing of such influence would be a challenging and Herculean labor, and indeed has never been seriously attempted.

More obvious and accessible is the subject defined by Prof. Kristeller as "the philosophical significance of the legal tradition."[4] Yet this topic is also one which has never been fully appreciated, it seems to me, except perhaps in the field of political thought. For within the study of law there were various powerful philosophical impulses: toward the discovery of a useful "method," toward the establishment of a suitable epistemology, toward the rational understanding of social behavior, and in general toward a structured view of the world. Civil law was a "science" by definition, since it tried "to understand things in terms of causes," [5] and at the same time it made a fundamental distinction between the world of nature (which was eternal and where general rules applied) and the world of society (which was mutable and where positive law applied). What is more, civil law furnished the motive and even the model for a number of encyclopedic schemes, notably those of Barthélemy de Chasseneux, Grégoire de Toulouse, Jean Bodin, and Le Caron himself.[6] It was not only Plato and Aristotle, in other words, not only Descartes and his contemporaries, who encouraged the philosophical system-building of modern times. Legal scholarship contributed in particular to the early creations of social science, from Bodin to Vico and Montesquieu, and in general helped to preserve a continuity between the "encyclopedic" thought of the

---

[3] *The Dawn of Humanism in Italy* (London, 1947), 5.

[4] *Renaissance Philosophy and the Medieval Tradition* (Latrobe, Penn., 1966), 43.

[5] Barthélemy de Chasseneux, *Catalogus gloriae mundi* (Geneva, 1617), 359, proving (with reference to Aristotle) that law, both civil and canon, was a *scientia* : "scire est per causas cognoscere"; and "legistae et canonistae cognoscunt per causas et rationes."

[6] Most ambitious, though least known, are Grégoire de Toulouse, *De Republica libri sex* (Frankfurt, 1609), and especially *Syntagma iuris universi* (Geneva, 1623).

Enlightenment and that of the Renaissance and medieval period, a continuity which the "new philosophy" of the seventeenth century has somewhat obscured.

It is in order to throw some small light upon these themes—the relationship of jurisprudence to the history of ideas, the intellectual role of the lawyer in society, and especially the philosophical significance of law—that I offer this discussion of the thought of Louis Le Caron. No author better exemplifies the compatibility and essential congruity of jurisprudence and philosophy.

"The divine Plato has elegantly declared that true philosophy concerns itself with the life and customs of men."[7] So the nineteen-year-old Louis le Caron expressed what was at once the point of departure, the central premise, and the binding principle of his intellectual development. Although his thought was eclectic and undiscriminating even by the standards of sixteenth-century humanism and although his achievement spanned a wide variety of disciplines, Le Caron remained true to this youthful vision of philosophy, to "cette noble science des choses divines et humaines."[8] What he found most vital in Platonism as he understood it was the fusion between systematic philosophy and the welfare of the community; that is, the organization of all knowledge around a single "idea" which could be identified with the "souverain bien" of the state. Le Caron's own career exemplified this same combination of fascination with system and attention to public service. In this sense he remained throughout his life a "philosophe."

The very same ideal seemed to Le Caron also to be embodied in his chosen profession, and and he was fond of citing the classic formulas of Ulpian to the effect that jurisprudence was literally a form of wisdom and that its practitioners were veritable "priests of the laws."[9]

---

[7] *Πειθανῶν, seu verisimilium libri tres priores* (Paris, 1553), "De restituendo et in artem redigenda iurisprudentia, praefatio" : "... ut non ineleganter divinus ille Plato eam veram philosophiam dixerit quae in hominum vita et moribus tota est."

[8] *La Philosophie* (Paris, 1555), dedication to Marguerite de France, and a quarter of a century later, in *Questions diverses et discours* (Paris, 1583), dedication to Barnabé Brisson, he referred to "la philosophie, à laquelle des ma jeunesse je me suis voué."

[9] *Pandectes ou Digestes du droict françois* (Paris, 1587), I, 3. "La Jurisprudence est (dit il) la cognoissance des choses divines et humaines, la science du juste et injuste et les Jurisconsultes sont les Pontifes et Prelats (ains j'ayme mieux interpreter sacerdotes) de la Justice"; citing *Digest* 1, 1, 10, 2, "Iuris prudentia est divinarum atque humanarum rerum notitia, iusti atque iniusti scientia," and 1, 1, 1, 1, "Cuius merito quis nos sacer-

Following his mentor François Baudouin then, Le Caron did not hesitate to identify jurisprudence with the highest kind of knowledge. "I say that true philosophy is contained in the books of law and not in the useless and inarticulate libraries of philosophers, who in effect are men of great learning but incapable in matters of public administration... Wherefore jurisprudence may indeed by called the true philosophy."[10]

For Le Caron the identity of jurisprudence and Greek philosophy had a historical as well as a logical basis. Like most other humanist lawyers he believed that the legal wisdom of Rome was the product of Hellenic philosophy. He accepted, in other words, the story told by the classical jurist Pomponius in his textbook on the origin of laws, that the *decemviri* had prepared for their work on the Twelve Tables by journeying to Attica to consult with the law-givers of Greece. In this way, as Baudouin taught, echoing the famous words of Thucydides, Athens was the school of all Greece, and beyond. It was only natural that Le Caron, following the trail blazed by Baudouin, should have devoted one of his first legal monographs to a reconstruction, out of classical sources, of the Twelve Tables. For this monument, this "image of antiquity," in the words of Cicero cited by both Le Caron and Baudouin, "surpasses the libraries of all the philosophers."[11]

Perhaps the most conspicuous sign of Le Caron's attempt to bring together jurisprudence and Hellenic philosophy was the literary name under which he published most of his works: "Charondas." Le Caron claimed to be descended from a Greek who had migrated in the train of Cardinal Bessarion (another great syncretist) and this could be taken as the original form of his name. But Le Caron was surely inspired

dotes appellet." Substituting "scientia" in the first part of this formula for "notitia" transforms it into the standard definition of "sapientia," a parallel idea whose career has been traced by Eugene Rice, *The Renaissance Idea of Wisdom* (Cambridge, Mass., 1957), including some discussion of Le Caron himself.

10 *La Claire, ou de la prudence du droit* (Paris, 1554), ff. 23-24. See also *Veresimilis*, f. 2. Also see diagram *in calce*; and cf. Baudouin, *Commentarius in quatuor libros institutionum iuris civilis* (Paris, 1554), in tit.: "Perspicuum est leges quae ad publicas actiones pertinent veram et summam philosophiam continere." The ultimate source of this identification is Ulpian in *Digest*, I, 1, 1, which declares the study of law to be "veram (nisi fallor) philosophiam, non simulatam adfectantes," to which Accursius' gloss adds, "nam civilis sapientia vera philosophia dicitur, id est amor sapientiae."

11 *Ad leges duodecim tabularum liber singularis* (Paris, 1554), citing Cicero, *De Oratore*, 1, 193, 195; *Digest* 1, 2, 2; and referring to the laws "a Balduino ... eleganter restitutas et explicatas," i.e., to Baudouin's *Libri duo in leges Romuli et leges XII tabularum* (Paris, 1554); passages cited in *Tractatus universi juris* (Venice, 1584), I, f. 268 and f. 225.

by the fact that the original Charondas—"who lived not many years before the decemvirs," as Baudouin remarked—was both a law-maker, and, according to a commonly accepted legend, a disciple of Pythagoras, as Le Caron himself was.[12]

Le Caron's account of his intellectual development is a love story—a Platonic love story. His lifelong search for truth and beauty began, he tells us, when he was sixteen years old (in 1550). His discovery of philosophy was so moving that he regarded it more as a passion than as a conversion, and in conventional poetic fashion he embodied his new love in the person of the lady "Claire." To her he dedicated two major books which are all the more interesting in that they were published without his consent.[13] The first of these was a little volume of poems, the second a pretentious set of neo-Platonic dialogues on jurisprudence. In the first of these Claire appears as an ideal of love, beauty, and moral perfection; in the second as intellectual enlightenment and the summit of jurisprudence. "Claire! Claire!" exclaimed Solon, the principal speaker of one dialogue, "You are the law which my eager mind seeks, the law which rules my heart and is obeyed as a sovereign..."[14] From every point of view she was the hypostasis of the Platonic *Idee.*

According to Le Caron's allegorical autobiography, he had been occupied with his college work when he became enamored of Claire and indeed a slave to her.[15] That is, while spending a conventional

---

12 A new study of Le Caron's career is needed. Still the best is F. Gohin, *De Lud. Charondae vita et versibus* (Paris, 1902); also Lucien Pinvert, "Louis le Caron, dit Charondas (1536 [sic]-1613)," *Revue de la Renaissance* 2 (1902), 1-9, 69-76, 181-88; Anicet Digard, "Etudes sur les jurisconsultes du seizième siècle. Louis le Caron, dit Charondas," *Revue historique de droit français et étranger* 7 (1861), 177-92; Louis Carolus-Barré, "Le Contrat de mariage de Loius le Caron dit Charondas avec Marie de Hénault," *Bibliothèque d'Humanisme et Renaissance* 7 (1945), 252-57. That Le Caron was born in 1534, not 1536, appears from the engraving in the Paris, 1607 edition of his *Pandectes.*

13 *La Poesie* (Paris, 1554), dedicated "à la Claire"; *La Claire* (n. 10), followed by "la Clairté amoureuse" and likewise dedicated "in Claram"; and "Claire, ou de la beauté," *Les Dialogues* (Paris, 1556), f. 149. In his *Panegyrique, ou Oraison de loüange au roy Charles VIIII* (Paris, 1566) Le Caron says that the first two were published "contre ma volonté."

14 *La Claire,* f. 9.

15 *La Claire,* "A tres excellente et tres vertueuse damoiselle cousine de sa Claire": "... je tombai es retz de la clairté, laquelle ravit mon entendement des premiers desseings douteusement pour-pensez en plus asseuré conception. Car de cette splendeur je me trouvai si ardemment epris, qu'en mes estudes ne voulois suivre autre guide que l'escorte du clin de ses celestes yeus. Ainsi n'aiant attaint l'an de mon eage dixeseptiesme,

youth in the study of the trivium (*la bienparlante literature, biendisante faconde, et subtile dispute*), he came into contact with "la clairté," the splendor of philosophy, in the form of the dialogues of the "divine Plato," as he always called him. Having completed his course in the liberal arts, Le Caron was given leave by Claire to move on to the study of law, on condition that he would remain faithful to her. It was while at Bourges that he received the terrible news of her death. Henceforth he would not be able to gaze upon her face, but he would always keep her memory : though now he was committed to the profession of law, in other words, he would always retain his original philosophical ideals.

The University of Bourges was the center not only of the "reformed jurisprudence" established by Andrea Alciato but also of the "so-called reformed religion" established by his one time student Jean Calvin. By the first of these (commonly referred to as the *mos gallicus*) Le Caron was profoundly and favorably impressed. Although he arrived too late to study with Alciato's first disciple, Eguinaire Baron (who died in 1550), he did work with two of the most distinguished legal humanists, François le Douaren and François Baudouin. By the new religion, on the other hand, though it was closely bound up with the new jurisprudence, he was wholly disgusted. He complained to his uncle Philip Valton about those "evil spirits" who "abandoned themselves to their furious passions" instead of working for the progress of knowledge.[16] This conflict claimed the life of at least one student besides dividing the faculty and causing friction between Le Douaren and Baudouin, who was forced to leave as a result. Characteristically, Le Caron refused to take sides; his syncretism extended also to his private life.

From his years at Bourges Le Caron derived a great familiarity with the techniques and goals of legal humanism, though as always within the framework of his Platonic vision. For a time at least he adopted all the views of this school. He lamented the brutal editorial policy

---

je feus d'une vaine et douteuse liberté, en utile et constante servitude transformé. Mais l'echange me feut heureuse, que l'excellent esprit de si divine Claire ne m'enflamoit que de plus en plus à la connoissance des artz dignes d'un noble cœur ... Elle me permit voir les academies de la plus civile prudence, sous condition de retourner à son premier mandement. Depuis elle m'appella de la fameuse université de Bourges et lors desolee pour la mort d'un tressavant et renommé Docteur [Baron]."

16 "Philippo Valtono, avunculo suo," prefacing his edition of Ulrich Zasius, *Catalogus legum antiquarum* (Paris, 1555). In general, see Louis Raynal, *Histoire du Berry* (Bourges, 1844), III, 372 ff.

of the Byzantine editor of the texts of civil law, Tribonian, who left only "torn and mutilated fragments of ancient jurisprudence"; and he devoted himself to such tasks of historical restoration as his studies of the Twelve Tables, the Digest, and a recently published manuscript of Ulpian.[17] He attacked the unhistorical and unphilosophical obfuscations of such "scholastic doctors" as Bartolus, while praising the work of the humanists, including Budé, Alciato, Cujas, Le Douaren, Baudouin, and Zasius, whose catalogue of ancient Roman laws he edited. Throughout his life he would retain a deep interest in the newly emerging field of legal history.

Yet unlike such humanists as Baudouin and Cujas, Le Caron was really not interested in history and philology for their own sake. He accepted the view of Ulpian that the rules of grammar did not necessarily apply to legal terms, and he endorsed the conventional derivation of *jus* from *justitia*, for example, on grounds of logical and legal priority. Similarly, he was unable to take their complacent attitude toward the so-called "antinomies" in civil law. To him these contradictions were not so much instances of historical change as departures from the legal ideal, and so almost in scholastic fashion he offered a "rule for the resolving of antinomies found in legal authorities." *Doctrina multiplex, veritas una* held for law as well as for philosophy : "As there were various sects of philosophers in Athens, so there were among jurisconsults in Rome," Le Caron declared, and he deplored such discord in both cases.[18] For him as for Plato, reality was both transverbal and suprahistorical.

What is more, Le Caron was attracted to a branch of the new jurisprudence which inclined rather toward logical reorganization of civil law than toward philological and historical exegesis. Like Le Douaren, Hugues Doneau, François Connan, and to some extent Jean Bodin, he wanted not only to restore the law to its original state but also re-form it in a more systematic way. Such was the theme of his first

---

17 *Versimilis*, "De Restituendo" referring to "haec abscissa et mutila veteris iurisprudentiae fragmenta quae sic a Triboniano disposita sint"; *Tituli xxviii. ex corpore Ulpiani* ... (Paris, 1554); his edition of the *Digest* (Antwerp, 1575), dedicated to the Parlement of Paris and discussion (p. 2) of the most controversial of the interpolations in the *Digest* (1, 2, 2) : "Sunt qui non sine iudicio hoc caput a Triboniano ex diversis auctoribus sub Pomponii nomine compositum esse existiment, aut certe multa ab illo addita."

18 *Veresimilis*, f. 82^{v}; cf. I, 1, and II, 1 : "Dissolvendarum antinomiarum quae in iuris authorum libris inveniuntur ratio." On the problem of *antinomiae*, see Le Douaren's commentary on Justinian's prefaces to the *Digest* in his *Opera omnia* (Lucca, 1765-68), I, 2.

work, a discussion of that well known humanist topic, derived from Cicero, concerning the restoration of jurisprudence and its reduction to an "art" (*de restituendo et in artem redigenda jurisprudentia*), and such would be the intent of a number of later works.[19] In this way, too, Le Caron showed his fundamentally philosophical cast of mind.

In one important respect Le Caron differed from his mentors at Bourges and indeed from all of the established "legal humanists" of his day, and this was in his attitude toward vernacular culture. From the beginning he was a great enthusiast for the French language and indeed a kind of minor satellite of the Pléiade. He particularly admired his friend Pierre Ronsard and indeed credited him with "the renaissance of true poetry."[20] Le Caron's "vernacular humanism" was displayed most conspicuously in two of his earlier books: one his poems (surely among the most tedious of that epoch) dedicated to Claire, Ronsard, "the demon of love," and others; the other a set of neo-Platonic dialogues on philosophical subjects. Although he never completed the dialogues, he planned to honor a number of literary friends, including Claude Fauchet and "the great Pasquier, who puts Plato to shame."[21] Later Pasquier returned the compliment, though a bit less hyperbolically, by recalling Le Caron as one of that vernacularist avant-garde which had fought for the French language.[22] With Pasquier, too, Le Caron shared the fashionable *gaulois* interests of the 1550's, and later joined him, Fauchet, Antoine Loisel, the brothers Pithou, and others in a concentrated assault upon "French antiquities."[23]

---

19 Cicero, *De Oratore*, I, 42; cf. Quintilian, *De Oratore*, XII, 3, 10, and Aulus Gellius, I, 22, 7; see also n. 41.

20 *La Claire*, ff. 4v-5, referring to "ce divin Pindare François Pierre Ronsard auquel à bon droit j'attribue la renaissance de la vraie poësie, sans frauder du Bellai, de Thiart et autres ..." Le Caron's poetical work is discussed in various works devoted to the Pléiade such as M. Raymond, *L'influence de Ronsard sur la poésie française (1550-1585)* (Geneva, 1965), 249-54.

21 *La Poesie*, f. 67, "Au Seigneur Pasquier :

"Le grand Pasquier, qui à Platon fait honte,
Le plus divin des immortelz espritz
Philosophant au giron de Cypris
Par son amour, Amour mesme surmonte."

Les Dialogues, including "Ronsard, ou de la poesie"; according to the table of contents, Book II was to include "Pasquier, ou l'orateur," "Fauchet, ou de l'utilité qu'apporte la congnoissance des choses naturelles," and others.

22 *Les Recherches de la France* (Paris, 1621), VII, 11.

23 On this aspect of Le Caron's work, see my *Foundations of Modern Historical Scholarship* (New York, 1970), 241 ff.

Yet in Le Caron's linguistic nationalism there was very little nostalgia. In that endless "quarrel of ancients and moderns" he stood very definitely on the side of youth. "I say and always have said," he wrote, "not only that our language is not poor but that it is richer than Greek, Latin, or any other foreign tongue."[24] A generation before the great humanist Guillaume Budé had conceded this for such barbaric pastimes as the hunt, but Le Caron would recognize no such qualifications. In particular he agreed with the thesis which, contradicting Budé, had been offered just a few years before by Joachim du Bellay in his classic defense of the vernacular : "that the French language is not unsuited to philosophy." Nor was it, of course, to jurisprudence : the old view, shared by Budé and most philologists, that philosophy was a peculiar possession of the Greeks (as law was of the Romans) was quite unacceptable to an idealist—and a Frenchman—like Le Caron.

It may be true to say that Le Caron, like Pico, found the true source of wisdom in history, and it is certainly true that he had a deep interest in the history of philosophy.[25] Yet again his attitude was essentially unhistorical—or rather his perspective was that of sacred not human history. The vehicle of philosophical tradition, Le Caron suggested, following St. Ambrose, was the Holy Spirit;[26] Plato was indeed "divine," beyond time as well as criticism; and as for himself, Le Caron was a kind of Plato redivivus (*à la française*). Conceptually, then, Le Caron's attitude was just the same as that of Luther, Melanchthon, Calvin, and other Protestants toward religious "tradition" : just as they affected to trace the anticipations and doctrinal continuity of the *vera ecclesia*, so he tried to trace the anticipations and doctrinal continuity of the *vera philosophia*, or "La Philosophie chrestienne," as he sometimes called it. Like Pico, in short, Le Caron aimed

---

24 *Les Dialogues*, f. 2 : " ... je ne suis ne trop serf admirateur, ne trop arrogant despriseur de l'antiquité." *La Philosophie*, dedication : "Je di, et l'ai tousjours soustenu, que nostre langue non seulement n'est pauvre mais aussi plus riche que La Grecque, Latine, ou autre estranger, tant brave soit elle." See also *La Claire*, f. 9. Cf. Budé, *De Philologia* (Paris, 1532), p. 186. And Du Bellay, *La Défense et illustration de la langue française*, ed. L. Séché (Paris, 1905), ch. X, "Que la langue française n'est incapable de la philosophie." Le Caron was responsible for the coining of many new terms; e.g., "droitconseillant," "avant propos," "humaniser."

25 Rice, *Renaissance Idea of Wisdom*, 100, n. 27; cf. the remarks of Ernst Cassirer, "Giovanni Pico della Mirandola," *Journal of the History of Ideas* 3 (1942), 123-44, 319-46.

26 *Discours philosophiques* (Paris, 1583), p. 34 (revised ed. of *La Philosophie*), and *Pandectes*, I, 1; in general, P. Fraenkel, *Testimonia Patrum* (Geneva, 1961).

not at the establishment of a new philosophy but rather at the recovery of a *philosophia perennis.*

The career of philosophy, as described by Le Caron, began with Moses and passed on, by way of Egypt (through Hermes Trismegistus), to the pre-Socratic philosophers of Greece (Le Caron calls them "ancients"), culminating finally in the vision of Plato. Thereafter, though preserved to some extent by Aristotle ("Stagyrite le plus subtil des Platoniciens" is the highest praise Le Caron can find for him), this tradition was corrupted into various sects.[27] Finally, revived and perfected by Christianity, it passed on to the European nations, or more specifically, according to the old conceit, by the "translation of studies" from Athens to Rome to Paris.[28] And at the end of this tradition stood none other than Louis le Caron, called Charondas : *sic transit sapientia mundi.* A very contrived story, but perhaps not so different, after all, from the way in which the history of philosophy has usually been written.

The cultural imperialism inherent in the notion of *translatio studii*, which was an inseparable companion of the *translatio imperii*, is quite in keeping with Le Caron's general view; for philosophy itself, he believed, had an *imperium.* Several times he referred to philosophy as the "sovereign science," and it was his intention to declare the "sovereignty of philosophy" over all other disciplines.[29] Thus he hoped to impose some order upon that unwieldy "encyclopedia" of humanist learning. This purpose was also reflected in his philosophical method, which likewise moved from the top down in legislative fashion : his preference was to proceed not from particulars to universals, or as he put it, from things perceived to things hidden, but rather from first principles to particulars.[30] Such was the flexibility of this method,

27 *La Philosophie*, ff. 22 and 17v : "Je dirai ... que nul plus gravement, amplement, philosophiquement, et divinement a traicté la philosophie que Platon, mais les autres l'ont plustost corrumpue et obscurcie que descrite." This pioneering contribution to the history of philosophy may be compared to the contemporary sketch by another French Platonist, Louis le Roy, "L'Origine, progres et perfection de la philosophie, avec la comparaison de Platon et Aristote," prefacing his translation, *La Phedon de Platon* (Paris, 1553).

28 *Nouveau commentaire ... sur la coustume de ... Paris, ou droit civil Parisien* (Paris, 1613), "avant propos."

29 *Discours philosophiques*, f. 16v ("la souveraineté de la Philosophie"), f. 12 ("la souveraine sagesse"), f. 9 ("la souveraine science").

30 *La Philosophie*, f. 40, and diagram. Le Caron's intense belief in sorcery appears in a curious "Discours sur le proces criminel faict à une sorciere condamnee à mort ...," in *De la Tranquillité d'esprit* (Paris, 1588), 159.

so ecumenical, omnivorous, and amorphous was his thought, so "neo-" his Platonism, that he was able to accommodate to it learning of every variety and of every age. From this kingdom of philosophy not even magic was excluded.

In general Le Caron accepted the conventional division of philosophy into things divine and things human, corresponding to wisdom and prudence. From this he drew an epistemological distinction very similar to that made by Vico between the *verum* and the *factum* : that is, between being, "which is without beginning, one, eternal, and immeasurable," and non-being, "which has been created from being, but which is mutable, in motion, and subject to corruption."[31] The first can be comprehended only by divine intelligence, but the second, emerging and disappearing in time, is accessible to human sense perception, and so represents in effect the historical forms of human culture. So philosophy comprehended the entire range of human behavior and indeed was the principal sign of "the dignity of man."

Le Caron was concerned more with the structure than with the substance of philosophy, but more than either he was interested in the "office of the philosopher." In another early dialogue between a "courtier" and himself he discussed the value and purpose of philosophy. The courtier stated all the standard skeptical objections : philosophy had no practical use, its conclusions had never been agreed on by its professors, and it was at bottom nothing more than a pedantic game.[32] In answering these objections Le Caron returned to his central thesis concerning the social basis of philosophy. In the first place he agreed completely with the critique of scholastic philosophy and resumed the line of argument established by such earlier humanists as Ermolao Barbaro and Melanchthon, that true philosophy was inseparable from eloquence. "One who divorces eloquence from wisdom, which are closely bound together," Le Caron said, "seems to me to be

---

[31] *Discours philosophiques*, f. 10^v : "... il faut premierement distinguer ce qui EST, lequel sans commencement est toujours UN, Eternal et immesurable, de ce qui a esté crée n'estant jamais. Au Permenide, il [Plato] monstre que l'ESTANT ne differe de l'UN... Mais ce qui n'est à la verité (lequel imitans les Grecs et Latins, nous appellons NON ESTANT) a esté crée d'iceluy ESTANT ; toutesfois il est muable, mortel et suiect à corruption ... Et ce qui N'EST, peut estre touché de la pensée irraisonable, puis qu'il naist, et perist n'estant jamais à la verité."

[32] *Dialogues*, f. 48^v ff.

throwing society into a wretched state of disorder."[33] The companion of philosophy, in short, should be not dialectic but rhetoric. And in the second place, as Plato himself taught, philosophy was not a simply private pursuit but the very foundation of public life. The achievement of the Platonic tradition, in his view, was to bring philosophy down from the heavens, from "contemplation," not only into the households of men (as Cicero had said of Socrates) but also into the forum, the council chamber, and even the law courts.

The "office of the philosopher," then, was not merely to follow the ancient precept, "know thyself," as Le Caron's disillusioned contemporary Montaigne was teaching.[34] Nor was it to determine the "souverain contentement" of the individual, which implied the still more reprehensible hedonism of Rabelais. True philosophy was aimed rather at "public utility" and the "sovereign good" of the whole community. In short, this "royal philosophy," prescribed by Le Caron for the education of the prince and indeed of any "politic," was equivalent to "la science politique."[35] For Le Caron, of course, the term "politique" had very different connotations than it did for many of his contemporaries, who were beginning to use it in a derogatory way, often as a synonym for "Machiavellian" or even atheist or as a party label. He accepted the rather old-fashioned usage which included also the notions of legality, morality, and public welfare, and which is perhaps best expressed in the remark of Baudouin : "Homo politicus, hoc est, juriconsultus." That is, Le Caron would add, *philosophe*, for

---

33 *Dialogues*, f. 64 ("Oraison pour la philosophie"), f. 64v. On this controversy in general, see A. Bernardini and G. Righi, *Il concetto di filologia e di cultura classica* (Bari, 1953), ch. II, and Q. Breen's translation of the essential documents in *Journal of the History of Ideas* 13 (1952), 384-426.

34 *La Philosophie*, f. 15v ("office du philosophe"), f. 12, discussion of the Apollonian precept "COGNOI TOI-MESME," and again in *Questions diverses et discours*, f. 62v : "Mais je diray que la trop grand recherche de soy-mesme n'est que vaine et inutile curiosité." *La Philosophie*, f. 7v : "J'ai dict parcidevant le philosophe (lequel justement merite tel nom) estre celui qui d'une amore de sagesse recherche la verité, estudiant à l'utilité publique." Cf. f. 113v, on the "souveraine contentement" or "volupté" of Rabelais.

35 *Dialogues*, f. 3, "Le Courtisan, que le Prince doit philosopher, Ou, de la vraie sagesse et Roiale philosophie"; *Panegyrique*, Biv ("la science Royale"); and Eiiiv ("la science politique"); *La Philosophie*, f. 69, "Le Philosophe, Ou, que la philosophie est toute roiale." There are other questions relating to the "institution du prince" in *Questions diverses*.

as Ulpian said, "jurisconsults desired and professed, or rather taught, the true philosophy."[36]

In several respects Le Caron's political position was markedly different from that of most of his colleagues in the French magistracy. Not that he rejected any part of royalist ideology : he rehearsed the old Gallican formulas that the king was the "image of God" and "emperor in his kingdom" and of course attributed to him the *merum imperium*, or sovereignty.[37] But for Le Caron reason was enshrined not in monarchy but in law, and the true "mark of sovereignty" was not the legislative power, as Jean Bodin argued, but justice itself.[38] Le Caron placed great emphasis upon the role of magistrates and the judiciary and upon their discretionary judgment. The delegation of *haute justice* in particular he found "very *politique* and in accord with the opinion of our Plato."[39] What is more, he did not hesitate to associate the notion of justice as much with custom as with formal laws and indeed argued that time and experience operated as a corrective upon the inequities of legislation : *usus legum corrector* was the old precept he cited.[40] The legislator had an important function, of course, but it was rather that of a doctor prescribing for health than that of a ruler trying to control the behavior of his subjects.

Equally unorthodox were Le Caron's views about the historical foundations of the French "chose publique." He offered an even more fundamental rebuke to Bodin by endorsing the argument for "mixed monarchy," regarded as treasonable in some circles. "I accept the opinion of Polybius," he wrote, "that of the three types of government, that is, monarchy, aristocracy, and democracy, one cannot exist alone; rather the three together, organized and balanced, form a true

---

[36] *Pandectes*, I, 3. Cf. Baudouin, *Commentarius de jurisprudentia Muciana* (Halle, 1729), 31.

[37] *Au Roy nostre souverain prince et seigneur* (Paris, 1588) and *Pandectes*, I, 18, "Le Roy est Empereur de France." On the *merum imperium*, see Le Caron's edition of [Jacques d'Ableiges'] *Grand Coustumier de France* (Paris, 1598), p. 531; *Responses et decisions du droict françois* (Paris, 1637), p. 574; and *De Iurisdictione et imperio*, in *Ad Tit. de verborum obligat.* (Paris, 1553), f. 46 ff. There are discussions of Le Caron's political thought in M.P. Gilmore, *Argument from Roman Law in Political Thought 1200-1600* (Cambridge, Mass., 1941), 82-85, and in Vittorio de Caprariis, *Propaganda e pensiero politico in Francia durante le guerre di religione* (Naples, 1959), 214-24.

[38] *Pandectes*, I, 1. (Cf. Bodin's famous remarks in his *Republic*, III, 8.) *Dialogues*, f. 46^{v} : "... la loi ... est la raison universelle de tout le peuple."

[39] *Les Dialogues*, f. 29.

[40] *Memorables observations du droict françois* (Paris, 1637), 34, and *Pandectes*, I, 3.

republic..., such as that of France."[41] Le Caron also showed a certain sympathy with the general idea of popular sovereignty. It certainly applied to Rome, according to the famous *lex regia*, one of his favorite texts. "As for the French government," he wrote, "it was established not by force but by election." [42] Finally, Le Caron was an admirer of the Estates General and argued that, like the English Parliament, they had once enjoyed a much greater authority than recently.[43]

These were dangerous opinions and in fact resembled nothing so much as the treasonable views spread by the Huguenot propagandist François Hotman. Yet in Le Caron's case they stemmed from no real sympathy for resistance; even as a deputy of the third estate at Blois in 1588 his political position was positively obsequious. As always the shaping force was his oecumenical and neo-Platonic cast of mind and his professional commitment to jurisprudence. As a result of the first he attached more importance to justice than to authority in his republic, and as a result of the second he attached more importance to private than to public law. According to Le Caron, discord was the product not merely of resistance of subjects to oppressive rulers (though there was certainly an excess of that at this time) but more fundamentally of the conflict between "mien et tien," which has always disrupted human tranquillity.[44] The remedy for this was a kind of harmonic justice which Le Caron described in elaborate, neo-Pythagorean terms. This "eunomia" was two-fold, depending both upon a justice that was general and common to all, and a justice that was particular and proportionate to one's individual status, and also upon a sovereign who respected this harmony, whether or not he was a philosopher-king.[45]

---

[41] *Responses et decisions*, "Response politique" : "Je cognois l'opinion de Polybe estre veritable, que les trois especes de Republique qu'on estime les meilleures, à savoir, Monarchie, Aristocratie, et Democratie, l'une ne peut estre seule, ains de trois ensemble composees et temperees se forme une vraye Republique ... Comme est celle de France, en laquelle y a un Roy, qui se gouverne par le conseil des Pairs de France..., et la peuple obeyssant volontairement ... C'est ceste belle et excellent harmonie qui entretient la societé politique..."

[42] *Pandectes*, I, 1 : "La Republique françoise ... n'a esté establie par force, ains par election du peuple ..." On the *lex regia*, see I, 4, and "Leges ... additae" in *Catalogus legum*, f. 142^{v}.

[43] *Pandectes*, I, 15.

[44] *La Philosophie*, f. 70.

[45] *Panegyrique*, Hiii.

Many traditions went into the making of Le Caron's political views : the ancient notion of the mixed constitution, medieval and modern writings on German history, the mirror-of-the-prince genre, civil law and its various schools of commentary, feudal law, especially those who wrote on the French *coutumes*, movements of legal reform in the sixteenth century (ordinances and the "reformation of customs"), the venerable tradition of French legists, including writings about the estates as well as the sovereign courts, and above all that antiquarian renaissance of the later sixteenth century to which Le Caron himself made important scholarly contributions.[46] Yet even in his political thought Le Caron remained constant to the memory of the lady Claire and to the abstract *idee* of justice, so much so that it is hardly an exaggeration to regard Le Caron as in effect a philosophical constitutionalist—even a Platonic constitutionalist.

The final proof of this observation is Le Caron's lifelong fascination with the idea of a universal system of laws. The ultimate source of this idea as far as law was concerned was of course Roman law itself, especially the plan of Justinian, though of more immediate importance was the contemporary movement toward reforming or systematizing civil law sponsored by such French jurists as Le Caron's teacher Le Douaren, Hugues Doneau (another contemporary at Bourges), François Connan, and to some extent Jean Bodin.[47] These attempts

---

[46] *Grand Coustumier*, preface to son : "Ceux qui de nostre eage ont travaillé et travaillent encores à retirer des tenebres d'oubliance les escrits des anciens Grecs et Latins, et les illustrer d'observations et annotations, ont merité grandement des sciences, n'estans moins loüables que ceux qui publient des nouveaux livres de leur façon. A leur example les François amateurs de leur patrie se doivent dedier à rechercher et remettre en lumiere les anciens livres de leur langue pour la decoration d'icelle. J'en ay veu de diverses sciences, d'histoires, de poësie et d'oraison soluë, qui ne cedent en rien aux Grecs et Latins..." Of Le Caron's fellow researchers, those he cites include Pasquier, Fauchet, Pithou, Choppin, Du Tillet, Du Haillan, Dumoulin, Brisson, Argentré, Bacquet, as well as L'Hôpital and Christofle de Thou.

[47] The tradition of legal system-building from the sixteenth to the eighteenth century, especially in its relations to philosophy, needs further investigation. In general, see R. Stintzing, *Geschichte der deutschen Rechtswissenschaft* (Munich, 1880), I, 139 ff; A. Eyssell, *Doneau* (Dijon, 1860); C. Bergfeld, *Franciscus Connanus (1508-1551)* (Cologne, 1968); F. Ebrard, "Über Methoden, Systeme, Dogmen in der Geschichte des Privatrechts," *Zeitschrift für schweizerisches Recht* 67 (1948), 95-136; Aldo Mazzacane, *Scienza, logica e ideologia nella giurisprudenza tedesca del sec. XVI* (Milan, 1971); Hans Troje, "Arbeitshypothesen zum Thema 'Humanistische Jurisprudenz'," *Tijdschrift voor Rechtsgeschiedenis* 38 (1970), 519-63; and my "The Development and Context of Bodin's Method," in *Jean Bodin : Verhandlungen der internationalen Bodin Tagung in München*, ed. H. Denzer (Munich, 1972).

to rationalize civil law, to find a *ius perennis*, were very obviously grounded in philosophical motives and are linked historically with the grander designs of the seventeenth and eighteenth centuries, such as those of Domat, Pufendorf, Vico, and Montesquieu, for systems of universal law.

But once again Le Caron was diverted by his vernacularist bias and his professional commitments. He came to doubt whether classical antiquity was any more relevant to modern French society than classical languages were to French literature. "Frenchmen," he declared, "you have enough examples in your histories without inquiring into those of Greece and Rome." [48] This was even more obvious in the case of law, since Le Caron shared the growing hostility of many of his colleagues toward the substance, if not the form, of Roman law, both civil and canon. He accepted and indeed insisted upon the conventional Gallican doctrine that, as he declared to King Charles IX, "You are not subject to the laws of the Greeks and the Romans, nor are your magistrates bound by them, except to the extent that they are in accord with reason."[49] Le Caron joined in the growing chorus of complaints by Pasquier, Hotman, and others about the evil effects of Roman law, which in France had brought about a lapse from "the simplicity of ancient manners," and had turned the country into a veritable paradise for litigators. The problem was to find the original tradition of French law.

Thus Le Caron, in the company of many fellow legists, turned from civil law back to the customs of the French countryside. What began as a plan to translate the Digest into French ended up twenty years later as Le Caron's masterpiece, the *Digest of French Law*, which preserved the form of the Digest but concentrated on the substance of French law, institutions, and history. This work was the descendant of a long series of feudist compilations, including those of Philippe de Beaumanoir (a thirteenth-century forerunner of Le Caron as royal official in Clermont in Beauvaisis), Jacques d'Ableiges (whose *Grand Coustumier de France* Le Caron edited), and Charles Dumoulin (like Le Caron a commentator on the Parisian *coutume* and a promoter of a native French code of laws), and various collections of judicial decisions and royal legislation (Le Caron himself

---

[48] *Responses et decisions*, "Avant-propos." "Vous avez, hommes François, assez d'exemples en vos Histoires sans en rechercher aux Grecques et Romaines..."

[49] *Panegyrique*, Dii. Cf. *Pandectes*, I, Juvenal, *Satire*, VII, 148.

produced several of these, as well as an edition of Barnabé Brisson's famous *Code of Henry III*).[50] The work was also among the first in a series of attempts, including those later made by his friends Pasquier and Loisel, to bring some order into the chaos of French customary law by fashioning a system out of medieval history, classical jurisprudence, and philosophy.[51]

In general this work, technical and overloaded with other people's erudition as it is, may be taken as the fulfillment of Le Caron's original philosophical ideal : for here philosophy could exercise its "sovereignty" not only over fields of learning but over "the life and customs of men in general." Into the vulgar and vernacular field of French law, moreover, Le Caron brought all of his general assumptions about jurisprudence. "French law," he wrote, "is composed of all the parts of universal law, the science of which is called jurisprudence, civil science or wisdom, referred to as 'royal' by some. It is the major part of moral as well as political philosophy, which is most useful to human society."[52] So Le Caron brought together, as he believed, all the materials necessary for the formation of an ideal republic in France. So he continued to carry on the task of the jurisconsult as defined by Ulpian and the "office of the philosophe" as conceived by Plato.

---

[50] *Responses de droict françois* (Paris, 1583); also a manuscript (Paris, BN, Fonds français, 21,569), "Responses et arrests de la cour de parlement remarquez par Charondas Iurisconsulte Parisien"; *Ordonnance du domain, et droicts de la couronne de France* (Paris, 1637); *Coustumes ... de Paris* (Paris, 1595); Brisson, *Le Code du Roy Henry III* (Paris, 1609); and n. 31.

[51] *Panegyrique*, Diii : "... ains comme vos sujects vous emportent et appartient tous autant les uns que les autres, aussi doit avoir entre eux une communauté des loix que soyent toutes escriptes en langue François, pour estre entendues non moins de ceux qu'on appelle rustiques et paysans que de plus subtils practiciens... à fin qu'ils cognoissent tous que c'est que vostre Majesté leur command pour vivre politiquement en vostre Royaume." Cf. Loisel, *Institutes Coustumieres* (Paris, 1607), and Pasquier, *L'Interpretation des Institutes de Justinian*, ed. M. le duc Pasquier (Paris, 1847), approximately contemporaneous.

[52] *Pandectes*, I, 3 : "Le droict François est composé de toutes les parties du droict universel, duquel la science est appellee Iurisprudence, science ou sagesse civile, et par aucuns Royal, laquelle est la principale partie de la Philosophie morale, d'autant que c'est la politique qui est la plus utile à la societé humaine. La Philosophie consiste ou en la recherche des secrets ou en l'institution des mœurs; l'une se propose une contemplation et l'autre s'exerce en action; toutes les deux loüables et qui se doivent estre embrassees par les grands et nobles esprits, mais l'action est plus necessaire à la vie commune."

The general effect of jurisprudence upon philosophy, to judge from Le Caron's work, was to shift emphasis from "theoretical" to "practical" knowledge, from the *vita contemplativa* to the *vita activa*, and so from natural to social science. This tendency, so characteristic of Renaissance humanism as a whole, may be seen in a longer perspective and suggests in particular a link with eighteenth-century thought. Clearly, one of the agents of this shift was jurisprudence, which combines, at least potentially, the cultural values of humanism with the systematizing features of formal philosophy. This combination is obviously present in the work of Vico and Montesquieu, who were both, like Le Caron and Bodin, educated in the law and authors of quasi-legal systems of thought. Both sought above all the "spirit of the laws," and it is significant that this concept (*mens legum*), meaning intention or reasonableness as distinct from the letter of the law and implying a moral or philosophical standard transcending the accidents of history and the particularity of specific texts, was itself derived from civil law.[53]

There are other such parallels with the same provenance. It has been noted, for example, that Le Caron's discussion of the origins of society, likewise based on civil law, seems "strangely like eighteenth-century thinking on the subject."[54] Various assumptions crucial for political thinking from the sixteenth to the eighteenth century were preserved in civil law, such as the distinctions between private and public law, between civil society and a pre-legal state of nature, and at least implicitly between the methods of natural and of social philosophy. So were certain interpretations of historical development (from barbarism and oral tradition, corresponding to unwritten custom, to a literate and enlightened society based upon rational and perhaps codified laws) and the endless search for a universal "law of nations" (the *jus gentium* inspired not only Grotius' contributions to international law but also one aspect of Vico's "new science"). Most important, jurisprudence contained what is perhaps the ultimate ideal of a social science, that is, a rational system of understanding human behavior in terms of cause and effect on the basis of accumulated human experience.

---

53 Alciato, *Parerga*, in *Opera*, IV, 323 : "... quod ipsi [*grammatici*, such as Lorenzo Valla] scilicet ad sola verba attenderent, mentem legum ignorarent." See Vicenzo Piano Mortari, "Il problema dell'interpretatio iuris nei commentatori," *Annali di storia del diritto* 2 (1958), 29-109.

54 M. P. Gilmore, *Argument from Roman Law*, 83.

In these and other ways Le Caron may, like Bodin, be regarded as a "predecessor of Montesquieu" and, since he combined the ideals of Roman law with Platonic philosophy, even more conspicuously of Vico. Although there is no evidence of direct influence, the parallels are striking. Both men stand in the mainstream of the humanist tradition; both linked their philosophic vision with a formative personal experience and turned to autobiography to express it; both looked to jurisprudence as a source of inspiration and as a conceptual model; both chose Plato as their first authority; and finally, both represent a kind of latter day Socratic revolution—a shift of focus from the "secrets of nature," as Le Caron put it, to the "life and customs of men."

In conclusion, then, we may place Le Caron between two enlightenments—that emanating from the "divine Plato" and that of the eighteenth century. In style and superficiality of thought Le Caron seems to stand closer to the latter, for his interest in philosophy was not really professional, and he was in his own words an "amateur de sagesse."[55] Yet like many eighteenth-century thinkers, and for the same reasons, he regarded himself as the best of all possible philosophers. He, too, found in history some of the most essential lessons about human behavior. He, too, wanted to apply the "knowledge of things divine and human" to problems of government and society for purposes of reform. Though a good Catholic, he, too, attacked papal usurpation and championed ecclesiastical reform. And finally, he, too, hoped to accomplish these things through education and above all through legislation. So it seems appropriate to bestow upon Le Caron the title by which he referred to his own calling, and at the same time to extend to him the observation once made about his more famous colleague Bodin—that he was at once one of the last of the legists and first of the *philosophes*.[56]

University of Rochester

---

[55] *La Philosophie*, f. 8^v. In his *The Enlightenment : An Interpretation* (New York, 1966-69) Peter Gay argues for the exclusive application of "philosophe" to eighteenth-century thinkers; I would not want to stretch the meaning further but only to point out the historical background of the usage he discusses. I make the connection more directly in "Vico's Road," in *Giambattista Vico's Science of Humanity*, ed. G. Tagliacozzo and D. Verene (Baltimore, 1976), 16-29.

[56] Etienne Fournol, *Bodin prédécesseur de Montesquieu* (Paris, 1896), especially p. 27, and most recently, G. Cotroneo, "A Renaissance Source of the *Scienza nuova* : Juan Bodin's *Methodus*," in *Giambattista Vico, An International Symposium*, ed. G. Tagliacozzo and H. White (Baltimore, 1969), 51-59.

APPENDIX

Organization of Knowledge

- Knowledge–
  - Philosophy —
    - Divine Metaphysics or Theology
    - Human : understanding–
      - Physics : natural in gen. —
        - Mathematics
        - Physics, in special sense —
          - Arithmetic
          - Geometry (incl. optics)
          - Music
          - Astronomy
        - Medicine
      - Ethics : moral in gen. —
        - Ethics (private)
        - Economics
        - Politics (incl. legislation or jurisprudence)
  - Art —
    - Liberal-
      - grammar
      - rhetoric
      - dialectic
    - Mixed
    - Mechanical

Louis le Caron, *Discours philosophiques* (Paris, 1583), f. 35.

X

Murd'rous Machiavel in France: A Post Mortem*

The better to betray, be false;
Lie, cheat, and try to hide the facts;
Always wear your sheep's disguise;
And never shun hypocritical acts.

Flatter and follow only the great;
Study Man, his plans and his deeds;
Worship not the soul but the State,
And God—when it suits your needs.

Demand peace when there is no peace;
Make friends with the Turk if you can;
Protect and arm the heretic;
But remember Machiavel is your man.

Of Providence, finally, don't bother to ask;
Just never discard your political mask.[1]

* Preliminary versions of this paper were offered at the Columbia University Seminar on Political and Social Thought on November 20, 1969 and at the American Historical Association Convention in Washington, December 29, 1969 in a session devoted to "Five Hundred Years of Machiavelli Interpretations." Special thanks to Felix Gilbert for his comments, private as well as public.

[1] Pour mieux trahir faire la chatemite,
Mentire, piper, deguiser verité
Couvrir le loup de fainte saincteté,
Sembler devot et n'estre qu'hypocrite,—

In such accents Machiavelli seemed to speak to Christian readers, Catholic as well as Protestant, in the sixteenth century. Throughout Europe he created at once a shock of recognition and a wave of revulsion, and it is not surprising that a caricature of his views should have arisen. What needs explaining is not the caricature—we possess several equally gross distortions even today—but rather the extent to which it was broadcast, the uses to which it was put, and the ferocity with which it was attacked.

Unusual happenings suggest unusual explanations, and here is one of the most plausible. Contemporary reports to the contrary, Machiavelli did not really die in 1527. Half a century later, as Christopher Marlowe has told us, he was alive and well and living in France.[2] There he led a busier and certainly more successful career than he had ever had as a Florentine secretary and author. The evidence for his activities is quite as overwhelming as that for the contemporary phenomenon of witchcraft, and we have exactly the same obligation to accept it. Among other things, Machiavelli inspired the persecution of French Protestants by the Valois kings; he became a trusted adviser of the Guises and a constant companion of Catherine de' Medici and her children; he provided aid and comfort to the Jesuits and to the Catholic League as well as to the party of the *politiques;* and finally, so the story goes, the massacre of St. Bartholomew was a celebration held expressly in his honor. More generally, he helped to corrupt French

---

Flatter les grans, se renger a leur suite,
D'homme et de chair faindre une deité,
Sonner l'estat, et non la pieté,
Forger son Dieu au fond de sa marmite,—

Demander paix où paix estre ne peult,
Prest de coiffre le turban si l'on veut,
Nourrir soubz main et armer l'heretique,—

Pour Evangile Machiavel tenir,
De l'autremonde en rien se souvenir,
Sont les couleurs du masque Politique.

"Sonnet du Politique" from *De Jezabelis Anglae parrecidio varii poemata latina et gallica* (s.l.n.d.), cited by G. Ascoli, *La Grande-Bretagne devant l'opinion française* (Paris, 1927), I, 297.

[2] *The Jew of Malta,* l. 1-2:
Albeit the world think Machiavel is dead
Yet was his soul but flown beyond the Alps. . . .

morals on every level and to infect French society with every Italianate vice from Ciceronianism to sodomy. It is this formidable bit of historical demonology, the posthumous career of Machiavelli in France, that is the subject of this paper.[3]

Although Machiavelli became the embodiment of a real "devil theory of history," there was nothing supernatural or even suspicious about his journey across the Alps. As the French translator remarked to his customers in 1544, "This Florentine merchant . . . has voluntarily left his own country to be received into yours. . . . Do not be so ungracious as to refuse him citizenship." From all appearances he was welcomed with open arms, or at least open minds. Within the next eight years the *Discourses on Livy*, the *Art of War*, and the *Prince* (in two different versions) appeared in French dress, while the *Florentine Histories*, though not translated until 1577, was read and cited in Italian. Within a few years, one of his admirers declared that he was a prophet honored more in France than in his own country.[4]

One reason for this, no doubt, was the somewhat extravagant advertising campaign that accompanied his works. According to the translator Jacques Gohory, for example, the *Discourses* offered "a mirror of universal history that could wonderfully instruct all manner of people." One of the first of those so instructed was Guillaume de la Perrière, who in 1555 displayed his own mirror, a "political mirror," which reflected the views of Machiavelli as

[3] Discussions of anti-Machiavellian literature are repetitive and not very critical. The best are G. Cardascia, "Machiavel et Jean Bodin," *Bibliothèque d'humanisme et renaissance*, III (1943), 129-67; Albert Cherel, *La Pensée de Machiavel en France* (Paris, 1935); and J. R. Charbonnel, *La Pensée italienne au XVIe siècle et le courant libertin* (Paris, 1919), 13 ff. Others include Charles Benoist, *Le Machiavélisme* (Paris, 1936), III; Giuliano Procacci, *Studi sulla fortuna del Machiavelli* (Rome, 1965); Andrea Sorrentino, *Storia del'antimachiavellismo europeo* (Naples, 1936); Antonio Panella, *Gli Antimachiavellici* (Florence, 1943); Oreste Tommasini, *La Vita e gli scritti di Niccolò Machiavelli* (Turin, 1883), I; and, of course, the classic work of Meinecke, *Die Idee der Staatsräson in der neueren Geschichte* (Munich, 1924). And see now S. Mastellone, "Aspetti del anti-machiavellismo in Francia," *Il Pensiero politico* (1969), II, 376-416.

[4] Adolf Gerber, *Niccolò Machiavelli, Die Handschriften, Ausgaben und Ubersetzungen seiner Werke im 16. und 17. Jahrhundert* (Turin, 1962), III, 21; and the Italian sonnet prefacing the French translation of the *Discorsi* (1548) in Gerber, III, 23. I have relied heavily on this indispensable work.

well as of Aristotle and so, hopefully, enhanced the image of the French monarchy.[5] The *Art of War*, too, was promoted vigorously. Jean Charrier suggested that his translation might teach Frenchmen not only how to acquire universal empire but perhaps even how to recover the holy land.[6] This book, too, was soon put to use, notably by Raymond de Fourquevaux, who published his highly derivative treatise on the practice of war just two years later.[7]

The appeal of the *Florentine Histories* was more limited, but this book had at least one practical application of interest. In their search for a "usable past," Protestant historians were willing to accept aid from any quarter. So it is not surprising, though it has passed unnoticed, that they should have applauded Machiavelli's criticism of the papacy. Flacius Illyricus in his fundamental *Catalogue of the Witnesses of Truth* of 1556 even admitted Machiavelli to his honor roll of proto-Protestants, along with such disparate authors as Marsiglio of Padua, Jean Gerson, Lorenzo Valla, and Guillaume Budé.[8] Thus Machiavelli contributed, if only in a negative way, to the reconstruction of Lutheran "tradition."

Reform-minded Frenchmen, too, welcomed his assistance. In 1551 Charles Dumoulin published a curious and indeed unique work of scholarship, a Protestant gloss upon that most glossed of texts, the corpus of canon law; and the following year he used this material in a scathing attack upon the Roman curia. In both of these books, which constitute a thoroughgoing re-evaluation of ecclesiastical history, Dumoulin included Machiavelli among his authorities and ranked him far above such "wholly popish" historians as Flavio Biondo. "In the history which he wrote in the Tuscan language, especially in the first book," Dumoulin declared, "Nicholas Machiavellus depicted marvelously well the origin, rise, and expansion of the papacy, along with the ruses of the popes by which this was accomplished. At the beginning, as he said, the Roman pope had no authority except what was given through

[5] *Le Miroir politique* (Paris, 1567), f. 5^{v}. In the introductory *epistre* there is an elaborate discussion of the terms *police* and *civilité*.

[6] Gerber, III, 28.

[7] *Instructions sur le faict de la guerre*, (ed.) G. Dickênson (London, 1954); originally published in 1548.

[8] *Catalogus testium veritatis* (Basel, 1556), 993.

reverence for religion and doctrine." Dumoulin agreed that the real trouble began in the eighth century. The coming of the Lombards, he concluded, "led the pope to *farsi piu vivo*, as Machiavelli put it, that is, to take courage and to act." With the alliance between the papacy and the Carolingian Franks, the fortunes of Italy and France converged. Like Machiavelli, though from the opposite point of view, Dumoulin believed that the calamitous results of this encounter were still being felt in the sixteenth century.[9]

Then as now, of course, Machiavelli was normally identified with his *Prince*. In 1557 this work was honored with a place on the first papal index (not to be joined by his other books for another half century). Yet in France it seemed to raise few eyebrows at first. Machiavelli did use "somewhat intemperate language," admitted his translator Guillaume d'Auvergne, and he seemed "to loosen the ties of conscience."[10] But the blame for this should not be placed on Machiavelli, he argued; it belonged rather to "the naturally vicious law of the world" which required princes sometimes to exceed the normal bounds of morality. Machiavelli's purpose was simply to teach the powerful (the *seigneur Politiq*) how to conserve and augment their domain. What is more, in contrast to the many authors who described princes of superhuman perfection, he "accommodated the form of his precepts to experience." As Machiavelli's other translator, Guillaume Cappel, summed it up, "One might accuse him of portraying an excessively severe prince, and yet we may excuse him through the parallel of a good doctor, who looks not to his patient's pleasure but to his sickness, and so prescribes strong medicine."[11]

At this very time, there was a large and growing market for such strong medicine. There were French books on the theory and practice of politics, of course, but on the whole they tended to be either oppressively legalistic or blandly moralistic—either conventional lists of royal privileges or traditional "mirrors" of the prince. Closest in form to Machiavelli's work was the *Institution of*

[9] *Les Commentaires analytiques sur l'edit des petites dates* and *Annotationes ad jus canonicum*, in *Opera omnia* (Paris, 1681), IV, 464, 68.

[10] Gerber, III, 32.

[11] *Ibid.*, 34.

the Prince compiled just a few years later by the great humanist Guillaume Budé.[12] Budé's "science politique," or "prudence civile," was loaded down with an impossible weight of moral, philosophical, and literary ornamentation. Closest in spirit to Machiavelli's work and also approximately contemporary was Claude de Seyssel's *Grand Monarchy of France.* Seyssel also emphasized experience, both diplomatic and military, and he framed his analyses in terms of what he called "natural and political reasons." His general purpose was "the conservation and augmentation of the French monarchy" through political and, if necessary, military means. Yet Seyssel very explicitly insisted that "la police" be tempered by religion and justice. Such, indeed, were the indispensable "bridles" restraining princely power.[13]

It is no wonder that Machiavelli spoke more directly to members of the next generation, who were beginning in a much more single-minded way to seek a "science" of politics. In 1567 Louis le Roy published a short history of political philosophy, thereby giving it a respectable pedigree and further definition.[14] He lamented its neglect and especially its divorce from experience, and although he was a disciple both of Budé and of Seyssel, he turned rather to Machiavelli as the most valuable modern supplement to Aristotle. Jean Bodin, who knew Machiavelli better than any other sixteenth century author, was still more enthusiastic. To him Machiavelli was "the first . . . for almost 1200 years after barbarism overwhelmed everything" to write intelligently about government.[15] Bodin's own ambition was to walk a little farther down Machiavelli's "untrodden path."

In other ways too, it would seem, Machiavelli had chosen a favorable time to settle in France. For it was precisely during the third

[12] *De l'Institution du prince* (Paris, 1547), 19. See the new edition and commentary in Claude Bontems *et al., Le Prince dans la France des XVIe et XVIIe siècles* (Paris, 1965).

[13] *La Monarchie de France,* (ed.) Jacques Poujol (Paris, 1961), 115 ff.

[14] *De l'Origine, antiquité, progres, excellence, et utilité de l'art politique* (Paris, 1567). For his use of Machiavelli see his translation, *Les Politiques d'Aristote* (Paris, 1568), 614, 745, 788.

[15] *Methodus ad facilem historiarum cognitionem* (1566), in *Oeuvres philosophiques,* (ed.) Pierre Mesnard (Paris, 1951), 167. In his *Six livres de la république* (Paris, 1583), 939, Bodin criticized Machiavelli for his defense of "mixed government."

quarter of the sixteenth century that men were beginning to distinguish and to define the public side of human behavior. In fact, even before Machiavelli became a public figure, French scholars were celebrating the arrival of the "homo politicus," in the words of François Baudouin.[16] At about the same time, in 1560, Etienne Pasquier published his own little dialogue on the "prince" and personified this point of view by calling his most important interlocutor "le politique";[17] fourteen years later, so would the author of the famous *Reveille-Matin*. It was during the 1560s, too, that *politique* was used as a highly charged, often derogatory way of characterizing anyone who placed public utility above religious principle. A later critic of *politiques* defined them as "those who refer all religion to policy or to government" and along with many others professed to detect in this practice the fine Italian hand of Machiavelli.[18]

Yet in the years between Pasquier's *Pour-parler du prince* and the *Reveille-Matin, politique* underwent a change in usage through that common process by which a contemptuous epithet becomes a proudly worn party label. Pasquier's friend Claude Fauchet argued that it was possible to be at once a Christian and a "bon politique," and many Protestants agreed. Thus the author of the *Reveille-Matin* caused his *politique* in the company of his colleague the *historiographe* to become converted to the true, which is to say the reformed, religion.[19] The basic reason for this shift in meaning, of course, was the massacre of St. Bartholomew. Long before this there had been a group of moderates (*moderatores*) inclined to a *via media*, but "Machiavelli's holiday" made some such program much more urgent. As one well-informed observer, and near victim of the massacre, wrote in the spring of 1574, "In Paris more than a thousand persons—nobles, magistrates, and merchants—have been

[16] *Commentarius de jurisprudentia Muciana* (1559) (Halle, 1729), 20. A similar discussion of "notre politic" appears in *Les Dialogues* (Paris, 1556), f. 40r, by Baudouin's former student, Louis le Caron.

[17] *Pour-parler du prince*, in *Recherches de la France* (Paris, 1633), 993. Cf. *Le Reveille-Matin des François* (Edinburgh, 1574), attributed variously to Nicolas Barnaud, Hugues Doneau, and even (impossibly) to François Hotman.

[18] Leonardo Lessius, *De Providentia numinis et animi immortalitate* (1613), cited by Charbonnel, 33.

[19] *Documents concernant la vie et les oeuvres de Claude Fauchet*, (ed.) J. Espiner-Scott (Paris, 1938), 189.

thrown in prison. They have taken the name of *politiques [politici]*, and . . . they demand the restoration of the ancient constitution through the convocation of the Estates General."[20] The author of this passage, François Hotman, was one of the most active propagandists both for this party and for the so-called "ancient constitution," which he had already celebrated in his notorious *Franco-Gallia*.

Hotman was no friend of Machiavelli, of course, nor of any of the "Italianized Frenchmen" who followed his doctrine. On the contrary he and the men of his party, who were "nouveaux reformateurs" as well as "bons politiques," according to one admirer, seized upon Machiavelli as the very embodiment of tyranny, atheism, and intolerance.[21] Machiavelli became not only a legend but a seed-bed of legends. He was regarded as the father-confessor to a whole tribe of frauds, fiends, and *fuorusciti*, and more especially to Catherine de' Medici, daughter of the man to whom he had dedicated his *Prince*. Stories were told that she took this book as her bible, that she brought up her children on it, that one of them, the future Henry III, carried it around in his pocket,[22] and that the massacre of Coligny and thousands of Huguenots was a direct application of the counsel given in the eighth chapter.

Such at least were the charges made by the Huguenot exiles in Switzerland, who began to sound the alarm against this monster. The *Reveille-Matin*, for example, adopted a frankly conspiratorial view, arguing that Machiavelli's evil genius had inspired official policy ever since the massacre of Vassy in 1562. The peace of St. Germain, concluded in the year of the first Machiavelli centennial, was represented as an offspring of the Cardinal of Lorraine—the "tiger of France," as Hotman had called him a decade earlier—and

[20] François Hotman to Gualter, 27 April 1574. Zürich, Zentralbibliothek, MSS, F. 39, f. 196^{r}.

[21] Nicolas Barnaud(?), *Le Miroir des François* (Paris, 1581), 291. Hotman's complaints against Machiavelli appear in a single letter to Wualter, 27 Sept. 1580, in Zürich, Staatsarchiv, E. II. 358, f. 79^{v}; also in *Epistolae Hottomannorum* (Amsterdam, 1700).

[22] *De iusta Henrici tertii abdicatione e Francorum regno* (Lyon, 1591), II, 33; see also Franciscus Portus, *Ad Petri Carpentarii virulentam epistolam responsio* (s.l. 1573), 31-32. In September 1572, William of Hesse said the *Prince* was the Italian bible (*die welsche Bibel*); A. Kluckhohn (ed.), *Briefe Friedrich des Frommen* (Braunschweig, 1870), II, 496.

of Catherine de' Medici, descended, in one vivid if implausible image, from a long line of Italian "buggers." Together, this "devil of a Guise" and his "whore" had created a "Sodom of horrible atheism" and the bloodbath of August 1572.[23] What was more shocking, even Frenchmen went along with this policy. The first president of the parlement of Paris, Christofle de Thou, allegedly edpressed his approval by remarking, "He who knows not how to dissemble knows not how to rule." This maxim was not Machiavelli's, but it came from the next most likely source—Philip de Commines, who as everybody now knows was the "French Machiavelli."

The biggest blast "against Machiavel"—indeed the *primum in genere*—was that by Innocent Gentillet, who seemed almost literally to believe that Machiavelli had risen from the dead and that it was his mission to destroy Machiavelli once and for all. Under the reign of Henry II, Machiavelli's name was unknown in France, Gentillet wrote, but with the coming of the wars and the coming of the Italians, his doctrine began to infect every level of society.[24] While recognizing that "Doctor Machiavel" was the world's leading authority on tyranny, ranking even above Bartolus, Gentillet was not impressed with his method. Machiavelli had known no history, he had merely "fished stories" out of Livy, and in truth every useful thing in his writings had been stolen from other authors.

Gentillet's own method had even less to recommend it. What he did was to reduce Machiavelli's views, derived from the *Discourses* as well as the *Prince*, to a series of simple-minded "maxims" and

[23] *Le Reveille-Matin*, introductory poem on "La Paix Valoise"; see especially pp. 37, 71, 141. The author indicates his debt to Hotman's *Franco-Gallia* (p. 191). Etienne de la Boétie's *Discours de la servitude voluntaire* was first printed as part of the *Reveille-Matin*, though it was composed in about 1548. There is no reason to suppose, as does Joseph Barrère, *Estienne de la Boétie contre Nicolas Machiavel* (Bordeaux, 1908), that the work was a retort to the *Prince*.

[24] *Discours sur les moyens de bien gouverner et maintenir en bonne paix un royaume ou autre principauté . . . contre Nicolas Machiavel Florentine* ([Geneva], 1576), now in a critical edition (Geneva, 1968) with notes and introduction by C. Edward Rathé, who has published an analysis, "Innocent Gentillet and the First 'Anti-Machiavel,'" *Bibliothèque d'humanisme et renaissance*, XXVII (1965), 186-225, citing other literature, of which the most important is H. J. Schäfer, *Innocenz Gentillet* (Cologne, 1929).

then to refute them by logical argument and historical example. He pressed his attack on three fronts: counsel, religion, and "pollicie." In the first place, Gentillet rejected the notion of absolute and arbitrary power in favor of a monarchy limited by fundamental laws, a faithful aristocracy, and an assembly of estates. Secondly, he attacked Machiavelli's "atheism" and defended not only the Christian religion but the Gallican church, which had long since found remedies for the usurpations of papal government so well described by Machiavelli himself. Finally, Gentillet condemned Machiavelli's prescriptions for cunning, cruelty, and hypocrisy as medicine worse than any disease; as a counter-remedy Gentillet suggested tyrannicide, resurrecting for this purpose the old arguments of Jean Petit. Such views inspired much of the revolutionary propaganda of these years, including the still more notorious *Defense of Liberty against Tyrants*, which likewise took "diametric opposition to the evil arts of Nicolas Machiavel."[25]

The Huguenot thesis, in short, was that the real guilt for France's plight in general and the massacre in particular lay neither with the tiger nor with the whore but with Machiavelli himself. He was also the moving spirit behind the Jesuit infiltration of France and, later, behind the Spanish League, argued Pasquier. Not only was he a policy-maker, he was also a perverter of youth. According to François de la Noue, he had converted a million to atheism; and curiously, a Catholic like Pierre Gregoire of Toulouse agreed that Machiavelli was a "most pernicious atheist."[26] In the face of such charges one hardly knows whether to applaud the sociological sophistication which permitted Huguenot critics to analyze the moral, social, and political corruption of France or to denounce the superstition that could attribute such conditions to the evil influence of a single man. (And *influence*, by the way, is a most appropriate term, being Italian in origin and having overtones both of pathology and of astrology, which happened to be a favorite pursuit of the Queen Mother.) In any case, we may conclude, a spectre was beginning to haunt Europe in the last quarter of the sixteenth

[25] *Vindiciae contra tyrannos* (1579), preface, in Latin edition of Machiavelli, *Princeps* (Leiden, 1648), 213 ff.

[26] La Noue, *Discours politiques et militaires*, (ed.) F. Sutcliffe (Geneva, 1960), 160; Gregoire, *De Republica* (Toulouse, 1582), XIII, 12.

century—the spectre of "Machiavellism," for such was the term which men like Pasquier, Henri Estienne, and others were introducing at just this time.[27]

Thus Machiavelli's image was raised to the level not only of metaphor but of myth. He was identified quite literally by some with the *Zeitgeist.* "The misfortunes of our age," wrote Pasquier, "are such that in order to be counted an able man one must be a Machiavellian"; the phrase he coined was "il faut Machiavelizer."[28] Yet at the same time Pasquier could see far enough behind Machiavelli's political mask to realize the symbolic nature of his target. "There are the Machiavellisms of which the world was delivered before Machiavel was born," he admitted elsewhere; "and there be a great many Machiavels among us at this day, who never read his books."[29] Pasquier was thinking in particular of his own *bête-noir,* Loyola, but of course every man could select his own personal Machiavel to villify.

Had he been honest with himself, Pasquier might have added that there is a little bit of Machiavel in every man, even in a loyal Gallican like himself. Although he pronounced Machiavelli's books "fit to burn," in his own political work Pasquier aimed at "political demonstrations no less strict than those of mathematics for its professors."[30] Nor was Machiavelli's moral relativism unpalatable in itself. Nothing was more common among French political writers than the assumption, as La Popelinière wrote in his own embryonic "Anti-Machiavel," that the prince should rule "according to the humors of the men of his time rather than the laws of reason."[31] One of Pasquier's friends, Louis le Caron, told Henry IV—who hardly needed telling—that the public good (*l'utilité publique*) "changes often according to circumstances and events." Another of his friends, and a fellow Jesuit-hater, Pierre Ayrault, thought that it

[27] *Les Lettres,* XII, 9, in *Oeuvres* (Amsterdam, 1723), II, 348, also in the critical edition of Dorothy Thickett (Geneva, 1966), 321; and Estienne, *Principum monitrix musa* (Basel, 1590), 252.

[28] *Recherches,* 459.

[29] *The Jesuites Catechisme* (London, 1602), f. 64r.

[30] *Recherches,* 22; cf. *Les Lettres,* IX, 7 (*Oeuvres,* II, 236).

[31] Bibliothèque Nationale, Manuscrits, Fonds français, vol. 20787, f. 19v ("Contre-Machiavel"); and yet he regarded Machiavelli the historian as "homme iudicieux," in *Histoire des histoires* (Paris, 1599), 104.

might even override private morality. At any rate he distinguished between "things unjust in themselves, unjust in private terms, and unjust in public terms" and went on to suggest a formula that Machiavelli might have endorsed completely: "In republics one does not always consider what is just in itself, but what is relevant to the state, which maintains itself here in one way and there in another."[32]

Yet no French author, not even Commines or Machiavelli's imitator Jean de la Taille, could "match a villain" like Machiavelli. (The pun is contemporary and not of my making.)[33] His medicine was too strong for even his greatest admirers. Le Roy, for example, called him "an author without conscience and without religion." Even Bodin, who himself had a somewhat diabolical reputation among his countrymen, was of two minds about his works: after having praised him extravagantly in 1566, Bodin chose, a decade later, to decry the "tyrannical ruses . . . poured like a poison into his book *The Prince*."[34] And La Taille, who in 1573 offered a doggerel version of this book to Henry III, found it advisable to bowdlerize Machiavelli's arguments a bit.[35]

What made Machiavelli's views so indigestible to French readers? One reason was sheer and (if the phrase is not tautological) unadulterated xenophobia. From Petrarch to Machiavelli Italians had scorned the French as "barbarians"; now Frenchmen returned the compliment with interest. One particularly clear manifestation was murder "Italian style," as Henri Estienne described it in 1566. French gentlemen, who preferred duelling, did not even

[32] Le Caron, prefatory letter to Henry IV in Barnabé Brisson, *Code du Roy Henry III* (Paris, 1622), and Ayrault, *De l'Ordre et instruction judiciaire* (Paris, 1576), f. 29^{r}.

[33] Edward Meyer, *Machiavelli and the Elizabethan Drama* (Weimar, 1897), 28. On Shakespeare's "murd'rous Machiavel," see p. 60.

[34] *Methodus*, 167. *Six livres de la République* (Cambridge, Mass., 1962), p. A70; preface, translation by K. D. McRae in his English edition.

[35] René Pintard, "Une adaptation de Machiavel au XVIe siècle: le 'Prince nécessaire' de Jean de la Taille," *Revue de littérature comparée*, XIII (1933), 385-402. It is amusing to see Catholics and Protestants using Machiavelli's name in vain against each other. In 1575, L'Estoile, *Journal de l'Estoile pour le règne de Henri III*, (ed.) L. R. Lefèvre (Paris, 1943), 89, characterized Hotman's critics as "corrumpus machiavélistes et Français italianisés," mentioning in particular Antoine Matharel, who himself, in his *Ad Franc. Hotmani Franco-Galliam . . . responsio* (Paris, 1575), 155, remarked that Hotman was even worse than Machiavelli.

have a name for this unspeakable practice and so had to import a foreign term.[36] "Assassination" thus became a familiar part of French public life. But such outlandish conduct—unchivalric if not uncivilized—was symptomatic of a deeper disorder. Not only Protestants like Estienne, Gentillet, and Hotman, but Catholics like Pasquier and Ayrault seemed to detect a vast and growing Italian syndrome in the body politic. Whatever the etiology of the disease and whatever its remedy, the source of the contagion could be located precisely. "As among all nations in craft and subtiltie Italy beareth the name," declared Estienne in his diagnosis, "so in Italy Tuscane, and in Tuscane Florence excelleth."[37] And of all symbols to express this disease, of all scapegoats to blame it on, who was better qualified than Machiavelli?

But there was another and perhaps more fundamental antagonism, and this goes to the heart of Machiavelli's political methodology. According to Gentillet, there are two roads to knowledge, and Machiavelli was unable to keep his footing on either.[38] On what contemporaries would have called the "regressive road," the empirical approach moving from effects to cause, he showed his atheism, perversity, and general ignorance. On the deductive road, which moves from cause to effect, he lost his way entirely. He did not even realize, apparently, that its destination is not political science but mathematics. This fallacy above all—that is, the abstract, coldly logical, reductionist, and what we might call behaviorist method—alienated French intellectuals. Not even Machiavelli's supposed irreligion disturbed them more deeply; after all Bodin too acquired a reputation as an "atheist" and even a sorcerer, and yet he continued to be respected as a political philosopher.[39]

The fact is that Machiavelli and his French critics disagreed fundamentally about the very substance of history. For one thing French scholars, including *politiques* like Pasquier and Bodin, had

[36] *Apologie pour Hérodote,* (ed.) P. Ristelhuber (Paris, 1879), I, 353. Cf. Pasquier, *Recherches,* IX, 20; CSP For., Eliz., 1563, p. 92.

[37] *A mervaylous discourse upon the lyfe, deeds, and behaviours of Katherine de Medicis* (Heidelberg, 1575), 6. A sampling of popular anti-Italian literature may be found in *Journal de l'Estoile pour le règne de Henri III,* 90-103 *passim.*

[38] *Contre-Machiavel,* preface.

[39] *Scaligerana . . .* (Amsterdam, 1740), I, 500.

an appreciation for ideological factors, which the limitations of Machiavelli's method hardly permitted him to acknowledge. They realized, of course, that some men were driven by material rather than spiritual motives, that for example there were "malcontents" as well as Huguenots struggling against the domination of the Guises; but they did not doubt that the wars were essentially religious in character. Contact with Calvinist and Jesuit ideologues intensified this attitude. On the other hand, they were aware of the force of tradition and the role of such institutions as the parlement and the university in fostering inertia. They had a sense of the complexity as well as the tragedy of history, and it is not surprising that they turned with renewed interest to the balanced kind of political analyses represented by Seyssel, whose work enjoyed a revival in the last quarter of the century.

Between Machiavelli and most French authors, moreover, were enormous differences in education and experience. Machiavelli's mind was shaped by the military and diplomatic services he performed for the Florentine Republic, while most Frenchmen followed academic and especially legal careers. François Baudouin had indeed referred to the "homo politicus," but he immediately added, "hoc est jurisconsultus." Most Frenchmen were cut off from power and from policy-making questions in general, and they were increasingly disillusioned about its uses and potential as one civil war succeeded another. Pasquier, listening to the harangues during the meeting of the Estates of Blois in 1588, seemed to be hearing only the "swan's song" of the monarchy; in general, he felt, men were losing control of their own fates.[40] These are perhaps some of the reasons why French scholars of this generation were concerned more with description than with causal analysis, more with the nature of institutions than with the laws of politics, more with the temper of society than with individual psychology. If their work was less probing than Machiavelli's, it was also more comprehensive; they preferred a net to a harpoon, as it were, in the reassessment of their past. It is not surprising that men like Pasquier should look upon history less as a store of vicarious experience to be used in future calculations than as a drama, an increasingly tragic drama, to be watched. In a sense history was retreating from politics and

[40] *Les Lettres*, XIII, 7 (*Oeuvres*, II, 378; [ed.] Thickett, 383).

reverting to its moral function.

Yet there was a positive side to this. In general, French scholars had a much deeper sense of individuality and of historical differences. Machiavelli deliberately ignored questions of cultural tradition, specific social context, and institutional peculiarity, but Pasquier, Bodin, and Hotman, worlds apart as they might be on religious or political grounds, took such problems and indeed "national character" in general as the substance of history and of any possible science based on history. Because they were "barbarians" they could not—and by this time would not—connect their own traditions with ancient Rome. They could not even use Rome, as Machiavelli did, as a model of political experience. Such were the assumptions of Hotman's "anti-Tribonianist" arguments and Pasquier's reconstruction of French culture and of that comparative method developed by Bodin and other French jurists.[41]

What I am suggesting, in short, is that the anti-Machiavellian backlash in sixteenth-century France stemmed not only from offended political and religious sensibilities but also from a clash between different modes of perceiving reality—not only from a doctrinal *Kulturkampf* but from a fundamental, though not always fully articulated, *Methodenstreit*. Machiavelli frightened, while at the same time he fascinated, his French readers by that political mask which he never seemed to discard. Indeed, because of the brutality and cynicism of his political analyses he seemed to be, in an intellectual sense, more of a tyrant than his "prince." Now obviously this contrast between Machiavelli as a hawkish policy-maker and his French critics as sophisticated and inhibited academic doves can be overdrawn, and perhaps I have overdrawn it. Yet, in a sense, these men brought it upon themselves by conjuring up this devil which modern scholarship has still not completely exorcised. For it is largely because of these worshipful French scholars that Machiavelli remains, at least in one of his reincarnations, the demon of power. Because of their needs and fears he became not only an "advocate of tyranny," he emerged as the bogeyman of the western world.

[41] See the remarks of Jean Moreau-Reibel, *Jean Bodin et le droit public comparé* (Paris, 1933), 53, and J. G. A. Pocock, *The Ancient Constitution and the Feudal Law* (Cambridge, 1957), especially chap. I.

XI

HISTORY, ENGLISH LAW AND THE RENAISSANCE

What should they know of England,
Who only England know?

KIPLING'S QUESTION CONTAINS MORE TRUTH THAN POETRY, BUT IT IS not one which English historians have been disposed to consider very seriously. For them it has not required a formal indoctrination in British empiricism — or a "storm in the channel" — to keep the continent isolated; it has been enough for them to feel that dissenters, who would like to see English history set more firmly in a European context, will be in a small, unheeded, unpublicized, and probably unsubsidized minority. The example set by Maitland, and Selden before him, has not often been imitated. Nor, in view of the pressures and self-perpetuating tendencies of professional scholarship, is any major reformation to be expected in the near future. Old-fashioned constitutional history has been deepened and enriched through the study of administration and class-structure, but this has not been accompanied by any appreciable widening of national horizons or even interchange between special fields. In this respect Holdsworth seems hardly to represent an advance over Maitland, or for that matter Messrs. Richardson and Sayles over Stubbs. In England (and in America as well, which in this respect at least seems to have clung to its colonial status) the result has been in particular to play down the influence of continental law and institutions and in general to cast the comparative study of society into neglect, if not disrepute. Consequently, Maitland's explanation of "Why the history of English law is not written" still seems painfully appropriate:

> In the first place I think we may say, because of the traditional isolation of English law from every other study . . . . History involves comparison, and the English lawyer who knew this and cared nothing for any other system than his own hardly seems to come in sight of the idea of legal history.[1]

[1] F. W. Maitland, *Collected Papers* (Cambridge, 1911), i, p. 487. Maitland's famous Rede lecture of 1901 on *English Law and the Renaissance* (Cambridge, 1901) is of fundamental (and even eponymous) importance here, though it does not deal with legal history as such; nor do the standard recent studies of historiography by F. S. Fussner (cited below in notes 22 and 33), May McKisack (cited below in note 37) and F. J. Levy (*Tudor Historical Thought* [San Marino, 1967]). The only book to do so directly is H. Arneke, *Kirchengeschichte und Rechtsgeschichte in England* (Halle, 1937), esp. pp. 194 ff.

In general the present paper is a by-product of and a kind of excursus to my *Foundations of Modern Historical Scholarship* (New York, 1970), which discusses the relations between history and the main varieties of continental law, particularly in France, that is, civil, canon, customary and royal legislation.

Maitland's observation was not only a lament about the state of historical studies, it was an indictment of one aspect of the whole common law tradition. The scholarly insularity he noted was not simply a reflection of the "splendid isolation" of the nineteenth century or the shrinking empire of the twentieth, it was an enduring feature, a conditioned reflex if not a national trait, of English scholarship. Though associated most often with Victorian Whiggery, this attitude obviously has deeper roots. It figured perhaps most conspicuously in times of crisis, notably during the wars against France at the end of the eighteenth century and during the constitutional conflicts of the seventeenth century. A *locus classicus* is the work of Edward Coke, whose whole career was dedicated to the proposition that English common laws "are the most equal and most certain, of greatest antiquity, and least delay, and most beneficial and easy to be observed".[2] But even then this was an old refrain, and in fact Coke was doing little more than rehearsing the arguments of his famous predecessor Sir John Fortescue. There were other societies, of course, that accepted the doctrines of "juridical nationalism",[3] but in England the movement was unique both in intensity and in durability. By Fortescue's time it had attained the level of a national mythology; and useful as it may have been for the rights and privileges of the propertied classes, it was a serious impediment to any kind of historical understanding.

"Comparisons are rightly to be judged odious", observed Fortescue, and so they are, at least as he employed them.[4] In order to enhance his "Praise of the Laws of England" he indulged in a whole series of odious comparisons between common law and civil law, that is, the civil law practised in French courts as far as Fortescue understood it. Interesting as this book has been to historians of political thought, it has seldom been taken very seriously as a description of fifteenth-century government. In fact, what Fortescue did was to juxtapose an idealization of the laws and character of England (from the vantage point of the King's Bench) with a caricature of those of France, and his purpose was transparently polemical. Civil law he represented in terms of its arbitrariness (such as establishing truth by witnesses

[2] Sir Edward Coke, *Les reports de Edward Coke . . .*, 11 parts (London, 1600-15: *S.T.C.* 5493 etc.; London, 1738 edn.), ii, preface.

[3] Vittorio de Caprariis, *Propaganda e pensiero politico in Francia durante le guerre di religione* (Naples, 1959), p. 261; and Vincenzo Piano Mortari, *Diritto romano e diritto nationale in Francia nel secolo XVI* (Milan, 1962), p. 79.

[4] Sir John Fortescue, *De Laudibus Legum Anglie*, ed. S. B. Chrimes (Cambridge, 1942), pp. 42 ff.; see also the remarks of H. D. Hazeltine in the introduction, pp. xix ff.

instead of the sworn judgement of a jury), its cavalier treatment of family property (allowing bastards to succeed), its brutality (the use of torture) and above all its tyranny (as reflected in the famous civilian formula, "what pleases the prince has the force of law"); and he found the French monarchy guilty by association. By contrast the "political and regal" government of England belonged to a wholly different species. Now this was, at least in part, professional cant. Only in the provinces of written law in the south of France, in fact, was civil law accepted as "common law", and even there it was restricted to those matters for which there were no customary rules. It was applied, as one jurist put it, "by reception not by domination", and it was feared at least as much as it was admired.[5] Fortescue's contemporary, Etienne Bertrand, for example, was no less careful than the Chief Justice to give first place to native French custom.[6]

In general the contrast between English and French government was not nearly as sharp as Fortescue represented it. At the beginning of the sixteenth century Claude de Seyssel, who had also been a jurist, sketched out a portrait of the "grand monarchy of France" as a mixed polity with various limiting traditions and institutions that was not at all dissimilar to Fortescue's "regnum politicum et regale"; and representative monarchy, the theory as well as the practice, survived throughout the sixteenth century.[7] What is more, even those French jurists who conceded a significant difference between the two monarchies assumed a close historical connection. "In the kingdom of England", remarked Louis le Caron, "one sees many traces and vestiges of the ancient laws of France, of which unfortunately only a shadow remains".[8] From the French point of view, at least, the difference between the two governments was one not of kind but of degree, or perhaps of historical divergence.

Equally striking, French lawyers in the fifteenth and sixteenth centuries were quite as eager as Fortescue to condemn the tendencies of Roman law toward political tyranny, legal brutality and social rigidity. They too looked with suspicion upon the principles *quod*

[5] Jean Ferrault, *Tractatus . . . jura seu privilegia aliqua regni Franciae* (Paris, 1545).

[6] Paul Ourliac, *Droit romain et Pratique méridioniale au XVe siècle : Etienne Bertrand* (Paris, 1937).

[7] Claude de Seyssel, *La monarchie de France*, ed. J. Poujol (Paris, 1961), ch. 8. In general, see A. Lemaire, *Les lois fondamentales de la monarchie française d'après les théoriciens de l'ancien régime* (Paris, 1907); C. H. McIlwain, *Constitutionalism, Ancient and Modern* (Ithaca, 1940); and J. R. Major, *Representative Institutions in Renaissance France* (Madison, 1960).

[8] Louis le Caron, *Pandectes ou Digestes du droit françois* (Lyon, 1596), p. 278.

principi placuit and *patria potestas*, and the provisions of civil law that threatened the integrity of the "grandes familles". They too were careful to uphold the independence of their legal traditions and to reject any notion of a formal "reception". This they argued on the grounds that their king "had no superior in temporal matters" (and it is interesting to note that English lawyers were not above turning this old Gallican formula to their own uses).[9] Finally, French scholars too assumed that law was a reflection of national character as well as a means of controlling social behaviour, and that the vernacular ought to be the vehicle of ordinary judicial proceedings. A classic example of this attitude, and of the suspicion of Romanism in general, is François Hotman's *Antitribonian* of 1567. Once again the similarity with English attitudes is conspicuous. Indeed, Hotman might almost have been summarizing the argument that appeared eight years before in John Aylmer's defence of England's law (as well as her queen) against Knox's blast. Aylmer, who may have known Hotman during his exile in Strasbourg, protested against the "burden" of civil law, the "cannon shot" of pontifical law, and such practices as testamentary succession, "for nothing soner destroieth great houses, than the division of thenheritance, as it appeareth in Germany". If civil law were the "best ever made", "yet comprehendeth it not al things in al countris . . .". Like Hotman he concluded that "our law must direct us, because it best agreeth with our country".[10] Needless to say, in England as well as in France the professional distrust of foreign law was reinforced by a protestant hatred for still more insidious forms of "Romanism".

Nevertheless the divergence between English and French scholarship became ever more pronounced. One of the underlying reasons for this was the curious reluctance of the English to consider historical perspective or context. Their tendency was rather to move directly from the most abstract principles of natural law to the most technical practices of English courts without any reference to contacts or parallels with continental jurisprudence. So Sir Thomas Littleton discussed English land law without any reference to its feudal back-

[9] Charles de Grassaille, *Regalium Franciae libri duo* (Paris, 1545), pp. 67 ff.; Etienne Pasquier, *L'interprétation des Institutes de Justinian*, ed. M. le Duc Pasquier (Paris, 1847), i, pp. 26, 490; Antoine Loisel, *Institutes coustumières* (Paris, 1646), ed. M. Reulos (Paris, 1935). In *The History of the Common Law of England* (London, 1713), pp. 28-9, Sir Matthew Hale remarks that civil and canon law have no force in England because the king "recognizes no superior" but that a "Reception" is allowed in certain courts.

[10] John Aylmer, *An harborowe for faithful and trewe subiectes* (Strasbourg, 1559: *S.T.C.* 1005), sig. K4v. Cf. François Hotman, *Antitribonian* (Paris, 1603), ch. 17.

ground and defined the fief in wholly unhistorical terms.[11] So Christopher St. Germain and Edward Hake discussed the notion of equity in terms of Aristotle's conception but with no consideration of the forms that this was taking in modern times.[12] So John Rastell, who was Thomas More's brother-in-law, derived "comyn law" directly from nature and proceeded to discuss its vocabulary without any regard for continental practice or Latin equivalents.[13] In general the assumption seemed to be that, as Dugdale later put it, "common law is no other than pure and tried Reason".[14]

This was literally worlds apart from the practice of continental jurists. Not only humanists like Guillaume Budé and university teachers like Jean Pyrrhus d'Angleberme, but also practising lawyers — "Bartolists" — like Barthélemy de Chasseneux, André Tiraqueau and René Choppin habitually discussed French customs in comparison with civil, canon, and several sorts of feudal law.[15] Though quite as professionally-minded as the common lawyers, these men never hesitated to draw upon the learning and experience of others, and they frequently established parallels between the three chief varieties of continental law. In a sense the habits of comparative law were built into the legal profession on the continent, especially in France, with its multiple heritage and complex system of lay and ecclesiastical courts, of written and unwritten law, and with the close ties between the universities and the *barreau*. These habits were not at all shared by the English, although the background of their law was ostensibly no less mixed. Englishmen drew extensively upon the arguments of sixteenth-century French propaganda, but hardly at all upon the scholarship and perspective of which this was, in part, a

[11] Sir Thomas Littleton, "Tenores Novelli" [1481], in Sir Edward Coke, *The first part of the institutes of the lawes of England* (London, 1628; *S.T.C.* 15784), 15th edn., 3 vols. (London, 1794), i, p. 1.

[12] Christopher St. Germain, *Doctor and Student* (London, 1532: *S.T.C.* 21568), and Edward Hake, *Epieikeia*, ed. D. E. C. Yale (Yale Law Lib. Pub., no. 13, 1953). Much the same leap from the "timeless" concept of equity directly to English practice is made in the most recent discussion of the problem, Stuart Prall, "The Development of Equity in Tudor England", *Amer. Jl. of Legal History*, viii (1964), pp. 1-19.

[13] John Rastell, *Expositiones terminorum legum anglorum* (London, 1527: *S.T.C.* 20703), prohemium.

[14] Sir William Dugdale, *Origines juridiciales* (London, 1666), 2nd edn. (London, 1671), p. 3.

[15] See especially J. Brejon, *André Tiraqueau (1488-1558)* (Paris, 1937), pp. 317 ff.; J. Moreau-Reibel, *Jean Bodin et le droit public comparé* (Paris, 1933), ch. 1; and my "Development and Context of Bodin's Method", in H. Denzer (ed.), *Jean Bodin: Verhandlungen der internationalen Bodin Tagung in München* (Munich, 1973), pp. 123-50.

product.[16] In 1550 Eguinaire Baron published an elaborate comparative treatise of civil and customary law, perhaps the first of a distinguished genre, which both drew upon and contributed to historical scholarship.[17] The study of English law enjoyed no such cosmopolitan treatments.

What was at issue between English and French scholars was not only a particular interpretation of history, it was a question of basic method; even given identical evidence, they would not come to the same kind of conclusions. Consider the sensitive problem of outside "influence". In general, French scholars recognized such a process, whether through "imitation" or through conquest, in their own Gallican past. Thus Etienne Pasquier, who did not doubt the superiority of French law, admitted that the provincial customs were "formed in a largely Roman spirit".[18] For him the model for — and the measure of — such influence was the French language, which amply reflected its variegated past. Such a thesis, along with its philological assumptions, would not be likely to win favour with English scholars. If they were embarrassed at the language of their sources, at the "Hotchpot French", as one common lawyer put it, "stuffed up with such variety of borrowed words",[19] they did not attach any fundamental historical significance to this. "We have a few hunting terms and peddlars French in the lousye law", Aylmer admitted, "but the language and the customs bee Englyshe and Saxonyshe". His countrymen's blood might be French, he added, but their hearts were English.[20] In contrast to scholars like Pasquier and Hotman, English lawyers would not be impressed with the mere appearance of alien formulas, such as *quod principi placuit* in Bracton, nor would they be willing to admit that the teaching of civil law in the universities or the practice of ecclesiastical courts had introduced any significant change in English government. They had too strong a faith in a permanent and unchanging tradition — comparable to the "true" doctrinal tradition envisaged by Luther, Melanchthon and Calvin. This was, in Butterfield's use of the term, "Whiggery" with a vengeance.

[16] See J. H. M. Salmon, *The French Religious Wars in English Political Thought* (Oxford, 1959).

[17] Eguinaire Baron, *Institutionum civilium ab Justiniano Caesare editarum libri IIII* (Poitou, 1550), organized as "commentaria bipartita".

[18] Pasquier, *L'interprétation*, i, p. 64. Pasquier's studies of French linguistic and legal history are collected in his *Recherches de la France* (Paris, 1621), books VIII and IX.

[19] Abraham Fraunce, *The lawiers logike* (London, 1588: *S.T.C.* 11343), dedicated to the lawyers of Gray's Inn.

[20] Aylmer, *An harborowe*, sig. Q2v.

Perhaps the most remarkable thing about the English tradition was the way it resisted the great transformations of sixteenth-century scholarship. It is certainly going too far to say, with Maitland, that this was the time when English law was "saved but isolated", but not to suggest that it was the time when English historical scholarship was isolated but stagnated (except in a quantitative sense). In France historians and lawyers had quietly disposed of many of their cherished professional beliefs — that the "Salic law" and the Parlement of Paris were derived from the early Franks, for example, and that their laws were older than those of the Romans. The English, on the other hand, clung even more tenaciously to their myths, and they continued to rest their case upon the aboriginal character and prehistorical origin of common law. The fact that between Fortescue and Coke lay over a century of exploration into European legal and institutional history, much of it by professional jurists, did not seem to matter. On the contrary, as J. G. A. Pocock has said, "Between 1550 and 1600 there occurred a great hardening and consolidation of common-law thought".[21] It is something of a paradox that this should have happened precisely when the continent was enjoying a golden age of legal and historical scholarship and when a kind of "historical revolution" was beginning in England itself. Here, as in France, many of the participants in this movement, including several original members of the Society of Antiquaries, were recruited from the legal profession, but this did not make them any less parochial. Most remained, as one recent admirer has admitted, "insular scholiasts", and their activities appear more as a riot than a revolution of learning.[22]

* * * *

One major source of trouble lay in the very nature of the common law tradition, especially by comparison with the profession of civil law. "The study of English law", Erasmus remarked early in the century, "is as far as can be from true learning",[23] and things had not

[21] J. G. A. Pocock, *The Ancient Constitution and the Feudal Law* (Cambridge, 1957), p. 31. My indebtedness to this fundamental book is too great to permit, and too obvious to need, further specification.

[22] F. S. Fussner, *The Historical Revolution* (London, 1962), p. 99 — a valuable book despite its extravagant, rather un-English, and (in my opinion) inappropriate title. R. J. Schoeck, "The Elizabethan Society of Antiquaries and Men of Law", *Notes and Queries*, cxcix (1954), pp. 417-21, lists 38 antiquaries associated with the Inns of Court.

[23] *Opus Epistolarum Des. Erasmi*, ed. P. S. Allen, iv (Oxford, 1922), p. 17.

changed for the better by Coke's time. "It were to be wished", wrote one English civilian, "that God would vouchsafe our Innes of Court with some second Budaeus, that is a third Varro, whose skill in the lawes might be exquisite . . .".[24] What both Erasmus and Fulbecke had in mind was the non-academic, not to say anti-intellectual, character of England's so-called "third university". Fortescue had called the Inns of Court the "studia generalia" of English law, but though they were not wholly impervious to humanist learning, they were essentially technical schools.[25] Even a man like Abraham Fraunce, a great admirer of Hotman and of other French civilians and an enthusiast for Ramist logic, displayed a relatively narrow professionalism. If he drew a comparison with common law, it was to establish that the two traditions were separate but equal. Fraunce excused the "rudeness and barbarism" of English law with the same arguments applied by continental jurists to medieval law, namely, that the fault lay not with the men but with "the misery of their obscure age", and he pointedly denied the relevance of the literary standards of the humanist school of jurisprudence. "Both Bartolus his Latin and Brytton his French in some mens judgment is sufficiently elegant", he inelegantly concluded, "because it is fully significant".[26] In any case, as the most recent historian of the Inns of Court has concluded, Fraunce's book "seems to have made no mark on the legal profession".[27] In general, if the Inns of Court added strength to the legal profession, by the same token they served to separate the practice of law from scholarship much more sharply than on the continent.

It should be added, of course, that legal education encouraged a certain empirical cast of mind, "for generalities", as Coke observed, "never bring anything to a conclusion".[28] But clearly such concern for evidence stemmed not from curiosity about the process of history but only from the desire to build up a case. Justinian's Digest was compiled at least in part for antiquarian purposes, and so were some of the sixteenth-century inventories of French law; but English collections, such as *A newe boke of presidentes* (1543), were

[24] William Fulbecke, *The second part of the parallele or conference of the civill law, the canon law, and the common law of England* (London, 1602: *S.T.C.* 11415a), dedication.

[25] Fortescue, *De Laudibus*, *cap.* 49.

[26] Fraunce, *The lawiers logike*, dedication.

[27] Wilfred R. Prest, *The Inns of Court under Elizabeth and the Early Stuarts* (Totowa, N. J., 1972), p. 146.

[28] Coke, *Reports*, vii, preface.

purely utilitarian in character.[29] This is not to say that English law was inflexibly conservative; on the contrary common lawyers could be remarkably imaginative in adapting their tradition to the needs of the day. But their work was neither graced nor constrained by the newly emerging discipline of history.

The archetype of this intellectual insularity was Edward Coke, and he expressed better than any other the common law mythology which has now become part of history. That English institutions in general were self-generating and self-sufficient — were "immemorable" and the product of "time out of mind" — was for him, in the phrase of Justice Holmes, an "inarticulate major premise". The minor was the inferior and absolutely alien character of other systems; and the conclusion, articulated only too often, was that English law was, quite literally, incomparable.[30] For preserving the liberties of the English nation (and the privileges of the English legal profession) this may have been a useful syllogism; for the development of legal and historical scholarship it was, to say the least, constricting.

Coke's guild-mentality contrasts sharply both with the attitude of the French "historical school of law", which had wanted to promote a marriage of history and law for the benefit of both, and even with the rival Bartolist school, which had its own, often very sophisticated, appreciation of the processes of history. Coke took the contrary view that history was the source not only of poetic legends, such as that of Brut, but of legal misconceptions, such as the opinion that the offices of sheriff and justice of the peace had been introduced by the Normans — or for that matter, according to some of his colleagues, trial by jury. So Coke warned men to "beware of Chronicle law reported in our Annals, for that will undoubtedly lead thee to error".[31] "To the grave and learned writers of Histories", Coke concluded, "my advice is that they meddle not with the Laws of this Realm, before they confer with some Learned in that Profession". It is true that Coke himself did not hesitate to make use of historical writings, but this was merely because as a lawyer he believed the more arguments the better — there was no telling, he remarked, what might persuade some people. But it was not in history that one learned about the law; on the contrary it was in the study of law that one found "the faithful and true Histories of all Successive Times". The truth of the

[29] *A newe boke of presidentes in maner of a register* (London, 1543: *S.T.C.* 3327), with a preface by Thomas Phaer.

[30] Coke, *Reports*, ii, preface.

[31] *Ibid.*, iii, preface. Cf. Roger Twysden, *The Commoners Liberty* (London, 1648), p. 2.

matter is that Coke was not interested in "history" at all. When he recited the hackneyed old Ciceronian formula, "the Witness of Times, the Light and Life of Truth", when he referred to real "vestiges of antiquity and truth", he meant his own canon, the sacred records of English law.[32] But his assumption about these records was that they reflected, however imperfectly, the timeless and unchanging body of common law. Just as Calvin asked "What was the church really like in the time of Christ and the Apostles", so Coke wanted to know what common law was like before the statutes. His legal ideal, in short, was not only pre-historical, it was supra-historical; his attitude was based not merely on "wrong history", as Herbert Butterfield has suggested, but on anti-history.[33]

In order to preserve this innocence it was necessary to maintain the old doctrine of the hermetic character, or at least the incomparability, of common law. Since this was no longer easy to do by scholarly argument, Coke was obliged to take refuge in professional ethics. He called it "a desperate and dangerous matter for Civilians and Canonists . . . to write either of the Common Laws of England, which they profess not, or against them which they know not".[34] For his part Coke would never presume to pass judgement on foreign laws, although he was not altogether ignorant of them, and naturally he expected the same abstention from foreign scholars. When Hotman, after looking over a copy of Littleton on tenures loaned to him by Pasquier, expressed an unfavourable opinion, Coke became almost speechless with anger. To Englishmen Littleton's book was sacred: Camden had compared it to Justinian's collection, and Coke himself thought it as close to perfection as humanly possible. About many matters — about the existence of an ideal "ancient constitution" and immutable "fundamental laws" — Coke would have agreed with Hotman, but about the monuments of English law there was no room for debate. In England there was only one law, and to hear Coke tell it, he was its prophet.

Coke made no pretence of being a historian, of course; he was in the

[32] Coke, *Reports*, i, preface. In general see my "Clio and the Lawyers: Forms of Historical Consciousness in Medieval Jurisprudence", *Medievalia et Humanistica*, new ser., v (1974), pp. 25-49.

[33] H. Butterfield, *The Englishman and his History* (Cambridge, 1944), an interesting companion piece to his famous *The Whig Interpretation of History* (Cambridge, 1929). Recently F. S. Fussner, *Tudor History and the Historians* (New York, 1970), p. 236, has repeated this charge of Coke's "wrong interpretation" of history, but in general seems to take a positive view of the influence of common law on historiography.

[34] Coke, *Reports*, x, preface. Cf. François Hotman, *De Feudis commentatio tripertita* (Lyon, 1573), in *Operum*, 3 vols. (Lyon, 1599-1600), ii, col. 913.

tradition rather of those "professional remembrancers" who, learning their law by hearing in court, were bound to oral if not mythical modes of thought.[35] As Maitland said, he was "of all mankind the most credulous"; and according to Pocock, his mind "was as nearly insular as a human being's could be".[36] But he was not alone on his island. The most distinguished of English antiquaries, William Lambarde, displayed much the same cast of mind. By the time he had published his learned survey of the English court system, Lambarde had already gained distinction as a local historian, and he planned a work on the topography of England until he was forestalled by Camden. He was familiar with legal records and once won praise from Elizabeth herself for helping her to understand certain terms of law from those earlier days when, as she put it, "force and arms did prevail" and before the "wit of the fox" was afoot.[37] Later he was appointed deputy keeper of the Tower records. He had enjoyed a good classical education and knew the writings of such continental scholars as Valla and Paulus Emilius. In his *Archion* Lambarde proposed to view the English courts "Historically, as the time it selfe begat them", but in fact he was more solicitous of the conventions of "la comen ley" than of the fashions of historical scholarship.[38] At this time he had been an associate of Lincoln's Inn for some dozen years, and he wrote in much the same tone he used when charging local juries.[39] On the whole he stayed with English sources and showed only a perfunctory interest in parallel or related developments in other societies or indeed in any "foreign" imports into England. Like Coke and Fortescue, in short, he was more interested in celebrating than in understanding "the native liberty and ancient pre-eminence of the English policy". Again this attitude contrasts with that of such continental authors as Vincent de la Loupe, Charles de Figon and Claude Fauchet, who wrote similar books about the offices and courts of the French government.[40] They too praised the

[35] See M. T. Clanchy, "Remembering the Past and the Good Old Law", *History*, lv (1970), pp. 165-76.

[36] Maitland, *Collected Papers*, iii, p. 453, and Pocock, *The Ancient Constitution*, p. 56.

[37] M. McKisack, *Medieval History and the Tudor Age* (Oxford, 1971), p. 82.

[38] William Lambarde, *Archion; or a commentary upon the High Courts of Justice in England* (London, 1635: *S.T.C.* 15143), ed. C. H. McIlwain and P. Ward (Cambridge, Mass., 1957), p. 20. See Wilbur Dunkel, *William Lambarde* (New Brunswick, 1965), pp. 130 ff.

[39] "Charges to Quarter Sessions" (Maidstone, 28 Sept. 1591), in Conyers Read (ed.), *William Lambarde and Local Government* (Ithaca, 1962), p. 108.

[40] Vincent de la Loupe, *Origines des dignitez* (Paris, 1572); Charles de Figon, *Discours des estats* (Paris, 1579); Claude Fauchet, *Origines des dignitez*, in *Oeuvres* (Paris, 1610).

"pre-eminence" of the French monarchy, but this did not blind them to its manifold institutional inheritance, Celtic as well as Roman and German. But Lambarde recognized but one source, and that was pre-Conquest England.

Or was it a more remote "Gothic" past? For Lambarde was an enthusiastic, almost a utopian, "Germanist". As Hotman had traced French institutions back to an idealized "Franco-Gallic" state, so Lambarde assumed that English society was essentially Anglo-Saxon in character and likewise that Tacitus's account of the early Germans applied also to the forebears of the English. He insisted upon the basic "continuance" of Parliament from Anglo-Saxon times and regarded Magna Carta as "the first letter of manumission of the people of this Realme out of the Norman servitude". Not surprisingly, Lambarde preferred custom to written laws. "For written Lawes must needs be made in a generality", he wrote, "and be grounded upon that which happeneth for the most part, because no wisdome of man can fore-see everything in particularitie, which Experience and Time doth beget". It was the need to take into account the variables of time, place and circumstance that justified the principle of equity and the jurisdiction of Chancery. Such jurisdictions did not open the door to arbitrary government, Lambarde argued; on the contrary they actually prevented "a rigid and Arithmeticall Government" such as that of ancient Rome.[41] But that such jurisdictions also opened the door to judgements based upon civil and canon law Lambarde did not permit himself to acknowledge.

In order to preserve the virgin character of English institutions Lambarde was obliged to make some rather special and revealing linguistic assumptions. In particular he proposed a distinction between the "name" and the "nature" of an institution — a view quite contrary to that of the new science of philology. With this distinction in mind he went on to discredit the notion of any significant foreign influence. The Norman invaders, for example, "did not so much alter the substance as the name of the Saxon order, which they found at their coming hither".[42] The word "court" itself, taken from the French "cour" and Latin "curia", stemmed ultimately — according to what we might call a functionalist etymology — from the word "cura", signifying "that heed and care ought to be taken in the deciding of controversies". But more fundamentally, the English constitution had its origin in (and preserved the connotations of) the

[41] Lambarde, *Archion*, p. 44.
[42] *Ibid.*, p. 12.

Saxon *gemot*, which referred to the popular assembly held by the king. So too with Parliament, despite its French etymology. Lambarde paused long enough to dismiss the older derivations — from the "peer's lament (*parium lamentum*)", or from "speaking one's mind (*parler la ment*)", which Valla had long ago discredited — and to notice the parallels with the French "assembly des Estates" and the German "Dyet". But in general Lambarde's conclusion was, "I see not how I can derive it from any other time, than from that, in which the German or English did first set foot on this land, to invade it".[43] So it was with the entire judicial structure of England, which was "no new-made Law or first brought by the Norman Conquest".

With Coke, in short, Lambarde shared a profound indifference to comparative legal studies, to the teachings of humanist philology, and to the conception of history associated with these. Despite his love of "authentick records" and his attention to detail, his perspective was strikingly naïve and abstract. His investigations seemed to be inspired not by historical curiosity but by the needs of jurisprudence. His *Archion* opens not with a discussion of the problem of historical origins but with a vague and highly theoretical statement, suggestive of Lockean political theory, of the contractual basis of government and the general function of courts of law. To indicate whence the courts of Admiralty and Chancery "fetched their beginning", he contented himself with citing statutory law — whereas Choppin and la Popelinière, the French historians of the court of the domain and the admiralty, traced these institutions from ancient times with numerous comparative digressions.[44] As for the various contradictions or conflicts of jurisdiction (Lambarde uses the civilian term "antinomia"), such as the perennial "tossing of this Ball to and fro, between the Councell and the Commons", he resolved such problems in a logical or legal rather than a historical fashion. In general he preferred to derive specific institutions from, or at least justify them in terms of, principles of reason and justice. This was also why Lambarde avoided consideration of Roman law, although he possessed books on the subject. "The law or policy of this realm of England . . . is a peculiar government", he told one of his juries, "not borrowed from the imperial or Roman law (as be the laws of the most part of

[43] *Ibid.*, pp. 123 ff. This etymology, rejected by Laurentius Valla, *De Elegantia Linguae Latiniae* (Rome, 1471), book VI, ch. 36, was accepted by Coke, *First part of the institutes*, sect. 164, as well as by Henry Swinburne, *A brief treatise of testaments and last willes* (London, 1590-1: *S.T.C.* 23547), p. 3.

[44] Lambarde, *Archion*, pp. 29 ff. Cf. René Choppin, *De Domanio Franciae* (Paris, 1574), and Lancelot Voisin, seigneur de la Popelinière, *L'Amiral de France* (Paris, 1584).

other Christian nations) but standing upon the highest reason selected even for itself". In his scholarly work he eschewed such obiter dicta on just the same grounds, refusing to deal, as he remarked, with "what pertaineth to another learning, I mean the Civill and Canon Lawes" because they "do not . . . peculiarly . . . belong to our nation".[45]

* * * *

To Lambarde, as to all common lawyers, "English law was like a wall built of stone and oak to defend a city". The enemies at the gates, of course, were those twin menaces, civil and canon law, which — coiled like two snakes about Mercury's wand, as Selden put it — Englishmen tended to regard with a sort of fascinated horror. The prejudice was deeply embedded in the legal profession. In 1547, for example, a group of students from the Inns of Court presented a "supplicacion" to the Protector Somerset to arrest the decay of common law by curbing the jurisdiction of Chancery, and they complained bitterly about those "who, being Civilians and not learned in the Common Laws, determyne the waighty causes of this realm according either to the saide Lawe Civile or to their own conscience".[46] To seventeenth-century common lawyers, as to Fortescue a century and a half before, the difference was still most simply expressed in the notorious formula *quod principi placuit.* To men like Coke, reading the extreme views expressed in John Cowell's famous *Interpreter* of 1607[47] and watching the alarming practices of James I, it meant purely and simply that "the people have given power to their prince to be a tyrant and tread them under foot at liberty".[48] No wonder Coke had contempt for continental jurisprudence in general and for "Doctor Cow-heel" in particular, whose book was burned by the common hangman. William Fulbecke pleaded that men should not "enter into disdainful comparisons", and the king himself protested that he in no way

[45] Read, *William Lambarde and Local Government*, p. 100.

[46] *Acts of the Privy Council of England*, ed. J. R. Dasent (London, 1890), ii, p. 49.

[47] John Cowell, *The interpreter* (Cambridge, 1607: *S.T.C.* 5900).

[48] [Anon.], *Englands Monarch* (London, 1644), fo. lv, written in response to Albericus Gentilis, *Regales disputationes tres* (London, 1604: *S.T.C.* 11741). Similar views are expressed by Coke and, e.g., Roger Twysden, *Certaine Considerations upon the Government of England*, ed. J. M. Kemble (Camden Soc., xlv, 1849), pp. 84-5.

favoured civil above common law;[49] but the chauvinism of common lawyers as well as the political extremism of certain civilians made this a vain hope.

It is unfortunate that Roman law should have been so exclusively associated with authoritarian political theory. This in itself was somewhat arbitrary to scholars with a broad perspective. About the formula *quod principi placuit*, for example, Pasquier remarked sensibly that "it is not necessary to take this phrase cruelly";[50] and this was essentially the position of English civilians as well. Indeed, on the basis of the *lex regia* from this same formula it was possible to justify active resistance to tyranny, as some English civilians, including Isaac Dorislaus and the antiquarian John Hayward, realized.[51] What is more important, no one could deny the traditional and actual utility of Roman law. Among others Richard Hooker remarked on "the great use we have thereof, both in decisions in certain causes arising daily among ourselves, and especially for commerce with nations abroad, whereunto that knowledge is most requisite".[52] Civil law was still of vital importance for many diplomatic, maritime and ecclesiastical matters, as well as in the prerogative courts and other jurisdictions outside common law. These included the Council and the courts of Admiralty, Star Chamber, Requests, the Marshal, the Constable, and above all Chancery, where, in the words of one of Coke's colleagues, "lextremitie et rigor al common ley est qualifie".[53] Until the end of the century most Masters of the Rolls, too, were civilians. As for canon law, which had never been distinguished clearly from civil law, it continued in force in many civil matters, except where explicitly forbidden by statute. "And I think that if it should bee taken away", declared James I in 1609, "it would make an entrie into Barbarisme

[49] Fulbecke, *A parallele*, introduction; and *The Political Works of James I*, ed. C. H. McIlwain (Cambridge, Mass., 1918), p. 307.

[50] Pasquier, *L'interprétation*, i, p. 26. Cf. Robert Wiseman, *The Law of Laws* (London, 1656), p. 19.

[51] Brian P. Levack, *The Civil Lawyers in England 1603-1641* (Oxford, 1973), pp. 111-14.

[52] Richard Hooker, *Of the lawes of ecclesiasticall politie* (London, [1594]-7: *S.T.C.* 13712), preface. See Swinburne, *A brief treatise*; R. Cosin, *An apologie: of, and for sundrie proceedings by jurisdiction ecclesiasticall* (London, 1591: *S.T.C.* 5820); Thomas Ridley, *A view of the civile and ecclesiastical law* (London, 1607: *S.T.C.* 21054); and Richard Zouch, *The Jurisdiction of the Admiralty* (London, 1663). Cf. W. S. Holdsworth, *Sources and Literature of English Law* (Oxford, 1925), ch. 5.

[53] R. Crompton, *L'authoritie et iurisdiction des courts de la maiestie de la roygne* (London, 1637: *S.T.C.* 6050). According to W. J. Jones, *The Elizabethan Court of Chancery* (Oxford, 1967), p. 18, the contrast between common law and the procedure of prerogative courts in general has been exaggerated.

into this Kingdome".[54] In many respects, indeed, the situation was not markedly different from that in France, which likewise relied extensively upon civil law while at the same resisting any general "reception". Various attempts were made to harmonize civil and customary law. Why should the same not be done for England? "The common law is the daughter, the civil law is the mother", remarked Henry Marten; "I am sorry to see such a strangeness between them".[55] They should not be opposed like the two faces of Janus, as Fulbecke put it, but should rather be joined like the three graces.[56]

To most lawyers, in fact, what was most attractive about civil law was not its absolutist connotations but its logical underpinnings and its philosophical superstructure. The "law of laws", as Wiseman wrote, formed "one body and system", and it was for this reason that it survived the Empire and alone deserved to be regarded as a "science".[57] After the Reception of civil law by the imperial courts in 1495, there was much talk about reform in other countries along similar lines. Even in England Cardinal Pole, deploring the rude customs of the Normans, recommended that his countrymen "receuyue the cyuyle law of the Romaynys, the wych is now the commyn law almost of al Chrystyan natyonys".[58] In France complaints about the confusion and inequity of local customs echo and re-echo through books of law and royal ordinances. Such civilians as François Connan, François le Douaren and Hugues Doneau worked to provide France with a legal system based upon a reconstructed and reorganized Roman law — and likewise faced resistance from feudists like Charles Dumoulin and Hotman, who preferred to

[54] *The Political Works of James I*, p. 310.

[55] Levack, *Civil Lawyers*, p. 139.

[56] Fulbecke, *A parallele*, preface. In general, Maitland's view of the "Reception" was derived from German scholarship and was not applicable to the continent as a whole; he was followed in the main by W. S. Holdsworth, "The Reception of Roman Law in the Sixteenth Century", *Law Quarterly Rev.*, xxvii (1911), pp. 387-98, and *The History of English Law* (London, 1903-66), iv, p. 218. The whole problem needs a general reassessment. Maitland's interpretation of a possible reception in England has been totally rejected by Samuel Thorne, "English Law and the Renaissance", in *La Storia del diritto nel quadro delle scienze storiche* (Florence, 1966), pp. 437-45.

[57] Wiseman, *The Law of Laws*, epistle to reader. Cf. Arthur Duck, *Treatise of the Use and Authority of the Civil Law* (first published, in Latin, London, 1653), trans. J. B[eaver], in C. J. de Ferriere, *The History of the Roman or Civil Law* (London, 1724).

[58] Thomas Starkey, *A Dialogue between Cardinal Pole and Thomas Lupset*, ed. J. M. Cowper (Early Eng. Text Soc., xxxii, 1898), p. 194.

fashion a "common law" out of native customs.[59] A generation later Pasquier and his friends Antoine Loisel and Louis le Caron, though critical of many features of Justinian's collection, relied heavily upon it in their various "institutes" and "pandects" of French law. In England too jurists were attracted as much by the structure as by the substance of Roman law. Just as Pasquier arranged the maxims of feudal law, the writings of medieval jurists, and royal ordinances according to the titles of Justinian's Institutes, so Cowell used this Byzantine textbook to give shape to the raw materials of English law, including the writings of Littleton and Fortescue, the law reports and statutes, with even stronger insistence upon the agreement between English and Roman law.[60] Another of Coke's favourite enemies, Francis Bacon, endorsed the idea of an English "digest" and in 1594 even made the proposal to a group of common lawyers (in a contribution to a Christmas revel in Gray's Inn).[61] Needless to say his audience must have been unalterably opposed to such a plan. Even if it had not been for the suspect character of its sponsors, the patently un-English nature of the plan would have been enough to alienate them.

If common law was a fortress to defend against the incursions of Roman law, the English Reformation seemed to represent the beginning of aggressive warfare against this foreign influence. In 1535 Henry VIII ended the teaching of canon law, and in general, as one eighteenth-century historian observed, "The books of Civil and Canon law were set a-side to be devoured of Worms, as savouring too much of Popery".[62] Yet a tenuous tradition of Romanism managed to survive in the sixteenth century and even to attract a few protestants. This was not only because some Englishmen continued to go abroad, especially to the University of Padua, to take degrees in the subject, but also because this tradition maintained a significant institutional basis. In 1511 an organization of civilians, a kind of bar association like the Inns of Court except that it performed no teaching

[59] See the recent analyses of W. Vogt, *Franciscus Duarenus 1509-1559* (Stuttgart, 1971); C. Bergfeld, *Franciscus Connanus 1508-1551* (Cologne, 1968); and V. Piano Mortari, "La Sistematica come ideale umanistico dell'opera di Francisco Connano", in *La Storia del diritto*, pp. 521-31.

[60] John Cowell, *Institutes of the Lawes of England* (London, 1651); cf. William Fulbecke, *The pandectes of the law of nations* (London, 1602: *S.T.C.* 11414), and the work of le Caron cited in note 8, above.

[61] J. S. Spedding, *The Letters and the Life of Francis Bacon* (London, 1874), vii, pp. 358-64, and vi, pp. 57 ff.

[62] John Ayliffe, *The Antient and Present State of the University of Oxford* (London, 1714), i, p. 188.

functions, was founded by a lawyer with the rather inappropriate name of Richard Bodewell. During the sixteenth century there were over two hundred members of this Doctors' Commons, including such distinguished scholars as Cuthbert Tunstall, Stephen Gardiner and Thomas Smith.[63] For some jobs, moreover, particularly for diplomatic missions, Henry VIII actually preferred civilians. For this reason he established in 1540 regius professorships in this subject both at Cambridge and at Oxford, posts which were first held by Thomas Smith and Joseph Story respectively. The Protector Somerset was still more favourable to civil law, and in 1547 an effort was made to establish separate colleges of civil law at both universities.[64] The royal commissions submitted their plans, but little was accomplished at this time. According to a statute of Edward VI, the professor in the "jure school" of Oxford was obliged "to shew in his Lectures the difference of the Common Law of this Land from the civil", but there is no way of telling how seriously this was taken.[65] Still, there were a few signs of life — eight bachelors of law at Cambridge before 1551, and one doctor, Walter Haddon, a pupil of Smith soon himself to succeed to the regius chair.

These were the lean years. Under Elizabeth, however, the fortunes of civil law improved, and by 1560 it could reportedly be studied as well at Caius College as on the continent. The situation at Oxford also seemed encouraging. In 1566 the queen herself came to hear legal disputations, and later a number of foreign scholars, including Pierre Pithou and Jean Hotman, came to be incorporated as doctors of civil law. Jean Hotman's more famous father François was apparently invited to occupy a chair, but he was too involved with Huguenot politics to accept.[66] In 1587, however, an equally renowned jurist, Alberico Gentili, was installed at Oxford as regius professor. For a time the fortunes of civil law seemed to be improv-

[63] The 201 English civilians of the sixteenth century are listed in Coote's *Catalogue of English Civilians*, published with F. Hargrave, *Sketches of the Lives and Characters of Eminent English Civilians* (London, 1804). Besides Holdsworth, see Ernest Nys, *Le droit romain, le droit des gens et le collège des docteurs en droit civil* (Brussels, 1910).

[64] See Somerset's letter in *The Letters of Stephen Gardiner*, ed. J. A. Muller (Cambridge, 1933), before 25 March 1548; and *Letters and Papers, Domestic (1547-80)*, ed. R. Lemon (London, 1856), p. 17. More generally, C. E. Mullett, *A History of the University of Oxford* (New York, 1924), ii, pp. 83 ff., and J. B. Mullinger, *The University of Cambridge* (Cambridge, 1844), ii, pp. 57, 129.

[65] Anthony Wood, *Historia et antiquitates Universitatis Oxoniensis* (Oxford, 1674), English trans. by J. Gutch, *The History and Antiquities of the University of Oxford*, 2 vols. (Oxford, 1792-6), vol. ii, part ii, p. 772.

[66] P. Nevelet, *Vita Francisci Hotomani*, prefacing *Epistolae Hotomanorum* (Amsterdam, 1700).

ing. The old canon law fellowships were transferred to civilians. By the end of the century there were twenty-five bachelors and eleven doctors of civil law and soon thereafter, which was more alarming to common lawyers, a king that looked with favour upon the profession in general. Unfortunately for the civilians, however, this was more than counterbalanced by the increased self-consciousness and aggressiveness of their common law rivals. Political unpopularity, dependence upon the crown, and isolation from "the country" plunged the civil lawyers into a professional crisis in the early seventeenth century.[67]

From the standpoint of historical scholarship, civil law in England displayed a more serious deficiency. During the sixteenth century the most spectacular development in continental jurisprudence was the remarkable success of legal humanism, a movement generally associated with that philological triumvirate Guillaume Budé, Andrea Alciato and Ulrich Zasius. In England a few scholars, especially such friends of Erasmus as Vives and Tunstall, followed this well publicized "reformed jurisprudence" with some interest. "More than Perotto, Valla, and even Ermolao [Barbaro] and Poliziano", Tunstall wrote in 1517 to Budé, "you have contributed to the revival of ancient eloquence of centuries past and to the restoration of the humanities".[68] Within a generation this "historical school of law" was assured by its reception into a number of universities, especially in France, and it began to work a veritable revolution in legal education and scholarship, if not in legal practice. Its criticisms of the old Bartolist school of scholastic jurisprudence even penetrated the common law tradition, so that Coke, in very Budaean terms, could lament the "many interpretations, and commentaries and diversities of opinions" that overlay the texts of civil law.[69] It was precisely the uncovering of the ancient splendour of Roman law that constituted the scholarly programme of this so-called "French method".

In England one man attempted, almost single-handed, to introduce the teachings and methods of legal humanism. This was Thomas Smith, graduate of the University of Padua and first regius professor of civil law at the University of Cambridge. In his two extant

[67] Levack, *Civil Lawyers*, pp. 50 ff. This is a valuable social and political study but leaves practically untouched the formative Tudor period.

[68] *Opus Epistolarum Des. Erasmi*, ed Allen, ii (Oxford, 1910), p. 539, Tunstall to Budé, April 1517; for Vives's remarks, see *ibid.*, iv, pp. 273-4 (4 June 1520).

[69] Sir Edward Coke, *The Second Part of the Institutes of the Lawes of England* (London, 1642), proeme.

lectures, "On the Method of Studying Civil Law" and "On the Dignity of Laws and the Utility of Studying Civil Law", Smith advertised, in highly conventional terms, the virtues of the "French method".[70] In his rather self-congratulatory introduction he outlined his own studies of language, history, philosophy, and especially, in Italy and France, of law. After the customary attack upon those ignorant guildsmen (*sectatores*) of scholastic jurisprudence, including Accursius, Bartolus, and their partisans, who "took as true history the stupidest and hoariest fables", Smith paid tribute to the founders of legal humanism, Valla and Poliziano, and to those "two luminaries of modern jurisprudence", Alciato and Zasius. In Budé's very words he declared that there were more than six hundred places in the Digest which could not be understood without the help of medicine, philosophy, rhetoric, poetry, and other arts.[71] Without such encyclopaedic knowledge teachers of law would resemble those who disseminated "barbarous grammar, sophistical logic, Scottist philosophy, and quack medicine". Most important was history, by which "old rites are explained, the customs and original institutions of the ancients are interpreted, and new and recent law is established".[72] In general the teacher of civil law should proceed "in the order of history, from the founding of a city, or from the king who established the government, or from the origin of a war, progressing by years and days according to the continuing sequence". For such was the method of the historical school of law.

To Smith, as to such systematizing continental jurists as Connan and Bodin, civil law had a transcendent as well as a historical dimension. In particular it provided a basis for communication with foreign nations to which the customs and speech of England were alien. Philosophy served the same purpose, but since philosophy is known only to a few, as Smith pointed out, "civil law is truly common law" to all grades of men.[73] In general he believed that civil law

[70] Cambridge Univ. Lib., Baker MS. xxxvii, fos. 212r-20v and 202r-11v: "D. Thomas Smith Doctoris LL. et Regii apud Cantabrigienses Professoris, Oratio prima, de suis auditoribus, et de ratione studii juris civilis", and "... Oratio Secunda, De Dignitate legum atq[ue] utilitate studii juris civilis". This manuscript has never been published, though extracts were printed by Maitland, *English Law and the Renaissance*, and by Mullinger, *University of Cambridge*, ii, pp. 129 ff.

[71] "Oratio prima", fos. 213r, 217v. Smith mentions his young student Walter Haddon ("Oratio secunda", fo. 210r), who later praised Smith in return, in "Oratio, quam habuit, cum Cantabrigiae legum interpretationes ordiretur", *Lucubrationes* (London, 1567-8: *S.T.C.* 12596), p. 68, but without showing any enthusiasm for legal humanism.

[72] Smith, "Oratio secunda", fo. 211r.

[73] *Ibid.*, fos. 206r, 203r.

was a "divine science", superior to other fields because its value was public as well as private, general as well as particular. In later years Smith's enthusiasm for Roman law abated somewhat, and he came to appreciate the "barbaric and half-Gallic laws" of England, as he called them at this time. Yet he preserved the broad perspective which civil law had given him. Like Bodin (whether or not there is any direct influence) Smith came to advocate a comparative view of law and politics. In his famous discourse on the commonwealth of England Smith admitted, as did most civilians, that specific laws originated in custom (*lex ex facto oritur* was the formula) and that English laws often differed from those of continental nations, "which doe not follow the civill lawe of the Romans compiled by *Justinian* into his pandects and code".[74] Nevertheless, he emphasized the parallels between English, Roman and Greek institutions, and he deliberately avoided certain biases of the common lawyers. He did not hesitate to call the king "absolute", for example, and he specifically rejected Littleton's old characterization of the fief (*idem est quod hereditas*) in favour of the civilian doctrine, legally orthodox though still historically incorrect (deriving it from the Latin *fides*).[75] In general Smith invited men to compare English government with others, either those "which at this day be in *esse*, or doe remain described in true histories . . .". This ideal, which he shared with Bodin and other commentators on the *jus gentium*, was very largely the product of Roman legal science, and of legal humanism in particular.

Unfortunately, Smith was not only the first effective advocate for legal humanism in England, he was practically the only one. Neither his work nor his following fulfilled the ideals set down in his youthful lectures. Holdsworth has observed that "the common lawyers knew only their own system while most of the civilians were compelled to know not only their own system, but also something of the common law. This led them to compare the two systems . . . ".[76] Yet this had little effect upon historical scholarship, certainly nothing comparable to the fruitful interchange between legal and historical studies so conspicuous in France in the later sixteenth century. English civilians did help to preserve some knowledge of Roman law, if not its historical significance, and even of certain scholarly problems,

[74] Sir Thomas Smith, *De republica Anglorum* (London, 1583: *S.T.C.* 22857), ed. L. Alston (Cambridge, 1906), pp. 142-3. Cf. Ulrich Zasius, *Paratitla*, in *Operum omnium* (Lyon, 1550), i, col. 17 (on Digest 1. 2. 2).

[75] Smith, *De republica Anglorum*, pp. 48, 135. In general, see my "De Origine Feudorum: the Beginning of an Historical Problem", *Speculum*, xxxix (1964), pp. 207-28.

[76] Holdsworth, *Sources and Literature of English Law*, p. 235.

such as the origins of feudalism, long discusssed by continental authors but practically unknown to Englishmen.[77] But for the rest they seem to have clung to the same sort of narrow professionalism as their common law rivals. Because of this very rivalry, perhaps, it was natural that they should have rejected the "new jurisprudence" and maintained their conservative stance.

The attitude of English civilians was well expressed, if not caricatured, in the work of Alberico Gentili, who was at once the most distinguished Roman lawyer in sixteenth-century England and the sharpest critic of the humanist school. In his *De iuris interpretibus*, published in London in 1582, Gentili — with that flagrant anti-intellectualism which established intellectuals can often muster — refuted every single major premise of the "new sect" of Alciato, as he called the historical school of law. He rejected the "encyclopaedic" programme of Budé which required that law students also be "theologians, metaphysicians, musicians, rhetoricians, poets, dialecticians, and even mariners", not to add farmers, craftsmen, and other such artisans.[78] He denied the need not only for Greek — the old Bartolist scholium "Graecum est, non potest legi" sufficed — but also for Latin eloquence, by which he meant the philological method as well as the affected anachronism of humanist style. He denied the value of an elaborate dialectic, especially that overwrought brand of logic hawked by the offspring of Ramus (*larvi Rami*) and later celebrated in the book of Abraham Fraunce.[79] He refused even to admit the existence of those "antinomies" of which "anti-Tribonianists" from Valla to Hotman had made so much. Finally, Gentili denied the utility of history, which Bodin, Baudouin, and others had urged so strongly, even if law students had the time to spend on such luxuries.

What Gentili was calling for in general was a repudiation of the new-fangled French method (*mos gallicus*) and a return to the old-fashioned professionalism of the Italian school (*mos italicus*). In England, one suspects, he was preaching to the converted. The fact is that English civilians were quite as resistant as common lawyers to the infiltration of literary and historical standards. They admired the work of Hotman, for example, but they could not go along with his extra-legal critiques of authoritative texts. Thus when he questioned Ulpian's famous characterization of natural law ("what nature teaches

[77] For example, Ridley, *A view of the civile and ecclesiastical law*, p. 61.

[78] Albericus Gentilis, *De iuris interpretibus* (London, 1582: *S.T.C.* 11736), fos. 14r, 29r.

[79] *Ibid.*, fo. 44v (and see above, note 19).

all animals"), William Fulbecke complained that he was "cavilling" and "following his forefather Valla", whom conservative jurists had always associated with the excesses of classicism.[80] Like Gentili, in short, English civilians refused to believe that history or philology had anything to do with the science of law. In this respect if in no other, the civilians were in agreement with the common lawyers. This guild mentality, with the compulsive utilitarianism accompanying it, constituted perhaps the major obstacle to the historical and comparative study of law.

In other ways, too, English historical scholarship lagged behind that of the continent. One example is the relative neglect, by historians at least, of legal records. Reasons for this are various. For one thing, the English archives were notoriously decentralized; for another, they were closely guarded, expensive to use, and organized largely for the benefit of lawyers. In any case it was not until the seventeenth century that public records could be used with any convenience. From this period date the principal calendars and catalogues, including those of Lambarde, Arthur Agarde and Thomas Powell, which served as guides to the main collections.[81] In France the archives, though more centralized, were in a similarly chaotic condition, and similar complaints about decay and confusion echo through the royal ordinances. Yet the records of the *Trésor des chartes* and the Parlement had been long and fruitfully utilized by lawyers and historians alike. The best example of this was the great *Recueil des roys de France*, which the archivist and antiquary Jean du Tillet began assembling in the 1550s and which was published posthumously in 1578.[82] In England there were later some archivists who were also antiquaries, such as Lambarde and Robert Bowyer, but before the seventeenth century there was nothing comparable to du Tillet's inventory of French history, relied upon by generations of historians — and nothing like the convergence between the archival and historiographical traditions in general.

* * * *

It was not until the seventeenth century that things began to change. Even then there was no thoroughgoing revolution; there was only a

[80] William Fulbecke, *A direction or preparative to the study of the Lawe* (London, 1600: *S.T.C.* 11410), fo. 63r.

[81] On this large subject see Levi Fox (ed.), *English Historical Scholarship in the Sixteenth and Seventeenth Centuries* (London, 1956), ch. 2; Fussner, *The Historical Revolution*, pp. 69 ff.; and McKisack, *Medieval History*, pp. 75 ff.

[82] Jean du Tillet, *Recueil des roys de France* (Rouen, 1578).

handful of scholars who, though they were not civilians, looked more to continental than to English traditions. Sir Henry Spelman had been appalled by his experience in Lincoln's Inn, where he encountered "a foreign language, a barbarian dialect, an uncouth method, a mass which was not only large, but which was to be continually born on the shoulders; and I confess that my heart sank within me".[83] Spelman was a member of the original Society of Antiquaries and acquired a remarkably broad knowledge of European law, feudal as well as civil and canon, and many contacts with continental scholars. As Pocock has suggested, "His role may be compared to that of the 'grammarians' of legal humanism", though his work had little impact until after his death.[84] This was even more conspicuously true of Sir John Selden, who was perhaps the only Englishman to rival Scaliger in range (if not in precision) of scholarship. In his *Ad Fletam Dissertatio* he retold the legend of the miraculous discovery at Amalfi by the Pisans of the famous manuscript of the Digest which was later made part of the Medici collection and which became the principal vehicle of, as well as inspiration for, the critical study of Roman law from Poliziano's time onward.[85] This book also contains one of the most comprehensive and panegyrical descriptions of the renaissance of Roman law in the fifteenth and sixteenth centuries. Clearly, it was to the great tradition of legal humanism, especially to the French school so derided by Gentili, that Selden felt his closest allegiance.

Both of these men were deeply involved in the study of English law, and yet they consciously kept themselves apart from the conventions of common law. Spelman specifically warned against the Whig fallacy — "viewing what is past by the present" — and Selden used just such an argument to justify his study of ecclesiastical antiquities, which might seem no longer relevant to protestant England. Spelman's method was rather, in a famous phrase, "to seek the *Fountaines* and by that . . . judge the *Rivers* . . .".[86] But the fallacy

[83] Prest, *Inns of Court*, p. 142.

[84] Pocock, *The Ancient Constitution*, p. 234.

[85] John Selden, *Ad Fletam Dissertatio* (London, 1647), ed. David Ogg (Cambridge, 1925), p. 95; "Notes on Sir John Fortescue's *De Laudibus* . . .", and "England's Epinomis", in *Opera omnia*, 3 vols. (London, 1725), iii, cols. 1, 891 and 1,895. In general, besides the work of Fussner, see H. D. Hazeltine, "Selden as Legal Historian", *Festschrift Heinrich Brunner* (Weimar, 1910), pp. 579-630, and Sergio Bertelli, *Ribelli, libertini e ortodossi nella storiografia barocca* (Florence, 1973), pp. 257-64.

[86] *The English Works of Sir H. Spelman* (London, 1723), 2nd edn. (London, 1727), ii, p. 62.

at the opposite extreme from presentism was still more to be guarded against. For Selden this was best illustrated by Fortescue, whose barbarous Latin might be excused but whose chauvinism and credulity could not. Inquiring into the ultimate origin of common law was a "trivial demand" in the first place; to exaggerate its age was worse than useless — as French historians had been arguing for a generation. "Little then follows in point of honour or excellency", Selden concluded, "specially to be attributed to the laws of a nation in general, by an argument thus drawn from difference of antiquity, which in substance is alike... Those which best fit the state wherein they are, clearly deserve the name of best laws".[87] Such arguments from antiquity were hardly more acceptable than the eponymous myths of Brutus, Francus, "and divers such, which are all mere fictions or impostures". These are two of the ways in which Selden and Spelman followed the values of continental historical thought, especially as expressed in the work of the historical school of law and its alumni.

Because of their familiarity with continental scholarship these men had an unprecedented awareness of the whole context of English history. At the same time, along with many continental historians, they shared a generally Germanist outlook and a full measure of that racial pride which modern vernacular authors had begun to affect. In England this attitude was first actively promoted by Richard Verstegan, but of course the arguments for the "honourableness" of a German ancestry had long been advanced by such French authors as du Tillet and by German writers before them.[88] In the same style Spelman celebrated the defeats of the Romans at the hands of the Germans, "a prime and most potent people", and praised in particular their libertarian institutional heritage. So, in keeping with Spelman's policy of judging rivers by the fountains, did Selden, who presented a whole series of parallels between the customs described in Tacitus's *Germania* and those of medieval England. Despite the diversity of western nations they were, as Spelman put it, "all from the same root".[89]

What is more, the fortunes of these nations continued to cross and recross. Like Smith, Spelman objected to Littleton's unhistorical

[87] Selden, "Notes on Sir John Fortescue's *De Laudibus* . . .", col. 1,892.

[88] Richard Rowlands [i.e. Richard Verstegan], *A restitution of decayed intelligence* (Antwerp, 1605: *S.T.C.* 21361). In general, see Samuel Kliger, *The Goths in England* (Cambridge, Mass., 1952), pp. 126 ff. Cf. du Tillet, *Recueil*, pp. 1 and 386.

[89] Selden, "England's Epinomis", col. 12; cf. Spelman's preface to his *Archaeologus* (London, 1626: *S.T.C.* 23065).

view of feudalism. Following Pasquier and his teacher Cujas, Spelman attempted for the first time to discuss English land law in the context of European feudal society, and indeed of the *jus gentium.*[90] Selden too rejected the notion of a unique and pristine English tradition. "But questionless the *Saxons* made a mixture of the *British* customs with their own", he commented, "the *Danes* with old *British*, the *Saxon* and their own; and the *Normans* the like . . .".[91] The same argument held for Roman law, civil and canon, and Selden took a position remarkably similar to that of his older contemporary Pasquier. A remark in Selden's "Table Talk" suggests that his philological assumptions were also substantially the same:

> If you look upon the language spoken in the *Saxon* time, and the language spoken now, you will find the difference to be just, as if a man had a cloke that he wore plain in queen *Elizabeth's* days, and since, here has put in a piece of red, and there a piece of blue, and here a piece of green, and there a piece of orange-tawny. We borrow words from the *French, Italian, Latin,* as every pedantick man pleases.[92]

To judge from language, at least, history was more of a crazy-quilt than a seamless web. So it had been too with Roman law, whose effects upon English society Selden fully appreciated. Spelman was in agreement and even went on to cite Cowell for this purpose. He summed up his interpretation in this way: "I think the Foundation of our Law to be laid by our *German* ancestors, but built upon and polished by Materials taken from the Canon Law and Civil Law . . .".[93] If this was blasphemy to common lawyers, it was a hypothesis that could significantly broaden and enrich the study of English legal, institutional and social history.

The work of these men pointed the way to a broader and deeper approach to the investigation of the cultural past, but on the whole it was exceptional and represented a brief interlude in the course of English historical scholarship. The ideological conflicts of the seventeenth century made disinterested inquiry into the English past a luxury, a dangerous one at that, and clearly the triumph of Parlia-

[90] *The English Works of Sir H. Spelman*, ii, pp. 1-46, "The Original, Growth, Propagation and Condition of Feuds and Tenures by Knight-Service in England".

[91] Selden, "Notes on Sir John Fortescue's *De Laudibus* . . .", col. 1,887.

[92] Selden, *Opera,* iii, col. 2,040. About English laws Bacon made this remark (see note 61): "It is true that they are as mixt as our language, compounded of British, Roman, Saxon, Danish, Norman customs: and surely our language is thereby so much the richer, so our laws likewise by that mixture the more complete".

[93] *The English Works of Sir H. Spelman*, ii, p. 100, "The Original of the four Terms of the Year".

ment did not provide a more congenial atmosphere for the kind of cosmopolitan-minded work exemplified by Selden and Spelman. Under any conditions, perhaps, they were too eccentric to attract a following among their countrymen; in the explosive age of revolution — and in the complacent age of Whig ascendency which succeeded it — they seemed outlandish. The next generation of English historical scholars seems distinctly inferior to them in breadth of vision, if not in precision and technique. These "worshipful men", whose work has been so carefully described by David Douglas, were concerned largely with the collection and edition of texts, local history, or the partisan celebration of insular traditions, whether royalist or parliamentary.[94] They were antiquaries of a distinguished and fruitful but extremely narrow school. Nor, on the other hand, were there any significant changes in the habits of the common lawyers. They succeeded deplorably well in avoiding what one learned Victorian author defined as "the risk principally incidental to the Historical Method . . . , that is to lapse either into mere antiquarianism on the one side, or into general political and social history on the other".[95]

In this polarity, perhaps, we have one of the major reasons for the narrowness of English historical scholarship — though admittedly, to revert to Spelman's metaphor, it is a long way back up this river to the fountain of historiographical insularity I have located in the sixteenth century. Here is the way Maitland saw the paradox:

> That process by which old principles and old phrases are charged with new content, is from the lawyer's point of view an evolution of the true intent and meaning of the old law; from the historian's point of view it is almost of necessity a process of perversion and misunderstanding. Thus we are tempted to mix up two different logics, the logic of authority, and the logic of evidence. What the lawyer wants is authority and the newer the better; what the historian wants is evidence and the older the better.[96]

Continental scholarship had long ceased to be obstructed by such professional conflicts; and only an Englishman could remark (as Maitland remarked) that François Baudouin's arguments about the congruity of law and history "have a wonderfully modern sound".[97] It was precisely because England lacked a "historical school", it seems to me, that the study of English laws and institutions has seemed to alternate between the poles of "mere antiquarianism", which has

[94] D. C. Douglas, *English Scholars 1660-1730*, 2nd edn. (London, 1951).

[95] James Bryce, *Studies in History and Jurisprudence* (Oxford, 1901), ii, p. 185.

[96] Maitland, *Collected Papers*, i, p. 491.

[97] Maitland, *English Law and the Renaissance*, note 28.

preserved the worst as well as the best features of British empiricism, and the Whig fallacy, which has preserved the worst as well as the best features of the common law tradition. The one thing common to both of these attitudes is the guild mentality which tends to deny the relevance either of a comparative approach or the utility of contact with other disciplines. In law such exclusiveness is narrowing; in history it may be fatal. No man, in the words of another English poet, is an island: not even a professional historian. Not even a professional English historian.

University of Rochester

XII

VICO'S ROAD: FROM PHILOLOGY TO JURISPRUDENCE AND BACK

> The Vico Road goes round and round
> to meet where terms begin.
>
> James Joyce, *Finnegan's Wake*

"History does not yet have its principles."[1] When Giambattista Vico made this observation in 1720, he was already at work on a remedy. It is hardly too much to say that his entire intellectual life was taken up with an unwavering, though not quite single-minded, attempt to do for the human past what Isaac Newton had done for nature, that is, literally to fashion a *Principia* of history. Over two decades before, in his first inaugural lecture at the University of Naples, he had announced the primacy of human culture for the attainment of true wisdom; and in the subsequent quest he became increasingly convinced that, given the weakness of human nature and the corruption of human intelligence, the only route was, not through pure reason, but through the investigation of humanity's past in all of its richness and depravity, in all of its grandeur and absurdity. This lifelong search took Vico along a very circuitous and often unmarked trail. Sometimes he lost his bearings, doubled back, and tried again to find the right path; but never did he give up the journey, which began as early as 1700, when according to Vico's own recollection he "entertained in his mind a new and grand idea of uniting in one principle all of human knowledge."[2] This aim was pursued through an encyclopedic variety of works ending in the successive metamorphoses of the *New Science*.

Vico's lament about the disorder of history applies also to his own career, for his biography likewise lacks its "principles," in his sense of the term, though his *Autobiography* certainly provides materials for such a project. The first and perhaps most significant of Vico's axioms is that one has to begin at the beginnings: "Doctrines must take their beginnings from that of the matters of which they treat."[3] It is the curse of human nature, he assumed, that men cannot apprehend things through pure reason but must proceed gradually, by empirical and historical means, the way children learn. Analogously, on the level of metaphysics, Vico

[1] *Diritto universale*, bk. 1: *De uno principio*, ch. 104, *Opere* 2: 95: "Historia nondum habet sua principia." Cf. *Scienza nuova prima*, bk. 2, ch. 57, *Opere* 3: § 208: "Scoverta de' veri elementi della storia."

[2] The Autobiography, *Opere* 5: 31.

[3] *Scienza nuova*, *Opere* 4: § 314.

tended to assume that the properties of any changing thing are present in some fashion from its inception, so that in order to understand the character of anything—the *ingenium* of a nation, for example—one had to begin *ab ovo*. As applied to biography this is not quite an invitation to psychoanalysis, but it does imply that a man's ideas and attitudes may be understood most directly in terms of his early studies and enthusiasms, not in terms of his final philosophy. And this assumption is quite in line with certain other features of Vico's thought: that formal philosophy is vastly inferior to the natural workings of the human mind;[4] that the study of language and topics belong to childhood, while philosophy and criticism belong to old age; and that in general mature and reasoned wisdom is actually "derived" from the more creative thought processes of youth—the child is literally father of the man. Moreover, since Vico's "methods" were designed specifically to help historians in the reconstruction of complicated, obscure, and unrecorded processes, it seems most appropriate to apply them to his own mental life.

How does this genetic approach apply to Vico? The pattern seems clear, though the details are few. At the age of seven Vico fell on his head and was unconscious for five hours or so. Now it would be unkind to suggest that this misfortune had a formative impact upon his thinking; yet it was the first event of his life that he thought worth recording, and if nothing else it interrupted his studies and forced him to become his own teacher for some three years. It marked his first departure from conventional education and so the first stage of his growing intellectual independence, and to this extent he never fully recovered from his fall. At the castle of Cilento he continued his solitary habits of study for nine years, continuing to be, in his own word, an "autodidact," and proud of it. Later he "blessed his good fortune in having no teacher whose words he had sworn by. . . ." He was used to being alone in his opinions and out of step with his times—to being, as he put it, "a stranger in his own land." The result was to broaden but hardly to discipline his mind. Despite later vanity about the mathematical design of his work, he had little use and less aptitude for the niceties of geometry, which he thought proper rather to "minute wits" than to "minds already made universal by metaphysics." For logic he had even less patience, and he gave it up altogether. What he wanted was to range over the whole spectrum of human knowledge, especially the preserve of the humanities, in order to find relationships grander than those of Euclid or even of Newton. In Vico's own terms his point of departure, and indeed his final destination, was not philosophy but "philology."[5]

Although we may think of Vico as a philosopher, in fact the subject that he taught for most of his active life, over forty years, was rhetoric; and

[4] First Inaugural Oration, *Opere* 1: 10.
[5] The Autobiography, *Opere* 5: 3, 9–22.

so he was, in the most traditional sense, a professional humanist. He was an accomplished poet, and towards the end of his life he was appointed royal historiographer as well.[6] That he belonged to the grand tradition of Renaissance humanist scholarship is indicated by the substance of his erudition, his ideas about language, his concerns with such problems as world chronology, and even his encyclopedic plan to establish a unified system of knowledge. This allegiance was increasingly obscured by tendencies in his later writing: by the penchant for generalizing and turning every insight into a "principle"; by his fascination with system, geometric design, and circular form; and by the tendency (illustrated in the successive versions of the *New Science*) to suppress citation of "authorities," as if literally to proceed, as he promised in his *Autobiography*, "as if there were no books in the world." Yet beneath the eclectic exterior of this rococo philosophy it seems apparent that Vico's main achievement—his basic inspiration, key concepts, and scholarly instincts—derived from his peregrinations about that humanist circle of learning centering about the *studia humanitatis* and the attitudes associated with these. "How many new arts have been devised!" marveled Vico in a formula that had been part of humanist litany for centuries. "How many new sciences!"[7] He was thinking, too, of course, of the achievements of men like Galileo and Descartes; but it is important to remember that his own great enterprise, his own "new science," was a reconstituted version of that central creation of Renaissance scholarship, *philologia*, which he began by celebrating in the same "encyclopedic" terms as those employed by Lorenzo Valla, Guillaume Budé, and Erasmus. The first phase of Vico's intellectual road, then, coincided with the later stages of Renaissance Humanism.

> A prolonged visit to a house
> of call at Cujas Place.
>
> *Finnegan's Wake*

Yet if Vico was a humanist by calling and by training, he did not want to spend his entire professional career within the confines of the *trivium*, teaching liberal arts to children. His particular goal was not philosophy, however, but jurisprudence, a subject which had been the secondary focus of his studies almost from the beginning and which figured most prominently in his early scheme of learning, as it had in the descriptions of the *studia humanitatis* by many earlier humanists. His approach was through

[6] See the addendum to the Autobiography by the Marchese di Villarosa, *Opere* 5: 84.

[7] *De mente heroica, Opere* 7: 19; cf. *De studiorum ratione, Opere* 1: 78. The orientation of the present discussion, general and specific, arises from my *Foundations of Modern Historical Scholarship: Language, Law, and History in the French Renaissance* (New York, 1970).

the textbooks of Hermann Vulteius and Henricus Canisius and the legal history by Vincenzo Gravina; then he moved on to the sources of civil and canon law and took his degree *utriusque*. He was won over to the tradition of legal humanism associated with the names of Valla, Budé, Andrea Alciato, and especially Jacques Cujas (*interpetri eruditi, Alciatani,* or *Cujaciani*) because of its criticism and critical method, but at the same time he respected the medieval jurists (*giureconsulti medesimi*) because of their philosophical standards.[8] The trouble with modern jurisprudence, he believed, stemmed from the conflict between these two schools. "Why has philology been alienated from philosophical studies?" he asked.[9] The fault lay not only with the traditional hostility of scholasticism and humanism, he suggested, but also with the fashionable naturalistic bias of Descartes and his disciples. The major objective of Vico's legal quest was, by building on the work of a few pioneers like Grotius, to reunite the soul and body of jurisprudence and to restore its essential "constancy."

One of the turning points in Vico's life came in his attempt to achieve professional status by obtaining the chair of law at his University of Naples. His account of the competition is at once comic and pathetic. He described his assigned lecture as a triumph of wit, strategy, and learning. His subject was the *Digest* title "On Prescriptions," and he displayed both his learning and his characteristic eclecticism by defending medieval jurists like Accursius, as well as the humanists Alciato, Cujas, and Hotman.[10] But Vico's curious erudition did not carry the day; and in view of the overreaching and rather bizarre notions expressed in his *Universal Law,* composed with an eye to this chair, the decision of the university authorities may not seem surprising. In any case he spent the rest of his life in his lowly position. Thenceforward Vico was not only isolated, he was without chance of professional advancement. His only hope lay in the future, that is, in literary fame, and the vehicle of this fame would be his *New Science,* already prefigured in his *Universal Law,* in which Vico would create and preside over his own world.

From a genetic and historical—a Viconic—point of view, however, the key work of Vico's career, in Vico's characterization, was the earlier one, the *Universal Law*. Here we can see the first effects of the union between Vico's "new science" of philology and that most perfect form of wisdom, which was jurisprudence. The direction of this, the first major phase of Vico's road, is clear. Vico explained,

[8] The Autobiography, *Opere* 5: 7ff.; cf. *De studiorum ratione, Opere* 1: 100–13; *De Italorum sapientia, Opere* 1: 145–46; *Diritto universale,* "De opera proloquium," §§ 17–18, *Opere* 2: 31–32. In general see Fausto Nicolini, *La giovinezza di Giambattista Vico (1668–1700)* (Bari, 1932), and Benvenuto Donati, *Nuovi studi sulla filosofia civile di G. B. Vico* (Florence, 1936).

[9] *Diritto universale,* bk. 2: *De constantia jurisprudentis,* pt. 2, ch. 1, § 24, *Opere* 2: 318.

[10] The Autobiography, *Opere* 5: 44–47.

Philology is the study of speech and it treats of words and their history, then shows their origin and progress, and so determines the ages of languages, thus revealing their properties, changes, and conventions. But since the ideas of things are represented by words, philology must first treat the history of things. Whence it appears that philologists study human governments, customs, laws, institutions, intellectual disciplines, and the mechanical arts.[11]

If mathematics was the language of the book of nature, as Galileo had taught, philology was indispensable for anyone who hoped to penetrate the book of humanity. As for the target of this philological method, it would be that subject which was at once a cornucopia of learning, the most comprehensive expression of ancient culture, and the most complete reflection of human society and its ideals—namely, jurisprudence, and particularly Roman jurisprudence. Although Vico chose Greek poetry, and specifically Homer, as the vehicle of his masterwork, the *New Science*, it should be understood that most of his insights and ideas and general line of argument were developed first of all in the context of, and with the aid of, the Western legal tradition—the great *respublica jurisconsultorum*, as one of Vico's Neapolitan contemporaries called it, which included all of Europe and almost two millennia within its boundaries.[12]

The debts owed by Vico to jurisprudence are incalculable and in some cases almost indemonstrable, at least in terms of conventional *Quellenforschung*, for they involve matters not only of content but of form and method, not only *exempla* but, much more significantly, also *principia* of human behavior. In many ways Vico may be understood as another in the long line of commentators on the texts of civil law.[13] His discipleship is most clearly apparent in his discussion of such classic rubrics as "On law and justice," "On the origin of law," and "On the meaning of words," as well as in his investigation of such sources as the Law of the Twelve Tables and the post-Roman *Consuetudines Feudorum*. The main difference between Vico and other commenators is that Vico, following the lead of such freewheeling Renaissance jurists as Jean Bodin, departed from convention, not only by changing the order and meaning of topics and, in typically eclectic fashion, by adding extralegal material, but by transmuting

11 *Diritto universale*, bk. 2: *De constantia jurisprudentis*, pt. 2, ch. 1, § 1, *Opere* 2: 308.

12 Giuseppe Aurelio di Gennaro, *Respublica jurisconsultorum* (Leipzig, 1733).

13 A "born glossator" Vico is called by Frank Manuel, *The Eighteenth Century Confronts the Gods* (Cambridge, Mass., 1959), p. 150. Certain aspects of the juridical tradition on which Vico drew I discuss in "The Development and Context of Bodin's Method," in *Jean Bodin: Verhandlungen der internationalen Bodin Tagung in München*, ed. Horst Denzer (Munich, 1973), pp. 123–50; in "Clio and the Lawyers: Forms of Historical Consciousness in Medieval Jurisprudence," *Medievalia et Humanistica*, n.s. 5 (1974); and in "Louis le Caron Philosophe," in *Philosophy and Humanism: Renaissance Essays in Honor of Paul Oskar Kristeller*, ed. Edward Mahoney (Leiden, 1975), pp. 16–35. Unfortunately, there is no useful general treatment of the legal tradition between the late Middle Ages and Vico's time.

them into almost unrecognizable form in order to elaborate his philosophical view of history. Most of his ideas about the origins and processes of historical change, of the structure and values of civilization, and even of the nature of human consciousness can be correlated with, if not derived from, legal formulas. Topics should be studied in youth, when memory is strongest, Vico believed, and philosophy in maturity, when reasoning powers are greatest; and the pattern of his own thought seems to follow this prescription, for it was Roman jurisprudence that provided the topical basis for the first expression of Vico's science of humanity.

No less important, though less obvious, was Vico's reliance upon the hermeneutics developed within the legal tradition; and characteristically his adaptation of the *ars interpretationis* of the jurists was a conflation of humanist and scholastic methods of exegesis—another manifestation of the fusion of philology and philosophy. Like the humanists, he insisted on understanding laws in their specificity and historical context, and in particular he carried on their pursuit of interpolations, that is, of "Tribonianisms," and anachronisms.[14] Yet he transformed these attitudes into a highly theoretical way of "divining" and interpreting antiquity. He was especially fascinated with the possibilities of etymology, though again he refused to be bound by a narrowly literal interpretation. So he rejected Valla's famous criticism of a conventional derivation of "testament" (from a "testifying of the mind") on the grounds that law was not restricted by grammar. His view was not unlike that of another fifteenth-century jurist, namely, that etymology was not merely historical but was designed to get at the "quidditas" of a term (*ex rerum ipsarum vi et potestate*, as Vico put it); and the result was sometimes derivations as outlandish as some of those of Isidore of Seville.[15] But in general Vico preserved the goal of Renaissance jurisprudence: to determine not only the letter but also the spirit (*voluntas, mens, ratio*) of laws, and even to "correct" them according to rational standards. Vico may have gone further than his predecessors, but not necessarily in another direction. In any case the second stage of his road is marked by his adaptation of the forms, methods, and attitudes of Roman legal science.

[14] *Diritto universale*, bk. 1: *De uno principio*, chs. 85 and 211, *Opere* 2: 84–85 and 243–45; and in general, Vincenzo Piano Mortari, *Ricerche sulla teoria dell'interpretazione del diritto nel secolo XVI* (Milan, 1956), and Pietro de Francisci, "L'antitribonianismo di G. B. Vico," *Rivista internazionale di filosofia del diritto* 5 (1925): 428–36. This entire issue of the *Rivista* is devoted to the subject of Vico and law.

[15] *Diritto universale*, bk. 1: *De uno principio*, ch. 170, *Opere* 2: 184–85; *ibid.*, bk. 2: *De constantia jurisprudentis*, pt. 2, ch. 7, *Opere* 2: 342–44; *Scienza nuova prima*, bk. 2, ch. 60; *Opere* 3: §§ 212–18. Cf. Lorenzo Valla, *Elegantiae latinae linguae*, VI, 36, in *Opera omnia*, ed. Eugenio Garin, 2 vols. (Turin, 1962), 1: 217, and Claude de Seyssel, *Speculum feudorum* (Basel, 1566), p. 11.

Long Livius Lane . . .
by New Livius Lane

Finnegan's Wake

"To jurisprudence," Vico declared, "the Romans gave the same definition as the Greeks gave to wisdom, 'the knowledge of things divine and human.'"[16] For Vico this famous formula, derived from the first title of the *Digest*, had a threefold function. First, it provided him with a vehicle for his conception of culture, which was essentially a projection of this traditional idea of *sapientia*. Second, this fundamental distinction, which corresponded to that between philosophy and philology, established, in a temporalized form, the *termini a quo* and *ad quem* of the trajectory of cultural history, which in a sense recapitulated that of individual education. Finally, it offered the Roman experience as the paradigm of historical change.

Remember. O Romans, you keep universal rule over nations
In these ways: by maintaining peace through law,
By doing justice to the lowly, by bringing down the haughty.[17]

These lines of Vergil, which Vico was fond of citing, symbolized also Vico's own adaptation of Roman law, which likewise gave conceptual order to the chaos of human history, gave new significance to primitive creations, and placed the most exalted constructs of civilization in critical perspective. In Vico's vision of history, then, Rome again ruled the world of the *gentes* and established the conditions for *humanitas*, or rather for Vico's science thereof.

The supreme model of *Romanitas* was that great "image of antiquity," as Cicero called it, the Twelve Tables; and in his discussion of this alpha and omega (*finis et fons*) of civil law, Vico once again was carrying on a leading theme of humanist scholarship, which had tried to reconstruct this monument since the sixteenth century.[18] Here was displayed the "heroic

[16] *De studiorum ratione*, *Opere* 1: 101. Cf. also the Sixth Inaugural Oration, *Opere* 1: 66; *Diritto universale*, "De opera proloquium," §§ 2–6, *Opere* 2: 26–28. See also the *Digest*, I, 1, 1, and in general Eugene F. Rice, Jr., *The Renaissance Idea of Wisdom* (Cambridge, Mass., 1958), and Benvenuto Donati, "La definizione di Ulpiano di 'juris prudentia' e l'interpretazione del Vico," *Archivio giuridico "Filippo Serafini"* 98 [4th ser., 14] (1927): 51–74.

[17] *Diritto universale*, bk. 1: *De uno principio*, ch. 186, *Opere* 2: 214, and "Sul diritto natural delle genti," *Opere* 7: 27. See in general Giovanni Baviera, *Giambattista Vico e la storia del diritto romano* (Palermo, 1912); Max H. Fisch, "Vico and Roman Law," in *Essays in Political Theory: Presented to George H. Sabine*, ed. Milton R. Konvitz and Arthur E. Murphy (Ithaca, 1948), pp. 62–88; Elio Gianturco, "Vico's Significance in the History of Legal Thought," in *Giambattista Vico: An International Symposium*, pp. 327–47; and especially Dino Pasini, *Diritto, società e stato in Vico* (Naples, 1970).

[18] *Diritto universale*, bk 1: *De uno principio*, ch. 176, *Opere* 2: 197; *ibid*., bk. 2: *De constantia jurisprudentis*, pt. 2, ch. 36, *Opere* 2: 564–71; *Scienza nuova*, *Opere* 4: § 154, and the first *ragionamento* appended to the *Scienza nuova*, *Opere* 4: §§ 1412–54.

wisdom" of Rome, of which Vico recognized three elements. The first, as always, was the divine origin and character of primitive law, which caused the founding fathers to enshroud their handiwork in secrecy and led later jurists to style themselves, in Ulpian's phrase, "priests of the law" (*sacerdotes legum*).[19] Second, and correlative to this, was the poetic character of this law, which Vico later referred to as a "serious poem" both because of its mythical overtones and because traditionally it had in fact been chanted. Recalling Justinian's own remark about the "fables of early law," Vico declared that "ancient jurisprudence is poetic throughout."[20] Last, and a function of these, was the extreme formalism of ancient law, which reflected the literalism of a preconceptual period when words had a magic power: "As the tongue has declared so shall it be binding," Vico quoted, and "When the words fail the cause is lost."[21] From these elements came the conservative and almost hermetic nature of Roman law and its intimidating historical force, which, as Vico pointed out, inspired even in the reforming Justinian a great "reverence for antiquity." *Patrios mores servandos* ("the ways of the fathers must be preserved") was the formula Vico cited.[22]

Through the Twelve Tables Vico gained some of his most important insights about the conventional legal *quaestio de origine juris* and so the *principia historiae* which constituted the primary target of his *Universal Law*. Prehistorical times (*tempus obscurum heroicum* or *fabulosum*) were no golden age, no Thomist state of innocence, but rather were filled with crime and acquisitiveness—the brute rule of "mine" and "thine" described by jurists like Lucas de Penna and Bodin.[23] Regulation of this primitive anarchy began with individual action, which is to say, in terms of private law. *Lex ex facto oritur* ("law originates in fact") was the old formula. Vico illustrated this process through the etymologies of terms designating early means of acquiring possessions, such as *mancipatio* (*res manu captae*, "by hand"), *usucaptio* ("by use"), and *heredity* (related to *hero*), and also through discussion of paterfamilial practices and the notorious *patria potestas*. Testamentary succession itself was a legal act based on individual will and thus, according to Vico, an antecedent of the famous political principle that the prince's will was law (*quod principi placuit legis habet vigorem*). In general, he assumed, "familial or domestic authority" (*aucto-*

[19] *Diritto universale*, bk. 1: *De uno principio*, ch. 168, *Opere* 2: 180; cf. *Digest*, I, 1, 1, 1.

[20] *Diritto universale*, bk. 1: *De uno principio*, ch. 182, *Opere* 2: 200–201; cf. Justinian's prefatory edict to the *Digest*, "Tanta." See also *De uno principio*, ch. 124, *Opere* 2: 114; *Scienza nuova*, *Opere* 4: §§ 469 and 1027.

[21] *Diritto universale*, bk. 1: *De uno principio*, ch. 180, *Opere* 2: 198.

[22] *Ibid.*, chs. 141 and 215, *Opere* 2: 132–34 and 250.

[23] *Ibid.*, ch. 104, *Opere* 2: 95–101. Cf. Jean Bodin, *Method for the Easy Comprehension of History*, trans. Beatrice Reynolds (New York, 1945), p. 297, and Lucas de Penna, cited by Walter Ullmann, *The Medieval Idea of Law as Presented by Lucas de Penna* (London, 1946), p. 47.

ritas oeconomica seu familiaris) constituted the "first foundation of government" (*rerum publicarum rudimentum*).[24] At one point Vico departed from the common view of Bodin and others, and that was in his belief that aristocracy, not monarchy, was the first type of government. According to the formula of Pomponius cited by Vico, "When the institutions themselves dictated it, kingdoms were founded."[25]

For Vico, then, might made right, or rather right originated in might: at first, as he put it, *bonus* meant simply *fortis*. This heroic form of justice he called the "law of private violence" (*jus privatae violentiae*), and within this he recognized three protolegal categories. These were lordship, liberty, and self-defense (*dominium, libertas, tutela*), of which the last two comprised what the jurists had called "prior natural law," and the first, "posterior natural law." To these correspond also, it is important to note, a series of other basic and completely homologous triads which expressed, in Vico's characteristically systematizing way, various aspects of *humanitas*. These included the three parts of human nature, which are knowledge, will, and strength (*nosse, velle, posse*); the three heroic moral qualities, virtue, temperance, and fortitude; the three parts of jurisprudence, philosophy, history, and judgment; and even the three species of government, monarchy, aristocracy, and democracy.[26] It was in terms of these categories that the historical process itself unfolded, and here again the pattern was juridical in nature. The movement was from a private to a public sphere, specifically to the political categories of eminent domain, civil liberty, and sovereignty (*summum imperium*). "Out of lordship, liberty, and self-defense," as Vico summed it up, "all republics are born." So in that "adolescence of the human race" men passed from a fabulous and heroic age into historical time (*tempus historicum*), and so Vico laid the foundation for another of his theories of humanity, that "the order of ideas proceeds according to the order of things."[27]

The remaining question was the cause of this social transformation, and again Vico had recourse to a legal convention. What impelled men to move from a state of nature to a state of society was not mere natural utility, as such infidels as Machiavelli and Grotius had argued. Rather it was that fundamental concept of civil law, equity—*aequum bonum* was the term Vico adapted from Ulpian's famous definition of law as *ars boni et aequi*—which was the "source of all natural law" (*fons omnium naturalis juris*); and this in turn was inseparably bound up with that motive

[24] *Diritto universale*, bk. 1: *De uno principio*, chs. 100ff., *Opere* 2: 90ff.

[25] *Scienza nuova*, *Opere* 4: § 584.

[26] The heroic moral qualities and protolegal categories are discussed in *Diritto universale*, bk. 1: *De uno principio*, chs. 71ff., *Opere* 2: 75ff.; corresponding triads appear in the "De opera proloquium," esp. §§ 2, 25, and 28, and in chs. 10 and 138ff., *Opere* 2: 26, 34f., 44, and 128ff.

[27] *Diritto universale*, bk. 1: *De uno principio*, chs. 87, 108, and 124, *Opere* 2, 86, 104, and 114; *Scienza nuova*, *Opere* 4: § 238.

force of civilization, the drive toward truth (*vis veri*).[28] Here is another conspicuous illustration of Vico's aversion to naturalistic explanations. Utility was merely the occasion for social organization; the cause was a kind of moral instinct (*honestas*). "The true reason of state" (*giusta ragione di stato*) was not animal self-interest but human equity (*aequitas civilis*). So the "principles of history" were linked directly with the "principles of jurisprudence" (*legitimae scientiae principia*).[29] This transmuted and temporalized form of jurisprudence, Romanoid if not Roman, constitutes the third stage of Vico's road.

> Panoptical purview of political progress and the future Presentation of the Past.
>
> *Finnegan's Wake*

In his own eccentric and eclectic fashion Vico fulfilled another part of the enterprise of late medieval and early modern jurisprudence, which was to rationalize and to systematize law and especially to raise it above its Romanist context. Yet even this work was carried out in terms provided by the civilian tradition; namely, the field defined by ancient jurists as "the law of nations" (*jus gentium*), though as usual Vico transformed this concept. In the first place Vico, again like Bodin two centuries before, in effect equated this field with that of universal history, which represented the combined life stories of all the *gentes* and their customs and institutions. Secondly, he altered the *jus gentium* in historical terms by distinguishing between the law of the greater nations (*jus majorum gentium*) and that of the lesser (*jus minorum gentium*)—that is, between the "heroic" jurisprudence and wisdom of the fathers and the civil institutions of the first governments. Vico summed it up in this way: "From the principle of self-defense [*tutela*] comes the *jus gentium*, which can be defined as the law of violence, and as self-protection is the first law of human life, so it holds first place in history, which is the life of the human race."[30]

[28] *Diritto universale*, bk. 1: *De uno principio*, chs. 34ff. and 55, *Opere* 2: 49ff. and 61–62; cf. *Digest*, I, 1, 1. In general see Nicola Petruzzellis, "*Vis Veri e Societas Veri* nel pensiero di G. B. Vico," in *Giambattista Vico nel terzo centenario della nascita* (Naples, 1971), pp. 37–51, and for the Renaissance background, Guido Kisch, *Erasmus und die Jurisprudenz seiner Zeit* (Basel, 1960).

[29] *Diritto universale*, bk. 1: *De uno principio*, chs. 46, 53, 179, and 185, *Opere* 2: 54–56, 60–61, 198, and 209–13; cf. *Scienza nuova*, *Opere* 4: §§ 320 and 948.

[30] *Diritto universale*, bk. 1: *De uno principio*, ch. 100, *Opere* 2: 90. Among many studies, see Guido Fassò, *Vico e Grozio* (Naples, 1971), Girolamo Cotroneo, "A Renaissance Source of the *Scienza nuova:* Jean Bodin's *Methodus*," in *Giambattista Vico: An International Symposium*, pp. 51–59, and Elio Gianturco, "Character, Essence, Origin and Content of the *Jus Gentium* according to Vico and Suarez," *Revue de littérature comparée* 10 (1936): 167–72, and "Bodin and Vico," *ibid.* 22 (1948): 272–90.

One of the consequences of this principle was that, on a priori grounds, Vico could not accept the idea of appreciable cultural "influence" in the early stages of a national history. Although every nation experienced the same general process, each had its own *ingenium* (*genius* was the humanist term) and cultural style. In general terms Vico accepted the humanist commonplace about the antihistorical character of Greek thought and the nonphilosophical character of Roman thought, and so he rejected as a fable the account, given by Pomponius and accepted by all previous commentators, about the trip made by the *decemviri* to consult with the wise men of Athens before drawing up the Law of the Twelve Tables.[31] This view was reinforced by Vico's study of feudal law, that is, of the *Consuetudines Feudorum,* which jurists had persisted in regarding as an authentic part of Roman law. According to the *communis opinio,* the institution of fiefs was Roman in origin, and the usual source, suggested by humanist and scholastic jurists alike, was the ancient *clientela.* Only a minority argued, largely on terminological grounds, that feudalism had to be acknowledged as modern, and specifically Germanic, in origin. Here again Vico constructed a kind of metahistorical synthesis out of these two interpretations. While agreeing that fiefdom and vassalage were Germanic in character and in no way an imitation of Roman practices, he nonetheless insisted upon the analogy with the ancient *clientela.* But he reversed the practice of the jurists by applying "barbaric" terminology to early Roman society instead of applying classical terminology to feudal institutions. "Roman law emerged from feudal law," as he expressed it, "not feudal from Roman," by which he meant that "feudalism" represented an early stage of every society.[32] So the old rubric *de origine feudorum* became the starting point for another of Vico's principles of history.

For Vico the period of barbaric culture, or "heroic wisdom" (*heroica sapientia*), was crucial in the establishment of these principles; thereafter it was simply a question of the way in which they were worked out. In general the pattern of civilization was remarkably similar to the evolution of jurisprudence—as well as to the education of a legal-minded scholar like Vico. The movement of history was from particularity to uniformity, from the private sphere to the public, from anarchy to order, and from philology to philosophy. The signs of this transformation in the period of "human jurisprudence" included the appearance of standards of comfort instead of

[31] *Diritto universale,* bk. 1: *De uno principio,* ch. 176, *Opere* 2: 197; *Scienza nuova, Opere* 4: § 1031, and the first *ragionamento* appended to the *Scienza nuova, Opere* 4: §§ 1412–54; cf. *Digest,* I, 2, 2: "De origine juris."

[32] *Diritto universale,* bk. 1: *De uno principio,* chs. 129 and 192, *Opere* 2: 119–20 and 222–23; *ibid.,* bk. 2: *De constantia jurisprudentis,* pt. 2, ch. 21, esp. § 41ff., *Opere* 2: 450–78, esp. 467ff.; *Scienza nuova prima,* bk. 2, ch. 31, *Opere* 3: § 149; *Scienza nuova, Opere* 4: § 599. See also Fausto Nicolini, *Commento storico alla seconda Scienza nuova,* 2 vols. (Rome, 1949–50), 2: § 1057, and more generally my "De Origine Feudorum," *Speculum* 39 (1964): 207–28.

utility, natural equity instead of special interests, and popular government rather than oligarchy. Similarly Roman jurisprudence had been organized in rational terms, and jurisconsults had become philosophers of the law (*philosophi legum*) instead of mere practitioners (*pragmatici*, the traditionally derogatory term of humanists).[33] Law became at once more equitable and more general: cases became members of instead of substitutes for general categories, and the primitive *ingenium* of Rome was transformed into true wisdom. In this final period of enlightenment there also emerged what Vico called the "constancy" of jurisprudence, philosophy, and philology, and consequently the means for acquiring a true understanding of humanity. It is precisely at this point, indeed, that for the first time Vico proclaims: "a new science is attempted."[34]

On the most general level of all, Vico saw the process of history as operating between another set of terminals corresponding to what was perhaps the most fundamental of all of Vico's concepts, distinguishing between the certain (*certum*), which belonged to human consciousness, and the true (*verum*), which was the province of nature and of God.[35] In law the distinction was between the standards of authority, which extended from human will, and reason, which applied to "the necessity of nature"; and human experience, historical as well as individual, naturally proceeded from the first to the second—from standards that were *de facto*, arbitrary, and perhaps irrational to those that were *de jure*, equitable, and perhaps philosophical. Before being amenable to reason, Vico said, men had first to become accustomed to authority; and so it was not always possible (according to an admission which Vico adapted from Justinian) to understand the rationale of some early laws. In general, Vico thought, "ancient jurisprudence neglected the true for the certain," that is, equity for the "propriety and origin of words." On the other hand the medieval "interpreters" tended to dogmatize unhistorically without a proper understanding of philological "authority." These were the conditions of that discord of philology and philosophy which Grotius, that philologist of universal understanding—"jurisconsult of mankind" Vico called him—began to repair, and which spurred Vico to his effort to reconstruct the essential "constancy of jurisprudence" and to establish the "natural law of nations" (*jus naturale gentium*).[36] This system of universal law constitutes one facet of the *New Science* (where it is termed *diritto naturale delle genti*) and one of the last stretches of Vico's road.

[33] *Diritto universale*, bk. 1: *De uno principio*, chs. 19 and 84, *Opere* 2: 46 and 84.

[34] *Ibid.*, bk. 2: *De constantia jurisprudentis*, pt. 1, ch. 1, and pt. 2, ch. 1, *Opere* 2: 272 and 308ff.

[35] *Diritto universale*, "De opera proloquium," § 30, *Opere* 2: 35; *ibid.*, bk 1: *De uno principio*, chs. 83 and 180, *Opere* 2: 83–84 and 198.

[36] *Diritto universale*, bk. 1: *De uno principio*, chs. 136 and 218, *Opere* 2: 126–27 and 254–55; cf. *Scienza nuova, Opere* 4: §§ 31, 154, and 394, and "Sul diritto natural delle genti," in *Opere* 7: 25–31.

By a commodius vicus
of recirculation. . . .

Finnegan's Wake

"The true principles of history," Vico announced in the first version of his *New Science*, "are those rules of morality, politics, law, and jurisprudence of the human race, discovered by this new science of humanity, by which the universal history of nations is governed, and which determine their rise, progress, maturity, decline, and fall."[37] So at last we reach the final and most traveled portion of Vico's road, the part where it begins to circle around and join with its beginnings by considering the nature of poetry, myth, religion, and other aspects of "poetic wisdom" in terms of a number of hybrid pseudosciences, including a "philosophy of authority," a "civil theology," and a "rational chronology," as well as a "philosophical grammar," a "system of universal law," and a myriad-formed "philosophy of history."[38] As Galileo had begun to decipher the great book of nature through mathematics, so Vico began to decipher, likewise in a "new science," the book of humanity through language; and what finally emerged was not so much a *philosophia perennis* as a *philologia perennis*.

Despite "geometrical affectations," the orientation of Vico's thought was always historical and indeed (one need not be a Crocean to say) historicist; and his principal sources of inspiration were the *studia humanitatis* and the human "science" of law (*legitima scientia*, it is called in the *Digest*). Jurisprudence was scientific, as jurists had argued for centuries, both because it dealt with things in terms of cause and effect and because it was universal, though, unlike natural philosophy, it had as its goal human welfare; and such were precisely the claims that Vico made for his "new science."[39] Jurisprudence differed from natural philosophy, moreover, in that its arrangement was topical (in a rhetorical sense) rather than logical, and its categories—persons, actions, things, relations—were those of society rather than metaphysics. It was this human system of moral, social, and political thought, it may be suggested, rather than the tradition of Greek, scholastic, or Cartesian metaphysics that provided Vico with his principal model and central ideas. Indeed, in laying the foundations for his new science of humanity, Vico was quite directly fulfilling the old Roman ideal set down in the very first sentence of the *Digest* (and quoted approvingly by him), that "jurisprudence is the true philosophy."[40]

Even while transcending the European legal tradition, however, Vico

[37] *Scienza nuova prima*, bk. 2, ch. 57, *Opere* 3: § 208.

[38] *Scienza nuova*, *Opere* 4: §§ 385–99; *Diritto universale*, bk. 2: *De constantia jurisprudentis*, pt. 2, ch. 1, *Opere* 2: 308–19.

[39] A characteristic discussion is Barthélemy de Chasseneuz, *Catalogus gloriae mundi* (Paris, 1529), X, 9.

[40] *De studiorum ratione*, *Opere* 1: 101; cf. *Digest*, I, 1, 1, 1.

continued to be affected by its habits and techniques; for the older jurists, too, had transcendental pretensions—hoping, in Vico's terms, to understand not only the certain, from authority, but also the true, through reason. "To understand laws," according to the formula of Celsus cited by Vico, "is not only to know their letter but also their spirit and intention."[41] In legal terminology the "spirit of law" (*mens* or *ratio legis*) referred basically to the intention of the lawmaker as contrasted to the *verba* of the law itself, but it connoted also the rational justification of the text. Vico was quite in agreement with the standard sixteenth-century view that "the *mens* represents the soul of the law, the *verbum* its body," though as usual he fitted this idea into his own dialectical scheme. Specifically, his point was that the *mens legis* had to do with the authority of the law (and so belonged to the realm of the *certum* and to the standard of utility), while the *ratio legis* had to do with its rationality (and so involved the *verum* and equity). The consequence for Vico, as for Montesquieu, was that comprehension of "the spirit of laws" required both historical and legal—both philological and philosophical—analysis.[42] Indeed these two processes, together with their practical application to society, constituted the essence of jurisprudence, whose purpose was thus one of restoration of natural and divine law. What was true of jurisprudence held for wisdom in general: "The first principles of all sciences are from God," Vico declared at the outset of his *Universal Law*,[43] and yet the "true principles" of Vico's science lay only at the very end of his road.

> Old Vico roundpoint.
>
> *Finnegan's Wake*

"So turns the circle of divine law," Vico wrote.

> As all human law begins with divine law, so by the succession of things which we have followed, it returns to divine law. And as society was begun among men by God through that succession of the law of the major nations, common civil law, and the law of the minor nations through war, so it endures in God Himself.[44]

The parallel with the pilgrimage of Dante, noted over a century ago by Michelet and by many others since, is striking. Like Dante, Vico regarded language as the gateway to the truth and "poetic wisdom" as the most

[41] *Diritto universale*, bk. 1: *De uno principio*, ch. 84, *Opere* 2: 84; cf. *Digest*, I, 3, 17.

[42] *Diritto universale*, bk. 1: *De uno principio*, ch. 81, *Opere* 2: 82. Cf. Stefano Federici, "De interpretatione legum," in *Tractatus universi juris* (Venice, 1584), I, 210, and in general Piano Mortari, *Richerche sulla teoria dell'interpretazione del diritto nel secolo XVI*.

[43] *Diritto universale*, bk. 1: *De uno principio*, ch. 1, *Opere* 2: 43.

[44] *Ibid.*, ch. 156, *Opere* 2: 162.

essential starting point, yet a transcendental vision as the final destination. Like Dante, he took the experience and values of the Roman tradition as his guide. Like Dante, too, he traversed a number of circles, rising from the elementary learning of the liberal arts to the exalted certainty of philosophy and theology, of divine wisdom, before reaching his final vision. The difference is that Vico's path did indeed circle back upon itself, ending up with a system of human science, a theory of history, language, and culture, and with a revelation not about the destination of humanity but rather about its origins—about the *principia* of history and the roots of language, the baby-talk of the human race.

Vico's own intellectual *corso* exhibits a similar circular pattern, especially in the convoluted, multilayered, multiversioned *New Science*; for to arrive at his destination he had indeed to become as a child. He returned not only to the elements of grammar and primitive speech of childhood, to the credulity and creativity of that stage of life, but also—the main aspect of his new science—to his catechism. But in another sense, of course, he was not really back at his starting point at all: the element of self-consciousness was added; he was at the beginning of a *ricorso*, so to speak. Emulating the divinity, he had transcended humanity by—in intellectual terms—recreating it, and so finding his end in humanity's beginning. Having begun with a state of natural law as a divine given, Vico offered his own system of natural law as a rational construct, thus indeed, in his role of philosophical demiurge, transforming the *factum* into the *verum*, the realm of *coscienza* into that of *scienza*. There are countless ways of looking at Vico's grand construct—as an encyclopedic summary of centuries of Western scholarship, as a cornucopia of new and previously undefined disciplines, or perhaps merely as a giant cryptogram of curious learning—a "vicous circle," in one of Joyce's apter coinages. But as for comprehending the past of humanity, it must be said that Vico transcended rather than resolved the problem, offering instead a sort of codification of his own reading of the humanistic and especially the legal traditions and one of the largest *petitiones principii* on record. The original dilemma remains: "History does not yet have its principles."

XIII

THE PREHISTORY OF SOCIOLOGY: MONTESQUIEU, VICO, AND THE LEGAL TRADITION

In this article the history of sociology is set in the context of the European legal tradition, especially that of Roman law and its modern interpretations and transmutations; and Montesquieu and Vico are briefly examined as social thinkers illustrating a kind of paradigm-shift from the old art of law to the new science of society.

Over half a century ago, in what is still one of the most perceptive essays on the history of sociology, Albion Small rejected the common view of the discipline he helped to establish in this country. "Sociology is not a comet as popularly pictured, viz., a body coming from nowhere and bound nowhere," he declared. "Its lineage is as old as man's efforts to understand the human lot." [1] He did not try to trace this entire lineage, but he did offer an extraordinarily broad perspective on the immediate antecedents of this branch of social science, including not only various schools of economic and political thought but also historical scholarship. It is most striking that he opened his story not with Auguste Comte or Karl Marx but with an apparently irrelevant and (as it must seem today) obscure squabble between two legal scholars over the suitability of a code of laws for German society. He did this because it seemed to him that the debate between Friedrich Karl von Savigny and A. F. J. Thibaut posed a fundamental question about his subject; namely, what kinds of nexus are there between antecedents and consequents in human experience? Small's unfashionable attitude relates in two ways to the present paper. First, it suggests a link between sociology and the history of ideas and especially an access to the more remote background of this discipline; and second, it assumes a basic connection between the science of society and the art of law, the oldest and most social-minded discipline of all. It was the so-called historical school of law that Small chose as his departure for his *Origins of Sociology*. With the help of this insight I propose to take a new look at this problem in an even longer perspective.

The phrase "prehistory of sociology" is something of a novelty in more ways than one. Neither of its terms is much over a century old, the first dating from an antiquarian work of 1851, the second a coinage of Comte in 1830. Taken together they may seem not only unfamiliar but even contradictory or meaningless. Certainly they correspond to no considerable body of investigation undertaken either by sociologists or by historians. True, there have been historical studies of *Sociologie* and *Wissensoziologie* going back to antiquity—"from lore to science," as Harry Elmer Barnes put it in his quaint Baconian fashion.[2] But neither of these approaches is entirely adequate. The latter is altogether too general, consisting as it does of little more than a macrohistory of political philosophy with a slightly different emphasis. The first, exemplified by Emile Durkheim and Werner Stark, seems on the other hand both too literal and too doctrinaire, cleaving as it does to the immediate "forerunners" of the Positive Philosophy or of Karl Mannheim's sociology of knowledge. Neither approach views efforts to establish a science of society in a broad historical perspective, as distinguished from a doctrinal genealogy suggestive of that notorious "Whig fallacy" exposed to ridicule by Herbert Butterfield.[3] Of course the history of ideas may always be the search for intellectual fathers in some sense, but it need not be limited to ideological brethren. The "proper study of mankind" is the property of no single church, party, or elite; this should be one of the first rules of historical—as well as sociological—method.

It is curious, though it seems to have provoked little curiosity, that few other fields of intellectual endeavor have taken so restricted a view of their past. The histories of philosophy, literature, art, science (as well as individual philosophies, literatures, arts, and sciences), and history itself are all well established, have standard textbooks, courses, departments, and even research centers devoted to them; and all define themselves by subject matter rather than by nomenclature or ideological commitments. Yet sociology, and in its company various anthropological disciplines, has attracted no comparable historical or antiquarian interest. Is this because the science of society is so sophisticated and modern that pre-Comtean and pre-Marxian efforts must be relegated to the garbage can of error, sham, and quackery? Only extraordinary ego- and ideocentricism, it seems to me, could make us think so. And even if prerevolutionary social thought be disparaged as feudal or standing in the same relation to social science as magic to natural science, it constitutes a field worth looking into if only to see how far we have emerged from the darkness of the old regime. Thomas Kuhn's argument about the nature of the scientific enterprise applies also, I would suggest, to sociology: here too there is a "role for history," not only to correct professionally ingrained myopia but also, at least potentially, to help construct a new and more dynamic image of social science.[4]

This is hardly the place to enter into the conceptual problems involved in Kuhn's extravagantly publicized and interminably discussed thesis, especially since Kuhn himself has objected (largely in vain) to applications outside of the "hard sciences." For present purposes I would not claim any revolutionary effects from attempting to open up a longer perspective on the history of social science, nor can I see for this effort anything yet approaching the "historical revolution in the study of science" detected by Kuhn in 1962. It does seem to me, however, that Small's demand for a more broadly historical view of sociology needs emphasizing now even more than in his day. Conceptually as well as practically, "presentism" seems to be enjoying increased favor; and while arguments on its behalf may have a certain professional and pedagogical validity, the notion that historical perspective is bound to irrelevant antiquarianism ought to be resisted.[5] Human society is in its very essence historical, and so are the sciences thereof. There is no single methodology for particular purposes of social analysis, and penetrating certain problems will always require sharp (and therefore narrow) instruments; but a deeper (and perhaps dynamic) understanding of social and cultural behavior and thought must take into account the dimension of time and the process of history. If this is true of the natural sciences, how much more appropriate is it for disciplines like sociology?

The analogy with natural science is appropriate in many ways. "The history of science," A. C. Crombie has said, "is the history of systems of thought about the natural world." [6] However important the requirement of "system," it seems clear that this definition does not entail any special premises, methods, or terminology; and it certainly does not deny "science" to those unenlightened times before God "let Newton be." On the contrary, in Kuhn's "historiographical revolution" such scholars as Pierre Duhem, Anneliese Maier, Marshall Clagett, Crombie, and Kuhn himself have devoted themselves precisely to these antediluvian ages in the effort not only to celebrate worthy "precursors" but also to throw light on the historical context and the process of scientific discovery. It is understandable that few practitioners of what Kuhn calls "normal science" welcome or even need enlightenment from such quarters, but it is otherwise with those who hope either to understand the unfolding of the story of scientific enterprise or to prepare for the transformation of normal science and perhaps even for the emergence of a new "paradigm." The ultimate benefit of this sort of investigation, in other words, may be some deeper understanding of what, in a more or less happy analogy with Kuhn's work, might be called "the structure of sociological revolutions." [7]

Gaining access to this problem demands a certain openmindedness about the direction as well as the values of the general subject, which by analogy should be "the history of systems of thought about the social world." What is needed is not merely a preconceived criterion of scientific validity, which can only be a consensus of the scientific community at any given time, but rather a curiosity about historical actuality to the extent than it can be reconstructed; not the selection of congenial-minded "precursors" but the search for similarly motivated investigators; and specifically not the idolization of a few eponymous heroes but the appreciation of a wide range of inquirers. Clagett writes:

> It is an obvious fact to the historian of science that the physical concepts of a Galileo or a Descartes, or even a Newton, radical as they may seem, were conditioned in many ways by the ancient and medieval learning that survived into the early modern period. And thus anyone who is honestly interested in the enormously complex *historical* process of the formation of modern science must examine in detail the germinal concepts of the preceding periods. This examination will give some insight into how a proto-scientific theory was criticized and emended until it was no longer a cogent whole. It will also show how the very points of criticism of the older system became points of departure for the new.[8]

There is a major difference between "the logic of scientific discovery" (in Karl Popper's famous phrase) and the history thereof.[9] Ideological pressures, professional totems and taboos, and even the patterns of generational conflict reinforce this distinction.

My question here is why a similar extended perspective should not be opened on—and similar energies directed to—the early phases of the science of society, a field in which logic has traditionally played an even slighter role. In sheer methodological terms, not to speak of the substance of intellectual history, the benefits would seem to be at least as promising as those of the history of medieval mechanics, say, or of ancient planetary astronomy. More promising, in fact, considering the intrusion of human values and the need for self-understanding and self-criticism even for those who still hope to create a value-free science of society. Such a perspective would not radically revise our view of the immediate antecedents of nineteenth-century sociology.[10] It would not, that is, obscure the significance of those eighteenth-century thinkers of an historical and anthropological turn of mind, such as Herder, Heeren, Ferguson, and certain of the French encyclopedists; and it would not challenge the central position of Montesquieu and Vico, which seems to be agreed upon. In many ways they remain the Newton and the Descartes—the lawmaker and the epistemologist—of modern social thought. This perspective would give us a more comprehensive understanding of the system, or systems, of social thought being criticized and emended by these men. For both Montesquieu and Vico undeniably represent not only new points of departure but also summings-up of older enterprises which should be (yet seldom are) regarded as integral parts of the sociological tradition.

Bluntly stated, my thesis is that the principal source of inspiration of these two unorthodox scholars, and even much of the substance of their knowledge, is what I call, with appropriate vagueness, the legal tradition. This tradition centers on the enormous body of Roman law along with its medieval and modern commentaries but includes also canon, feudal, and other varieties of customary law along with various critiques and spinoffs not only too numerous to mention but almost too complex to classify. What has been regarded as the birth of social science, in fact, can also be seen as the fulfillment in certain ways of legal tradition—or perhaps the establishment of different paradigms of the social thinking embodied in law. This is in no sense to deny the primacy of economics in the emergence of nineteenth-century "sociology," but it is to suggest the underlying significance of jurisprudence for both the form and content of this discipline. This is not very conspicuous in the case of English sociology (except for the extraordinary and still insufficiently appreciated contribution of Henry Sumner Maine), at least partly because of the nonacademic, if not anti-intellectual character of the common law. Nor has it been true of modern French sociology in the wake of positivism, although at least some disciples of Durkheim have lamented this.[11] But it is certainly true for the dominant tradition of German sociology culminating in the work of Max Weber, who came to this field from law and brought with him many of the attitudes and categories of his first profession, although few interpreters have made much of this connection.[12]

Most illuminating of all is the case of Karl Marx, a pivotal as well as a central figure who reflects directly the transition from old-regime juridical-mindedness to postrevolutionary market- and class-mindedness, thus illustrating the replacement of law by economics as the principal vehicle of social science. Through his study of Roman law with Savigny and the Hegelian Eduard Gans, Marx became convinced of the priority of jurisprudence in his own intellectual plans. Because of the vital relationship between law and philosophy, he told his father in 1837, he spent time reading not only such modern authors as Thibaut and J. G. Heineccius but also the sources of law, and he translated the first two books of Justinian's *Digest* into German.[13] He even composed some three hundred pages of his own philosophy of law—private law, at least, for he stopped short of public law—before he "saw the fallaciousness of the whole." Specifically he rejected the systematizing "metaphysics of law," which was reflected in his own scheme and which he associated with Kantian idealism. Thereafter he concentrated on "positive studies only," though this still included civil and canon as well as Germanic law. But within five years he had passed through his juristic apprenticeship and, characteristically, rejected it, especially in its embodiment in the dominant German school of jurisprudence headed by his former mentor Savigny and founded by Savigny's mentor, Gustav Hugo. Marx's criticism appeared in the *Rheinische Zeitung* in 1842 as "The Philosophical Manifesto of the Historical School of Law," lamenting the conservatism and obscurantism of this school and its goal, as Sidney Hook expressed it, "to nail the present upon the cross of the past." [14] Yet it was through these legal studies, and especially Savigny's discussion of property, that Marx found his own way in social philosophy.[15]

If it is impossible to appreciate the genesis of Marxian thought apart from jurisprudence, such neglect is still less justifiable for the seminal age of Montesquieu and Vico (whom Marx himself thought it essential to read). According to Raymond Aron, author of one major historical survey of the subject, "Montesquieu was more of a sociologist than Auguste Comte." [16] The reason for this is that Montesquieu better fits Aron's prescription that sociology should be (1) scientifically objective and (2) concerned with the "social as such." This is a good example of how "precursors" are born, or rather canonized. The historical truth is that the purpose of Montesquieu's major work was that most traditional goal of jurists for centuries, "the spirit of the laws." In legal jargon the *mens legum*, or *ratio legum*, referred to the intention of the lawmaker, or more generally the reason behind the text, the "spirit" as contrasted with the "letter" of the law.[17] This had been the avowed aim of Montesquieu's great seventeenth-century predecessor Jean Domat; and even a century before that the term *mens legum* had had a philosophical dimension. So Montesquieu was operating under a heavy weight of precedent when he expanded the concept into a protosociological program. In short it was legal professionalism that provided Montesquieu both with his supposedly modern "objectivity" and with his fundamentally social angle of vision.[18]

Keeping this in mind may also help to clarify one of the central puzzles of Montesquieu's *L'Esprit des lois*, which is its structure, or lack thereof.[19] It seems to me undeniable that, notwithstanding digressions and intrusions, this book reflects the workings of a mind incorrigibly conditioned by the legal tradition—not only by the civil law in which Montesquieu was educated but also by the French parlement in which he served. From Justinian's time onward jurists had been in the habit of beginning with a general definition of law, its species and sources—"Quid jus," according to the rubrics of one sixteenth-century commentator, "De divisione juris," "Unde jus"—and going on to take up the law of things, persons, family, succession, and so on.[20] So, in his more freewheeling and reflective way, did Montesquieu, who began with a general definition corresponding to the *Digest* title "De jure et justitia," went on to discuss the three species of constitutions in the fashion of the second title "De origine juris," and then proceeded to the law of things (commercial law), the status of persons (liberty and servitude), family, and succession. In the course of this he made abundant use not only of standard Roman authorities but also of commentators and such modern discoveries as the fragments of Ulpian published in the sixteenth century. The protosociological system which Montesquieu was criticizing and emending, and indeed restructuring, was the *Corpus Juris Civilis* in its various transmutations.

In his departures from civilian convention Montesquieu continued to be faithful to the legal tradition in unmistakable ways. The last sections of his book, for example, correspond exactly to the collections of feudal law, the so-called *Libri Feudorum*, which medieval jurists had anachronistically accepted as "Roman." More fundamentally, Montesquieu's impressive forays into the wilderness of comparative law likewise followed trails already blazed by French legists, who for centuries had wrestled with the "conflict of laws," specifically that between the civil law taught in the universities and the customs applied in the courts, and who had also to take into account the principle of territoriality that prevented the use of laws of alien provinces or countries. The geographic and historical relativism reflected in the attitudes of such authors as Jean Bodin, Pierre Dubois, and even Pierre de Beaumanoir, was also part of Montesquieu's intellectual inheritance, as it has been of French sociology in general.[21]

It goes without saying that Montesquieu had no intention of adding just one more commentary on Roman and feudal law: his philosophical concern for the inner relationship between laws and political forms and ideals prevented any such narrow professionalism. Yet again his large intellectual ambitions were not entirely innovative, and certainly not in the context of modern systematic jurisprudence. Philosophically minded jurists from the time of Baldus, and more specifically from the time of Bodin, had shown a deep interest in larger questions of public law, and had begun what we might call the sublimation of the legal tradition. Systematic jurists, including François Connan, François le Douaren, and Hugues Doneau, promoted this by trying to reorganize civil law in the light of modern social conditions.[22] Bodin, Louis Le Caron, Gregory of

Toulouse, and others went still further by making the ideal "republic" their principle of organization, the framework for their cosmologies and encyclopedias, yet at the same time without abandoning that "ascending" approach to government (to adapt a phrase from Walter Ullmann) which gives a "sociological" style to their analyses.[23] Most important, they went beyond the Roman experience to universal history for their systems, in effect expanding the old *jus gentium* to include the customs and institutions of all nations, ancient and modern. This was the significance of Bodin's formula that history was the major source of universal law (*in historia juris universae optima pars est*).[24] This major premise of the sixteenth-century historical school of law was stated no less explicitly by Montesquieu, for whom "il faut éclairer l'histoire par les lois et les lois par l'histoire." [25] For these and other reasons Bodin has been taken as a "predecessor" both of Montesquieu and of Vico.[26] It seems no less valid than taking them as predecessors of Durkheim or Mannheim.

The debt of Giambattista Vico to the legal tradition is still more conspicuous.[27] Only academic mischance prevented him from assuming the chair of jurisprudence at the University of Naples. In any case, it was that hope which led him to erect his formidable system of law, the *De Universi juris* of 1720. Like Montesquieu, Vico sought the "spirit of the laws," citing to this effect the famous formula of Celsus, that "understanding laws is knowing not only their letter but also their force and intention." [28] Characteristically, Vico transmuted his old idea into a new principle consonant with his own evolving and increasingly abstract philosophy which took its final form in the *New Science* that occupied the remainder of his life. In particular he related it to his famous distinction between the *verum* and the *certum*; that is, between absolute truth, which is the province of nature and of God, and human certainty, which belongs to consciousness and society. For Vico the "spirit of the law" had a similar twofold structure: the *ratio legis* corresponded to the *verum* because it involved reason and equity, the *mens legis* to the *certum* because it had to do with human authority and social utility.[29] The consequence of this anti-Cartesian assumption that understanding came originally not from natural science but from self-consciousness—not from *scienza* but from *coscienza*—was that jurisprudence required historical as well as philosophical analysis. It is this combination, it seems to me, that accounts for the fundamentally sociological character of Vico's as well as Montesquieu's thought.

In general, Vico took Rome as the model of human legal, institutional, and social experience, and he made even more extensive use than Montesquieu of conventional Romanist sources, not only Justinian's collections but also the *Libri Feudorum* and especially the primitive law of the Twelve Tables.[30] Yet like Montesquieu he proposed to extract from this material a more universal pattern of development—a *corso* through which all the *gentes* passed. In particular he tried to show how jurisprudence developed from custom, based on simple force and authority, to rational and even codified law, based on reason. This shift corresponded to the literary development from poetry to philosophy and, in general, the passage of nations from a mythical age (a *tempus obscurum* or *fabulosum*) to enlightenment (a *tempus historicum*). The key to this interpretation was the Twelve Tables, a "serious poem," as Vico called it, which embodied the "heroic jurisprudence" and "poetic wisdom" of that earliest stage of history. And as the Twelve Tables represented the beginning of the Vichian *corso*, so the *Libri Feudorum* represented the beginning of a *ricorso*—"barbaric," to be sure, but in the sense of a primitive new phase, not the degenerate aftermath of the civilian tradition as lawyers had long regarded it.

In the *Scienza Nuova* Vico replaced this juridical vehicle of "poetic wisdom" with the richer substance of the Homeric poems, but the connecting links with the original legal model were by no means lost. Nor were the links with the *nova scientia* in its original form, which was identified directly, in Vico's characteristically anti-Cartesian fashion, with the human science of philology. "Philology is the study of speech," he explained, "and it treats of words and their history, then shows their origin and progress. . . . revealing their properties, changes and conventions. But since the ideas of things are represented by words, philology must first treat the history of things. . . , [that is] human governments, customs, laws, institutions, intellectual disciplines, and the mechanical arts." [31] Like Bodin and Montesquieu, then, Vico set about to ransack the histories of all nations (*gentes*) within the expanded framework of the *jus gentium*, though again he injected his own reformulation, distinguishing between the "law of the greater nations" (*jus majorum gentium*), and that of the "minor nations" (*jus minorum gentium*), that is, between the heroic phase and the first civil governments. But throughout his work Vico kept in mind the goal of reconstructing a "universal system of law"—a *jus naturale gentium* or, in its final form, a *diritto naturale delle genti*.[32] This was at once one of the faces of the "new science" and one of the landmarks in the prehistory of sociology.

It is at this point that a concrete historical link between modern social science and ancient legal science becomes visible. The relation between the Vichian paradigm and legal tradition is most conspicuously revealed in the formula, taken by Vico from the very first title of the *Digest*, which declares flatly that "Jurisprudence is the true philosophy." This commonplace, *jurisprudentia est vera philosophia*, was repeated, glossed, and elaborated in legal and rhetorical terms by hundreds of jurists from the thirteenth century onwards.[33] One line of development can be traced through such sixteenth- and seventeenth-century Romanists as Doneau and Domat down to the French Civil Code of 1804. "It is philosophy that is the true source of jurisprudence," wrote one of Domat's disciples cited in that code.[34] Beyond this tradition of systematic jurisprudence this theme was almost a conditioned response of liberal as well as legal education, hence part of the common stock of ideas of many literate Europeans between the Renaissance and the Enlightenment, no matter how disillusioned they might be with legal practice. In general, the history of this *topos*, and of various attempts to realize it, constitutes a central theme of modern social thought.

The common ground between jurisprudence and sociology is so extensive that, from a certain point of view, the latter may seem to be a collateral descendant of the former. It was Weber himself who defined the general tradition out of which, in the longest perspective, he operated; namely, that of the *honoratiores*, the empirical and theoretical or "scientific" experts in the law who judged individual cases by applying reason to fact.[35] Of this international type the highest representative was the ancient Roman jurisconsult, whose business was not only to issue authoritative *responsa* on specifics but also, ideally, "to elaborate a rigorously abstract system of juristic concepts." The French and German codes were the most conspicuous product of this impulse but hardly less directly affiliated were such philosophic structures as Domat's *Civil Laws* and Gregory of Toulouse's *Syntagma Juris*, which likewise retained the primal categories of persons-things-relations or actions.[36] It may not be too farfetched to classify Weber's own systematizing attempts with such old regime creations, and ultimately with those of his *honoratiores*. For Weber, too, proceeded by judging specific (historical) cases, such as the Puritan ethic, and thus built an empirical base for an abstract (sociological) system. In a sense, Weber not only issued *responsa prudentium* concerning particular historical phenomena but also acted as a legislator, even a codifier, of social thought.

Perhaps the most obvious common denominator of jurisprudence and sociology is the insistence on the "scientific" status of each. Generations of jurists acclaimed their discipline as a "science" and promoted it above such fields as medicine because of its universality and especially its method, which was to treat its subject matter in terms of cause and effect.[37] Civil law is a *scientia*, declared Johann Oldendorp in the sixteenth century, "that is, the knowledge of social things through causes" (*cognitio civilium rerum per causas*), which at that time meant the four Aristotelian causes.[38] Out of such presumptions, too, came the impulse toward systematization which emerged, or reemerged, in the sixteenth century and which displayed not only a cordiality toward new logical systems, such as that of Petrus Ramus, but also—long before Descartes—an *esprit géométrique*. Law began with axioms and propositions, wrote François Le Douaren, "just as geometry with points, lines, surfaces etc." [39] For centuries, moreover, civil law was reputed to be "written reason" (*ratio scripta*), and even in nations where it had not been officially "received" it was often applied as a common law, "not by reason of empire," according to one sixteenth-century formula, "but by the empire of reason." [40] Through the efforts of several generations of jurists between that time and the age of Vico and Montesquieu the civil law tradition underwent a process of criticism, rearrangement, and transmutation that went further toward the realization of this philosophical and rationalistic ideal. In many ways this ideal was shared, if not inherited, by the discipline of sociology.

But it is easy to exaggerate the natural-law aspect of the legal tradition. Equally significant and "scientific," though less appreciated, is the "positive" side of jurisprudence (*jus positivum* was a conventional term from the twelfth century), which concentrated much more directly on what Aron called "the social as such." Society, as François Connan, another sixteenth-century jurist, put it, "turned away from nature" (*deflexit de via naturae*); and legal "reason" was human and practical, not speculative.[41] Nor, Althusius would add, should it be confused with the more abstract field of politics. "Where the political scientist ceases," he wrote, "the jurist begins"; for it was the latter's task not to ask grand questions about social ideals (despite the attempts of Bodin and Gregory of Toulouse) but rather "to derive and infer right (*jus*) from fact (*factum*)." [42] *Lex ex facto oritur* was one old formula of sociological jurisprudence, and another was the still more famous proposition of Gratian, the codifier of canon law: "Custom is inviolable and may not be avoided either by human law or by sacred canon." [43] The implication was that jurists had to judge social process and structure as well as to establish legal norms. Fundamentally, law had to be assessed by social custom (*consuetudo legum interpretatur*), as Connan explained; and similarly custom had to be confirmed by human judgment (*res judicatae consuetudinem confirmant*).[44] Jurists had to be aware, too, of the process of degeneration (*desuetudo*), of the necessity of adjusting laws to social conditions by corrective legislation (*leges correctoriae*) as well as equity, of the "conflict of laws," and of interpreting laws, in the canonist phrase, "according to the variety of places and of ages." [45] Such consciousness of the mutability and relativity of laws was also needed in the effort to realize the ideal of jurisprudence as the "true philosophy."

Obviously this entire line of argument needs more careful and concrete development. Obviously, too, Vico and Montesquieu were not the only, not the most representative, and perhaps not even the most distinguished members of the tradition of philosophical or sociological jurisprudence in the old regime, at least from the somewhat eccentric perspective suggested here. The quantity and quality of citizens in this *Respublica Jurisconsultorum*, as one of Vico's contemporaries called it,[46] is indicated, though by no means exhaustively, in the magisterial survey of the history of German corporative law made in the late nineteenth century by Otto von Gierke, the fourth volume of which treats some two hundred authors, mostly jurists, who busied themselves with the theory of society between 1500 and 1800.[47] There are undeniable drawbacks to Gierke's work as an introduction to social thought. Aside from being dated, it overemphasizes doctrines of natural law, hence the relations of law to natural philosophy, to the neglect of positive law and comparative law. It suffers also from a certain (at least retrospective) discredit because of associations with romantic—some might say protofascist—views of *Genossenschaft*. But despite an antiquated conceptual and ideological context, the work does not seem less useful for historical purposes than many exercises in Comtean and Marxian precursor-hunting; and certainly it constitutes a study of social thought unparalleled in scope if not depth. Individual figures such as Johann Althusius, Hugo Grotius, Samuel Pufendorf, and Jean Domat have received special attention in recent years; but many others, comparable to the *calculatores* and *speculatores* disinterred by historians of natural science, remain to be investigated and placed in context. And even more important than such soundings is the task of surveying and remapping the terrain as a whole.

How can this more general exploration be planned and undertaken? Robert Nisbet, surveying what he calls "the sociological tradition," singles out five "unit ideas" for discussion in the somewhat *ideengeschichtlich* style made famous by Arthur O. Lovejoy; and although they are subjected to the sort of foreshortened treatment characteristic of the "normal science" of sociology, they do help to define a range of problems basic to any science of society and suggest some intellectual bridges to the prehistorical age of sociology.[48] These ideas are defined generally—and, it would appear, in a "value-free" manner—as community, authority, status, the sacred, and alienation. I say "value-free," but in a deeper sense this approach is indeed value-ridden, as was that of Comte, Marx, and many others. For modern sociology has always seemed to emphasize social forces and groupings between the individual and the sovereign (as conceived by classical political theory), or between the individual and the market (as conceived by classical economics). To this extent "the sociological tradition" seems to turn back to the patterns and groupings of an older and more juridically oriented society—a society in which the rule of law (positive if not natural law) was much more closely identified with social reality. At least on the conceptual level it may be concluded that sociology seems to reverse the rule of Toennies, moving from *Gesellschaft* back to *Gemeinschaft*—or, to reverse that of Maine, from contract back to status.

In some form or other each of Nisbet's unit-ideas figures in the legal tradition and was the object of extensive discussion in analytical as well as normative terms. The examination of communal structures on all levels constituted much of the substance of civil, canon, and customary law. On the lowest—for Althusius the natural—level is the community of kinship, the family; and under the rubric "Grades of cognation and affinity" this received elaborate treatment with a view especially to intricate problems of property and succession.[49] The complex diagrams and argumentations accompanying this title seem to prefigure (in ways that may deserve investigation) those of modern structural anthropology. Still more elaborate were the discussions of civil or private associations (*collegia*), guilds, corporations, and the like, along with various obligations, tacit, contractual, and legal, that furnish coherence and continuity.[50] On the highest level are public associations, such as the city, province, and state itself, which involve a still wider range of social problems—police, economic and fiscal management, public services and welfare, communication, religion and culture, and, in general, the subpolitical ties between citizens and government.

Similar leads can be suggested for the idea of authority, from sovereign to political power, and for the enormously complicated question of status (*conditio personarum* in legal terminology), from free and privileged citizenship to various kinds of subordination, servitude, and slavery, which again overlaps with the law of property. These are all subjects familiar to the historian of law, although their significance for social thought has received at best marginal treatment. More problematical is the idea of the sacred, the religious and sacramental basis of society; but in various explicit and implicit ways it has been fundamental to civil as well as canon law, connected as it was not only with the church but also with familial, representative, and royal institutions. Aspects of this topic have been opened up by such medieval historians of law as Walter Ullmann and especially by Ernst Kantorowicz, whose study of "political theology" is of prime relevance.[51] The idea of alienation, the extrasocial as it were, is at least latent in criminal law and the legal consideration of heresy, poverty, and madness.[52] Indeed the very definition of madness as a social problem, and the attendant institutionalization (that is, isolation) of this form of alienation, as Michel Foucault argues, was a creation of lawyers and legislation. In general, as Ullmann has remarked, "By viewing law as a social phenomenon, medieval jurisprudence was forced to elucidate some basic principles about society, and thus was led to consider topics which, under modern conditions, would be dealt with, not by the lawyer, but by the sociologist"; and this continued to be true of modern commentators on law.[53]

In any case, legal discussion of these and many analogous topics adds up to more than reflections of curious customs of times gone by. They underlie the "history of systems of thought about the social world" and so form part of an intellectual continuum in which both the legal and the sociological traditions have participated. It is not possible here to suggest in particular what might be uncovered in such explorations; I have here only defined the territory in a rather speculative way based on the sporadic and limited expeditions I have made in recent years. It may be that connections between law and sociology are largely in the eye of the beholder, but of two points I remain persuaded. One is that scholarly "amnesia," as Pitrim Sorokin called it, leads social scientists to claim "that nothing important has been discovered in their fields during all the preceding centuries. . . and that the real scientific era in these disciplines began only in the last two or three decades with the publication of their own researches and those of members of their clique." [54] No doubt this is an exaggeration, made in Sorokin's characteristically cranky and self-serving style, but it does point to a deficiency of perspective which historians may help to correct in at least an extradisciplinary way. The second is the point that, in any case, the enormous and continuous enterprise of jurisprudence between the thirteenth and eighteenth centuries constitutes a wilderness of intellectual history that beckons social theorists and historians alike.

Notes

1. Albion Small, *Origins of Sociology* (University of Chicago Press, 1924), pp. 19, 41. This book was first published serially in *American Journal of Sociology*, 1923-1924.

2. Harry Elmer Barnes, *Social Thought from Lore to Science* (New York: Heath, 1938). Cf. Emile Durkheim, *Montesquieu and Rousseau, Forerunners of Sociology*, trans. Ralph Mannheim (Ann Arbor: University of Michigan Press, 1960), and Werner Stark, *Montesquieu, Pioneer of the Sociology of Knowledge* (London: Routledge and Paul, 1960).

3. Herbert Butterfield, *The Whig Interpretation of History* (Cambridge: Cambridge University Press, 1931).

4. Thomas Kuhn, *The Structure of Scientific Revolutions* (Chicago: University of Chicago Press, 1970), introduction.

5. For example, in their different ways, Allan R. Buss, "In Defense of a Critical-Presentist Historiography: The Fact-Theory Relationship and Marx's Epistemology," *Journal of the History of the Behavioral Sciences* 13 (1977): 252-260, and David Hill, "In Defense of Presentism," *History and Theory* 18 (1979): 1-15. Cf. the well-known discussion of G. W. Stocking, "On the Limits of 'Presentism' and 'Historicism' in the Historiography of the Behavioral Sciences," *Journal of the History of the Behavioral Sciences* 1 (1965): 211, 218.

6. A. C. Crombie, *Augustine to Galileo*, 2 vols. (London: Falcon Press, 1952), 1: 1.

7. In *A Sociology of Sociology* (New York: Free Press, 1970), chap. 1, Robert W. Friedrichs discusses "the structure of social scientific revolutions" on the analogy of Kuhn's theory (though in defiance of Kuhn's strictures) and counsels interpreters to take a more pluralistic view of intellectual transformation and "paradigm shifts."

8. Marshall Clagett, *The Science of Mechanics in the Middle Ages* (Madison: University of Wisconsin Press, 1959), p. xix.

9. Karl Popper, *The Logic of Scientific Discovery* (London: Hutchinson, 1959); and see Lewis Feuer, *Einstein and the Generations of Science* (New York: Basic Books, 1974).

10. The most recent survey is Ronald Fletcher, *The Making of Sociology*, 2 vols. (New York: Joseph, 1971), typically discussing the pre-Comtean "beginnings" very cursorily.

11. According to Henri Levy-Bruhl, "Rapports du droit et de la sociologie," *Archives de philosophie du droit* 3-4 (1937): 21: "On peut seulement s'étonner qu'il y ait été fait relativement peu de place au droit dans l'école sociologique française. Cela tient à ce que le fondateur de cette école, Durkheim, était lui-même philosophe et non juriste, et la plupart de ses élèves philosophes, moralistes, historiens de religion."

12. Marianne Weber, *Max Weber: A Biography*, trans. Harry Zohn (New York: Wiley, 1975), p. 114, discusses Weber's connection with Mommsen and others.

13. Letter of 10-11 November 1837, translated in *Collected Works*, 8 vols to date (New York: International Publishers, 1975), 1: 10 ff.

14. Sidney Hook, *From Hegel to Marx* (Ann Arbor: University of Michigan Press, 1962), p. 142. In general see Christoph Schefold, *Die Rechtsphilosophie des jungen Marx von 1842* (Munich: Beck, 1970), and Hasso Jaeger, "Savigny et Marx," *Archives de philosophie du droit* 12 (1967): 65-89.

15. According to Eugen Ehrlich, *Fundamental Principles of the Sociology of Law*, trans. Walter Moll (New York: Russell and Russell, 1962), p. 320: "I have gained the conviction in my travels that in the literature of the world there is not another monograph the name of which and, in part, the content of which is so well known to the jurists of each and every legal system as Savigny's *De Possessione*."

16. Raymond Aron, *Main Currents in Sociological Thought*, 2 vols. (New York: Penguin, 1965), 1: 14.

17. These and related points are discussed further in my "Vera Philosophia: The Philosophical Significance of Renaissance Jurisprudence," *Journal of the History of Philosophy* 14 (1976): 267-279.

18. Eugen Ehrlich responded to a privately expressed criticism by Justice Holmes that he had overlooked Montesquieu in his book (see note 15) by remarking, "In fact *L'Esprit des lois* must be considered the first attempt to fashion a sociology of law." See his "Montesquieu and Sociological Jurisprudence," *Harvard Law Review* 29 (1916): 583.

19. See Franz Neumann's introduction to Montesquieu, *The Spirit of the Laws*, trans. Thomas Nugent (New York: Hafner, 1949), p. xxix.

20. François le Douaren, *Opera omnia*, 3 vols (Lucca: J. Rochius, 1765), 1: 3.

21. Discussion in my "Development and Context of Bodin's Method," in *Verhandlungen der internationalen Bodin Tagung in München*, ed. Horst Denzer (Munich: Beck, 1973), 123-150, and for the more general context of historical investigation into society and institutions before the eighteenth century my *Foundations of Modern Historical Scholarship* (New York: Columbia University Press, 1970).

22. Among recent studies of this crucial subject see in particular Christoph Bergfeld, *Franciscus Connanus 1508-1551* (Cologne: Böhlau, 1968); Walter Vogt, *Franciscus Duarenus 1509-1559* (Stuttgart: Kohlhammer, 1971); Aldo Mazzacane, *Scienza, logica e ideologia nella giurisprudenza tedesca del sec. XVI* (Milan: Giuffrè, 1971); Emilio Cortese, *La Norma giuridica*, 2 vols. (Milan: Giuffrè, 1962-1964); Vincenzo Piano Mortari, *Ricerche sulla teoria dell'interpretazione del diritto nel secolo XVI* (Milan: Giuffrè, 1956); and Hans Troje, *Graeca Leguntur* (Cologne: Böhlau, 1971).

23. Walter Ullmann, *Principles of Government and Politics in the Middle Ages* (London: Methuen, 1961).

24. Kelley, "Bodin's Method," p. 138.

25. Montesquieu, *De l'Esprit des lois*, 2 vols. (Paris: Garnier, n.d.), 2: 412.

26. Etienne Fournol, *Bodin prédécesseur de Montesquieu* (Paris: A. Rousseau, 1896), for example, and Girolamo Cotroneo, "A Renaissance Source of the *Scienza nuova*," in *Giambattista Vico, An International Symposium*, ed. Giorgio Tagliacozzo and Hayden White (Baltimore: Johns Hopkins University Press, 1969), pp. 51-59.

27. Discussion in my "Vico's Road: From Philology to Jurisprudence and Back," in *Giambattista Vico's Science of Humanity*, ed. Giorgio Tagliacozzo and Donald P. Verene (Baltimore: Johns Hopkins University Press, 1976), pp. 15-29, and "In Vico Veritas: The True Philosophy and the New Science," *Social Research* 43 (1976): 601-611.

28. Giambattista Vico, *Diritto universale*, ed. Fausto Nicolini (Bari: G. Laterza & Figli, 1936), p. 84, citing Digest, 1, 3, 17.

29. *Diritto universale*, p. 35.

30. Ibid., p. 197, 119. Cf. Max Fisch, "Vico on Roman Law," in *Essays in Political Theory Presented to George H. Sabine* (Ithaca: Cornell University Press, 1948), pp. 62-88.

31. *Diritto universale*, p. 308.

32. Giambattista Vico, *The New Science*, trans. Thomas Bergin and Max Fisch (Ithaca: Cornell University Press, 1968), p. 31.

33. See note 17.

34. See A. J. Arnaud, *Les Origines doctrinales du Code civil français* (Paris: Librairie générale de droit et de jurisprudence, 1969), and Jacques Vanderlinden, *Le Concept du code en Europe* (Brussells: Editions de l'Institut de Sociologie de l'Université libre de Bruxelles, 1967).

35. Max Weber, *On Law in Economy and Society*, trans. Edward Shils and Max Rheinstein (Cambridge, Mass.: Harvard University Press, 1954), pp. 198-223.

36. Jean Domat, *Les Lois civiles dans leur ordre naturel* (Paris: Jean Baptiste Coignard, 1689), and Pierre Grégoire, *Syntagma Juris Civilis* (Lyon: Pillehotte, 1587), and *De Republica* (Lyon: Pillehotte, 1609).

37. Vicenzo Piano Mortari, *Richerche*, and Eugenio Garin, *La Disputa delle arti nel Quattrocento* (Florence: Vallechi, 1947).

38. Johann Oldendorp, *Certissimae politiae* (Lyon: Sebastian Gryphius, 1551), p. 79.

39. François le Douaren, *Opera omnia*, 1: 1.

40. Aubépin, "De l'Influence de Dumoulin sur la législation française," *Revue critique de législation et de jurisprudence* 5 (1854): 305.

41. François Connan, *Commentariorum juris civilis libri X* (Naples: Antonius Tivano, 1724), p. 16.

42. Johann Althusius, *The Politics*, trans. Frederick Carney (London: Eyre and Spottiswoode, 1964), p. 3.

43. Emile Friedberg, ed., *Corpus Juris Canonici*, 2 vols. (Graz: Akademische Druck- u. Verlagsanstalt, 1959), 1: 23.

44. François Connan, *Commentariorum*, p. 43.

45. Walter Ullmann, *The Medieval Idea of Law* (London: Methuen, 1946), p. 57. These themes are pursued in my "Clio and the Lawyers: Forms of Historical Consciousness in Medieval Jurisprudence," *Medievalia et Humanistica*, n.s., 5 (1974): 25-49.

46. G. A. di Gennaro, *Respublica Jurisconsultorum* (Naples: S. Abbatis, 1752).

47. Otto von Gierke, *Natural Law and the Theory of Society 1500-1800*, trans. Ernest Barker (Boston: Beacon Press, 1957).

48. Robert Nisbet, *The Sociological Tradition* (New York: Basic Books, 1966), p. 47 ff.

49. François Hotman, *De Gradibus cognationis et affinitatis* (Paris: J. Bogardus, 1547).

50. Johannes Althusius, *The Politics*, p. 28 ff.

51. Ernst Kantorowicz, *The King's Two Bodies* (Princeton: Princeton University Press, 1957).

52. Michel Foucault, *Madness and Civilization*, trans. Richard Howard (New York: Vintage, 1971), p. 160.

53. Walter Ullmann, *The Medieval Idea of Law*, p. 163.

54. Pitrim Sorokin, *Fads and Foibles in Modern Sociology* (Chicago: Regnery, 1956), chap. 1.

XIV

The Metaphysics of Law: An Essay on the Very Young Marx

"IN A WORD I HATE ALL THE GODS!" Karl Marx took this defiant cry of Prometheus, "the eminent saint and martyr of the philosophical calendar," as the motto and point of departure of his doctoral thesis presented at the University of Jena in 1841, and in many ways it was symbolic of his entire career.[1] As a student at the Gymnasium of Trier in 1835, the seventeen-year-old Marx, still a practicing Lutheran, was already celebrating the power of man to determine his own fate and envisaging the Promethean task of re-creating the world by uncovering its first principle, its *arche*, and using it for the benefit of all mankind. "History calls those men greatest," he wrote in his reflections on the choice of a profession, "who have ennobled themselves by working for the common good"; and this heaven-, or rather earth-, storming goal Marx also preserved for the rest of his life.[2]

Too little attention has been paid to the profession first chosen by Marx, namely, that of the law. For centuries the law had been represented by its practitioners as the most direct path to the "common good" (*bonum publicum*). In general (and intellectually genetic) terms it was by pursuing jurisprudence—not always the substance and methods, perhaps, but certainly the ideals of jurisprudence—that Marx began the heroic task by which he hoped to attain greatness. Needless to say, his enterprise was not without setbacks, and of these one of the first was Marx's disillusionment with conventional jurisprudence as it actually related to political and social matters. Another was the resistance of political authority, and with it professional law, to the pursuit of the social ideals embodied in jurisprudence. This resistance Marx felt most directly in the censorship legislation directly aimed at the *Rheinische Zeitung*, on which he served his apprenticeship in practical politics in the two

My thanks for the proddings and suggestions of friends and colleagues at the Institute for Advanced Study, who heard one version of this paper, and of those at the University of Rochester (especially Peter Linebaugh), who have shown forbearance toward still another perspective on Marxism.

[1] Marx, "Dissertation und Vorarbeiten über die Differenz der demokritischen und epikurischen Naturphilosophie," in *Marx-Engels Gesamtausgabe* (Berlin, 1927–32), 1, pt. 1: 10 (translations throughout from *Marx-Engels Collected Works* [New York, 1975–], 1: 30). Also see G. Cottier, *L'Athéisme du jeune Marx* (Paris, 1959).

[2] Marx, "Betrachtung eines Jünglings bei der Wahl eines Berufes," in *Marx-Engels Gesamtausgabe*, 1, pt. 2: 167 (*Collected Works*, 1: 8).

years after receiving his doctor's degree. In 1843 Marx resigned in protest, and, interestingly enough, his statement was accompanied by a representation of Prometheus with his entrails being devoured.[3] Yet Marx's own Promethean enterprise continued, and it may not be too fanciful to see his system of political economy as the final metamorphosis of his first calling.

Marx's commitment to a legal career began in the fall of 1835, when he entered upon the study of civil law at the University of Bonn. Even then, he showed distressing signs of unorthodoxy, and his father worried about his romantic notions. "In connection with the lectures on law," Heinrich Marx wrote in November 1835, "you must not demand [that they] . . . should be touching and poetic"; and he continuously urged his son to be more practical-minded.[4] In a stream of letters father taxed son with a variety of time-honored adolescent failings that seemed to reflect idealism and rebelliousness. Most prominent among these were disorder ("One expects *order* even from a scholar, and especially from a practical lawyer"), financial irresponsibility (". . . and you know quite well I am not rich"), selfishness (". . . in your heart egoism is predominant"), and a dangerous tendency to violence[5] ("Is duelling then so closely interwoven with philosophy?"). Karl had indeed been charged with "rowdiness and drunkenness at night." Despite such compulsive "sermonizing," the elder Marx tried not to insist on his authority, but the "wild goings-on at Bonn" made it clear that his son was willful and defiant and had set his sights on a goal higher than a conventional legal or cameralistic career. Academically, however, Marx was declared "diligent" and even "very diligent and attentive" (*sehr fleissig und aufmerksam*) in all ten of the courses he took during 1835–36, six of which dealt with branches of law and legal history.[6]

His transfer to the University of Berlin in the fall of 1836 marked a turning point in Marx's life and very noticeably strengthened his attachment to legal studies. Although its most eminent philosopher, Georg Wilhelm Friedrich Hegel, had been dead for five years, the university was still among the most impressive in Europe, and its faculty of law in particular was a center of intellectual ferment. The most eminent professor was Friedrich Karl von Savigny, one of the greatest legal scholars of the century and regarded as leader of the intimidating "historical school of law," which emerged in opposition both to natural law theories and to rationalistic efforts at codification, especially that of Napoleon. The second most renowned professor was the Hegelian Eduard Gans—"a versatile Jew," sniffed Heinrich von Treitschke, "acute rather than intelligent"—who had emerged as a leading critic of this same historical school. The tendency of the historical school was, as Sidney Hook has put it, "to nail the present upon the cross of the past";

[3] *Marx-Engels Gesamtausgabe*, 1, pt. 1: frontispiece (*Collected Works*, 1: 374).

[4] Heinrich Marx to Marx, Nov. 18–19, 1835, in *Marx-Engels Gesamtausgabe*, 1, pt. 2: 186 (*Collected Works*, 1: 646). Also see the forthcoming biography by Jerrold Seigel.

[5] Heinrich Marx to Marx, early 1836, Mar. 19, 1836, May-June 1836, Dec. 9, 1836, in *Marx-Engels Gesamtausgabe*, 1, pt. 2: 188, 191, 192, 226 (*Collected Works*, 1: 650, 652, 653, 689).

[6] "Abgangszeugnis der Universität Bonn für Marx," Aug. 22, 1836, in *Marx-Engels Gesamtausgabe*, 1, pt. 2: 194 (*Collected Works*, 1: 658). On Marx's legal studies, see August Cornu, *Karl Marx et Friedrich Engels*, 1 (Paris, 1955): 81ff.

and Savigny himself had to defend his school against the charge that it proposed to surrender to the "tyranny of the past" (*die Herrschaft der Vergangenheit*).[7] In contemporary debates Savigny and Gans were at odds over the reform of Prussian law as well as the academic problem of "possession" in civil law. One concerned French scholar, who in 1827 had published a thesis on Savigny, observed, "The war is spectacular. In the historical school they are afraid of philosophy. . . . In the philosophical camp they look down with pity on purely historical jurists . . . ."[8] In 1839 this war between the "realism" of Savigny and the "idealism" of Gans became public. At least three years earlier, however, Marx had already been exposed to this juridical and philosophical *Kulturkampf*. In his first year at the university he studied "Pandekten" with Savigny and "Kriminalrecht" with Gans, and there is little doubt that their altercation had a shaping effect on Marx's own developing social views.[9]

If the perspective here seems eccentric, it is nevertheless precisely the one that the young Marx presented in the one autobiographical statement of his prerevolutionary years. This is the famous confessional letter which he wrote to his father at the end of his first year at the University of Berlin (November 10, 1837). "There are moments in one's life," he began, "which are like the frontier posts marking the completion of a period but [which] at the same time clearly indicate a new direction."[10] Looking back, he saw the beginning of a "new life" linked with his love for Jenny von Westphalen and expressed in his efforts to write lyrical poetry. During that same year, in fact, he wrote two "wild songs" on "nocturnal love" and a Faustian "fiddler," reflecting some of his adolescent pangs and "striving for poetic fire." But, like Dante Alighieri, whose "new life" was also associated with passion and poetry, Marx was impelled to turn from love to learning—from the "remote heaven" of his literary art, as he put it, to more adult aims. "Poetry, however, could be and had to be only an accompaniment," he continued in the letter to his father; "I had to study law and above all felt the urge to wrestle with philosophy."

What is essential to understand at this point is that Marx did not distinguish at all sharply between these two disciplines, for the identification of law and philosophy was among the first lessons learned by law students. "Jurisprudence is the true philosophy" is a formula taken from the very first

[7] Hook, *From Hegel to Marx* (Ann Arbor, 1950), 142. In general, see Adolph Stoll, *Friedrich Karl von Savigny*, 2 (Berlin, 1929): 184–88; Hans Günther Reissner, *Eduard Gans: Ein Leben in Vormärz* (Tübingen, 1965), 123, 159; and Hermann Kantorowicz, "Savigny and the Historical School," *Law Quarterly Review*, 53 (1937): 326–43.

[8] E. Lerminier, *Introduction générale à l'histoire du droit* (Paris, 1829), 270, and *De Possessione Analytica Savignianae Doctrinae Exposito* (Paris, 1827). See Max Lenz, *Geschichte der königlicher Friedrich-Wilhelms-Universität zu Berlin*, 2 (Halle, 1910): 384.

[9] "Abgangszeugnis der Universität für Marx," in *Marx-Engels Gesamtausgabe*, 1, pt. 2: 247 (*Collected Works*, 1: 703). According to the contemporary student catalogue, Marx must have taken "Privatim ius Pandectarum" from nine to eleven every morning with Savigny and "Ius criminale universale" from noon to one every afternoon except Wednesday with Gans as well as a third course on "anthropologia" with H. Steffens. See *Index lectionum . . . in Universitate Friderica Guilelma* (Berlin, 1837).

[10] Marx to Heinrich Marx, in *Marx-Engels Gesamtausgabe*, 1, pt. 2: 213–31 (*Collected Works*, 1: 10–21); and "Nachtliebe" and "Spielmann" in *Marx-Engels Gesamtausgabe*, 1, pt. 1: 147–48 (*Collected Works*, 1: 22–24).

sentence of the Pandects, that seminal collection of classical jurisprudence which Marx had not only studied (with Savigny the previous year) but had even begun to translate into German.[11] The justification for this identification had been two-fold: first, that law constituted a true "science" (*civilis scientia*), since it was universal and viewed the world in terms of cause and effect, and, second, that unlike natural science it proposed as its principal object the common good of society. From the thirteenth century to Marx's own time the theme *jurisprudentia est vera philosophia* was pursued by jurists, commentators, and systematizers of law, including contributors to the French Civil Code of 1804. Whatever the relations between mature Marxism and classical "civil science," the young Marx, at least the very young Marx, started in the old tradition. "The two," he wrote of law and philosophy, "were so closely linked that, on the one hand, I read through Heineccius, Thibaut and the sources quite uncritically, in a mere schoolboy fashion; thus, for instance, I translated the first two books of the Pandect[s] into German, and, on the other hand, tried to elaborate a philosophy of law covering the whole field of law."[12]

In these youthful experiments Marx carried out academic assignments at the same time he was also carrying on the great tradition of systematic jurisprudence which grew out of the work of the scholastic jurists (surveyed in Savigny's classic history of Roman law in the Middle Ages) and which gained maturity in the "reformed jurisprudence" established in the sixteenth century, most prominently at the University of Bourges. From here, especially through the efforts of Hugues Doneau (after his transferral to Heidelberg and, later, to Altdorf), the values and program of this philosophical school made their way into German academic jurisprudence; and the tradition was preserved and extended by generations of "Systematiker," as Savigny called them, down to the nineteenth century.[13] Among these were two distinguished

[11] For the general orientation of this paper, see my "Vera Philosophia: The Philosophical Significance of Renaissance Jurisprudence," *Journal of the History of Philosophy*, 14 (1976): 67–79, "Louis le Caron, Philosophe," in *Philosophy and Humanism: Renaissance Essays in Honor of Paul Oskar Kristeller*, ed. E. Mahoney (New York, 1976), 16–35, and "Vico's Road," in *Giambattista Vico's Science of Humanity*, ed. G. Tagliacozzo and D. Verene (Baltimore, 1976), 15–29.

[12] Marx to Heinrich Marx, Nov. 10, 1837, in *Marx-Engels Gesamtausgabe*, 1, pt. 2: 215: "Nun durfte und sollte die Poesie nur Begleitung sein; ich musste Jurisprudenz studieren und fühlte vor allem Drang, mit der Philosophie zu ringen. Beides wurde so verbunden, dass ich teils Heineccius, Thibaut und die Quellen rein unkritisch, nur schülerhaft durchnahm, so z. B. die zwei ersten Pandektenbücher ins Deutsche übersetzte, teils eine Rechtsphilosophie durch das Gebiet des Rechts durchzuführen suchte. Als Einleitung schickte ich einige metaphysische Sätze voran und führte dieses unglückliche Opus bis zum öffentlichen Rechte, eine Arbeit von beinahe dreihundert Bogen. Vor allem trat hier derselbe Gegensatz des Wirklichen und Sollenden, der dem Idealismus eigen, sehr störend hervor und war die Mutter folgender unbehilflich unrichtiger Einteilung. Zuerst kam die von mir gnädig so getaufte Metaphysik des Rechts, d. h. Grundsätze, Reflexionen, Begriffsbestimmungen, getrennt von allem wirklichen Rechte und jeder wirklichen Form des Rechts; wie es bei Fichte vorkömmt, nur bei mir moderner und gehaltloser. Dabei war die unwissenschaftliche Form des mathematischen Dogmatismus, wo das Subjekt an der Sache umherläuft, hin und her räsonniert, ohne dass die Sache selbst als reich Entfaltendes, Lebendiges sich gestaltete, von vornherein Hindernis, das Wahre zu begreifen."

[13] In this wilderness of juridical literature, almost wholly uncharted by historians except through the Hegelian connection, these are just a few of the most relevant works: the various systematic efforts of the Enlightenment jurist and historian Heineccius, notably the *Elementa Juris Naturae et Gentium* and the two volumes of *Elementa Juris Civilis*, arranged respectively according to the order of the Pandects and the Institutes of Justinian, in many editions and translations (including one by Thibaut); Gustav Hugo, *Institutionen des römischen Rechts*; Thibaut, *System des Pandekten-Rechts*; Gans, *System des römischen Civilrechts*;

names on Marx's reading list, Johann Gottlieb Heineccius and A. F. J. Thibaut, and his teachers at Berlin, including A. F. Rudorff as well as Savigny and Gans. All of these scholars followed variations of the old scholastic method associated with the fourteenth-century jurist Bartolus, a method based upon civil law principles that had been correlated and rationalized by generations of "authorities" working to achieve greater consistency, generality, and equity. In particular, they directed their efforts to the creation of an intelligible (and teachable) scheme of law based upon classical principles or organization, especially the Pandects.

So, evidently, did Marx. The three-hundred-page "unhappy work" referred to in his letter has not survived, but Marx did set down a brief outline for his father's edification. He began by making the conventional civilian distinction between private and public law, dividing the former into the equally conventional rubrics of the law of persons, things, and persons in relation to property, with special emphasis on the law of contracts. In its ramifying and trichotomizing (*trichotomische*) approach, Marx's scheme could not have differed substantially from innumerable such schemes devised by students of law over the centuries, especially in connection with eighteenth-century movements for codification.[14] What was unconventional was Marx's reaction to his own work, and he laid bare its deficiencies in his usual intemperate language. "The whole thing is replete with tripartite divisions, it is written with tedious prolixity, and the Roman constitutions are misused in the most barbaric fashion in order to force them into my system." Worst of all, it embodied the basic contradiction of the law of the old regime. Significantly, when Marx reached the public law section of his treatise, that is, the point at which civil rules joined up with political goals and questions of the common good, he "saw the falsity of the whole thing" and broke off the project.

The source of the error lay with what Marx was pleased to call "the metaphysics of law," which he defined as "basic principles, reflections, definitions of concepts, divorced from all actual law and every actual form of law." According to Marx, the "metaphysics of law" was akin to Kantian idealism and to allegedly "scientific" systems of natural law, such as that constructed by Johann Fichte, but it was even worse because of the way it manipulated social reality. The difficulty stemmed from the time-honored "opposition between what is and what ought to be," which in turn was "the source of the hopelessly incorrect division of the subject matter." "Mathematical dogma-

Savigny, *System des heutigen römischen Rechts*; as well as other works referred to by Marx. See note 18, below. In general, see Paul Koschaker, *Europa und das römische Recht* (Berlin, 1953); E. Landsberg, *Geschichte der deutschen Rechtswissenschaft*, 3 (Berlin, 1910); Franz Wieacker, *Privatrechtsgeschichte der Neuzeit* (Göttingen, 1967); and Guido Fassò, *Storia della filosofia del diritto*, vols. 2, 3 (Bologna, 1968–70).

[14] See A.-J. Arnaud, *Les Origines doctrinales du Code civile français* (Paris, 1969); and Klaus Luig, "Institutionen-Lehrbücher der nationalen Rechts im 17. und 18. Jahrhundert," *Ius Commune*, 3 (1970): 64–97. Marx's own contribution to this tradition followed the Roman form of Justinian and Gaius, which likewise distinguished the *ius publicum* from the *ius privatum* and divided the latter into the laws of persons, things, and actions (or, in Marx's terms for this last, persons in relation to property). In this Marxian trichotomy, the first two rubrics—persons (the basis of "subjective" law) and things (the objects in the natural world that are potentially property)—correspond in a general way to the Hegelian dialectic of subject-object but in a sequence that Marx rejected. See page 365, below.

tism" might be appropriate for the abstractions of geometry, which are bound neither by social context nor by historical change. "On the other hand," Marx explained, "in the concrete expression of a living world of ideas, as exemplified by law, the state, nature, and philosophy as a whole, the object itself must be studied in its development; arbitrary divisions must not be introduced, the rational character of the object itself must develop as something imbued with contradictions in itself and find unity in itself."[15] It seems significant that this, the first Marxian prefiguring of historical materialism, should be formulated in the context of a fundamental, and even revolutionary, critique of systematic jurisprudence. The subversive consequences were not lost on Marx's father, and his warning was prophetic. "Your views on law are not without truth," he wrote in response to his son's letter, "but are very likely to arouse storms if made into a system, and are you not aware how violent storms are among the learned?"[16]

Marx's break-through was certainly an act of scholarly dissent, even heresy, since he was defying authorities honored as "priests of the laws" (*sacerdotes legum*) in the Pandects and, hence, in legal tradition. But it was also a moral epiphany attended by a deep personal crisis. Disillusionment with the law sent him back to pure philosophy "with a good conscience," as he put it, and even to poetry; and these obsessions in turn so undermined his health that he was obliged to go to the country for a rest. The trip seemed to be effective. He returned not only with renewed strength but also with a resolve to turn away from youthful transcendentalism back to the substance of life. "I even joined my landlord in a hunting excursion," he wrote, "rushed off to Berlin and wanted to embrace every street-corner loafer." He returned with renewed interest in Hegel, whose works he read through for the first time in order "to bring genuine pearls into the light of day"; and this study coincided with his attendance at meetings of the radical Hegelian Doctors' Club. Such was the emotional context of Marx's initial revulsion from idealism. "A curtain has fallen, my holy of holies was rent asunder, and new gods had to be installed" is the way he expressed his traumatic experiences. "From the idealism which, by the way, I had compared and nourished with the idealism of Kant and Fichte, I arrived at the point of seeking the idea in reality itself. If previously the gods had dwelt above the earth, now they became its centre."[17] From this

[15] Marx to Heinrich Marx, in *Marx-Engels Gesamtausgabe*, 1, pt. 2: 215: "Das Dreieck lässt den Mathematiker konstruieren und beweisen, es bleibt blosse Vorstellung im Raume, es entwickelt sich zu nichts Weiterem, man muss es neben anderes bringen, dann nimmt es andere Stellungen ein, und dieses verschieden an dasselbe Gebrachte gibt ihm verschiedene Verhältnisse und Wahrheiten. Dagegen im konkreten Ausdruck lebendiger Gedankenwelt, wie es das Recht, der Staat, die Natur, die ganze Philosophie ist, hier muss das Objekt selbst in seiner Entwicklung belauscht, willkürliche Einteilungen dürfen nicht hineingetragen, die Vernunft des Dinges selbst muss als in sich Widerstreitendes fortrollen und in sich seine Einheit finden."

[16] Heinrich Marx to Marx, Dec. 28, 1836, in *Marx-Engels Gesamtausgabe*, 1, pt. 2: 199 (*Collected Works*, 1: 665).

[17] Marx to Heinrich Marx, in *Marx-Engels Gesamtausgabe*, 1, pt. 1: 218: "Ein Vorhang war gefallen, mein Allerheiligstes zerrissen, und es musste neue Götter hineingesetzt werden. Von dem Idealismus, den ich, beiläufig gesagt, mit Kantischem und Fichteschem verglichen und genährt, geriet ich dazu, in Wirklichen selbst die Idee zu suchen. Hatten die Götter früher über die Erde gewohnt, so waren sie jetzt das Zentrum derselben geworden."

position it was not far to a Promethean—and materialistic—denial of the "gods" altogether.

In this way, wakened as it were from his dogmatic slumber, Marx turned from the "ideal in itself" (*Begriff an sich*) to the "thing in itself" (*Ding an sich*), to use a Kantian expression that would not have pleased him. Yet he continued to think in juridical terms and, indeed, to apply to juridical sources for enlightenment, though in a very different style from the "metaphysics of law." "Shortly after that," he wrote, "I pursued only positive studies"; and he listed a variety of works on civil law by Savigny and others as well as Gratian's twelfth-century collection of canon law and some studies in early Germanic law.[18] Marx rejected the error, which he "shared with Herr v. Savigny," that separated legal form from content—that is, legal concepts from "positive" or "material" law. Instead, he believed that "positive law in its conceptual development" was exactly the same as "the formation of the concept of law," and so he concluded that philosophical understanding had to proceed, above all, through the *jus positivum*, since this law was the meeting place between legal norms and social reality. To fulfill the ideal of jurisprudence as true philosophy, in other words, one had to investigate first the material base. This train of thought quite likely led Marx not only to reject the "metaphysics of law" but also to turn to another discipline entirely as the principal vehicle of his social philosophy.

This interpretation of the very young Marx is made more plausible by examining the particular work in which he discovered the basic fallacy of the "metaphysics of law": the first book of his "positive studies," Savigny's great treatise on possession, *Das Recht des Besitzes*, which one authority regards as the most influential legal monograph of modern times.[19] In this work Savigny exhibited the same enormous range of learning as in his monumental history of Roman law, but in *Das Recht des Besitzes* he applied it in a practical and even polemical fashion. He discussed the whole complex of problems involved in possession and property with reference to the judgments of ancient authorities, especially those included in the Pandects, and of later commentators. The latter he divided into two classes: the "interpreters," including medieval and Renaissance jurists such as Portius Azo, Accursius the glossator, Andrea Alciato, and Jacques Cujas, as well as such modern authors as his colleagues Gans and Rudorff; and the "systematists," including Hugues Doneau, Doneau's mentor François le Douaren, R.-J. Pothier, and Savigny's rival A. F. J. Thibaut. In scholastic fashion he listed, criticized, and usually rejected the *opiniones* of these and many other jurists before presenting his own interpretation. In later editions the collecting of opinions and controversies continued (over fifty were treated in the seventh edition, published by Rudorff).[20]

[18] Marx mentions Savigny, *System des heutigen römischen Rechts*; Paul Feuerbach, *Lehrbuch des gemeinen in Deutschland gültigen peinlichen Rechts*; C. L. W. von Grolmann, *Grundsätze der Criminalrechtswissenschaft*; A. W. Cramer, *De Verborum Significatione*; J. N. von Wening-Ingenheim, *Lehrbuch des Gemeines Civilrechts*; C. F. Mühlenbruch, *Doctrina Pandectarum*; W. A. Lauterbach, certain titles on civil process ("einzelne Titel . . . Zivilprozess"); Gratian, *Concordia discordantium canonum*; and G. P. Lancellotti, *Institutionas Juris Canonici*.

[19] Eugen Ehrlich, *Fundamental Principles of the Sociology of Law*, trans. W. Moll (New York, 1962), 320.

[20] Savigny, *Das Recht des Besitzes* (7th ed.; Berlin, 1865), 10, 543. Also see Hasso Jaeger, "Marx et Savigny," *Archives de philosophie du droit*, 12 (1967): 65–89 (in a volume devoted generally to "Marx et le droit

The entire exercise was based on the assumption—rejected, of course, by Marx—that legal form, by which Savigny meant classification in the Roman system, could be distinguished from content, by which he meant specific formulation by Roman and modern jurists.

Even to the young Marx this book must have seemed a monstrosity of antiquarian learning without any reasonable relationship to the common good. At the outset the reader is instructed that the subject of the treatise is not the right to possess (*jus possidendi*), but rather the rights arising from simple possession (*jus possessionis*); and these rights Savigny grouped under two headings, usucapion and interdiction.[21] Usucapion signified uncontested possession (in the law of the Twelve Tables for one or two years), and it was related to the legal concept of prescription (the *praescriptio longae temporis* of Roman and canon law). Interdiction referred to the right to repossess something that had been seized by act of violence and so arose from redress of injury. Savigny also distinguished between "natural" and "civil" possession, that is, physical possession in the state of nature and the juridical condition that created "property," which was generally defined as "the totality of all real rights." Although he employed such legal concepts as *bona fides* and *justa causa*, Savigny's argument seemed to be based ultimately upon the accidents of Roman history, or prehistory, in which private property (such as the *ager privatus* discussed by the great Roman historian Niebuhr) arose out of the simple act of prehension, or willful seizure, and then somehow was given legal status by receiving customary acceptance and general social formulation. Out of *factum*, in juridical terms, came *jus*. Might makes right—perhaps even property is theft, if one can so render the euphemism "prehension"—so it may have seemed to a young and idealistic reader like Marx.

On this foundation, in any case, Savigny erected his theory of possession, and hence of property; and in reaction to this Gans launched an assault on the historical school of law in his own discussion of the problem of possession. This pamphlet, published in 1839, was an exercise in "scientific polemic" in which Gans bitterly attacked Savigny's sophistical habit of transforming hypotheses into demonstrated theses with the help of strategically placed "thuses" and "in facts." All Savigny really did was argue from Roman history, Gans charged; and for all their "practical sagacity" the Romans had no national claims to philosophical truth. "Possession is a fact, a natural condition and not a right"—so Gans stated Savigny's position—"but nonetheless the possessor has rights because of his possession." Such empiricist (and historicist) logic Gans totally rejected. When Savigny defined possession in terms of interdiction and usucapion, Gans complained, "he removed the subject to a field in which one cannot contend with philosophical weapons: as soon as pure theory is mentioned, he confuses the matter with terms which theory has

moderne"); Georges Cornil, "Philosophie et droit privé," *Revue de droit international et de législation comparée*, 2d ser., 10 (1909): 616–44; and Peter Landau, "Karl Marx und die Rechtsgeschichte," *Tijdschrift voor Rechtsgeschiedenis*, 41 (1973): 361–71.

[21] Savigny, *Das Recht des Besitzes*, 43.

nothing to say about . . . ."[22] It was obviously no way to go about realizing the ideal of jurisprudence as true philosophy.

Marx had no trouble choosing sides in this debate. Even if he had not shared Gans's Hegelian bias at this point, he would surely have been repelled by the method and, by inference, the morality of his other mentor, Savigny. In the first place, Marx had come to reject the idea of understanding and, still less, of legitimizing social institutions within the framework of an arbitrary system of civil law. Secondly, because of his concern for social justice he could have had little sympathy with Savigny's tendency to justify the entire range of property rights on the basis of the fact of possession, which is to say on the basis of an amoral and irrational state of nature. Clearly, it was a theory at odds with the view that Marx later came to adopt toward property, especially in relation to labor. For these reasons, it may be suggested that Marx's first act of academic subversion was to turn Savigny, not Hegel, on his head.

THIS INTELLECTUAL TRAUMA occurred in Marx's twentieth year, when he was still contemplating a legal career—in jurisprudence rather than cameralistics. In the next few years several things deflected him from this course. One was his immersion in traditional philosophy, not only that of ancient Greece for purposes of his thesis on Democritean and Epicurean philosophy, but also (and even more intensively) Hegelianism, which was situated at the vortex of many burning social as well as conceptual problems of the day. Another was the death of his father, whose moral pressure and financial support were both withdrawn in 1838. Finally, there was the official condemnation of the Left Hegelians, which blocked Marx from an academic career. In 1842 he began his career as a political journalist, first submitting articles to and then becoming chief editor of the *Rheinische Zeitung*. At last, he had occasion to contribute directly to the "common good" by commenting upon a variety of social issues, including freedom of the press and criminal law. Yet Marx still preserved some of his juridical-mindedness. He criticized the Prussian censorship legislation of 1841 on the grounds not merely of its injustice but also of its illegality. Again, he took up the theme of the contradictions between law and its professed ideals. "Is *truth* to be understood as being simply *what the government decrees* . . . ?"[23] Having overcome academic authority, Marx was setting his sights on more intimidating obstacles to the common good.

Marx kept coming back to the issues posed by his old teacher Savigny, who

[22] Gans, *Ueber die Grundlage des Besitzes, Eine Duplik* (Berlin, 1839), 7, 11. Gans had offered a similar, though milder, criticism of Savigny's famous *Geschichte des römischen Rechts im Mittelalter* in a review complaining that the work was merely literary history without conceptual value and concluding that "einer innerliche Geschichte" remained to be written; see his *Vermischte Schriften* (Berlin, 1834), 1: 46. For other entries in the contemporary debate over possession, see the list (not exhaustive) by A. Rudorff in his appendix to Savigny, *Das Recht des Besitzes*, 543–62. During the years 1836–42 there were over forty publications, not including popular discussions of the problem of property such as that of Pierre Proudhon; and throughout the century the literature continued to accumulate. For a modern discussion, see Gunter Wesener, "Ius Possessionis," *Festschrift für Max Kaser* (Munich, 1976), 715–42.

[23] Marx, "Bemerkungen über die neueste preussische Zensurinstruktion," in *Marx-Engels Gesamtausgabe*, 1, pt. 1: 154 (*Collected Works*, 1: 113).

in 1842 was appointed Prussian minister of justice for the reform of laws. "Are not," he asked, "most of your court cases and most of your civil laws concerned with property?"[24] A case in point was a recent statute concerning the theft of wood, which in effect had raised forest regulations to the level of criminal law. Even the penal code of the sixteenth century, Marx noted, had not gone so far in the protection of property. What he objected to was precisely the sort of proprietary claims argued by Savigny—"customs contrary to law, " as Marx put it, and benefitting only the privileged, landowning classes. "Their origin," he added, "dates to the period in which human history was part of *natural history*," that is, the "spiritual animal kingdom" of feudalism. Marx celebrated universal human law above such class privilege. "We demand for the poor a customary right, and indeed one which is not of a local character but is a customary right of the poor in all countries."[25] In this article Marx thought he had uncovered one of the basic flaws of modern "liberal legislation," which was "formulating and raising to a universal level those rights which they found already in existence," so raising *de facto* conditions to a *de jure* level. This is what came of arguing from the selfish individualism of a pre- and anti-social state of nature, instead of from the rational ideal of "the state as the great organism, in which legal, moral, and political freedom must be realized . . . ."[26]

Turning his journalistic attention to such practical problems, Marx began to formulate more clearly his views about the relationship between law and social reality—a problem that was congruent in many ways with that of the relationship between ideology and society's material base. These views have almost invariably been interpreted in terms of Marx's Hegelianism, and with justice. Yet it is clear that he was still involved in academic jurisprudence, for he devoted to that subject the most comprehensive and aggressive statement of his philosophic position up to that time: his pivotal and, as Sidney Hook has remarked, "strangely neglected" critique of the historical school of law. This school, whose manifesto was Savigny's celebrated essay on "the vocation of our age for legislation and jurisprudence," set itself against the optimistic and rationalistic philosophy of law which had prevailed in the previous century.[27] In his counterattack, "The Philosophical Manifesto of the Historical School of Law," Marx not only announced his abjuration of the profession of law but also suggested the premises for a more positive and critical basis for social thought and action.[28] In part, his attack was a typical act of academic

[24] Marx, "Der leitende Artikel in Nr. 179 der Kölnischen Zeitung," in *Marx-Engels Gesamtausgabe*, 1, pt. 1: 246 (*Collected Works*, 1: 199).

[25] Marx, "Debatten über das Holzdiebstahlgesetz," in *Marx-Engels Gesamtausgabe*, 1, pt. 1: 272 (*Collected Works*, 1: 230). Also see C. Vigouroux, "Karl Marx et la législation forestière rhenane de 1842," *Revue d'histoire économique et sociale*, 43 (1965): 222–33.

[26] Marx, "Der leitende Artikel," in *Marx-Engels Gesamtausgabe*, 1, pt. 1: 249 (*Collected Works*, 1: 202).

[27] Savigny, *Vom Beruf unserer Zeit für Gesetzgebung und Rechtswissenschaft* (Heidelberg, 1814), reproduced with other material relating to the quarrel with Thibaut in J. Stern, *Thibaut und Savigny* (Darmstadt, 1959).

[28] Marx, "Das philosophische Manifest der historischen Rechtsschule," in *Marx-Engels Gesamtausgabe*, 1, pt. 1: 251–59 (*Collected Works*, 1: 203–10). For a recent discussion, though largely in the Hegelian context, see Christoph Schefold, *Die Rechtsphilosophie des jungen Marx von 1842* (Munich, 1970). For the lexicon of Marx's juridical vocabulary and a historical commentary, see R. Guastini in *Materiali per una storia della cultura giuridica*, ed. G. Tarello, 3 (Genoa, 1972): 349–515.

rebellion, although he disguised his doctrinal parricide somewhat by taking as his ostensible target not *Herr Professor* and now *Herr Minister* Savigny (referred to only as "the most famous historical jurist") but rather Savigny's elder colleague Gustav Hugo, whom Marx called the "forefather" (*Ältervater*) and "original type" (*Naturmensch*) of the historical school of law. In any case, this declaration of independence was the first step in the enterprise of philosophical criticism that cleared the ground for Marx's own system of thought.

Like Savigny, Hugo affected a "reaction against the frivolous spirit of the eighteenth century"; but, in fact, Marx charged, it was the historical school that was frivolous and; worse still, irrational and immoral. In a sense the basic flaw was that of professional jurisprudence, that is, the eclectic, indiscriminate, and uncritical use of sources. Marx's complaints about Hugo (he "knows no distinctions") could have been applied as well to Savigny's treatise on possession. "Everything existing serves him as an authority, every authority serves him as an argument." Hugo's position was a travesty of Kant's and had been arrived at "by supposing that, because we cannot know what is true, we consequently allow the untrue . . . to pass as fully valid." Although insisting that the positive was irrational ("positive, i.e., uncritical" was Marx's gloss), Hugo held, nevertheless, that it, not reason, supplied the standard of human judgment, since in a sense it embodied natural law, undeniably and, indeed, tautologically reflecting the "natural" progression of events. This, Marx concluded, "is the frank, naive, reckless method of the historical school . . . . Hugo, therefore, profanes all that the just, moral political man regards as holy, but he smashes these things only to be able to honour them as historical relics; he desecrates them in the eyes of reason in order afterwards to make them honourable in the eyes of history and at the same time to make the eyes of the historical school honourable."[29]

What the historical school of law had accomplished, it would seem, was to make history self-justifying, to derive right from fact, as Savigny had done for property; and the result was the betrayal not only of reason but also of man himself. Absolute skepticism, absolute immoralism, and absolute relativism (if this is not a contradiction) were the foundations of the "positive" philosophy according to Hugo. "The sole juridical featur of man is his animal nature" was the proposition which Marx took to be the motto of the historical school and in particular of Hugo's *Natural Law as a Philosophy of Positive Law*, to which Marx's article was ostensibly devoted.[30] Among the consequences of Hugo's attitude was that slavery could be at least "provisionally lawful" and old regime jurists had indeed justified this argument foı centuries, largely on the basis of the "law of nations" (*jus gentium*), which was a repository for much of the indiscriminate and immoral "positive law" of the historical school.

[29] Marx, "Das philosophische Manifest," in *Marx-Engels Gesamtausgabe*, 1, pt. 1: 252, 254 (*Collected Works*, 1: 206, 209).

[30] Hugo, *Lehrbuch des Naturrechts als einer Philosophie des positiven Rechts* (Berlin, 1809), 43; Hugo discussed "Der Mensch als Thier" in an introductory chapter on "Juristische Anthropologie." Also see Arno Buschmann, *Ursprung und Grundlagen der geschichtlichen Rechtswissenschaft, Untersuchungen, und Interpretationen zur Rechtslehre Gustav Hugos* (Krefeld, 1963); and, most recently, Jürgen Blühdorn, "Naturrechtskritik und Philosophie des positiven Rechts," *Tijdschrift voor Rechtsgeschiedenis*, 45 (1974): 3–17.

What is more, Hugo argued, "slavery" was better than a state of war and "not much worse" than poverty, since the "slave-owner, even from well-understood economic considerations, is much more likely to expend something on the education of a slave who shows ability than on that of a beggar child." According to Marx, this was the import of Hugo's chapter on "freedom." The same "frivolous shamelessness" appeared in the succeeding chapters on marriage (though Marx's commentary was deleted by censors) and education, which are likewise treated on the positive and animal level. These views seemed to follow logically from the proposition that Marx extracted on civil law and cited with evident incredulity, that the "necessity of civil law in general is imaginary."

In Marx's view the full iniquity of Hugo's concept of law appeared in his chapter on constitutional law. Here the convergence between the authoritarian methods of traditional jurisprudence and the authoritarian assumptions of conservative government was complete. "It is a holy duty of conscience to obey the authorities in whose hands power lies." To this characterization of Hugo's position Marx added the gloss, "Has not Hugo proved that man can cast off even the last fetters of freedom, namely, that of being a rational being?" How, then, could his successors claim to be "the legislators of our times?" Though only Karl Haller, Friedrich Stahl, and Heinrich Leo were mentioned, Marx was again obviously thinking of his mentor Savigny, then occupied with revising the Prussian laws. In general, the historical school worked out of that great storehouse of German erudition in which Marx himself had begun, and to this they added trappings from modern fashions of mysticism, romanticism, and speculation. "Truly, however," Marx declared, "little criticism is needed to recognize behind all these fragrant modern phrases the dirty old idea of our enlightener of the ancien regime and to recognize behind all the extravagant unctuosity his dissolute frivolity." This idea, which betrayed the ideals of ancient jurisprudence as well as modern social conscience, was that law was mere animal law, not human but "positive" law, and its implication was "the right of arbitrary power."

The result of this line of criticism became clearer a year later when Marx, carrying out his resolution to place his arguments on a more philosophical basis, wrote an extended critique of Hegel's philosophy of law. These pages contain no poetry (though begun during the first months of his marriage to Jenny von Westphalen), little idealism in any sense, and a large amount of convoluted and ill-humored philosophizing; but old juridical issues figured prominently, and echoes of old scholastic quarrels can be heard. Marx was still incensed at Hugo and his progeny, that "school which legitimates the baseness of today by the baseness of yesterday . . . , a school to which history shows only its posterior . . . " (punning on the mindless empiricism, the *a posteriori* assumptions of the historical school).[31] In the introduction to his

[31] Marx, "Zur Kritik der Hegel'schen Rechtsphilosophie: Einleitung," in *Marx-Engels Gesamtausgabe*, 1, pt. 1: 609 (*Collected Works*, 3: 177), published in *Deutsch-Französische Jahrbücher* in 1844.

critique, Marx broadened his attack by criticizing both law and religion (here stigmatized with the famous phrase "opium of the people") as obstacles to the "common good." In this way jurisprudence seemed explicitly to fall victim to Marx's growing hatred of "all the gods" of established society. Guilty by association, too, was the political constitution (*politische Verfassung*), which Marx referred to as "the religion of national life, the heaven of its generality over against the earthly existence of its actuality."

For Marx, then, Hegelian philosophy had come to be another manifestation of the "metaphysics of law" and of the fallacies both of idealism and of the historical school. On the one hand, Hegel distorted social reality with an abstract and authoritarian system, and, on the other, he continued to accept uncritically the positive and subhuman, "animal" law of the old regime. The bases of this law were the caste divisions (*Stände*) that turned man, according to Marx, "into an animal that is directly identical with its functions. The Middle Ages are the animal history of human society, its zoology."[32] Hegel assumed an abstract and transcendent state and a concept of "sovereignty" that led him into triviality and tautology; yet he accepted without question the status quo of German political organization. His remarks on the executive, for example, "could stand word for word in the Prussian common law." What Hegel presented was not a system of philosophy, it might be concluded, but rather a system of "ideology" in a classically pejorative sense.

The fundamental contradiction in Hegel's *Rechtsphilosophie*—that between a received juridical system and the common good that ought to inform society—had troubled Marx since his first year at the University of Berlin. In Hegel's case it took the form of opposing the state to "the spheres of civil law and personal welfare, the family and civil society." Once again the central question concerned private property and, particularly primogeniture, which isolated property from the family as well as from civil society.[33] Marx pointed out that Roman law—although it provided for slavery, right of conquest, and class conflict—had never confused private property with political power. By keeping the *jus privatum* separate from the *jus publicum*, it had also prevented the sovereign will (the *imperium*) from becoming hereditary. Germanic law was quite different. Hegel epitomized the view that alienated private property—that is, inalienable landed property—from its "social roots" and from public wealth and that identified it with the ruling establishment. "The political constitution at its highest point is the constitution of private property," Marx declared. "The supreme political conviction is the conviction of private property." Here was another god to hate: "Primogeniture is private property become a religion to itself, lost in itself, elated by its own independence and power." It was "crass stupidity."

[32] Marx, "Kritik des Hegel'schen Staatrechts," in *Marx-Engels Gesamtausgabe,* 1, pt. 1: 499 (*Collected Works*, 3: 81); written in 1843, it was not published until the twentieth century. See the commentary by Joseph O'Malley in Marx, *Critique of Hegel's "Philosophy of Right,"* ed. and trans. O'Malley and A. Jolin (Cambridge, 1970).

[33] Marx, "Kritik des Hegel'schen Staatrechts," in *Marx-Engels Gesamtausgabe*, 1, pt. 1: 518 (*Collected*

Marx had not, at this point, fully developed his conception of class conflict, but it is evident that he had the makings of his theory. "Private property is the general category of the general political bond," he argued; but at the same time it was separated from public wealth, which is to say the common good, and this contradiction seemed to discredit the very foundations of jurisprudence and traditional political philosophy. Marx explained the rejection of his academic heritage in this way:

> The criticism of the German philosophy of state and law, which attained its most consistent, richest, and final formation with Hegel, is both a critical analysis of the modern state and of the reality connected with it, and the resolute negation of the whole German political and legal consciousness as practised hitherto, the most universal expression of which raised to the level of a science is the speculative philosophy of law itself.

This marked a watershed in Marx's thought, for as he had come to realize, "The criticism of the speculative philosophy of law turns not toward itself, but toward problems which can be solved only by one means—practice."[34] The first problem that came to mind was the relationship between industry and the political world. Some such aspect of "modern politico-reality" Marx proposed to substitute for the philosophy of law as his proper field of investigation.

So it was that Marx came to believe that the grounds for discussion of true philosophy had to be not formal rules of law but realities of possession and property, that is, what the English and French called political economy and what the Germans, more primitively and unscientifically, called national economy. Society had to be comprehended in terms not of its legal superstructure, in other words, but of its material base. This shift in Marx's thought coincided with a physical transition from Germany, a regime which was "decaying and destroying itself," to France, the promised land of rationality and revolution. There "Charles" Marx found a new vehicle for his increasingly intemperate views, the *Deutsch-Französische Jahrbücher,* and from its editorial board he looked forward to "the commencement and continuance of the new era we are now entering."[35] Marx's final rejection of the metaphysics of law and his conversion to the antithetical science of economics were accomplished in this Parisian period and are reflected especially in his critique of James Mill and the *Economic and Philosophic Manuscripts* of 1844, which has been the basis for so much discussion of so-called socialist humanism in Marx, a revisionist view that does not seem to have added much to the strictly historical appreciation of Marx's thought.

In any case, even in his revolutionary phase Marx had not yet finished with the old jurisprudence. "The first criticism of any science," he later acknowl-

Works, 3: 98).

[34] Marx, "Zur Kritik der Hegel'schen Rechtsphilosophie," in *Marx-Engels Gesamtausgabe*, 1, pt. 1: 613 (*Collected Works*, 3: 181).

[35] Marx, Draft Program of the *Deutsch-Französische Jahrbücher*, published for the first time in *Collected Works*, 3: 181.

edged, "is necessarily influenced by the science it is fighting against . . . ."[36] This position can be seen not only in his assumptions about the social functions of property but also in his celebrated view of "alienation," a concept which again has a legal as well as a Hegelian background, relating specifically to the transfer, surrender, or loss of patrimony or (in a political context) domain. "Alienation of domain" (or of sovereignty) was one of the most bitterly resented abuses of the old regime, representing as it did the most fundamental betrayal of the commonwealth. And, as in public law, so in the private sphere the effects of what civilians called *alienatio* were destructive. As Marx expressed it, "the loss or surrender of private property [*Entäusserung oder Entfremdung des Privateigentums*] is alienation of man, as it is of private property itself."[37] In the Roman experience, which continued to be Marx's principal model, the consequence of such alienation was the loss of identity, of citizenship, and, indeed, of the entire basis for social "belonging." From the point of view of political economy, it signified the separation of labor from landed wealth (the first form of capital), the need for a measure of exchange value—that is, money. Alienated from the natural wealth of the tribal community, men were "bound to life" by this "universal agent of separation," as Marx called money.[38] But the fundamental form of "alienation" was not that Hegelian state of inner isolation that has monopolized the attention of students of Marx. Rather, parallelling Marx's own shift from idealistic to materialistic premises, it was estrangement from *property*—a problem that was widely discussed by civil lawyers, especially with regard to the *ager publicus*, that original common land of the Romans that so fascinated Marx and that continued to concern him in *Das Kapital*.

For Marx the juridical fictions underlying such alienation were continuously reinforced by the fallacies of idealism, and he carried on the attack against this two-faced evil over the next two years, expecially in the *Holy Family* and the *German Ideology*. The "critical criticism" of the neo-Hegelian brothers Edgar and Bruno Bauer preserved the errors of Hugo by confusing fact and law, objective conditions and subjective consciousness. Edgar Bauer, for example, seemed to make mystical nonsense of Pierre-Joseph Proudhon's political-economic question, "What is property?"[39] On the other hand, Marx rejected the "illusions of the lawyers," who confused the Roman view of simple use and consumption (*jus utendi et abutendi*) with property, which was defined in terms of abstract and legalistic titles irrespective of any requirement of physical possession and which was, therefore, a major source of class

[36] Marx, *Die Heilige Familie*, in *Frühe Schriften*, ed. H. J. Lieber and P. Furth (Stuttgart, 1971), 1: 697 (*Collected Works*, 4: 31).

[37] Marx, Comment on James Mill, *Elements of Political Economy*, in *Marx-Engels Gesamtausgabe*, 1, pt. 3: 531 (*Collected Works*, 3: 218). The varieties of *alienatio* are taken up in all textbooks of Roman law; see in particular Adolph Berger, *Encyclopedic Dictionary of Roman Law* (Philadelphia, 1953). Also see Peter Riesenberg, *Inalienability of Sovereignty in Medieval Political Thought* (New York, 1956). For some recent studies, see Bertell Ollman, *Alienation: Marx's Conception of Man in Capitalist Society* (Cambridge, 1971); and Joachim Israel, *Alienation: From Marx to Modern Sociology* (Boston, 1971). Neither of these, however, deals with the legal dimension.

[38] Marx, Ökonomisch-Philosophische Manuskripte, in *Frühe Schriften*, 1: 633 (*Collected Works*, 3: 324).

[39] Marx, *Die Heilige Familie*, in *Frühe Schriften*, 1: 697 (*Collected Works*, 4: 31).

division. The "juridical illusion" was to reduce law to—or, rather, to inflate it into—an expression of abstract will, just as idealist philosophers expressed social relationships as "ideas." The Roman view of property was closer to reality: the relationship was not a legal fiction but the simple right of an individual to a piece of property, landed or movable, a right enjoyed by every Roman citizen (*dominium ex jure Quiritum*), stemming from *possessio*.[40] To neglect this was to fall into a confusion akin to that of Hegel's phenomenology, which Marx summarized cryptically in his notebook in November 1844: "Self-consciousness instead of man. Subject—object." And alienation was similarly subjectivized: "Abolition of estrangement is identified with abolition of objectivity."[41] For Marx, on the contrary, what needed abolishing was not the conscious state of isolation but the material condition of propertylessness, which left men open to exploitation.

In this way Marx continued to grapple with his intellectual heritage and to work on the problem that he stated in a note to the *German Ideology* as "Why ideologists"—including jurists, religionists, politicians, and moralists—"turn everything upside down." All of them stood in the way of the positive, materialistic, historical, and, ultimately, revolutionary view of society that Marx was seeking. Nor did political economists escape his ire. As he had rejected the "metaphysics of law," so he also turned against the "metaphysics of political economy," a phrase that he applied in particular to the views of Proudhon.[42] What first distinguished man from animals, according to Marx, was not consciousness or speech or religion as ideologists imagined, but rather production. The subsequent emergence of property and legal distinctions attached thereto marked the true beginning of history. "Civil law developed simultaneously with private proverty from the disintegration of the natural community." This process also continued in the modern European context. "With the exception of England it proceeded everywhere on the basis of the Roman Codex," he continued. "Even in England Roman legal principles had to be adopted to further the development of civil law, particularly in regard to movable property."[43] The most recent stage of this process was the transformation of movable property into capital, which has fallen into the hands of the legally dominant class with title to, though not necessarily possession of, this wealth.

At the end of this train of thought lay a number of the most fundamental elements of mature Marxism, not only concepts of class struggle and communism but also the aim of "changing the world" rather than merely interpreting it, as did the jurists, philosophers, and "bourgeois" economists.[44] But even as communism was beginning to haunt the conscience of bourgeois Europe, Marx himself continued to be haunted by the old learning, especially that embodied in civil law. Perhaps most essential was the notion of an

[40] Marx, *Die Deutsche Ideologie*, in *Frühe Schriften*, 2: 92–97 (*Collected Works*, 5: 89–93).
[41] Marx, Manuscript Note, in *Collected Works*, 4: 665.
[42] Marx, *Das Elend der Philosophie*, chap. 2, in *Frühe Schriften*, 2: 738 (*Collected Works*, 6: 161).
[43] Marx, *Die Deutsche Ideologie*, in *Frühe Schriften*, 2: 93 (*Collected Works*, 5: 91).
[44] Marx, *Thesen über Feuerbach*, in *Frühe Schriften*, 2: 4 (*Collected Works*, 5:5).

original communal property (the *ager publicus*) that ancient Romans cultivated, he argued, not as dispossessed laborers, but as owners (*nicht als Arbeiter, sondern als Eigentümer*) for purposes of subsistence (*Erhaltung des Einseln*), not the creation of exchange-value (*Wertschöpfung*).[45] In this revealing passage of the *Grundrisse*, Marx lapsed into English to make his point: "Das Individuum ist placed in such conditions of gaining his life as to make not the acquiring of wealth his object, but self-sustainance [*sic*] and its own reproduction as a member of the community . . . ." To underscore the practical character of Roman arrangements, Marx quoted in this connection the great historian Barthold Georg Niebuhr, who remarked of Numa Pompilius that, after being assured of divine approval of his election, he turned his attention not to religious but to human business (*nicht Tempeldienst, sondern menschlich*). "He distributed the land conquered in war by Romulus and left to be occupied . . . . All great law-givers, and above all Moses, founded the success of the arrangements for virtue, justice, and good morals upon landed property, or at least on secure hereditary possession of land, for the greatest possible number of citizens." Afterwards, this tribal and communal condition was destroyed by migration, conquest, and the differentiation into higher and lower tribes (*gentes*), and so began the period of recorded history—"the history of class warfare," according to the opening words of the *Communist Manifesto*.

Long before the experience of revolution, then, Marx realized that his pursuit of true philosophy had to take a different path from those of his juristic and philosophic mentors. By 1845 he was already contemplating a "critique of politics and economics" to rival the systems of the legal tradition, though he did not begin to lay out "the whole shit," as he called it, until the late 1850s.[46] Like the treatise on jurisprudence planned in adolescence, this work began with the sphere of private law. This time, however, the target was not property but capital, and the basic issue was not the theoretical "condition of persons," as in civilian convention but rather with exchange-value and money, which had made such abstract questions irrelevant in Marx's mind, and then with landed property and wage labor. Thereafter, again as in the youthful work, Marx intended to move into the public sphere, beginning with the state seen, of course, from a broader perspective (*naturae politico-economicae*, as he characterized his approach to Engels), followed by discussions of international trade and the world market. This enterprise, of course, constitutes another story entirely and must be understood in a very different context.

IN GENERAL, THE PURPOSE OF THESE REMARKS has not been to resurrect another "Young Marx," nor even to revise any particular interpretation of the old one;

[45] Marx, *Grundrisse der Kritik der Politischen Ökonomie* (Berlin, 1953), 378–80, "Formen, die der kapitalistischen Produktion vorhergehen," translated by J. Cohen as *Pre-Capitalist Economic Formations* (New York, 1965), 72–74.

[46] Marx to Engels, Apr. 2, 1858, in *Karl Marx/Friedrich Engels Briefwechsel* (Berlin, 1849), 2: 383–87. Also see Marx to Engels, Jan. 7, 1851, in *ibid.*, 1: 152.

it has merely been to open up a neglected perspective on the genesis and early development of Marxist social thought. Marxism has, of course, generated a massive scholasticism—glosses, commentaries, and interpretations by hostile as well as friendly students—but little of this has even attempted to offer a strictly historical construction. Even when various ideological totems and taboos have been avoided, the tendency has been to place Marx exclusively in the traditions of classical economics and philosophy, especially of German idealism. Although this approach is not improper in itself, it is insufficient as a basis of appreciating the richness of Marx's intellectual heritage. His conception of the world emerged from a surpassingly deep and wide-ranging assault upon Western humanistic, historical, and legal scholarship, going far beyond the names that have become familiar from general post-Marxian surveys of philosophy and economic, social, and political thought.[47] Only by entering into the less familiar terrain of old regime scholarship can one hope to appreciate fully the extent of Marx's intellectual base and of the conceptual struggles underlying his mature philosophy.

Within Marx's intellectual heritage, jurisprudence may not occupy a central position, but it does have a kind of temporal priority. The young Marx was steeped in legal erudition and his thoughts about social problems shaped by legal issues, especially those attendant upon the historical school and its opponents, though students of Marx have not tried to follow up his early enthusiasms and distastes.[48] What is more, jurisprudence provided not only an early focus for Marx's studies but a system of thought that continued to possess at least a negative importance. If it did not furnish him with the "true philosophy" he had been taught to expect, it did give him a satisfying target—a comprehensive secular religion and a paradigm of idealist social thought, in a pejorative sense of "ideology"—for his atheistic as well as his materialistic and socialistic urges. If it did not contain the divine fire, the means of understanding and of changing human society, it did offer him a socially meaningful way of venting his Promethean hatred of "all the gods" and of finding a way out of the trap of idealism. The juridical problems of possession and property led directly to the key, which was the iconoclastic new discipline of economics. In this Marx was to find his Promethean fire, the *arche* of his own true philosophy, perhaps of his religion, and a way of exorcizing all the gods that had oppressed mankind—an enterprise altogether worthy of classical jurisprudence as conceived of by the very young Marx.

[47] Survivals of old concerns are also illustrated in Marx's later studies of anthropology, a subject originally part of academic jurisprudence as well as philosophy; see notes 9 and 30, above, and *The Ethnological Notebooks of Karl Marx*, ed. Lawrence Krader (Assen, 1974).

[48] The importance of Marx's legal studies and his associations with Gans and Savigny have been pointed out by his biographers, especially Isaiah Berlin and August Cornu; but it has been so uniformly neglected by interpreters of the young Marx and of the documentable genesis of his thought up to 1842 who have favored the specifically Hegelian connection that I have not thought it relevant to refer to the works of Georg Lukács, Herbert Marcuse, David McClellan, and others, much less to analyses of the sources of Marxian economic and formally philosophic thought. For a more general discussion, see J. E. Seigel, "Marx's Early Development: Vocation, Rebellion, and Realism," *Journal of Interdisciplinary History*, 3 (1972–73): 475–508, which will appear in revised form in his forthcoming book.

XV

Hermes, Clio, Themis: Historical Interpretation and Legal Hermeneutics

I

The theory of interpretation has enjoyed a considerable revival of interest in recent years, especially in relation to historical methods.[1] Intellectual fashion aside, the main attraction of hermeneutics seems to be its promise of alternatives to intimidating behaviorist, quantitative, or abstract-structuralist approaches to the human sciences. In the pandemonium of "scientific" methods for the study of society and culture the one common feature has been the attempt in one way or another to do away with the thinking subject. In the name of scientific objectivity, psychoanalysts and Marxists have likewise looked for impersonal forces below, or beyond, the level of consciousness; functionalists and structuralists have sought patterns, or codes, which likewise transcend, or subsume, human behavior; "deconstructionist" literary critics have subordinated authorial intention and consciousness to the medium of discourse, whether language or "writing"; and "new" economic and social historians have cast their explanations in statistical and serial terms which make personality, quality, and perhaps values irrelevant. Each of these lines of inquiry undeniably has value and its own insights, but each is also threatened by some sort of reductionism, and none can tell the whole truth. In particular each tends to neglect, or to misconstrue, the role of the observer, which is to say the interpreter, usually by affecting to replace judgment by a technique. Now despite Kierkegaard's urging, subjectivity may not be truth, but neither is technique. What hermeneutics proposes is to accommodate

[1] Besides translations of the works of Gadamer, Habermas, and Ricoeur, recent studies include Karl-Otto Apel, *Transformation der Philosophie* (Frankfurt, 1973); Zygmunt Bauman, *Hermeneutics and Social Science* (New York, 1978); Joseph Bleicher, *Contemporary Hermeneutics* (London, 1980), and *The Hermeneutical Imagination* (London, 1982); David Hoy, *The Critical Circle* (Berkeley, 1978); Erwin Hufnagel, *Einführung in die Hermeneutik* (Stuttgart, 1976); T. K. Seung, *Structuralism and Hermeneutics* (New York, 1982), and *Semiotics and Thematics in Hermeneutics* (New York, 1982); and John B. Thompson, *Critical Hermeneutics* (Cambridge, 1981). For the most part I omit reference to the even larger bibliography from literary criticism.

both the inquiring subject and his intransigent object in its interpretive scope, to find a place in the routine of question-and-answer for the questioner-and-answerer, no matter what his perspective or scientific equipment.

"Interpretation" is pre- if not nonscientific, as old as literature, older than philosophy; and the theory of interpretation goes almost as far back. Indeed its origins are mythical, *hermeneia* being associated with the messenger-god Hermes and with the priests of the Delphic oracle, hence with the process of divination. From the beginning the aim of interpretation was to give human expression to superhuman, or general, truth; and philosophically, from Aristotle's *Peri Hermēnias*, it was regarded as the primary function of the intellect, that is, the formulation of statements preliminary to logical reasoning. But almost from the beginning, too, there was interest in finding the general "meaning" of human creations, especially written creations: there was, in other words, a philological as well as a philosophical hermeneutics, starting especially with criticism of the Homeric poems. Here was the first major encounter between Hermes and Clio; and their offspring, the science of philology, played an important part in the development of historical method, although the philosophical and theological varieties of hermeneutics have in large measure come to overshadow their literary cousin.

The classic historical survey remains Wilhelm Dilthey's *Entstehung der Hermeneutik*, which treats its subject as a cornerstone of the human sciences as well as a major dimension of Western history and indeed as an aspect of that "critique of historical reason" which was Dilthey's life task.[2] In Judaeo-Christian tradition, book-bound as it has been, hermeneutics has played a crucial and indeed shaping role. Talmudists and Christian exegetes alike expounded and explicated God's word as expressed in scriptures, and then extended their interpretations into larger earthly and heavenly domains. In the most elementary sense "interpretation" meant literary translation; and as biblical practitioners of this art from Jerome to Erasmus learned, it was a most demanding and even dangerous occupation: what man could presume to give human expression to the diving Logos? Fortunately, there was a hermeneutical dispensation. The old rule that "the letter killeth while the spirit giveth life" licensed not only translators but also more creative patristic and scholastic readers of the "sacred page."[3] The climax of medieval hermeneutics came with

[2] *Gesammelte Schriften* 5 (Munich, 1927): 334 ff.; and cf. Joachim Wach, *Das Verstehen, Grundzüge einer Geschichte der hermeneutischen Theorie im 19. Jahrhundert* (Tübingen, 1926).

[3] See Beryl Smalley, *The Study of the Bible in the Middle Ages* (Oxford, 1952), pp. 94 ff., and cf. Herman Hailperin, *Rashi and the Christian Scholars* (Pittsburgh, 1963), pp. 32 ff.

the famous three- or four-fold theory established by Origen and elaborated by the Victorine school of biblical criticism. History, allegory, tropology, and morality were the four conventional rubrics of the literal and various figurative modes of interpretration which allowed pious men to uncover the different levels of scripture, defined by Hugh of St. Victor as "the letter, the sense and the deeper meaning."[4] Despite protests of fidelity to texts—Latin *sensus historicus, fides historiae*; Greek *kyrios*; Hebrew *peshaṭ*—biblical hermeneutics developed into a complex "sacred science," a discipline which, by the Middle Ages, admitted the critical subject as well as the divine object into its domain.

Renaissance humanism at once broadened and simplified the theory of interpretation: broadened it by introducing notions of style, cultural context, anachronism, and a varity of critical tools; simplified it by insisting on the "historical sense" and discarding the conventions and apparatus of figurative interpretation. "Grammarians" like Lorenzo Valla and Erasmus had as little use for the etymological speculations of Isidore of Seville and allegorizing fantasies of the Victorines as they did for the metaphysical fictions of the scholastics; and they rejected all on the same grounds, that is, the metahistorical and metalinguistic character of such interpretation. The classic humanist treatment was Leonardo Bruni's *De interpretatione recta*, which inquired into the conceptual resources of Latin and the propriety of translating authors like Aristotle.[5] For Bruni the interpreter's basic skill was not philosophical depth, however, it was literary expertise and mastery of ancient authorities; and this scholarly requirement was even more essential for more complex interpretation, such as Valla's pioneering "higher criticism" of the New Testament and the conjectural emendations and "restitutions" made by classicists like Angelo Poliziano and Ermolao Barbaro.

It was in the sixteenth century, however, that hermeneutics emerged in a recognizably modern form. The philological "science" established by Bruni and Valla and developed by Poliziano, Budé, and Erasmus was perfected by the great generation of "critics," including Casaubon, Lipsius, and above all, the young Scaliger.[6] More famously, perhaps, this age of religious reform saw the emergence of the Protestant school of biblical criticism, which has conventionally been regarded as the point of departure of modern hermeneutics as formulated by Schleiermacher, extended to the world of human culture by Dilthey, and developed by such followers

[4] *Didascalion*, trans. J. Taylor (New York, 1961), p. 147.

[5] "De interpretatione recta," *Humanistisch-Philosophische Schriften*, ed. H. Baron (Leipzig, 1928), pp. 81–96.

[6] See Jean Jehasse, *La renaissance de la critique* (Saint-Etienne, 1976).

as Heidegger and Gadamer. In particular Flacius Illyricus, reacting to the definitions of Christian "tradition" set by the Council of Trent, had devised a "key" to scriptural criticism based on a combination of Renaissance philology and the Lutheran approach to biblical interpretation (which, though also devoted to the "historical sense," was by no means the simplistic fundamentalism some have misjudged it to be).[7] In the eighteenth century another stage was reached when G. F. Meier expanded theological hermeneutics into what (in 1757) he called "The Idea of a General Theory of Interpretation," while in the nineteenth century biblical scholars like Strauss extended their interpretations into the broader fields of mythology and cultural history.[8] From Dilthey's time this complex of intellectual traditions, chronicled with reverent detail in Joachim Wach's *Das Verstehen*, has broadened into a wide range of human sciences; and despite positivist resistance, its offshoots still thrive as special forms of "critical" philosophy. Through the partnership between Clio and Hermes the "thinking subject," *homo interpres* as he might be called, still lives; and so does hermeneutics.[9]

II

Yet if hermeneutics lives, indeed is enjoying a revival, it is not beyond reproach even by its admirers. Two basic criticisms may be suggested (not including the misguided charge of subjectivism), and they correspond neatly to the polarity evident in the theory of interpretation from its Greek beginnings. On the one hand there is the tendency of philological hermeneutics toward hypostasis and idolatry of the written text: Alexandrine *grammatikoi* do not look beyond Homer even when Homer nods; and Michel Foucault, Jacques Derrida, and other textualists have likewise, if more self-consciously, inclined to a fetishism of the printed page, a fixation on the "text-model." There are no doubt grounds on which such attitudes can be justified, and it is difficult to resist Paul Ricoeur's arguments for the "semantic autonomy of the text," if not for its exclusive identification with the "hermeneutical field."[10] The question here, however, is not the conceptual plausibility of textualism even in its extreme

[7] See Wilhelm Preger, *Matthias Flacius Illyricus und seine Zeit* (1859–61), 2: 478 ff.

[8] *Die Idee einer allgemeinen Auslegungslehre*, based on lectures at the University of Halle; and for the historical background of the "higher" criticism, David Friedrich Strauss, *The Life of Jesus Critically Examined*, 2nd ed., trans. George Eliot (London, 1892).

[9] Andres Ortiz-Oses, *Antropologia hermeneutica* (Madrid, 1973), pp. 79, "hombre-interpres," and 84, "animal hermeneuticum."

[10] *Interpretation Theory* (Ft. Worth, Texas, 1976), p. 29.

Derridean forms, but rather its methodological value for historical investigation and interpretation.

A similar reservation must be made about the philosophical school, which from Aristotle to Gadamer inclined toward what E. D. Hirsch deprecates as "metaphysical hermeneutics" or what Ricoeur characterizes more favorably as a shift "from epistemology to ontology," whether the surrogate text is secular or religious, phenomenal or noumenal.[11] In the "transformation of philosophy" pursued by German philosophers the key is also the fundamental "linguisticality" of the human condition; and again we seem to be confronted by an up-to-date version of the Baconian idols of the den, or perhaps the Vichian conceit of scholars. If for French devotees of *l'écriture* the book is seen as a world, for German defenders of *Sprachlichkeit* the world appears as a book; and neither metaphor, generative of so much scholastic debate, seems adequate for historical understanding. The fallacy of the first is the uncritical elevation of the subject above the object of interpretation, that of the second an existential, perhaps irreversible, leap into phenomenology. Perhaps from an aversion to old-fashioned "historicist" attitudes, both seem to have lost Dilthey's vision of a unifying and fructifying science of humanity, one by a literary ploy amounting to a sort of higher fundamentalism, the other by philosophical circumvention which in effect smuggles hermeneutics into metaphysical speculation. For the historian neither will do.

With the language model itself there are certain difficulties and diverting assumptions. "History is, as it were, the great dark book," Gadamer has written, "the collected work of the human spirit, written in the language of the past, the text of which we have to understand."[12] But let us not forget the "as it were," for the historical process is not merely a silent clamor of "intersubjective" thought. Much of its substance—actions, interactions, institutions, social patterns—may well escape the net of interpretive systems which bind themselves to conscious thought and expression, and so fall into the idealist fallacy expressed most famously in the Croce-Collingwood proposition that "all history is the history of thought" and preserved in the "existential subjectivity" of Gadamer. This would seem enough in itself to discredit the thinking subject, and indeed it has been the basis of one of the major complaints registered by positivist and behaviorist critics. It is a view which has implications

[11] Hirsch, *The Aims of Interpretation* (Chicago, 1976), p. 85, and Paul Ricoeur, *Hermeneutics and the Human Sciences*, trans. J. Thompson (Cambridge, 1981), p. 53.

[12] *Truth and Method*, trans. G. Barden and J. Cumming (New York, 1975), p. 156. Even more extreme is George Steiner, *Extraterritoriality* (New York, 1977), p. 62: "History, in the human sense, is a language-net cast backwards."

antisocial as well as antiscientific, and it needs a corrective from beyond the worlds of verbal behavior.

The point is that the "hermeneutical field" must accommodate not only the thinking subject and his medium but also the objects of his attention, which indeed serve to establish and to define his subjectivity. The world of "things," however remote and impenetrable in an ontological sense, needs to be accommodated as sphere of potential experience beyond the horizons of perception—an extension of the hermeneutical field to be explored and analyzed, perhaps civilized and socialized. A common failing of both philological and philosophical hermeneutics has been the general neglect of social and historical context. Gadamer's conviction that "Being that can be understood is language"[13] does not seem adequate to the problem of gaining access to the dimension of inarticulate human action, individual or collective, rational or irrational. Such indeed is the implication of the critique of Gadamer offered by Habermas, who has tried to provide remedies by attending (in Marxist or at least Marxoid fashion) to problems of ideology, to action theory and to "social systems."[14] Gadamer rejects this as in effect a reversion to dualism, while at the same time acknowledging the force of Habermas's concerns. How then can we overcome the subject-object paradox (which may itself be inherent in *Sprachlichkeit*) and at the same time accommodate the process of history without succumbing to reductionism, economic or political, or to the fallacies of "value-free" social science? Gadamer's answer is most provocative, though not systematically followed up. "Legal hermeneutics," he has declared, "is able to point out what the real procedure of the human sciences is."[15] This is the suggestion which, from a historical

[13] *Philosophical Hermeneutics*, trans. D. Linge (Berkeley, 1976), p. 31. It should be understood that the present critique is limited to questions of historical investigation and interpretation and does not confront the problem of Heideggerian "prejudice," which would in effect deny the possibility of historical understanding beyond our present *Kulturkreis*. This sort of epistemological relativism (which itself can be seen "historically" as well as logically and ontologically) is useful in suggesting the philosophical limits of historical knowledge and may even in effect reduce it, strictly speaking, to a form of imagination; but it can hardly be allowed to interfere with historical or anthropological inquiry; and indeed the aim of Gadamer, Ricoeur, et al. is precisely to salvage the philosophical standing of the human sciences.

[14] See Thomas McCarthy, *The Critical Theory of Jürgen Habermas* (Cambridge, Mass., 1981), p. 187, and Bleicher, *Contemporary Hermeneutics*, p. 153; also Martin Jay, "Should Intellectual History Take a Linguistic Turn? Reflections on the Habermas-Gadamer Debate," *Modern Intellectual History*, ed. D. LaCapra and S. Kaplan (Ithaca, New York, 1982), pp. 86–110.

[15] *Truth and Method*, p. 292.

rather than philosophical or literary angle, I propose to pursue here, beginning with a brief sketch of the historical background.

III

Unlike the long-standing relationship which Hermes has maintained with Clio, that with Themis, goddess of justice and social order, has hardly been noticed, except within professional legal scholarship—and that intellectual tradition has been largely cut off from the human sciences and even philosophy in the past century or more. This is a curious and lamentable circumstance, for legal hermeneutics has a history almost as long and colorful as those of the theological, philosophical, and literary varieties. What is more, it has enjoyed some of the same harvest times, most notably in medieval commentaries on civil law (corresponding to biblical exegesis), in Renaissance treatises on the *ars critica* in law, and in romantic theories of interpretation parallel (as well as contemporary) with those of Schleiermacher and Friedrich Ast. It has not, however, enjoyed a comparable revival, or historical appreciation, in the present century.[16] Preoccupied with Schleiermacher, his *Vorläufer* and his epigones, Dilthey did not even deign to mention the almost congruent legal tradition, nor is it touched on in the authoritative survey of Wach or later sketches known to me. Even Emilio Betti, though the law furnished his own intellectual provenance and though he touches on the subject (*interpretazione giuridica*; *juristische Auslegung*) says virtually nothing about the historical background.[17]

The starting point for such an inquiry must be Roman jurisprudence, although the debts to Greek philosophy and rhetoric were extensive and should not be forgotten. The pretension of Roman law to the status of true "science" and beyond that the highest form of human wisdom (*sapientia* as well as *scientia*) was based on two arguments: one that law was rational and universal, explicable in terms of "causes" and in accord with nature; the other that it took into account human values and social

[16] There is extensive literature on legal hermeneutics beginning especially with Savigny (see below, n. 25), but little carries over into historical or social thought. See, however, Manfred Thiel, *Interpretation: Philosophie, Jurisprudenz, Theologie* (Regensburg, 1980), pp. 320–493; Maximilian Herburger, *Dogmatik: Zur Geschichte von Begriff und Methode in Medizin und Jurisprudenz* (Frankfurt, 1981); M. Fuhrman, H. R. Jauss, and W. Panenberg, eds., *Text und Application: Theologie, Jurisprudenz und Literaturwissenschaft im hermeneutischen Gespräch* (Munich, 1981); Franz Wieacker in *Philologie und Hermeneutik im 19. Jahrhundert*, ed. H. Flashar, K. Gründer, and A. Horstmann (Göttingen, 1979), pp. 312–20; and P. Piovani, "Ex Legislatione philosophia," *Studi in onore di Emilio Betti* (Milan, 1962), 1: 392–428.

[17] See below, n. 30.

goals and worked, actively and "practically," to achieve them. It represented, in other words, both *theoria* and *praxis*. The great tradition of expertise in "legal science" began, as Max Weber has argued, with the empirical and theoretical masters called *honoratiores*, whose business was both to judge social reality (the facts of a case or, as legal reformers, the condition of a society) and to apply the reason of the law according to established method, eventually to contribute also to the analysis, conceptualization, and systemization of the law.[18] These professional scholars were at once practitioners (*prudentes*), scientists, and "priests of the law," but they were above all interpreters (*juris interpretes*), whose base was not only the accumulated (and accumulating) experience of civil law and the "law of nations" (*jus gentium*) but also the ill-defined concept of natural law. The legal hermeneutics developed by these forefathers of social science from at least the second century B.C. was the life principle of Roman, Romanist, and Romanoid jurisprudence for two millenia and more.

The great landmark in the history of Roman legal science is the work of legal codification carried out in the sixth century by the Emperor Justinian and his Byzantine editors, who tried to sum up and to systematize more than ten centuries of legal experience and interpretation. One of the premises of this effort was the hope of the Emperor that his law should "prevail forever, " and one corollary was the ban he placed on all "interpretation" whatsoever.[19] But to avoid what Justinian himself called "the vain discord of posterity" was an illusion, not only because of the instability of the human condition but also because of the demise of imperial authority in general. Beginning with the twelfth century revival of civil law, legal hermeneutics found new life and, through the ambitions and controversies of medieval *juris interpretes*, an astonishingly active career. For scholastic jurisprudence, "interpretation" was essential not only to discover the meaning or "spirit of the law" (*mens legum*, *ratio legis*) but also to give applicability to modern society and even to reform and to "correct" laws; and it did not hesitate to treat questions of political

[18] *On Law and Society*, trans. E. Shils and M. Rheinstein (Cambridge, Mass., 1954), pp. 198 ff. Classic discussion by Fritz Schulz, *History of Roman Legal Science* (Oxford, 1953), and for the medieval phase Ennio Cortese, *La norma giuridica* (Milan, 1962–64); more generally Helmut Coing, *Die juristische Auslegungsmethoden und die Lehren der allgemeinen Hermeneutik* (Cologne, 1959). There is a huge literature relevant to hermeneutics and to the cultural sciences more generally.

[19] Constitution *Deo Auctore* prefacing the Digest, on which F. Pringelsheim, "Justinian's Prohibition of Commentaries to the Digest," in his *Gesammelte Abhandlungen* (Heidelberg, 1961), 2: 86–106.

"power." In the course of such discussions there emerged practical awareness both to problems of subjectivity and to the necessity of making judgments in terms of times, places, circumstances, and persons: the science of law had also, in short, psychological, epistemological, and sociological dimensions.[20]

The first great age of modern legal (as of theological) hermeneutics was the sixteenth century. In connection with the widespread search for a proper scientific "method" in various disciplines, legal scholars also began to produce treatises on legal methodology and then specifically on the theory of interpretation (*De interpretatione legis* and *De extensionibus* being the conventional ways of defining the subject).[21] These discussions were informed not only by the issues of scholastic jurisprudence but also by the historical and literary insights of humanist scholars—"grammarians" who approached the legal canon of Justinian, as they approached holy scriptures, as human documents. As Erasmus interpreted the Bible in the light of philology, so his younger friend Andrea Alciato introduced similar critical methods into the study of civil law. This was the age, too, of the great methodological conflict between "legal humanism" and the old-fashioned scholastic jurisprudence, reflected most famously in Alberico Gentili's dialogue of 1582 but more profoundly in contemporary treatises devoted to the problem of legal systematics and its relation to history and philology.[22] This polemical and "scientific"

[20] More detailed treatment in my articles, "Vera Philosophia: the Philosophical Significance of Renaissance Jurisprudence," *Journal of the History of Philosophy* 14 (1976): 267–79; "Civil Science in the Renaissance: Jurisprudence Italian Style," *The Historical Journal* 22 (1979): 777–94; and "Civil Science in the Renaissance: Jurisprudence in the French Manner," *History of European Ideas* 2 (1981): 261–76. See also Pietro Costa, *Iurisdictio. Semantica del potere politico nella pubblicistica medievale 1100–1433* (Milan, 1969), and Pierre Michaud-Quantin, *Etudes sur le vocabulaire philosophique du Moyen Age* (Rome, 1970).

[21] Most essential are V. Piano Mortari, "Il problema dell'interpretatio iuris nei commentatori," *Annali di storia del diritto*, 2 (1958): 29–109, and *Ricerche sulla teoria dell'interpretazione del diritto nel secolo XVI* (Milan, 1956). The connections between the methods of law and history have often been noted, for example by Julian Franklin, *Jean Bodin and the Sixteenth-Century Revolution in the Methodology of Law and History* (New York, 1963).

[22] *De iuris interpretibus* (London, 1582). See also Aldo Mazzacane, *Scienza, logica e ideologia nella giurisprudenza tedesca del sec. XVI* (Milan, 1971); Hans Erich Troje, "Wissenschaftlichkeit und System in der Jurisprudenz des 16. Jahrhunderts," in *Philosophie und Rechtswissenschaft*, ed. J. Blühdorn and J. Ritter (Frankfurt, 1969), pp. 63–97, and "Alciats Methode der Kommentierung des 'Corpus iuris civilis,'" in *Der Kommentar in der Renaissance*, ed. A. Buck and O. Herding (Godesberg, 1975), pp. 47–61; and Piano Mortari, *Diritto, logica, metodo nel secolo XVI* (Naples, 1978).

defense of professional methods constituted a dramatic prelude to a long series of hermeneutical controversies, including that between Savigny and Thibaut in the romantic age and, more recently, those carried on by Gadamer, Apel, Habermas, and Betti.

It is worth noting, too, that the collateral descendant of Roman jurisprudence (that is, canon law) likewise, congruently and dependently, developed a theory of interpretation which was even more "extensive" and socially conscious than that of the civilians.[23] For in their efforts to give social meaning to laws canonists attended not only to doctrinal tradition and professional convention (the *communis opinio* which might also reflect tacit consent) but also to the variables and unpredictables of the human condition—time, place, social condition, and circumstances—basic to what from the twelfth century has been called "positive law." Canonists have had their own peculiarly flexible standards of judgment (*aequitas canonica*) because of their special need to join public and private spheres, and as a result they have had recourse to various interpretive strategies—exceptions, privileges, dispensations—in order to "relax" abstract laws and accommodate them to society as well as to transcendent demands. Most characteristic of all was the canonist technique of "harmonizing interpretation," which was consummated in Gratian's great collection originally entitled "Concord of Discordant Canons" and subject to the same sort of interpretive glosses and commentaries as Justinian's secular canon. It is significant that canonist interpretation came to maturity at just the time of that religious "Reformation" which, besides challenging canonist tradition, formed the context of that seminal phase of modern hermeneutics described by Dilthey.

Since the "golden age" of legal science in the sixteenth century there has been a fairly continuous tradition, or set of traditions, of interpretation theory down to modern times. For theology Dilthey has located some of the major figures between Flacius and Schleiermacher, but for jurisprudence the trail remains largely unexplored, as has the stage since the early nineteenth century. The rise of "historicism," which produced the "higher criticism" of the Bible, gave impetus likewise to controversies over that reincarnation of civil law which was the Code Napoléon of 1804. Like his prototype Justinian, the French emperor tried to forbid

[23] Important discussions by Charles Lefebvre, *Les pouvoirs du juge en droit canonique* (Paris, 1931); J. Salgado, "La méthode d'interprétation du droit en usage chez les canonistes," *Revue de l'Université d'Ottawa* 21 (1951): 201–13; and 22 (1952): 23–35; and Stephan Kuttner, *Harmony from Dissonance* (Latrobe, Pa., 1960); also Pierre Legendre, "L'historie du droit canonique et la science des cultures," *Proceedings of the Second International Congress of Medieval Canon Law* (Rome, 1965), pp. 281–94.

"interpretation" while succeeding in fact only in politicizing the issue and in intensifying the old conflict between legislative authority and judicial discretion.[24] Ensuing debates, especially after the publication of Thibaut's *Theorie der logischen Auslegung des römischen Rechts* (1799) and Savigny's later responses, were addressed not only to professional questions of adapting a purportedly rational system of law to a recalcitrant social reality but more generally to the relationship between human action and historical change.[25] "What is the influence of the past on the present? " as Savigny phrased the question, and "What is the relation of what is now to what will be ?" The effect of the historical school under Savigny's leadership was not only to reinforce ties between historical and legal scholarship but to introduce hermeneutics into the partnership.[26] This new trinity of Hermes, Clio, and Themis was involved, at some points collectively, in efforts of considerable importance for the human sciences.

Until fairly recently the achievements of this partnership have been limited mostly to historical scholarship and to the professional domain. On the one hand we have seen the proliferating offspring of the *historisches Rechtschule* in the form of investigations of legal, institutional, and certain kinds of social history; on the other hand the endless and divergent debates of jurists over the value of historicism, positivism, formalism, naturalism, and various sorts of socialism (not only Communist law but also *droit social* and *Rechtssoziologie*, which is also heavily endebted to Savigny). Less significant has been the theoretical contribution of specifically legal hermeneutics to history and the human sciences, though Weberian sociology certainly owes much to legal categories (Weber himself having been trained in the law) and Gadamer has touched upon "the exemplary significance of legal hermeneutics."[27] Only one philosopher has tried comprehensively to follow up this insight, however; and this is Gadamer's most searching critic, Emilio Betti, a man who has himself been a major figure in contemporary hermeneutics, though little appreciated

[24] *Code Civil*, art. 5, discussion in P. A. Fenet, *Recueil complet des travaux préparatoires du Code Civil* (Paris, 1827), 1: 20. In general see Julian Bonnecase, *La pensée juridique française* (Bordeaux, 1933), and Eugene Gaudemet, *L'interprétation du Code Civil en France depuis 1804* (Basel, 1935).

[25] See J. Stern, *Thibaut und Savigny* (Darmstadt, 1959); also Savigny's own great *System des heutigen römischen Rechts* (Berlin, 1840), 1 (book J., chap. 4); R. von Jhering, *Der Zweck im Recht* (Leipzig, 1893), and François Geny, *Méthode d'interprétation et sources en droit privé positif* (Paris, 1899); and cf. Edouard Lambert, *La fonction du droit civil comparé* (Paris, 1903).

[26] Further discussion in D. R. Kelley, *Historians and the Law in Post-Revolutionary France* (Princeton, forthcoming).

[27] *Truth and Method*, p. 289.

in the Anglophone world (and hardly at all by historians). Since Betti came to hermeneutics from jurisprudence, bringing with him essential juridical ideas and insights, he is ideally suited to appear here as the principal witness for the defense of the partnership of Hermes, Clio, and Themis.

IV

Betti was a center of professional controversy from at least 1927, when he published his Milanese inaugural lecture on Roman law and contemporary legal doctrines.[28] Ostensibly, his aim was to restore the normative value of Roman law (and in this sense, perhaps, to "return to Savigny"); but more importantly his hope was to restore the "autonomy" and neutrality of jurisprudence in a period when it was being threatened by the positivism of jurists like P. De Francisci and especially by the political priorities of Fascism. In this period of a "crisis" both of historicism and of jurisprudence[29] Betti wanted to reconcile historical tradition and legal system (*storia* and *dogma*) in much the same way that Savigny had tried to distill his historical reconstruction of the Roman tradition into an up-to-date "Pandectist" system intended to form the basis for a German Code. In another sense, however, Betti was pursuing, in the crucible of Fascist experience, the age-old goal of reconciling the ideals of justice with social reality, and especially with the intrusions of political power. It was a losing battle for the most part, but it did prepare him for a larger intellectual effort. Betti's transition to philosophy after the war represents a sort of expansion, or sublimation, of his original professional and "technical" goal, culminating in his monumental treatise, published in German as well as in Italian, on "the general theory of interpretation."[30]

It was via legal hermeneutics, then, that Betti passed from Crocean "idealist historicism" to a more concrete and differentiated (though non-

[28] "Diritto romano e dogmatica odierno," *Archivio giuridico* 99 (1928): 26–66; and see the articles of Antonio de Gennaro and Pietro Costa in *Quaderni Fiorentini per la storia del pensiero giuridico moderno* 7 (1978): "Emilio Betti e la scienza giuridica del Novecento," pp. 79–111, and pp. 311–93.

[29] See especially Karl Heussi, *Die Krisis des Historismus* (Tübingen, 1932).

[30] Betti's treatise is cited from both Italian and German versions, *Teoria della interpretazione* (Milan, 1955), and *Allgemeine Auslegungslehre als Methodik der Geisteswissenschaften* (Tübingen, 1967). A brief summary, *Die Hermeneutik als gemeine Methode der Geisteswissenschaften*, has been translated in Bleicher, *Contemporary Hermeneutics*, pp. 51–94. In general see the articles in *Quaderni Fiorentini* (above, n. 28), especially by Gadamer, Franco Bianco, Mario Bretone, Luigi Mengoni, Rudolf Malter, Giuliano Crifo, and Aldo Schiavoni; and those in the first volume of his Festschrift (cited above, n. 16), especially those of G. Funke, A. Heuss, G. Kandler and A. Plachy (vols. 2–5 treat technical legal subjects).

Marxist) theory of interpretation which encompassed a variety of disciplines besides jurisprudence, including art, language, science, law, and social and economic structures. The encyclopedic range of Betti's work opens up a richer historical perspective (as well as philosophical range) than the orthodox tradition. In significant contrast, too, with the existential and phenomenological concerns of Gadamer (and the "ideological" concerns of Habermas) Betti's purpose was to return to the tradition of the human sciences and to the enterprises of philosophers like Dilthey, Cassirer, Erich Rothaker, and Michael Landmann. What is more, Betti's approach was methodological and in this sense prescriptive, being directed (as Gadamer himself acknowledged) to the *quaestio juris* and not merely the *quaestio facti* of interpretation, which is to say to the possibilities rather than the limits of hermeneutics.[31] This may be the main reason, too, that Betti refused to be bound by either the text-model or even the privileged position of language.

Betti's point of departure was epistemology (*gnoseologia*; *Erkenntnistheorie*)—the relation of the thinking subject (*soggetto pensante*; *denkende Subjekt* or *subjectives Bewusstsein*) to a world inferrable through experience, yet identified not with the Kantian *Ding an sich* but rather with an "ideal objectivity" inseparable from subjective judgment. He joined subject and object in a single dialectical process mediated by hermeneutical constructs he called "representative" or "meaning-full forms," through which meaning is communicated and preserved, according to Betti's famous four canons of interpretation which define the whole continuum of understanding.[32] Here the legal connection is clear. Jurists were always supposed to respect the "meaning" of laws, the *mens* in the sense of will or intention of the original lawgiver; and to a large extent Betti preserved this professional "intentionalism." We may be the ones who pose questions of a text, but this text has a will of its own and literally "talks back" to the interpreter (or judge). As Betti put it, "We must assume that the text has something to say which we do not know from ourselves and which exists independently of our act of understanding."[33] This is what Betti meant by his first canon, which asserts "the hermeneutical autonomy of the subject."

Whence Betti's motto, *Sensus non est inferendus sed efferendus*: meanings are not to be imputed to objects of analysis but derived from

[31] See Bleicher, *Contemporary Hermeneutics*, p. 146.

[32] *Teoria*, p. 19, and *Auslegungslehre*, p. 16. Cf. *Teoria*, p. 119, "L'oggettivazione dello spirito in una forma representativa"; and *Auslegungslehre*, p. 78, "Objektivationen des Geistes der sinnhaltigen Formen."

[33] *Teoria*, p. 35; *Auslegungslehre*, p. 49; and see Richard E. Palmer, *Hermeneutics* (Evanston, Ill., 1969), p. 58.

them in their historical context, which in turn involves not only intuition but also an array of historical methods and techniques.[34] In this "objective" sort of interpretation (*Auslegung* as distinguished from *Verstehen*) Betti could hardly confine his view of the "methodology of the cultural sciences" to purely literary reconstruction; for the hermeneutical field was social and—again the legal analogy—concerned with things, actions, and institutions as well as verbal communication. Jurists had to establish the "facts" of a case, and necessarily such facts had to be given legal, which is to say social, meaning in order to be subjected to categorical or equitable judgment on the basis of legal principle. Similarly, the nonverbal materials of the historical process had to be given meaning through selection and interpretation. Like Habermas, in other words, though in a more integral fashion, Betti tried to confront problems of social context, historical tradition, and implicitly ideology. Beyond "philological," "critical," and "psychological" moments of exegesis in which an interpreter tried to recreate a cultural object or pattern there is also what Betti calls a "technical-morphological moment," which seeks particular structural meanings defined in relation to other fields, including economic and social action.[35] Gadamer would have none of this; but though he might seem to have the best of this debate in philosophical terms, Betti's broader, more encyclopedic (and more eclectic) vision seems better suited to the needs of historical understanding.

Historical interpretation is not simply a matter of apprehension and formal judgment, of course; it has also to take into account human volition and values, those of the interpreter as well as the object of study. Interpretation is itself a social process, in other words, depending on a species of "good faith" (*bona fides*) and carried out in a "world of values" (*cosmos di valori*; *Kosmos der Werte*) in which value judgments (*giudizia di valori*; *Werturteil*) were unavoidable.[36] Again the mediating position of the jurist suggests a model, since judgments had to involve not only original intention but also rationality and social values, such as equity or public utility. Historical judgment is not normative in this direct sense; and yet historical interpretation does have its own standards of larger meaning, which depend on the norms and direction of (professional) historical inquiry. Historians, too, must work within a "meaning system," not only to pass judgment but also to formulate meaningful questions. For the epistemological, sociological, and anthropological requirements of history and the human sciences jurisprudence offered benefits which

[34] *Teoria*, p. 100; *Auslegungslehre*, p. 65.
[35] *Teoria*, p. 291; *Auslegungslehre*, p. 204.
[36] *Teoria*, p. 11; *Auslegungslehre*, p. 10.

were wholly lacking in what Betti called the "mathematical" and "mechanical" (*automatica*) "surrogates" of naturalism.[37]

In general, it seems to me, the significance of Betti's work for the study of history is that it addresses itself precisely to the problem of how to accommodate the scholarly inquirer as well as the object of inquiry in discussions of "method" and "truth," and that it posits an object of interpretation(*oggettivazione della spirito in una forma representativa*; *Objektionen des Geistes der sinnhaltigen Formen*) in terms of a multiplicity of texts and testimonies. What he took from the law in particular was its "gnoseological" and "axiological" orientation—that is, its concerns with the problems of knowing and judging, of human will (conscious and, implicitly, unconscious), aspirations and values—in a context of structured social "reality." What he discarded was its formalism and professional estrangement from the human sciences in Dilthey's sense. Betti stands in somewhat the same relation to the tradition of legal hermeneutics as do Gadamer, Habermas, and perhaps Ricoeur to the theologico-philosophical tradition.

V

What does the legal model of hermeneutics have to offer to the study of history? I have suggested that it is superior to, or at least historically richer than, the more familiar philological, philosophical, and theological varieties because it is concerned more directly with social reality, human actions, and collectivities. Like "general" hermeneutics, the legal theory of interpretation further offers an alternative to conceptions of history which look to, or lust after, scientific models of one sort or another, especially Betti's "mathematical surrogate." This point is intended not to revive the old quarrel between "historicism" and "naturalism" (in the words of Ernst Troeltsch, characterizing the famous distinction made by Wilhelm Windelband and Heinrich Rickert between *Kultur-* and *Naturwissenschaften*) but only to avoid the naive fallacies about "objectivity" and "value-free" social science generated in particular by the *Werturteilsdiskussion* opened by Max Weber in 1914.[38] At the very least hermeneutics offers an alternative to this blind alley. Hermeneutics does not presume to ban investigations based on quantitative or behavioral assumptions but only to insist that the meanings attributed to such research are themselves the products of culturally conditioned human effort.

Hermeneutics has implications for the "philosophy of history" in both of the forms it has tended to assume in recent years—the "analytical"

[37] *Teoria*, p. 180; *Auslegungslehre*, p. 120.

[38] Survey of these problems in Pietro Rossi, *Lo storicismo tedesco contemporaneo* (Turin, 1956).

and the "speculative" or (as Arthur Danto calls it) "substantive."[39] Despite a long and distinguished heritage reaching from Toynbee and Spengler through Hegel back to Otto of Freising and Augustine himself, the speculative philosophy of history seems to have fallen on bad times, despite noble efforts by Peter Munz, Haskell Fain, and others to seek "the whole truth about history."[40] Emerging from theology and myth, this genre seems bound to return to its source, at least in its conventional universal (i.e., Judaeo-Christian) form. This is the classic sort of "metahistory" and has ties as well with the classical tradition of hermeneutics. Explicitly or implicitly, it is also tied to beliefs about prehistory, especially myth, and posthistory, especially prophecy. It is hard for critical historians nowadays to take seriously such neo-Augustinian efforts to find the "grand design," whether of God or a mindless, material "law." Yet it may be equally foolish for historians to pretend that they do not operate in effect from metahistorical assumptions, at the very least from those present in language; and one might wonder about the advisability of devoting some critical effort to deciding about some of the larger meaning of history from our perspective. Not to do so may condemn us to the predicament ascribed by Whitehead to those who affect to have no metaphysical presumptions—which is to be disadvantaged by the instinctive metaphysics of the nursery. Legal hermeneutics has long grappled with the question of the need of a large conceptual framework in order to achieve validity and consistency in judgment and interpretation, and the analogy may well hold for historical studies as well.

The "analytical philosophy of history" is something else again. Although it has been represented as a reaction to idealism (especially that of pre-1914 Germany) and uncritical speculative philosophy, it is historically as old as F. H. Bradley's *Presuppositions of Critical History* (1874). Obviously, this "critical" approach had little to do with that of neo-Kantian philosophers like Rickert or Dilthey; it intended, and portended, a recourse to logic and naturalism as a way of making history "scientific" beyond the dreams of Ranke or even J. B. Bury. As a consequence, especially in the past generation or two, the theory of history has been dominated by a new scholasticism whose stock in trade includes prescriptive talk about "holism," "covering laws," action theory, the most naively positivistic notions of research (as "data-gathering"), and the

[39] Arthur C. Danto, *Analytical Philosophy of History* (Cambridge, Mass., 1965). As in the case of hermeneutics this brief critique is offered from the point of view not of philosophy but of historical method and interpretation.

[40] Fain, *Between Philosophy and History* (Princeton, N.J., 1970), and Munz, *The Shapes of Time* (Middletown, Conn., 1978), the most learned and provocative of recent contributions.

most rigid insistence of the primacy of "explanation" in history.[41] Marginally, this literature, which has gained the status of a professional specialty, may have a cleansing effect; but mostly it has been irrelevant because of its tendency to focus on explanatory logic to the exclusion of concrete understanding—to empty form of its content, except as paradigmatic cases (and even then the cracking of a radiator or an automobile accident is often preferred to even a generic historical "event" like a war or a revolution). In such arid discussions one would like to recommend Clifford Geertz's arguments for "thick description" and that sort of evidence jurists would call circumstantial.[42]

The spectre haunting these discussions is that of causal analysis—and lurking behind, perhaps, that minor offspring of La Place's Demon, the "covering law." Here submission to a scientific model is most complete—and seems most inappropriate. No one has shown this more convincingly than the analytical philosophers themselves, notably Karl Popper, who has argued that the purpose and indeed the premise, of causal analysis is prediction. The historical counterpart of this operation can only be (as Isaiah Berlin and Paul Veyne have pointed out) "retrodiction," a process which has little utility and less verifiability.[43] Or rather, it introduces a serious misconception of historical understanding, representing another example of the "tendency among tough-minded philosophers," noted by Leon Goldstein, "to assimilate knowing the historical past to knowing the natural present."[44] The point is not that causal analysis is not useful for special lines of inquiry, only that it does not suffice for many interpretive and synthetic purposes and that it may often be illusory—a mockery of scientific procedure. As Berlin has pointed out, strategic placement of "thus's" and "therefores" does not necessarily constitute demonstration; and as Veyne has suggested, it may be more appropriate to offer some information on the grounds simply that it is "interesting" ("c'est intéressant que . . ."), the precise relevance being either indeterminate or yet to be determined, yet significant for evaluation and judgment. As in jurisprudence, meaning must be established not only through particular

[41] Standard literature collected in William Dray, ed., *Philosophical Analysis and History* (New York, 1966); Patrick Gardiner, ed., *The Philosophy of History* (Oxford, 1974), and *Theories of History* (Glencoe, Ill., 1959); and Sidney Hook, ed., *Philosophy and History* (New York, 1963); while various Beiheften of *History and Theory* have gathered more extensive bibliography.

[42] See Ronald G. Walters, "Signs of the Times: Clifford Geertz and Historians," *Social Research*, 47 (1980): 537–56.

[43] Berlin, "The Concept of Scientific History," in *Philosophical Analysis*, ed., Dray, p. 13, and Veyne, *Comment on écrit l'histoire* (Paris, 1971), p. 182.

[44] *Historical Knowing* (Austin, Texas, 1976), p. 161.

facts, their linkages and their classification, but also through what Geertz has called structures of signification and W. H. Walsh has termed "colligatory concepts," including correlations, coherences, and continuities which cannot be subsumed under the rubric of causation.[45]

"Interest" suggests another school of analytical philosophy, this one identified as "narrativist" (Maurice Mandelbaum calls it "reactionist"),[46] though it is not really concerned with the philosophy of history as commonly understood. Rather it is interest in history as the construction of "story" (the root meaning of "history") and so it has a closer affinity with the rhetorical tradition, which since the time of the sophists has carried on its own running warfare with philosophy. The strength of narrativism is that it has helped to redress the balance upset by the naive realism and naturalism which so often accompany the "normal science" of history. Yet it is also in danger of falling victim to the old "scissors-and-paste" fallacy criticized by Collingwood, to the extent that it tends to neglect or to undervalue the sort of intertextual criticism and controls by which historians try heuristically and imaginatively to restore earlier mental and social contexts. In any case narrativism, which takes its inspiration from literary criticism, tends to be, as Goldstein remarks of W. B. Gallie, "a philosophy of history for readers of history only."[47] This is especially the case with textualists like Hayden White, who focus more or less hermetically on "historical imagination" and its literary expression, and of course critics like Foucault and Derrida, who have thrown off the "burden of history" altogether. Indeed this school seems in the process of declaring its independence of historical scholarship in much the same way that literary criticism has at times (and especially in recent times) separated itself from literature. This would be a pity, for the study of history needs the sort of scrutiny offered by this descendent of philological hermeneutics.

VI

But let us look more closely at the model of hermeneutics suggested by jurisprudence. The point of departure of the legal tradition has always been the conscious, willful, and in some sense "interested" subject. That this subject may be prey to unconscious, natural, or social forces beyond his control or perceptual horizons limits but does not change this

[45] Geertz, *The Interpretation of Cultures* (New York, 1973), 3 ff., and Walsh, "Colligatory Concepts in History," in *The Philosophy of History*, ed., Gardiner, pp. 127–44.

[46] "The Problem of Covering Laws," in *The Philosophy of History*, ed. Gardiner, p. 51.

[47] *Historical Knowing*, p. 164.

premise. In contrast to natural science this human orientation defines an evenly observable field and, in a metaphorical sense, a "perspective." It has been the boast of science that it has overcome subjectivism on several levels—that it removed man from his sovereign position first in the cosmos, then in nature, and finally in his own psyche. Yet this is not a view which can be maintained in the practical business of living, achieving, or even surviving, and certainly not of observing the remoter reaches of the human condition in the past. Social life is necessarily anthropocentric and in many ways, because of linguistic limitations, anthropomorphic; and hermeneutics makes this circumstance an axiom of historical understanding.

The basic structure of conventional law derives from the ubiquitous juridical trinity of person, thing, and action (*persona*, *res*, *actio*), and I would emphasize four suggestive feautures of this arrangement.[48] First is the principle of personality, which is to say that law is subject-centered and, in a variety of ways, concerned with individual will, or at least responsibility, consciousness, and judgment. Secondly, from this anthropocentric point of view, a systematic attempt is made to comprehend the surrounding world of "reality," referring above all to social "things" (ranging from goods, or property, to complex institutions, culminating in the "public thing," the *respublica* itself). Third is the circumstance that legal interpretation must address itself not only to facts and "real" predicaments and to the "letter and spirit" of texts but also to questions of values, which implies problems of partisanship and "ideology" as well as social goals. Finally, like language but more broadly, law implies a large system of meaning in which facts and patterns acquire a significance in terms of location and relationship. In Betti's conception legal interpretation involves a two-fold operation which accommodates subject as well as object—attribution of human significance (*Sinngebung*) as well as determination of objective meaning (*Auslegung*).[49]

The historical observer struggles, then, with a cultural predicament as well as a recalcitrant and sometimes intractable object of study—a context as well as a text. He cannot observe and judge his domain with omniscient objectivity, and perhaps in his writing he should stop posing as the "omniscient observer" of Victorian fiction; for he is limited by cultural horizons, temporal perspective, and a largely impenetrable future.[50] Looking around, the observer sees a natural world challenging

[48] Further discussion in my "Gaius Noster: Substructures of Western Social Thought," *American Historical Review*, 89 (1979): 619–48. According to Betti's distinction this discussion focuses on "technical-juridical" interpretation in "historical" rather than "normative" terms.

[49] *Teoria*, p. 574; *Auslegungslehre*, p. 438.

[50] Cf. Martin Duberman, *The Uncompleted Past* (New York, 1965), pp. 43 ff.

him, relatives and neighbors facing the same challenge, more remote actors competing with and perhaps threatening him; and he sees, or at least feels, the pressures and demands of institutions, political as well as social and economic. Looking back, through various professional aids, he may perceive a tradition, a heritage, which sustains and weighs on—or obstructs—his own actions. Looking forward, he formulates hopes and aspirations, perhaps even programs of action, as well as doubts and fears. In all of these observations ego-centric value judgments and social interpretations must be formulated in a particular cultural and linguistic context. And as it is with the individual, so it must be, on a larger scale, with a society, with a meaningful social science, and with historical understanding in general.

But if the interested, participating, time- , space- , and culture-bound observer must remain content with a limited social science, he also occupies a field of inquiry in which social interaction—"intersubjectivity"—becomes plausible and self-criticism possible (as well as necessary). Habermas's "self-reflection of the cultural sciences" is a built-in condition.[51] Interpretation, involving interaction between subject and object, takes place in an intellectual continuum, and here the legal analogy is clear. Legal interpretation likewise has to give priority to the person (legal "subjectivity") and to judge in terms of times, places, and circumstances, yet within a social and cultural tradition. The task of the juridical *interpres* is not only to determine the "facts" and to apply principles but also to evaluate the appropriateness of principles, themselves derived from earlier experiences, just as the historian must find some standard or resonance—"prejudice" in a nonpejorative hermeneutical sense—in his own experience to give meaning in that of others. He observes and judges within a conventional social field and professional tradition which themselves represent both subject and object. In legal, and analogously historical, terms the interpreter makes transits of what is generally called the "hermeneutical circle."

Such interpretation involves not only a hermeneutical circle connecting alien and familiar experience but also, as Gadamer has argued, a double focus including judge and the observed "reality" to which he is professionally bound to "do justice." Hence it must also involve a double set of values, corresponding as it were to the home and alien territories. Here is one of the dilemmas of the hermeneutical process, familiar to critics through the quandaries involved in translation and historians in the form of anachronism. In methodological terms, for example, should nineteenth-century political, social, or psychological theory—institutional,

[51] *Knowledge and Human Interests*, trans. J. Shapiro (Boston, 1971), p. 161.

class- or psycho-analysis—be projected back into the Old Regime, and if so, how far? Or is it advisable to utilize what have been called "nativist theories," conceptualizations drawn and adapted from the cultural context of the object in question? In any case the past is indeed a "foreign country," and the guide books for which historians are responsible must try to show the ways in which "people do things differently there."[52] Since understanding the past depends in part on appreciating its values, while its significance depends on modern values, the hermeneutical circle involves a most complex axiology. By it are determined the selection and definition of "facts," the patterns inferred and reconstructed from these facts, the "genealogy" of particular generalizations, and the long-range interpretation of the historical process.

What preserves the integrity of the interpretive process, what makes it possible to complete the hermeneutical circle, is above all the medium of language, which like historical facts can only be understood in societal terms. "Everything in a given text which requires fuller interpretation," wrote Schleiermacher, "must be explained and determined exclusively from the linguistic domain common to the author and his original public."[53] One consequence of this premise (much criticized by phenomenologists beginning especially with Heidegger) is that historians must often be content with convention rather than logic in their analyses—with "humanly followed rules," as Peter Winch puts it, rather than with causal laws.[54] The persistence of myth, ritual, and other metalogical behavior must be kept in mind when the historian pursues what E. D. Hirsch and Betti have called "recognitive interpretation."[55] A corollary is that historical interpretation must take notice not only of language in general but of particular languages. It is a curiosity of most American and English work in the human sciences, especially sociology and most especially the analytical philosophy of history, that practitioners seem to assume that a science of society can be adequately formulated in a single brand of technical English devoted to generalized factors (and one may doubt that exclusive recourse to German—or Greek—is much more adequate). Hermeneutical understanding depends on the particularity and "thickness" which only varied linguistic experience can afford.

Yet the language surrogate, like the "mathematical surrogate," is surely insufficient for a hermeneutics of history; for while it makes plausible

[52] L. P. Hartley, *The Go-Between* (London, 1953), p. 1.

[53] Cited by Hirsch, *The Aims of Interpretation*, p. 76.

[54] "Concepts and Actions," in *The Philosophy of History*, ed. Gardiner, pp. 41–59, and cf. "The Idea of a Social Science" in *Rationality*, ed. Bryan R. Wilson (Oxford, 1970), pp. 1–17.

[55] Hirsch, *The Aims of Interpretation*, chap. 2; Betti, *Teoria*, p. 343, and *Auslegungslehre*, p. 255.

the completing of the hermeneutical circle, it suggests the impossibility ever of breaking out of it. According to the Whorfian view and what has been called "Gödel's theorem of language," language can yield no ultimate human meaning.[56] This is where the legal theory of interpretation seems to open up the frontier of historical understanding. Unlike philological hermeneutics, which confines itself to the text, and unlike philosophical hermeneutics, which expands its horizons to existence itself as the text analogue, and unlike theological hermeneutics, which devotes itself to a still higher transcendent object—unlike all of these legal hermeneutics has concentrated, however artificially, on a concrete expression of human society and culture. Unfortunately, while hermeneutical attitudes have made their way into social and cultural science (especially in the work of Gadamer, Habermas, Ricoeur, and especially Betti), with many a glance back at the classical theory of interpretation, little or no attention has been paid to the legal model.[57] By way of conclusion let me suggest some of the points at which the historical study of society and culture may draw (and perhaps inadvertently and uncritically have drawn) insight and inspiration from the tradition of European law.

VII

Contemporary hermeneutics seems to me monopolized by philosophers and literary critics, all of whom invoke the historical tradition but without a comprehensive grasp of it. The larger pattern of development should take into account not only the centuries-long interplay between philosophical and rhetorical interpretations—the debates of Platonism and sophism repeated in changing contexts, complicated by the intrusions of theology—but also the theories and practice of interpretation elaborated by ancient legal (and more recent social) science. Not that normative jurisprudence carrying on its strictly professional functions (any more than Christian theology, carrying on the pursuit of the "historical Jesus") can be imported directly into current hermeneutical discussions. The point is rather that the needs and interests of historians may be better served, their sense of the relevance of hermeneutics enhanced, by bringing into these discussions some of the questions, conventions, and connections made with the—nowadays unfortunately isolated—legal branch of the Western tradition of hermeneutics.

Legal hermeneutics is unrepentently anthropocentric. It starts with a conception of *personalitas*, of the individual and perhaps psychological

[56] Hirsch, pp. 50, 66.

[57] See the collection edited by Paul Rabinow and William M. Sullivan, *Interpretive Social Science* (Berkeley, 1979), and the work of Baumann (above, n. 1).

aspect of the human condition; then goes on to *realitas*, which is to say social reality, based above all on the institutions of property and economic behavior; and finally treats *actio*, action theory, collective as well as individual. Within the framework of this conventional legal-sociological triad legal interpretation confronts a wide range of essential social categories and concepts. Suffice it here to mention just a few types: ideas of social organization (family, kinship structures, corporative groups, subversive groups, administration, nationality), ideas of authority and power (popular and traditional as well as public, political, and administrative), ideas of social interaction (commerce, war, international problems), ideas of social continuity ("wills," succession, inheritance) and discontinuity (the whole range of criminal law), ideas of social change (not only legislation but legal reform and the rise and fall of custom, *consuetudo* and *desuetudo*) and ideas of causation (one of the grounds for the claim of law to be a true "science").[58] Of course modern legal science (since the thirteenth century) has been intensively interpreted and, through historical and comparative as well as philosophical methods, reinterpreted and transformed by these ideas.

Legal science has never been value-free, however, and all of these themes have been interpreted in normative and even teleological terms: social organizations have their own goals (families to ensure their future strategies, corporate groups their "interests," etc.), authority is joined to "public utility," social interaction is supposed to further the common good and continuity, and social change is intended to take place in the direction of legal ideas, especially peace and justice, perhaps prosperity and political expansion as well, while causation has indissoluble ties with "just" and "good" causes.[59] For the jurist these norms represent ideals, or at the very least professional pretexts; but for students of social and cultural structure and change they also reflect a basic dialectic of historical change. The point is not that historians should interject such values into their analyses but rather that the meaning of actions and perceptions should be assessed in terms thereof—and ideology be joined to society. For legal interpretation has always made an effort, according

[58] A sampling of relevant works includes Riccardo Orestano, *Azione, Diritti soggettivi, Persone giuridiche* (Bologna, 1978); Paolo Zatti, *Persona giuridica e soggettivita* (Padua, 1975); Carol Maiorca, *La cosa in senso giuridico* (Turin, 1937); Peter Stein, *Regula Iuris* (Edinburgh, 1966); Pietro Costa, *Iurisdictio* (see above n. 20); and more generally Eugen Ehrlich, *Fundamental Principles of the Sociology of Law*, trans. W. Moll (Cambridge, 1936). See also H. L. A. Hart and A. M. Honoré, *Causation in the Law* (Oxford, 1959), and the criticism of Maurice Mandelbaum, *The Anatomy of Historical Knowledge* (Baltimore, 1977), pp. 199–204.

[59] Cortese, *La norma giuridica*, 1: 179 ff.

to its own lights, to establish what Quentin Skinner has called "social meaning"; and jurisprudence, in its own fashion, represents in general what Clifford Geertz has referred to as a "meaning system," or set of meaning systems, and so potentially the basis for a fuller appreciation of the historical process in all of its social and cultural significance.[60]

In the nineteenth century the "scientific" pretensions of traditional jurisprudence came increasingly under fire, especially from the new disciplines of political economy and sociology, which had even more aggressive claims to universality and explanatory power. Bentham rejected the old legal tradition in favor of simplistic social calculus; Comte rejected it in favor of a naturalistic conception of society amenable to control by "positive" science; and Marx rejected it in favor of a dialectical method joined to economic analysis. For all of these jurisprudence was the ghost of a dead, or dying, culture, scientifically useless because of its freight of ancient conventions and "values"; for Marx, indeed, it was the very embodiment of bourgeois ideology.[61] In the past century and a half these disciplines, since become vast and imposing professions, have been dominated by scientism, especially in France and England, where the legacy of positivism has been intimidating; and in various ways the study of history has fallen under the spell of quantitative and explanatory social science. For anthropology, on the other hand, and for the science of culture and more generally speaking, the inadequacies of economic or sociological reductionism have become increasingly obvious, especially with the passing of old-fashioned ideas of objectivity (*Wertfreiheit*) and naturalistic "explanation." And this, for historical studies, is where hermeneutics comes in. Dilthey and his followers have reached back profitably to older and in some ways richer conceptions of historical change and understanding, drawing in particular upon romantic literary and biblical interpretation. It seems to me that this line of inquiry could be deepened and given a more social orientation by attending as well to the insights and suggestions to be found in the legal tradition, though without neglecting the criticisms of recent philosophers, including Gadamer, Habermas, and Apel, as well as Betti.

And so the old question, "What is history?"—this time in the light of the theory of interpretation associated with legal (and more recently

[60] Geertz, *The Interpretation of Cultures*, and Skinner, " 'Social Meaning' and the Explanation of Social Action," in *The Philosophy of History*, ed. Gardiner, pp. 106–26.

[61] Discussion in D. R. Kelley, "The Metaphysics of Law: An Essay on the Very Young Marx," *American Historical Review*, 83 (1978): 350–67, and "The Science of Anthropology: An Essay on the Very Old Marx," forthcoming in *Journal of the History of Ideas*.

social) science. To this question there have been many prescriptive answers, from the idealizations of Cicero ("the light of truth, the mistress of light," etc.) to those of E. H. Carr ("the study of causes"), from the mystifications of St. Augustine (the working out of God's "grand design") to those of Gadamer ("the great dark book . . . written in the language of the past"), and from the aestheticism of Pliny ("always pleases") to that of Hayden White (a story well told). My own preference lies between the extremes of philosophy, theology, and rhetoric. Like law and hermeneutics history is a human form of apprehension—*prudentia* or *phronesis* rather than *episteme* (or *praxis*, for that matter). And like legal interpretation, historical interpretation had the same ultimate aim, which according to Ricoeur remains "to make one's own what was previously 'foreign.'"[62] According to Johann Huizinga's still useful definition, "History is the intellectual form in which a civilization renders account to itself of its past."[63] Without being too rigid, this formulation seems to provide for the traits of hermeneutics listed above: it is anthropocentric, value-oriented, responsible to tradition, and grounded in a meaning system. Less formally, it envisions the study of history as a human operation aimed at finding answers about the human past. What better way to express the significance of the partnership of Hermes, Clio, and Themis?

[62] *Interpretation Theory*, p. 91; and see Richard Rorty, *Philosophy and the Mirror of Nature* (Princeton, 1979), pp. 315 ff., discussing the transition "from epistemology to hermeneutics."
[63] "A Definition of the Concept of History," in *Philosophy and History*, ed. R. Klibansky and H. Paton (Oxford, 1936), p. 5.

ADDITIONS TO NOTES

[1] Norbert Henrichs, *Bibliographie der Hermeneutik* (Düsseldorf, 1968).
[2] H.-E. Hasso Jaeger, "Studien zur Frühgeschichte der Hermeneutik," *Archiv für Begriffsgeschichte* 13 (1974): 35-84.
[7] Anthony Grafton, *Joseph Scaliger, A Study in the History of Classical Scholarship* (Oxford, 1983).
[16] *Archives de philosophie du droit* 17 (1972), "L'Interprétation dans le droit."
[27] On the significance of legal theory see Anthony T. Kronman, *Max Weber* (London, 1983).
[47] A recent attempt to join narrativism and the analytical philosophy of history is F. R. Ankersmit, *Narrative Logic* (The Hague, 1983).
[58] On the legal concept *res* see also Gadamer, *Philosophical Hermeneutics*, pp. 69-81.

INDEX